1,000,000 Books

are available to read at

www.ForgottenBooks.com

Read online
Download PDF
Purchase in print

ISBN 978-1-330-50477-2
PIBN 10070891

This book is a reproduction of an important historical work. Forgotten Books uses
state-of-the-art technology to digitally reconstruct the work, preserving the original format
whilst repairing imperfections present in the aged copy. In rare cases, an imperfection in
the original, such as a blemish or missing page, may be replicated in our edition. We do,
however, repair the vast majority of imperfections successfully; any imperfections that
remain are intentionally left to preserve the state of such historical works.

Forgotten Books is a registered trademark of FB &c Ltd.
Copyright © 2018 FB &c Ltd.
FB &c Ltd, Dalton House, 60 Windsor Avenue, London, SW19 2RR.
Company number 08720141. Registered in England and Wales.

For support please visit www.forgottenbooks.com

1 MONTH OF
FREE
READING

at

www.ForgottenBooks.com

By purchasing this book you are eligible for one month membership to ForgottenBooks.com, giving you unlimited access to our entire collection of over 1,000,000 titles via our web site and mobile apps.

To claim your free month visit:

www.forgottenbooks.com/free70891

* Offer is valid for 45 days from date of purchase. Terms and conditions apply.

English
Français
Deutsche
Italiano
Español
Português

www.forgottenbooks.com

Mythology Photography **Fiction**
Fishing Christianity **Art** Cooking
Essays Buddhism Freemasonry
Medicine **Biology** Music **Ancient
Egypt** Evolution Carpentry Physics
Dance Geology **Mathematics** Fitness
Shakespeare **Folklore** Yoga Marketing
Confidence Immortality Biographies
Poetry **Psychology** Witchcraft
Electronics Chemistry History **Law**
Accounting **Philosophy** Anthropology
Alchemy Drama Quantum Mechanics
Atheism Sexual Health **Ancient History**
Entrepreneurship Languages Sport
Paleontology Needlework Islam
Metaphysics Investment Archaeology
Parenting Statistics Criminology
Motivational

GUNTON'S MAGAZINE

GEORGE GUNTON, Editor

VOLUME XV

*July - Dec
1898*

NEW YORK
POLITICAL SCIENCE PUBLISHING CO.
34 UNION SQUARE

LIBRARY
JUL
19
1962
UNIVERSITY OF TORONTO

H
1
G9
v.15

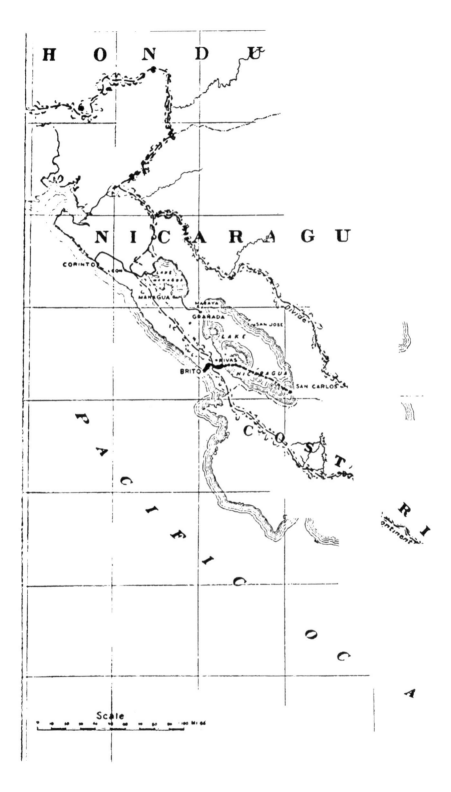

ECONOMICS AND PUBLIC AFFAIRS

CAN WE STAND VICTORY?

One of the severest tests of strength of character, alike in individuals and nations, is exceptional success. Most people can stand a large amount of adversity but few are equal to unexpected success. Except in rare cases, easy or extraordinary success produces a state of inflated egotism which dethrones sense, prudence, and wisdom; it causes what is known as "swelled head." Are we, as a nation, in danger of being afflicted with this malady? is a question of more than ordinary importance just now.

When the war broke out, officially and unofficially we declared to the world that we were pursuing a specific policy consistent with our traditional Monroe Doctrine; that our object was not conquest of territory or extension of political power, but solely to prevent the further continuance of an effete, decrepit and brutalizing monarchy with its revolting barbarism and inhumanity in this hemisphere. We declared that in the eyes of Christendom, judged by the ordinary standards of nineteenth century civilization, Spain had forfeited her right longer to be permitted to exercise her repressive and degrading authority over Cuba; that by all the standards of political efficiency she had utterly failed to maintain the right longer to govern this American island. We declared that to establish the right of self-government in Cuba and obtain proper reparation for the dastardly blowing up of our battleship, the *Maine*, was the sole aim and object of demanding Spain's exit from American territory.

Of course Spain affected to believe that our object was the conquest of Cuba, the Philippines, and eventually all other possessions belonging to European powers.

Shall we sustain the integrity of our declaration, or shall we justify Spanish predictions that we were "bluffing" and are really bent on conquest wherever we have the power?

During the first few weeks of the war it seemed difficult for the press and friends of the administration sufficiently to emphasize their absolute adherence to the non-conquest policy. The Monroe Doctrine was appealed to in numerous ways as laying down the gospel of our territorial policy. Since Dewey's victory at Manila and the manifest disruption of Spanish power in the Philippines, however, a radical change seems to have come over the tone of the press. Instead of talking about the spirit and letter of the Monroe Doctrine, confining our efforts and influence to the development and perfection of democratic civilization in the Americas, it is breaking out with glowing predictions of the Golden Age of an extended empire. This kind of rhetorical gush is finding expression in leading Republican papers throughout the country, like the Philadelphia *Press*, Boston *Journal* and New York *Tribune*, and is finding echo in some Democratic papers like the Washington *Times*, Atlanta *Constitution* and Cincinnati *Enquirer*, and even in some Mugwump papers, like the New York *Journal of Commerce*. If the Manila victory should prove to be such a self-inflating event as to cause the American people to revolutionize their public policy, abandon their hitherto almost sacred Monroe Doctrine, and change from a policy of industrialism to one of militarism and become seekers of conquest and owners of colonies, it will conclusively prove that we cannot stand victory.

This undoing of our traditional and avowed national doctrine received a special impetus from a recent after-dinner speech by General Wesley Merritt, the newly-appointed military governor of the Philippine Islands, in which he said: "The war was begun for the enforcement of the idea of human liberty, and with no thought of national aggrandizement, but the logic of events has brought about an unexpected result, and the government has taken the Philippines by right of conquest. What the navy has won the army will hold. The strong hand of the government on those islands ought never to be loosened. . . . . I believe in the new national policy of the United States which looks to the acquisition of additional territory represented in outlying islands that are requisite for the development of national strength and growth."

This appears to have been taken in many quarters as an authoritative expression of profound political wisdom. The words of General Merritt are caught up and enlarged upon as if they were the utterances of a renowned political philosopher to whom the nation looked for guidance in its longest-range statesmanship. This looking to a mere soldier for statesmanship, and taking an after-dinner remark as outlining a "new national policy," shows a lack of political principle and stability which, if shared in by the American people, would indeed be alarming. What has General Merritt ever said or done to entitle his views on a subject so vitally affecting the national welfare to any special consideration? He may be a brave and thoroughly efficient soldier and general, which fact tends rather to disqualify him as a political philosopher than to give his words special significance. He is a soldier and naturally sees and thinks through militarism. He sees government chiefly as military authority and national greatness as extent of empire and colonial possessions. Of course it is true enough for the present that what the navy has won the army must hold. In saying this General Merritt but expressed his immediate duty, the very purpose for which he was about to sail to the Philippine Islands. But to magnify this into a new national policy is sheer political ballooning. The journals or party which can take this seriously may well be distrusted as representing the principle of national policy or leadership in the movement of national destiny.

If the Monroe Doctrine ever contained sound political principle it does so to-day. The capture of Manila or military occupation of the Philippine Islands has done nothing to change the wisdom of that policy. If it is wise now suddenly to become a military, colonizing nation, it was always unwise to declare that' our destiny demanded an opposite policy. This sudden change is not the result of serious thought or new political light or deeper wisdom; it is merely a gush expression born of sudden victory. Of course our duty is to free Cuba, and, perhaps, deprive Spain of authority over Porto Rico and the Philippine Islands; and it may even be necessary to invade Spain itself and take possession of Madrid. This may be necessary, also, to secure proper indemnity covering the expenses incurred by the United States. But because all that may be required in the exigencies of war, to administer proper discipline to Spain and put her in a less harmful position towards civilization, it does not follow that it should radically change the policy of the United States towards the development of its own institutions and civilization.

It goes without saying that our national policy should be governed by our national interests. Our influence upon the world will be proportionate to the development of our own national character and institutions. As we have said, the only thing to do now is to take Cuba, Porto Rico, the Philippines and, if necessary, Spain itself. But this is a duty temporarily imposed by war. When the war is over our concern will be with the United States. Cuba will have to be entrusted with the experiment of self-government, and work out her own political salvation. Then, when the glamour of victory and military glory has subsided, the serious business of wisely directing the policy of this Republic will remain. What then will the United States have to gain by pursuing a military or colonial policy. When we say the United States we do not mean people in public life, who look only to lucrative political offices, nor do we mean ambitious generals who estimate civilization only by the size of standing armies; but we mean the eighty per cent. of the seventy-five million American people whose welfare depends upon the development of domestic industry and social improvement throughout the nation.

There are two classes of people who would naturally be interested in an aggressive colonial policy. First, the military class. All interested in army and navy life as a profession would naturally favor this new policy, because it would tend to furnish more positions of opulence and influence in these professions. Second, professional office-holders. Every expansion of the military and political machinery increases the bureaucratic function and opportunities for political appointments. These two classes may fairly be expected, therefore, to be in favor of an extended empire; but the people, the masses, the millions of American citizens, who are interested in peaceful industry and the social welfare of our people, have nothing to gain but much to lose by a change from an industrial to a military colonial policy.

In the first place, it would change the center of national interest from domestic to foreign affairs. This would be an effective check to all domestic reform movements for an indefinite time. Our new possessions would be a constant source of frictional diplomacy with suspicious European powers. This would be a fertile topic for political discussion, upon which party policies would be organized and political issues shaped, and would largely absorb public attention and effectively prevent the consideration of improvements in domestic public policy. The present little war is conclusive proof of this. It has completely submerged every other public question—finance, labor, municipal policies—in fact, everything is practically shelved by the war. Congress cannot seriously discuss any proposition of financial or economic policy affecting domestic conditions; party lines are practically obliterated, and patriotism calls for the sinking of everything in the support of the administration, because we are involved in foreign hostilities.

For generations, even centuries, foreign complications arising out of colonial policies have been the fertile resource of European statesmen to avoid facing domestic problems at home. Times without number have movements for industrial and political reform been shelved and effectively postponed for years and decades by the sudden advent of foreign complications. It is the most effective means of making a patriotic people forget its own needs in the needs of the government. There is no one thing which, during the present century, has permanently prevented or postponed the consummation of so many domestic reform movements; it is the last resource of undemocratic statesmanship.

The industrial and social reform movements which ought to make marked progress in this country during the next thirty years, such as greater diversification of manufacturing industries, adoption of an eight-hour working day, establishment of a general system of labor insurance for wage-workers, sanitary renovation of our cities, adoption of an American municipal policy which shall furnish free kindergartens and thoroughly

paved and clean streets, abolish sweat-shops from tene-
ment houses, supply adequate public libraries, open
parks, free gymnasiums and other improvements in the
condition of laborers in our large cities, cannot come
about save by concentration of political and social interests upon municipal and domestic affairs. Anything
which shall attract public discussion to foreign topics
will necessarily result in preventing or greatly checking the consideration and advance of all such economic
and social movements at home. The domestic employer, as well as laborers, will suffer neglect and stul-
tification by a change of policy which shall transfer the
center of political interest from the domestic to a military colonial policy. Besides suffering a practical arrest of industrial and social progress, the laborers and
business men will have to bear an increased weight of
taxation if this new policy is inaugurated.

Moreover, this policy, which is essentially military,
would involve not only a large standing army and a
large corps of political appointees, but it would necessarily tend to create a military instead of an industrial
type of public sentiment and interest. The one thing
which has given the United States pre-eminence over all
other nations in its national growth has been its immense industrial development, which is largely due to
the fact that our people have been essentially non-militant. The honors of success, the rewards of social po-
sitiou, the places of national honor, have all been in
the line of industrial accomplishments, and hence it is
that in the field of industry, of wealth production, of
social prosperity, of national development, our progress
has had no parallel in the world's history. Change the
center of interest, the center of public appreciation of
social honor, of national recognition, from industrial to
military accomplishment, and the very impetus for this
industrial progress is gone.

Moreover, this new policy is an abandonment, a practical reversal, of the freedom-giving political philosophy for which this country has stood pre-eminently above all other nations, *viz.:* the Monroe Doctrine, which is in effect the declaration that we stand for the peaceful evolution of an industrial democratic civilization. Armies and navies should only be instruments for protecting the industrial and social security and progress of our people, and never be used for conquest or political aggression. As political doctrine this is so supremely above the public policy of any other nation, it is so devoid of the predatory spirit of colonization and conquest, that the United States was fast coming to be regarded as the world's leader in peaceful, humane, liberty-giving institutions. If the so-called ''new policy'' is to be adopted and this high position abandoned, we at once drop to the level of the military nations of Europe and enter the scramble for conquest and political domination. The moment we assume that role we cease to lead and become followers of a lower type of national ambition. When it comes to armies, Russia and Germany are superior to us. When it comes to mere navies, England is ahead; but reckoned by the intelligence, wealth and self-sustaining moral power of free institutions, none of them are our peers.

If the American people can be induced to reverse the policy by which this country has become the richest, freest, most intelligent and prosperous country in the world, and sacrifice all the superiority it has stood for in national development for the purpose of an extension of empire and military authority, it will prove that after all we cannot stand victory and are not capable of maintaining the progress we have made.

INDUSTRIAL DANGERS IN ENGLAND

Industrial England is to-day menaced by certain serious dangers. Further progress along the lines of the last half century's development is being restricted by economic forces of rapidly growing importance, and unless wise statesmanship is applied to the problem an eruption may come. England's relation to the rest of the world, industrially, is gradually undergoing a great change, but her foreign policy is not being adapted to the new conditions. A pressure never before experienced is being felt more and more distinctly by her manufacturing interests, and capital (which feels the weight first) is transferring a part of it, at least, to labor. So far this new tendency has been shown in a slackening of progress rather than actual retrogression, but in a population long accustomed to progress the social effect is much the same. Not to gratify, measurably at least, a steadily rising standard of social wants is even more dangerous than to cut off something from a stationary, non-improving scale of living. It is a more difficult and serious thing merely to hinder the advance of an energetic, ambitious, progressive race than to push a spiritless, stagnant population down to a definitely lower level. India submits to periodic famines with less social disturbance than English workingmen would make over a general reduction of wages or increase of working hours.

The great engineers' strike in 1897 is the immediate case in point. The labor unions failed completely in this struggle and even lost some ground that had before been theirs. In the consequences of this failure lie some of the menacing dangers to which we have referred; chief in seriousness, perhaps, being the almost certain impetus to the socialist movement. So great a disaster to trades-unionism is naturally hailed by the socialists as conclusive proof of the permanent ascendancy of capital and hopelessness of labor's cause under the present economic system. That this is a wholly mistaken deduction we shall see later on; but its very plausibility, especially at a time when the defeated and embittered workmen are in exactly the mood for radical action, is cause for apprehension.

· The principal demand of the unions in this strike was for the eight-hour work day. Certain other points of less importance, such as regulation of the quality of work, manner of operating machinery and employment of non-union labor were also in dispute. The strike lasted six months — part of it eight months — and cost Great Britain, according to the English Labor Department estimate, about $75,000,000. The workingmen are said to have lost about $14,000,000 in wages and more than $4,000,000 in depletion of union funds to maintain strikers' families. The employers' loss is estimated at $14,000,000, not counting permanent diversion of business to other countries. The strikers were finally obliged to give up the struggle and returned to work without the eight-hour day and upon agreement that employers may freely hire non-union labor and settle with each workman as to the quantity of work, the piece-price, and hours of labor. The men accepted these terms in no submissive mood, but only from grim necessity. There can be no question but that an undercurrent of rancorous discontent is running deep and strong, and the inevitable gain to socialism from this situation is recognized in many quarters. The *Springfield Republican*, for instance, in an editorial on "Socialism in England," says:

"Ten years will show the truth or falsity of these forebodings. The socialist leaders themselves certainly view the situation with satisfaction. They have never been friendly to the powerful trade unions, deeming them selfish, exclusive and opposed to the solidarity of labor. The downfall, they assert, was inevitable and with so many of the unionists cast loose the socialists regard their own propaganda of root and branch, uncompromising war upon the existing economic system as the only hope to which the English workingman can turn. If this proves to be also the view taken of the situation by the defeated 'engineers,' the overthrow of collective bargaining by the employers will prove costly in the end."

Englishmen themselves are by no means blind to the danger in the situation. The *London Spectator*, while of the opinion that this particular strike could not have resulted otherwise than in defeat for the engineers, nevertheless says that it regards "the employers' victory with a certain grave apprehension." It believes strongly in the necessity and advantage of high wages, but doubts whether capitalists will see that their interest is in high wages, especially in view of the growing pressure of foreign competition. "The temptation as competition gets worse—" says the *Spectator*, "and it must get worse as new countries enter the field—will be more and more severe, and if it is met by reducing wages, we shall have everywhere a discontented city population, at war in its heart with Capital, and deprived even in America of the old refuge, flight to 'the land.' Not to mention that city workmen detest 'the land' and its thankless work as much as Jews do, they can get nothing out of the land, which since the wheatfields of the world were pooled by modern enterprise returns nothing, except to men who work in a way and live in a way for which artisans have become unfitted. The artisans, fiercely discontented, will look to the State for aid, as 'Populists' in America already declare that they do, and what with their power as voters, as conscripts, and as the class with which modern Christianity tends to sympathize in a very decided way, they will, we believe, force on many experiments not consistent with our present notions of social organization. We do not mean that they will adopt Socialism, which will always wreck itself on the hidden rock of human selfishness, the instinct implanted in man, like the love of life, for his preservation, but that they will rush at nostrums recommended to them as sources of salvation, as the Americans are now rushing at new currency laws with a belief, quite pathetic in its earnestness, that if the big people would only be fair there would be more hay obtainable from every field than there is grass in it. Those rushes may be very dangerous indeed, even if they leave the great fabric standing, and our fear is that the capitalists, once masters of the situation, will induce them by attacks, which they will consider just or necessary, upon the average of wages.   *   *   *   *   *   *

"Our only hope, we confess, for the beginning of the new century, is the intelligence of Capital; that is, the perception of its owners that its power must be very gently used."

English papers very generally attribute the failure of the engineers' strike to the fierce foreign competition which the masters are compelled to meet. "The foreigner is competing more keenly than ever with us," says the Liverpool *Journal of Commerce*, "and the gain that the workman secures comes not even out of his own employer's profit, but actually out of the latter's capital funds. This process cannot be continued forever."

The curious thing, however, is that none of these journals seems to see the significance of the situation as suggesting a new line of public policy. They see the labor discontent and growth of socialistic movements resulting from this set-back to trades-unionism; they trace the cause, correctly enough, to the foreign competition that is pressing English employers to the very margin of profitable operations; yet they seem to be at a loss to suggest a remedy. The *Spectator*, as we have seen,'says its only hope is in "the intelligence of Capital"; but what "intelligence" can solve the problem of granting labor's demands when bankruptcy would be the result? The Liverpool paper before quoted sees only disaster ahead "unless these suicidal demands be abated and truer theories about political economy learnt by labor leaders"; but it might as well try to sweep back the ocean as to "abate" labor's demands for improvement or induce the working people to accept any "theories about political economy" which require them to stop where they are and eventually, perhaps, to give up much of the ground already gained.

The truth is, this critical situation in England is but the outcome of a certain line of industrial evolution which we have often discussed and explained in these pages. English industry and English trades-unionism have progressed and grown strong, side by side, during the last fifty years. With a continually expanding foreign trade and no outside competition to fear, there was steady prosperity and out of the growing wealth of the nation it was possible for labor, by efficient organization, to obtain its share. Successive laws were enacted limiting the hours of work and prohibiting child labor and prescribing better conditions of factory toil; higher wages were granted in industry after industry, often as the result of strikes; and all this capital bore and went on to make new profits by new economies and new methods and larger trade. The situation of British industry with reference to the rest of the world permitted this steady progress both of capital and labor.

That situation, however, is changing. Years ago England—the birthplace of the factory system—was far beyond the reach of foreign competition in her own or any other markets. That is no longer true. Other nations have been copying her industrial methods and doing their own manufacturing; some of them have begun to compete with England in foreign markets and one at least — Germany — is steadily increasing her exports of manufactured goods to England itself. Our Consul at Hull, England, in discussing the British Board of Trade returns for the year ending October last, speaks of the decline in exports, particularly of cotton, woolen and worsted goods, and says:

"A significant fact in connection with this depression in the textile trade is that, while the steady decline in the exports is in progress, machinery and men are leaving the country for the Orient, where new competitive energies havé sprung into life and are gradually supplanting English cotton goods of the cheaper grades in the Chinese and Japanese markets. India has long since taken hold of the cotton business on its own account, and up to a very short time ago was able to undersell the imported fabrics in the Chinese and Japanese markets. The growth of cotton manufactures in the East has long been a serious problem to the merchants and manufacturers of Manchester and Lancashire and the adjoining districts of Cheshire, Derbyshire and Yorkshire. All the influence the Manchester Chamber of Commerce (one of the most powerful bodies in the Kingdom) could exert was brought to bear on the Government to retard this growing industry in the East, by regulations and laws similar to those which crushed the Irish woolen industry in days gone by. They found, however, that in India they had to fight British capital, invested there by Lancashire men, and stoutly protected by conditions and circumstances which made their ultimate triumph in India inevitable."

Germany is increasing her sales to England and

English colonies year by year. Her exports to Great Britain increased from $159,460,000 in 1893 to $169,-932,000 in 1896; to British colonies, from $22,372,000 to $26,418,000. During the same period her purchases from England declined from $134,470,000 to $131,-376,000, and from British colonies remained about stationary.

These are the causes of England's growing difficulty in maintaining the industrial pace of the last few decades. With no customs defence against this growing competition, her manufacturers have all they can do merely to hold their own, to say nothing of granting any new demands of labor. Formerly these employers would have found it cheaper to yield than to incur the expense of a prolonged strike; this time, however, they felt that to grant the demands of the engineers, in face of an increasing foreign competition, would be to put the whole industry on a losing basis. And so the strikers failed, and are beginning to distrust the economic system which no longer yields them the means of progress they require and insist upon having.

The conclusion seems inevitable. England must either be prepared to face growing revolutionary disturbances, and perhaps adopt despotic militarism at home, or abandon her free-trade policy. Having gained the industrial leadership of the world, under protection, she was able to adopt free trade with entire safety to her home industries and plain advantage to her foreign commerce; but with low-wage nations using her modern machine methods the case is being reversed. England is coming to need protection against continental Europe just as much as America has always needed protection against England, and for exactly the same reason, *i. e.*, the imperative necessity of maintaining a relatively higher wage level. Civilization and social safety absolutely require that no permanent backward step in the matter of wages shall be taken, but unless the higher levels are everywhere protected against the lower, just that backward movement is likely to come.

Here in America we are threatened with similar socialistic dangers because of our failure to apply the protective principle as our especial conditions require. We have tariff protection, but allow free immigration, discourage trades-unionism, neglect the hours-of-labor question and provide no method of insuring workpeople against disability and old age. In all these respects our attitude is like that of England on the tariff — *laissez 'faire*. Great Britain needs to return to the protective principle; America needs a broader application of it. Great Britain requires a new foreign policy, either of direct protection or of reciprocal tariff arrangements with her colonies on the Chamberlain customs-union plan; America's need is a broader domestic policy, to protect its labor against long hours, ignorance, unwholesome housing and old-age pauperism.

The protective principle is the same, whatever its particular application. Unless each higher group is effectively secured in every forward step it takes, it must soon fall back to the level of those below with whom it has to compete, and this process, continued, would mean the final grading down of all groups to the level of the lowest. It is because progressive tendencies are so strongly ingrained in the very character of the people, in modern countries, that any movement towards such a leveling down, or even any slackening of the onward march, produces social revolt. Unless England interposes the defensive hand which her situaation now demands, we may expect in a few years to see the complex fabric of modern industrial society assailed from the inside, in its chief stronghold and the very seat of its origin.

NEGRO LIFE ON A TURPENTINE FARM

J. C. WOOTEN

The southeastern part of the United States, along the coast and even as far up as the hilly section, is the home of the long-leaf pine. In addition to supplying lumber, these pine forests are made to yield a large quantity of turpentine. A kind of gum oozes from the pine, from which spirits of turpentine and resin are made by means of distillation.

A few decades ago North Carolina was known as the state of tar, pitch and turpentine, but as the supply of timber became exhausted the center of the turpentine interest moved further south, where the axe had not invaded. Georgia, Florida and Alabama are now the states in which the work is carried on most extensively. The commercial name for this product is naval stores. Savannah is the largest market in the world, and from there it is shipped to all nations. It requires much capital and labor to do this work on the extensive plan on which it is now done. The eastern part of North Carolina furnished not a few of the laborers on these farms before the law was passed against taking laborers out of the state under contract. Goldsboro, Wilson, Greenville and Kinston were the chief recruiting stations. Many were induced to go from having heard some emissary tell of the fabulous wages to be earned in the turpentine regions. The operators of the farms either came into North Carolina or sent their agents to seek laborers. The negroes in great numbers gathered around these agents and enrolled for the promise lands of Alabama and Georgia. These periodic excursions afforded a great opportunity for runaway couples, as well as for those not yet coupled.

The negroes would either go in a special car attached to the regular train, or on a special train called

the Black-flyer.   As the crowd was usually large enough
to fill many cars, the Black-flyer was most often the
means of transit.   It took about a day and night to
make the trip to Georgia and one additional day's ride
to reach Florida or Alabama.

It was formerly the custom to hire the negroes by
the year to do so much work and require them to wait
until December 15th to settle.   On account of the law
forbidding contracted labor leaving the state, the old
method of hiring by the year was abandoned.   Transportation is now furnished them on the promise to work
and pay it back as soon as possible.   They are now paid
either weekly or monthly.

When the negroes get to their destination they report to the commissary and buy a complete outfit for
their new life, which consists of a long-handle frying-
pan, a tin bucket, five pounds of hog meat, a peck of
meal and a plug of tobacco.   Then they go to the
quarters, which are mere shanties, 14x16, made of logs
and undressed planks, having stick chimneys and
windows with wooden shutters.   The only exterior objects to relieve the bleak dreariness of their habitations
are the tall pines that sing melodious anthems and serve
as protection against the wind and burning sun.   The
inside of a shanty is smoky and dirty; the walls are
decorated with fancy advertisements and illustrated
newspapers.   Such articles of furniture as a bureau or
wardrobe are not found.   A few nails driven in the
rough, undressed wall serve as a wardrobe, a small dry
goods box serves both as a chair and Saratoga, a pocket
hand mirror, a tin wash basin and a ten cent pine water-
bucket complete the furniture.

In the winter the homes are comfortably warmed by
a blazing fire made out of the unlimited supply of pine
taken from the Captain's cord wood near by.   Sometimes
the dross from the still is poured upon the wood to en-

liven the blaze.   Near the center of the quarters there
is generally a common well, unless nature has provided
a spring.

The negroes do not lose any time in unpacking and
getting their household goods arranged.   The first day
is spent in fixing their tools.   The men put handles to
their box-axes and sharpen the blades, while the boys
sharpen the hoes.   The hands report early the next
morning for duty.   The men, twenty-five in a squad, go
under the direction of a woodsman to the virgin forest,
where they cut cavities in the trees to catch the gum.
These are the boxes or depositories from which the crop
is taken.   It is slow work for the new men, but after one
or two weeks they become experts.   The axemen are
numbered, and when one cuts a box he halloos his
number, when the woodsman marks one for him on the
tally-sheet.   At noon or night, if one of the negroes
wants to find out how many he has cut, he goes up to
the tally-man and says: "Cap, how many for 99?" or
whatever his number may be.   It is strange how pro-
ficient they become in keeping account.   If a negro gets
in an extra tally on the scorer there is no correcting it,
but if the scorer fails to tally a single box the negro
knows it.   He can go through the woods and point out
every box he has cut during the day.

The "halloos" mingled with their songs (for they
always sing while at work) produce an effect not easily
forgotten.   Some of their melodies are of a pathetic
nature and when rendered by their deep, melodious
voices, tell in unmistakable language that they are thinking of their far-away homes.   This is the song with
which the more experienced ones console the new men:

> "Hard, but it's fair,
> "When you wuz home
> "You wouldn't stay dare."

This is answered by the new men in a way in which

only the homesick man can sing. The title of this song is "Five Hundred Miles from My Home."

After the first day's experience, ending, possibly, with a cut foot or back (for in throwing the long blade of their axes over and around their shoulders they do cut their backs), they return to the quarters to spend the night. Here it is even harder for them to repress the thoughts of home; but they find consolation in the banjo, accordeon, harmonica and dance.

With the boys who have been raking straw from around the pines, and racing all day, it is not so bad. It is a new experience with them and proves to be a pleasure until they come to the second and third year boxes, and have to rake the gum and scrape what has accumulated upon the ground from around the trees.

The negroes cut boxes and rake pines until March, when the box-cutters lay aside their axes for the hack, a steel instrument shaped like a half S fastened on to a handle and weight. The pine-rakers now use their dippers, a flat oblong piece of steel with a hollow end in which a handle is placed.

The work of cultivating and housing the crop now begins. It may occur to the reader to ask how it is possible to manage so many negroes and keep their work straight. It is done by blazing a line through the woods, thus making a "through" or "drift" of 2,100 boxes by actual count. Some of the chippers take four of these drifts for their crop, while others take five or six.

The chipper hangs his coat and bucket on the limb of a blown down pine and goes all day long from pine to pine freshening the streaks so that the pines will yield gum more freely. At noon he eats his dinner alone, which is made up of corn bread and white side meat. He rests awhile, takes a fresh chew of tobacco and goes back to his work.

The boys who do the dipping are not so lonesome, for they are always near each other, and at noon they form a group and play stick-frog, or skin, the latter being the great gambling game with cards. They bet as vigorously as blacklegs and frequently wind up the contest in a fight with lightwood knots or dippers. The coins used in these games are chews of tobacco, many of which can be made from a nickle's worth. These are the change and they are generally handled as cautiously as if they were real money. When one has lost his last chew and is five miles from the commissary, these tobacco coins are prized almost as much as gold dollars. While these boys are at work they not only clean turpentine boxes, but kill rabbits, polecats, rattlesnakes, gophers and anything else that comes in the way. The gopher is an animal peculiar to that section, very much like a turtle, except that it lives on land in a hole in which it burrows. It is said that they live on wire-grass in summer and lightwood knots and old tomato cans in winter. The gophers and rabbits which the negroes catch are carried home and cooked to become a part of the bill' of fare for the next day. The polecats and rattlesnakes are killed on general principles. In the summer season the hungry negroes sometimes venture into a neighboring cane field, watermelon patch or peach orchard, and feast themselves until frightened away by the sight of a man with a musket. After one of these escapades the initiated say : "Nigger, I told you Crackers git you.'

Pay-day in former times was quite different from what it is to-day. Now they get their pay every week or month, as the Captain's rule may be. The 15th is a time of rejoicing to the faithful and a time of mourning for those who have "gone broke." It is usually celebrated by a ball. There being fewer negro women than men on the farms, many women come in from the neighboring farms and towns to be present on that occasion. Usually it begins at dark Saturday night and lasts until Sunday morning at daybreak. It beggars description. The women are diked up in every imaginable style and in all the colors of the rainbow; the men in Prince Alberts, cutaways, bobtails—while their necks rise in misery above starched collars and flaming cravats.

The negroes who do not dance often build a fire in the yard, straddle a log and indulge in what is called the skin game. Any number may play the game and bet without limit. Having just been paid in cash for the month's work, they continue at this game until the dancers are worn out and asleep, and often until many of the men are dead-broke, sometimes playing all night and all day Sunday. A few wandering professionals usually come along, win all the money and then move on for fresh victims at another farm. Thus the professionals "make pay-day," as they call it. Many of these fellows are now serving sentences on chain-gangs. They become very much infatuated with the idea of making money without work, and often resort to arms to carry their point. However, on many farms these fellows are not allowed to stop.

Upon the average about 10 per cent. of the men on the farms are married; the others are a happy-go-lucky set. There are numerous churches and sects in the turpentine region and many of the negroes are exceedingly religious. Sometimes a chipper feels called upon to do the preaching and when he can work up a shout he is no longer to be relied upon to chop up his crop. His call to go preach is louder than the one to go chip.

Some of the preachers who serve the churches are devout Christians and elevate the negroes by their earnest appeals and godly lives, while there are others whose chief aim seems to be to feast at their special dinners and to fleece the poor negroes of enough money to buy a forty dollar suit. The men who contribute least to their spiritual life receive the most money. The negroes see the selfishness of these preachers, but cannot help giving to them because of their power to work upon the emotions.

They have no schools and little need for any. Few of them pay taxes or vote. Those who do vote always vote as the Captain directs. They are not intimidated, but do this because there is no organized party or leaders in that section.

The negroes are their own worst enemies. They are naturally hardy and few ever become sick or die, except from abuse of themselves. Very often a gunshot puts an end to their existence. It is nothing unusual to see one with a wounded foot or hand, caused from pranking with a pistol.

Their manner of life is altogether different in turpentine regions from what it is on the old farms in North Carolina. Notwithstanding the change in their lives some of their old habits are yet dear to them. They delight to have peddlers and patent medicine men come among them. They retain their love for brindle dogs and hounds, and make them do valiant service in helping them to get an old-time dinner of 'possum.

The negroes have a very friendly feeling for the white men on the farm. This fact is shown in that there is only one white man to fifty negroes. The operator has thousands of dollars invested with no protection whatever. The white families live in perfect peace, and never in ante-bellum days were the servants more attentive or more humble.

The negro women on these farms are lazy, slovenly and, as a rule, lewd. They think only of how they can spend their man's money. It is spent for dress and the gratification of their appetites and whims.

The commissary is the place where the negroes meet to trade and tell their experiences. It is their

Mecca.   Alone in the forest they plan how they intend
to go to the commissary and draw their money on the
15th December and then go home.   The hard-working,
frugal fellow may realize what he has longed for the
whole year, but the unfortunate are left behind as slaves
to the soil, because they are cursed by having found for
themselves a dusky damsel who squanders all their income.   Notwithstanding the wild life that the negroes
lead after coming on a turpentine farm they are easily
managed and always satisfied.   The Captain is everything to them ; his word is law and his storehouses
their chief pay and support.

The day is passed when there is a fortune in this
business.   The resin forests are fast becoming exhausted
and the farms are gradually being used for other purposes.   The operator now uses the pine for timber,
clears the land and raises agricultural products.   Para-
doxical as it may sound, the turpentine man builds up
the country by tearing it down.   He is indeed a pioneer
and the negro is his tool.

EDITORIAL CRUCIBLE

THE REFUSAL of General Blanco to exchange Lieut.
Hobson and his six comrades of the "Merrimac," and
his reported determination to use them as "defenses,"
shows the true Philip II. Spanish spirit.   Under these
circumstances it is the duty of President McKinley to
notify the Spanish government that General Blanco will
be held personally responsible for the lives of every one
of these heroes, and if, when Havana is taken, any one
of these men is missing, Blanco's head pays the penalty,
and Spanish officers of the next highest rank, beginning with Admiral Cervera, shall answer with their
lives for the remainder of the Hobson party.   Indeed,
the Minister of War at Madrid who issued this order
should be included in the number to atone for the
crime.

THE $200,000,000 war loan promises to be wholly
successful, without the aid of any syndicates or lump
subscriptions.   The new bonds are payable after ten
and due in twenty years, and will draw three per cent.
interest.   The smallest denomination is $20.00, largest
$10,000.   Subscriptions from individuals, and for the
lowest amounts will be accepted first; applications for
$500.00 and over will not be allotted until after the sub-
scription closes, on July 14th.   This method of popu-
larizing the loan ought to, and probably will, succeed.
The method of subscription has been made as simple as
possible.   Blank forms may be obtained at every money-
order post-office, and at most of the banks and express
offices, and on these forms is clearly indicated all that
it is necessary for the subscriber to fill out.   The subscriber may himself mail to the Treasury Department
at Washington the blank form filled out, together with
his remittance covering the par value of the amount of

bonds for which he wishes to subscribe. That remittance may be in whatever form best suits the subscriber's convenience—in currency, bank draft, check, post-office money order, or express money order. The day the currency is received, or the day the proceeds are received from the checks, drafts, or money orders, the subscription will be entered and will immediately begin drawing interest.

———

THE OREGON election appears to have somewhat disturbed the faith of the free silver people in their prophesied victory in 1898. Prominent silver men frankly admit that the prospects of the party, "which seemed so bright only a few months ago, have suddenly withered, and the future looks dark indeed." This shows that there is reasonable ground for hoping, and even believing, that the American people will finally reach a position of sustaining and even demanding a rational reform in our monetary system. The first step in this direction is to irrevocably establish a gold, or at least a full value, monetary standard, and rid us forever of the delusion that the value of standard money can ever be permanently maintained above its bullion equivalent. The defeat of the silver party in Oregon is a strong indication that permanent progress has been made in this direction. When this much is thoroughly assured we may expect to move on towards a comprehensive and scientific revision of our banking system, which shall make all paper money subject to coin redemption by the banks which issue it, and thus put all money (which is a commercial instrument) upon a sound economic and business basis. At any rate, it is encouraging to note that the educational work of the last few years has really begun to dispel the phantom of a forty-three cent dollar.

A SHORT time ago Mr. Debs was very sure that the only way to help the toiling masses to escape from the clutches of capitalistic society was to colonize them in socialistic groups, where no capitalist should have a foothold. To this end a Social Democracy party was organized and the millennium promised. But, alas! Mr. Debs has found out that he was wrong. He has concluded, probably from experience he does not care to relate, that ideal communities have much less of social perfection than he had imagined. He has learned that, after all, the only way any considerable portion of society can make progress is by the old fashioned road of leadership and followers—gradual improvement of social conditions through educational processes and opportunities; in other words, that there is no patent way to Paradise—that it is only by the road of human improvement, through character expansion, that a higher and better civilization can come. In proof of Mr. Debs' conversion, he and thirty-six of the delegates (out of a total of eighty-eight) bolted the Social Democracy convention and declared in favor of entering politics in the old fashioned way to obtain improvements for the laboring class. It would indeed be rash to predict that Mr. Debs has become rational on industrial matters, but it seems clear that from some cause he has been cured of the delusion that society can find economic salvation in socialistic colonization.

MOST OF our readers will probably remember that about one year ago a great furore was created by an anti-trust pamphlet written by President Gates of Grinnell College, Iowa, violently attacking the American Book Company. This pamphlet charged upon the Book Company all sorts of corruption, bribery and general misconduct, and described it as a "Foe to American Schools." The author and publishers of this pam-

phlet were prosecuted by the American Book Company
and, the case being brought to trial, the defendants
were entirely unable to substantiate any material item
out of the long array of the abusive charges made in
this pamphlet. The case was tried in Minneapolis,
before an average Western jury, and the verdict
(which was returned within thirty minutes) was one
of libel on the part of the defendants, with damages of
$7,700.

We call attention to this, not because of any interest in this particular case, but merely as an evidence
of the vicious and utterly flimsy character of most of
the attacks made upon large capitalistic organizations
in this country. It would be interesting to know just
what would be left of the other innumerable assaults
upon large corporations that are continuously made by
all sorts of newspapers and politicians, if the parties
attacked cared enough about it to bring their accusers
to the bar as the American Book Company has done.
This, at least, ought to have a sobering effect on those
who are willing to take every wild, incendiary attack
upon large industrial concerns as gospel truth, and as a
basis for radical hostile legislation.

THE IDEA of an Anglo-American Alliance seems to
be making steady progress. It is being observed with
some concern by the more military nations of Europe.
France, which has been extremely offensive in its anti-
American sentiment since the opening of the war, is
beginning to realize that, after all, it is just as well to
be on speaking terms with the United States. Several
of her prominent journals and public men have taken
occasion to say—rather apologetically—that they desire
to be counted among our friends. Similar expressions
have come from Germany, and Russia takes pains to
recall that she has always been our friend and, with a

true bear instinct, reminds us that we once had serious difficulty with England.

All this is just as it should be, and just as it is sure to be. The more closely the richest, most advanced and least military nations come into confidential relations, the more civil will the rest of the world become. It is in the nature of things that non-military and industrial people—living under democratic institutions—should have an increasing affinity for each other and a moral co-operation for extension of the political institutions, industrial methods and types of civilization they represent. This does not mean molestation or interference in any way with the peaceful progress of less advanced nations; on the contrary, it means a greater security for peaceful industrial expansion for the whole human race. To be sure, it may mean a check to the arbitrary extension of military despotism, for which everybody would be glad except a few Czars, Kaisers and Alfonsos, whose ultimate elimination from the direction of affairs it is the function of civilization to accomplish.

SPEAKER REED'S opposition to a colonial policy is bringing down upon him a good deal of rabid criticism, verging on abuse. The Memphis *Commercial Appeal*, for instance, asks: "Who is Reed anyway?" The *Commercial Appeal* may be excused for not knowing who Mr. Reed is. There are ever so many things that everybody else knows that this belated Memphis contemporary has not yet found out. Throughout Christendom people of ordinary information know that Thomas B. Reed is the strongest and most conspicuous character in American public life. For a number of years Mr. Reed has been so placed that he has been compelled to bear the brunt of the fight for his whole party; and he is probably the only man in the party, and for that matter in either party, who

could have done it. Almost any other man in his
position who was opposed to annexation of Hawaii
would have "fallen in line," for fear that to risk an open
expression of opposition to a policy which seemed to
have public endorsement would involve political disadvantage. Mr. Reed's very strength consists in the fact
that he opposed the annexation of Hawaii, as he
would oppose the annexation of Cuba and probably
of the Philippine Islands, because he believes as an
American and a statesman that a colonial policy is not
for the best interests and future progress of this country. Mr. Reed places the importance of a correct national policy above that of personal or party political
advantage. It is in this that Mr. Reed is greater and
stronger and more patriotic than those who merely
acquiesce in deference to public clamor or administration
favors. It is the function of the true statesman to lead,
especially on great national policies, and not to follow
the momentary market-place enthusiasm of the uninformed.

———

IT IS generally admitted that the new Primary Law
in New York has, on the whole, worked satisfactorily.
Still, to the astonishment and disgust of the reformers,
the machine men in New York City have been as triumphant in the primaries as ever. In the municipal
election it is claimed that as many Republicans voted
for Seth Low as for General Tracy. From this fact it
was assumed that the Low voters, the superior citizens,
would, under the new law, of course make themselves
definitely felt in the primaries, if they did not actually
carry them in a majority of districts. Yet the facts are
manifestly otherwise. Still this ought to surprise no
one. It only reveals what always occurs, viz., that
those who work most incessantly usually win. Any
movement whose cornerstone is anti-organization may

be set down as destined soon to fail. Organization is efficiency, and whether in the hands of saint or sinner is pretty sure to win. The Low movement, which abounded in moral ideas, lacked this essential element of practical sense and sound leadership. It built its house upon the sand of non-organization, and it has fallen to pieces with the first wind that blew from organized or machine efforts. New movements, to be lasting, must be constructive. Mere negative fault-finding or dislike of a personal leader can seldom do more than disrupt existing forces and give victory to the enemy. The Low movement was chiefly an anti-Platt movement; it was directed against an individual instead of for a public policy. Had it recognized the importance of organization and worked solely for a better constructive municipal policy it might have had some chance of success; at least, if it had not elected its candidate, it might have secured a permanent existence and future victory. But being only a negative movement, opposed to organization, inspired by dislike of an individual, it succeeded only in disrupting the existing organization and giving Greater New York the poorest specimen of a Tammany Mayor, without even laying the foundation for a superior movement in municipal politics.

CIVICS AND EDUCATION

TUSKEGEE AND ITS FOUNDER

That the negro race is capable of a high degree of intellectual and social development has been proven by experience. The advanced types already developed, few though they may be, are reasonable evidence that there is at least no impassable organic nor ethnological barrier to the final evolution of the Ethiopian up to practically the Caucasian type of civilization. However slow the process may be, however tortuous the road, the fact remains that what has been done can be done, and in truth is in course of being done, here in America, year by year.

Many decades of slave importations from Africa prepared the materials for a problem which the Civil War suddenly forced upon us for solution. We attempted to meet it, first, by admitting a half barbarous race to all the rights of full American citizenship. The carpet-bag era, Ku-Klux-Klan and wholesale disfranchisement stand out as three monuments to the failure of this policy. Deportation to Africa has been proposed and some colonies have actually been sent over, but the scheme is too utterly impracticable even to arouse public interest. As Mr. Washington has several times said, with reference to a certain expedition of 600 negroes to Africa some years ago, the people who hail that as a sign of an approaching solution of the race problem seem to forget that fully 600 negro babies were born that same morning south of Mason and Dixon's line. The situation is a sharp warning against the admission or annexation of any more types of inferior population, but those whom we already have with us must be dealt with here at home. Civilization demands this for our own sakes, humanity for theirs.

Within recent years the right method of treating this problem has been slowly gaining ground. That intellectual, social and moral culture and political capability must be preceded by material and industrial improvement is the law of progress, and it is becoming recognized as such. More and more it is seen that the southern negroes will never become politically free until they are able to meet the whites upon their own ground in the trade and industry of every-day life. Neither will the blacks ever become educated and socially refined until they are stimulated to actually desire and then to earn or produce the means of decent living and the leisure and disposition for a higher standard of social life; nor will they gain any fine sense of morality until the necessity of having their own rights and interests respected sharpens the line between *meum* and *tuum* so that the two cannot be confounded.

With this general principle to work from, the case has become more hopeful. Industrial development of the negro will eventually solve the negro problem. Two great factors in this process are already at work: one, the migration of manufacturing industries to the South, which will introduce order, precision and wage conditions; the other, industrial education. With the new factory system in the South should go a reasonable legal limitation of the hours of labor, in order that the more orderly habits and increased incomes of the natives, both black and white, may have opportunity to work themselves out in a higher standard of living and growth of social refinement. Meanwhile, this same kind of development is being powerfully aided by educational work of the sort going on at the Tuskegee Normal and Industrial Institute, in eastern Alabama.

Remarkable as this work is in itself, it is hardly less so than the history of its growth and the career of its founder. Booker T. Washington is at once the back-bone of this educational work and a proof of the negro's capacity to develop the higher characteristics which such training aims to produce. Though a small man physically, Mr. Washington has a magnetic personality, unlimited energy and a highly effective type of orator-ical ability. He is a quick, witty, graphic, manneristic speaker, possessed body and soul with enthusiasm for his work, and though not a great orator in the classic sense, yet not infrequently attains a lofty plane of action-inspiring eloquence. Best of all, perhaps, Mr. Washington's fund of practical common sense is so large and so well employed that practically none of his energy, either oratorical or administrative, is wasted. He is vividly conscious of the degradation of the south-ern blacks and the difficulty of rousing them to action, as only one who has lived and worked among them can be.

Mr. Washington was born a slave in Virginia two or three years before the war—he himself does not know the exact date. He was taken to West Virginia and there worked for some time in the coal mines. When still a mere lad he heard of the Hampton Insti-tute for negro education, and made his way thither on the meagre hope of finding some employment that would enable him to take the course. In this he suc-ceeded, and went out from Hampton with the deter-mination to do something to put similar opportunities within the reach of others of his race. Going down into the Black Belt of Alabama, where the negroes outnumber the whites three to one, and where the standard of life among the blacks is at its lowest depth of degradation, he began work, practically single-handed. This was in 1881, and the Tuskegee Nor-mal and Industrial Institute of to-day represents the labors of the last seventeen years. The institution

now owns 2,267 acres of land and 37 buildings, the
latter built almost entirely by the students themselves.
The whole is valued at $290,000, and is free from mort-
gage.   Last year there were 850 students and 86 instructors.   The average age of students was 18½ years,
nearly half of them being girls.   All students, in
addition to a regular English education, are taught
some useful trade or industry; 26 of these industries
are in constant operation as a part of the Institute.   The
cost of educating one scholar is $50 per year; board is
paid for by the students themselves, partly in money
and partly in labor.

At the seventh annual commencement, May 26th
last, 48 students were graduated; the total number
registered during the year being 1,047.   About 25
undergraduates have enlisted in the war for Cuban
freedom.   During the year just closed the total receipts of the Institute were about $114,000 in cash and
$52,000 worth of labor performed by students towards
their living expenses.   Of the cash receipts $62,000
were used for current expenses and $52,000 invested in
new plant.

The theory of this work is that young men and
women graduated from the Tuskegee Institute will
settle throughout the South and become stimulative
forces and centers of educational influence among their
own people.   The character of the training tends to
direct them naturally to this work, while at the same
time rousing their enthusiasm for it.   They are not
educated to be ministers or lawyers, but are fitted
especially for work which confronts them on every
hand as soon as they leave the Institute.   Some 300
graduates and ex-students, it is claimed, are now
settled all through the South, working as farmers, mechanics, school-teachers, housekeepers and in other
capacities, infusing the people about them with the

spirit of progress. The results, particularly in the
vicinity of Tuskegee, have been remarkable. Instead
of the dirty, one-room, unsanitary shanties in which
these people formerly lived, there are now neat little
cottages with well-tended gardens and a general atmosphere of cleanliness and self-respect. Most of the
"one-gallus" farmers, preparing their land by the aid
of a mule and wooden plow, mortgaging their crops far
in advance, at excessive interest, in debt for their farms
or behind on rent, borrowing money even to buy
cheap jewelry and gaudy clocks for their otherwise
destitute huts, when effectively reached by the Tuskegee influence become careful, economical agricult-
urists, paying up their debts, clearing off mortgages,
and transforming their homes into decent, habitable
cottages.

In his public appeals for this work Mr. Washington
shows a firm grasp of the fundamental principles of
social progress. The Tuskegee plan does not overlook
the importance of moral and religious growth, he says,
but simply recognizes the fact that any considerable
advance in these respects must be preceded by and
grow out of improved material conditions and industrial character. Where whole families are brought up
in one-room log cabins, living on the "skim milk of
industry," they cannot, as a class, be moral or develop
the highest qualities of life and character, however fervent their religious zeal. As Tuskegee's principal dryly
observes, a negro who goes home from prayer meeting
with an empty stomach to an empty pantry is pretty
sure to find something to eat before morning. Mr.
Washington gives an amusing illustration of the degree
of moral discernment that still prevails in a population
of the Black Belt type. One old negro in slave times,
he says, upon being convicted of stealing chickens from
his master argued in defence that since his master owned

both darkey and chicken there could have been no theft even if the chicken was now inside the man instead of the coop: "Massa's got less chicken, but he's got mo' nigger."

The negro must be raised to industrial equality with the whites before he can command either political freedom or social respect. We don't care very much for anybody, says Mr. Washington very truly, unless that person has something that we want; and it is because, in any given social group, each one does have something that the others want that people are bound together and made good neighbors and friends. When the negro becomes indispensable to his white neighbors as a tradesman, as a farmer, as a mechanic, as a factory hand, or when he accumulates money and loans it out to white men, he will no longer be driven from the polls or shot in his own house because of social and race prejudice. He can attain this industrial equality, not through any mere sentiment or sympathy on the part of reformers, but by becoming able to compete successfully with the white men on a free economic basis. People buy corn of a farmer not because of the farmer's needs or color or character, but solely because he can sell it cheaper than somebody else, and the way to enable the negro to sell corn and prosper in the business is to teach him how to produce cheap corn, by whatever improved methods of scientific farming the white man employs. Unless the blacks do occupy this responsible, efficient position industrially, it makes little difference what their political beliefs or social ambitions may be—they will not be permitted to express or attain them. They are like another negro of whom Mr. Washington tells, who, having "gone broke," tried to borrow three cents from an acquaintance to pay his ferry passage across the river, and was refused on the ground that when a man hasn't a cent in his pocket it doesn't make

much difference which side of the river he is on. Nor
does it.

The head of the Tuskegee Institute is entirely right
in saying that the negro problem of the South affects
the whole nation. The relations existing between the
races at present are morally degrading to the whites as
well as to the blacks. Probably no lynching ever took
place in which the perpetrators did not, in the very
brutalizing of their finer sensibilities and humane instincts, suffer more serious loss than their victim in
giving up his miserable life. The southern whites may
feel that civilization depends upon their disfranchising
the negro (and they may be right), but every act of
violence thus resorted to stunts the moral character and
deadens the sense of justice. This two-fold demoralization in the South has too long been a menace to the
political stability and ethical quality of the nation. Two
races were nominally freed by the Emancipation Procla-
mation, says Mr. Washington,—the white no less than
the black, and their destinies are the same. It remains
for us to make that freedom real on both sides by helping the negro up to the plane of industrial independence and competitive equality with the white men
among whom his lot is permanently cast. Industrial
training and the factory system are the great forces
which will bring about that end.

HOW STREETS ARE CLEANED IN EUROPE

Ex-Commissioner Waring's success in cleaning the streets of New York City was undoubtedly due in large measure to his careful study of the problem from the standpoint of a specialist. So far as possible he sought to reduce the whole process of street sweeping, garbage collection, disposition of refuse, organization of force and methods of work to a matter of scientific precision and efficiency. He made a thorough investigation of European methods of street cleaning, in order to learn whatever experience had to teach on the subject. During the summer of 1896, Col. Waring visited the principal cities of Europe with this object in view; his report to Mayor Strong is published in the June (1898) *Supplement to Municipal Affairs* and contains much important material. The greater age and more strongly centralized government of European cities seems to have produced a system of administration superior, in many respects, to our own; but it is worthy of note that the much-heralded cheapness of municipal government abroad is chiefly due to the lower wages paid to city employees. Col. Waring's report proves this so far as street cleaning is concerned. Some of his comments on the streets of Vienna, Budapest, Berlin, Paris, London, and Birmingham, and the methods of cleaning, are especially interesting.

Vienna. In Vienna, for instance, he was especially struck with the care shown by the citizens in refraining from littering up the streets. The contrast with New York in this respect was marked. "In the matter of street sweeping", however, says Col. Waring, "we are at no such disadvantage. Our best paved streets, though not so well paved as these, are better cleaned, and our worst streets, with a pavement that would not be tolerated anywhere in Europe, are cleaner than the average of all except the best, in Vienna." An excellent feature of street paving in Vienna is thus described:

"The tracks of the street railroads are grooved rails, somewhat like those on Broadway, but they are heavier, and the two sides of the rail are equally high and equally broad. The groove in which the flange of the wheel runs is narrower than the narrowest carriage-wheel, so that in driving, the wheel passes obliquely to and fro over the track without interference from it or from the pavement beside it. Contrasted with our 'centre-bearing rail,' with a deep, wide groove between it and the stone on each side of it, angering the driver, wrenching the vehicle and shortening its life, this Viennese device is most attractive. From the street cleaner's point of view, the small channel to be cleaned by the railway-man's scraper is a vast gain over the two deep wide ruts that no broom can clean properly."

Budapest. The methods of street cleaning in this city are nearly the same as in Vienna, but the system of disposing of the refuse is quite different. Everything is carried out of the city to Kleinpest, and, after some of the bulkier material is removed, the rest of the rubbish is dumped upon "endless aprons of heavy hemp cloth about two feet wide. These move slowly between two rows of women and children, who select the various treasures to which they are assigned, each after its kind. The white-bottle boy lets the green bottles pass, and the big-bone woman pays no attention to the small bones; these meet their fate further on. One group of children devotes itself entirely to corks, another to nails, another to strings, and so on. As the cloth finally turns over the end of the table it drops all of its rejected material into a conveyer, which carries it to the manure wagon. In the heap to which it is added there goes on a process of 'bacteriolysis' that reduces it all to the condition of a fine compost, fit for the fields."

Although conditions in New York are very different from those in Budapest, Col. Waring says that: " If we can ever reach the minute economy of the works at Kleinpest, we ought, with our richer refuse and our higher prices, to derive an income from our rubbish sufficient to pay nearly all the cost of running the Department of Street Cleaning."

Berlin.   This is the only large city in Europe in which the sweepers wear uniforms. Comparisons between the street cleaning methods of Berlin and New York are difficult because of the widely different conditions. To quote again: "For example, in New York we sweep every street at least once a day; we do not sprinkle the streets; we do not sweep the sidewalks; we remove all household refuse, and we are charged with the final disposition of street and household wastes of every kind. This last item costs us about $475,000 per year. In Berlin, on the other hand, the department sweeps the streets on an average of only three times a week; it sprinkles the street; it sweeps all the sidewalks; it has nothing whatever to do with household wastes of any kind, neither ashes, garbage nor refuse; it disposes only of the dirt swept up in the streets and from the sidewalks, and it pays a contractor for this removal only about $140,000."

In Berlin the relatively low wages explain the apparent cheapness of street cleaning as compared with New York. In fact, for the same number of employees, Berlin's system would be more than twice as costly as ours if the same wages were paid. " The rate of wages and the number of persons employed differ in a most important degree. Our force numbers about 2,700 of all grades, and we pay our sweepers and drivers an average of about $680 per year. In Berlin the force numbers only about 900, men and boys, and their average pay is not more than $260 per year. Our annual outlay is about $3,000,000; that of Berlin is about $760,000. The two cities are of very nearly the same population."

Paris. Paris has generally been exalted as the world's model in the matter of street cleaning, and it is somewhat surprising to find this impression not wholly confirmed by Col. Waring's report. Of the Paris streets he says: "After a close and careful examination I should say that they are quite as well swept as our streets, and that there is nowhere to be found the defective pavement of which we have so much. In the matter of litter, however, I think that New York is much better cared for. Except in the more frequented show streets, and to a certain extent even there, there is more paper scattered, and in many parts of the town much less attention seems to be paid to its collection and removal. On the whole, I think we lose nothing in the comparison. New York is as clean and at least as tidy as Paris. The methods of work in the French capital are in many respects different from what was found in other cities, and very different from the methods here. . . . All street sprinkling is done by the city, and under the direction of the engineers having charge of the cleaning. . . . In dry weather wood pavements are washed daily, asphalt every two days, and stone and macadam every three days."

Paris has had great difficulty with the problem of disposing of garbage collections. To carry them away by water transportation has been found too uncertain a method, and by rail too costly. The expense of an incineration plant has so far prevented any steps toward providing one. At present the garbage is carted out of the city by contractors, and dumped in various places, or parts of it sold to farmers for fertilizing purposes. "The whole question is still open, and it is an extremely knotty one. Everything points to a steady

and large increase of the cost of final disposition, whatever the methods resorted to."

Col. Waring seems to have obtained very few useful suggestions from the Paris system of street cleaning.
"Neither in street cleaning, in the removal of household wastes, nor in final disposition," he says, "did I
find any suggestions which would be of use in New
York, save as to the value of the salable refuse."

London. The methods of street cleaning in use in
the "square mile," or old city of London, are fairly
typical of those employed in the city as a whole. Of
this central city, he says: " The sidewalks are swept as
occasion requires, and in wet weather they are cleaned
with squeegees [rubber scrapers] in the daytime. The
collection of street sweepings, refuse and rubbish is
very large, and is increasing, as is the cost of work.
. . . The collections of all kinds are taken to a
wharf on the south side of the Thames, where they are
roughly sorted. What is valuable as manure is boated
away to the country. All else, after the salable refuse
is culled out, is shot into a 'destructor,' or cremator.
This apparatus works day and night throughout the
year, save for fifteen to twenty days, when it is stopped
for repairs and cleaning. By the last report it destroyed
in the year 23,117 loads (66 loads per day), leaving about 22½ per cent. of 'ashes and cinders more
or less hard but valueless, and for the removal of which
the Commission had to pay.' . . .

"The general appearance of the streets in London
as to cleanliness is much the same as that in New York
so far as its more important thoroughfares are concerned.
There is about the same amount of littering with paper
and other refuse. The less important streets, which
are swept only twice or thrice a week, are not so clean
as ours, which are all swept at least once every day.

But the pavement of such streets in London is *much* better." '

Birmingham. This city is evidently Col. Waring's model not only in street cleaning but in nearly every phase of municipal administration. Here again, however, the effect of relatively low wages in giving a low cost of operations is clearly seen. "The work in the streets, including repairs of pavement and macadam, sweeping and removal of sweepings, and all sprinklings, employs about 400 men (who work fifty-four hours per week) and about 160 horses. The gang leaders are paid from $6.00 to $7.00 per week, drivers get from $5.50 to $6.00, and sweepers, $5.25. Selected men of this force do the road-repairing, being paid, in addition to their regular wages, a price by the piece for this work."

Most of the streets of Birmingham have wood pavements, but there is a large amount of macadamized roadway of superior quality, and it is kept in repair by the city's own employees. The combustible refuse is burned, and several salable products, such as concrete, mortar, ammonia, fertilizer, etc., are realized from an utilization process.

The Ex-Commissioner's report closes (in part) as follows:

"In reviewing the whole subject of European street cleaning as it came under my observation, the most important and suggestive consideration is that which concerns the relation of the people to the work, and, largely as leading to that, the manner in which the police intervenes to prevent the littering of the streets. The regulations in European towns are no better than ours. The laws and ordinances are substantially the same, but there is the immense difference that in Europe laws and ordinances mean something and are executed, while here they are treated as mere matters of form. The policeman in Turin would as soon think of letting a highwayman escape his notice and official attention as of disregarding a man who deliberately threw littering material into the street. I have seen policemen in Europe accost gentlemen, apparently foreigners, and politely, but effectively request them to pick up a paper they had thrown away. I have seen policemen in New York—and the spectacle is observable at every turn—saunter in a dignified manner past a crowd of littering people, utterly unconscious of the fact that they were violating any rule or regulation, and apparently considering it beneath the dignity of their position to heed the suggestion of a citizen that they were not obeying their orders. Here lies, unquestionably, the great secret of the difference between our ways and European ways.

"As to methods available for the improvement of the New York system, very little was observed. As a rule, our carts are better than theirs, being lighter and tighter; our brooms are probably better; and our methods of final disposition are quite as good, owing, no doubt, to our much better conditions for dumping refuse. Indeed, the only country in which important differences were found was Austria. The method of separating wastes at the point of final disposition in operation at Budapest was suggestive of very important improvements available here. So in Vienna I found the best street-sweeping machine, the best sprinkling cart and the best snow-plow."

It is gratifying, indeed, as a sign of American municipal progress, to note that so little was observed in the street cleaning methods of these cities better than the New York system. Needless to say, however, this has only become true within the last two or three years, and it is practically certain that under Tammany's restored *regime* our standard of efficiency will be materially lowered.

CIVIC AND EDUCATIONAL NOTES

One of the best bills in the interest of labor passed by the last legislature in this State was that limiting the hours of service of druggists' clerks to 'TOO MUCH POWER" INDEED! sixty-six hours per week—an average of eleven hours per day. Every consideration of social decency and common humanity demanded the enactment of this measure. But, since it was a city bill, it had to come to Mayor Van Wyck for approval and it was promptly vetoed, with the trashy excuse that its provisions for enforcement gave the Board of Health too much power! In the large sense this was not a local bill at all, and ought to have been so framed as to escape being finally judged by the Tammany standard of political philosophy. Such legislation is an instrument of general social progress and necessarily includes cities in its operation because it is in cities chiefly that such progress takes place.

A law passed by the last New York Legislature authorizes cities of the first class in New York State to ART IN CITIES expend any amount not in excess of $50,000 annually, and cities of the second class any amount not to exceed $25,000, for the encouragement and development of art. These cities are authorized to purchase works of art executed in the United States by United States citizens and also to contract for artistic decorations on and in municipal buildings and other public works. This law is naturally hailed with great satisfaction by artists, but it will be pleasing to the public chiefly because of the higher standard of municipal art toward which it seems to point the way. To have our public works and institutions throughout the city beautified with examples of genuine art must exercise a refining influence on the general artistic taste of the public, and this would be a distinct feature of social progress. It is a much too narrow view of the state's proper functions to say that public improvements should be merely utilitarian; indeed, the cultivation of the higher social qualities is the most important object of progressive effort, and a municipality is as completely justified in encouraging art as it is in building school-houses or maintaining public parks.

The movement for vacant-lot cultivation in cities, as a measure of poor relief, has attained considerable headway in many quarters. This is the scheme started by ex-Mayor Pin-gree of Detroit, and it has since been tried in New York, Boston, Brooklyn, Philadelphia, Chicago, Minneapolis, Omaha, and other cities. A recent number of the *Charities Review* contains a long defence of this "potato patch" plan and description of its workings in various places. Such a method of treating the labor problem is at best only a temporary expedient and cannot possibly abolish the evil of non-employment. If carried to any great extent it would simply mean that legitimate farmers would have to diminish their potato crops and see that source of income steadily shrink. As a system of temporary relief, similar to wood yards, etc., vacant-lot cultivation is distinctly better than direct charity or commitment to almshouses. Nevertheless, the important thing, it seems to us, is continually to keep in mind the fact that any permanent solution of the labor problem must be sought in other and more fundamental lines of effort. To make poverty easy is but to increase the difficulty of abolishing it. To establish a permanent industry on a scale that yields only a bare subsistence is to perpet-uate a low standard of living and render it more and more difficult to raise the general social level.

VACANT LOT CULTIVATION

SCIENCE AND INDUSTRY

THE NICARAGUA CANAL .

Every great achievement in human progress is the resultant of numerous forces, working singly at first, and then welded together for a final stroke in the fire of some great uprising or crisis. For many decades forces have been growing up demanding that the isthmus between North and South America shall be pierced and the enormous waste of a useless trip around a whole continent saved to the world's commerce. The industrial development of our Pacific coast and need of closer relations with the Atlantic seaboard has been one of these forces; our growing trade in the Orient—China, Japan, and the Philippines—has been another; and the increasing danger of dividing our navy in such a way that a good part of it would be practically useless in case of a sudden dash upon either coast, has been an important and is now one of the principal reasons for prompt action in the matter of a trans-isthmian canal.

The war with Spain is the crisis that has finally welded all these forces into a movement with the definiteness and energy necessary to success. This new pressure has at last brought us to the point of saying not merely that the canal ought to be built, but that it must be built, almost regardless of cost. There are no engineering difficulties that are not resolvable into the question of cost, and cost is a problem that this country is especially qualified to solve. Whether or not the government should guarantee the bonds of a construction company depends largely upon the conditions accompanying the arrangement. If there is no other way of inducing private capital in this country to undertake the work, and at the same time retain to the United States government exclusive control of the canal,

then the guarantee had better be given; but it should
be under such conditions as will absolutely protect the
government's interests in the matter and yield it some
return for the risks and obligation assumed.

Furthermore, the charter to any construction company thus aided should absolutely prohibit the sale or
lease of the canal to any foreign government or foreign
company. Control of this canal, both financially and
politically, should be wholly kept in the United States.
There is a strong and very natural prejudice against
repeating the Pacific Railroad experience of the last
three decades, but it is only fair to say that the proposition to guarantee bonds for this canal is entirely different from the direct issuing of bonds by the government to the companies, as was done in the Union
Pacific case. Furthermore, if the government should
at any time be obliged to take possession of the canal it
could do so without overstepping the proper limits of
the state's functions, because, once constructed, the
operation of a canal is an almost purely automatic affair,
involving even less opportunity for change and improvement than does the post-office system. This, of course,
is by no means the case with railroads; these demand a
continual process of alteration, improvement and re-
adaptation which the government is least of all agencies
qualified to carry out, and an expert talent which popular election never can secure. While the canal might
better, perhaps, remain in private hands, no particular
economic disadvantage would result from its transfer
to governmental control and such an outcome would
have the additional justification of military necessity.

The Nicaragua route is the one for which our aid
is sought, and which, if constructed, we should control.
The Panama Canal is a French enterprise and, even if
it could be acquired without vexatious international
difficulties, the engineering problems to be solved

are probably greater than on the much longer Nicaragua route. Moreover, the distance between our Atlantic and Pacific coasts would be considerably less by the Nicaragua than by the Panama Canal. If this canal were constructed, vessels from New York to San Francisco would have to travel only about 4,900 miles, instead of the 15,660 miles necessary to round Cape Horn; a saving of 10,760 miles, or about two-thirds of the present distance. Even more striking is the fact that the Nicaragua Canal would bring New York City nearer the Pacific Ocean than it now is by any of the direct transcontinental railroad lines. The shortest rail line is *via* the Northern Pacific—3,237 miles; by the Nicaragua Canal the Pacific could be reached in 2,519 miles. The military advantage of this quick communication would be enormous; such a cruise as that of the *Oregon*, occupying more than two months, could be made in less than three weeks. A squadron stationed in Lake Nicaragua could reach either Atlantic or Pacific waters with equal promptness, to meet any sudden raid on the coast.

The Nicaragua route has been surveyed several times since 1850, and at least two companies—the Nicaragua Company and the Maritime Canal Company of Nicaragua—have been formed to build the canal. Some of the work has already been completed, but, owing to various complications operations were suspended about five years ago. At present the route is being re-surveyed by a government commission, with the purpose of reporting finally on the feasibility and probable cost of the undertaking. At the same time the route is being inspected by a party of American contractors under the guidance of a prominent member of the Western Society of Engineers. In a recent number of the bi-monthly *Journal* published by that society, the President, Mr. Alfred Noble, gives an exhaustive description of the Nicaragua route as projected by the Maritime Canal Company. For the sake of permanent information and reference we here reproduce a few paragraphs in which he outlines the more important general features of the Canal. These will be more clearly understood by reference to the frontispiece map, which is one of several that appeared in connection with Mr. Noble's article:

"The key to the Nicaragua route is Lake Nicaragua. This magnificent body of fresh water has a length of about 110 miles, lying in a northwest-southeast direction, nearly parallel with the Pacific Coast and at a minimum distance therefrom of twelve miles. Its maximum width is about forty-five miles and its area about 2,700 square miles. These figures are only approximate; the region has never been carefully surveyed, and no two maps agree.

"The elevation of Lake Nicaragua above mean tide is only about 102 feet at ordinary low water, and it rises in ordinary seasons about eight feet, making ordinary high water 110. Its outlet is near the southeast end, where its waters discharge into the San Juan River and thence to the Caribbean. This lake would constitute a vast reservoir for the supply of the summit level of the proposed canal."

Of the route itself and its engineering features, Mr. Noble says:

" The Pacific terminus of the route is at the mouth of a small stream called the Rio Grande. It ascends this valley, which in its upper portion is quite tortuous, for a distance of about 10½ miles, and then takes a tolerably direct course across the continental divide and descends the valley of the Lajas to the lake, a farther distance of 7½ miles, entering the lake 56½ miles from its outlet. After passing down the lake, it follows the river for a distance of 69 miles to a point 3½ miles below the mouth of the San Carlos.   From this point to Greytown, where one of the several mouths of the river discharges into the Caribbean, the river makes a considerable detour to the southward; the canal, however, is laid across the country through the small valleys above referred to, through the pass called the East Divide and across the swampy coast region to the Caribbean at Greytown. This cut-off follows a very direct line and is some 6 miles shorter than any possible route following the river.   The total length of the route from the Pacific to the Caribbean is about 174 miles. ·

"The depth of the canal as projected is to be 30 feet in the terminal harbors and also in the great rock cuts in the East and Continental divides and in the channel which is to be excavated at the lower end of Lake Nicaragua; elsewhere the depth is to be 28 feet except in certain short earth sections, where it is to be 30 feet at the centre of the channel, gradually reducing to 28 at the foot of the side slopes.   The bottom width of channel is to be 120 feet in the sea-level portions, which are really extensions of the harbors; 80 feet in other earth canal sections; 125 feet where excavation is required in the San Juan River; 150 feet where excavation is required in the open lake, and 100 feet with vertical sides up to 5 feet above water in the rock cuts across the divides.   The locks are to be 70 feet wide and 650 feet long."

Mr. Noble explains that the proposed minimum depth of 28 feet was suggested for a canal intended solely for commercial purposes; if it is now to be built or guaranteed by the United States the dimensions should be somewhat larger, so as to "afford passage for our largest warships."   Wider locks would also be necessary—"a change which would add little to the cost."

The question of water supply for the summit level is a very serious one in most canal projects.   "Lake

Nicaragua,"'says Mr. Noble, "provides abundantly for this one. Along the greater part of the sailing route in the lake, the depth of water is ample for any navigation, but for several miles near the outlet it is shallow and a channel will have to be dredged. It is easy to see that if the lake surface can be raised permanently a part of this dredging can be avoided."

To raise the lake surface it is proposed to build a great dam in the San Juan River at Ochoa, 69 miles east of the lake, at the point where the canal leaves the river channel and takes a northeasterly route direct to the Caribbean Sea. This dam would raise 69 miles of the San Juan River to the summit level of the canal, and greatly reduce the amount of dredging necessary to deepen the river and part of the route in Lake Nicaragua. "At the site of the Ochoa dam," says Mr. Noble, " the river banks are clay but the bed is sand. Borings have been made 18 to 24 feet into the sand without passing through it, and its depth is unknown. The dam is intended to raise the river surface 65 feet. If the foundations were of rock a masonry dam would undoubtedly be built, but is probably impracticable at the site chosen. No better site has been found in the vicinity.

" The plan adopted for the dam is to form a mound of loose rock across the river by dumping into the flowing stream from cableways; the rock is to be in large masses, five tons or more in weight. It is expected that as the sand is scoured out around and under the stones they will sink into the bed and finally become stable. It is also expected that the width of the dam at the base will be several hundred feet. Such a dam would not hold water, but it is intended to dump on the up-stream side smaller stone, gravel and clay until the interstices in the rock mass become filled and the whole structure sufficiently water-tight."

About half way between Ochoa Dam and the Caribbean Sea the canal crosses the "East Divide," which is a low pass through a mountain range averaging 2,000 feet in height. In this divide "the maximum depth of cut is 328 feet. In a distance of three miles there will be 3,400,000 cubic yards of earth and 8,300,000 cubic yards of rock excavation. The earth, which is clay, will be needed in the embankments between the divide and Ochoa; the greater part of the rock suitable for those purposes will be required in the Ochoa dam, the Greytown jetties and in concrete for locks and sluices in the vicinity.

"The descent from the summit level to the Caribbean is to be made in three or four locks placed at suitable points in the eastern slope from the East Divide. The sea-lock will be about 11 miles from the sea; immediately east of it the ground is only 15 feet above sea level and the canal to the sea coast will be made by dredging through clay, mud and sand."

The eastern terminus of the canal is at Greytown, and here a difficult problem is encountered by reason of sand bars formed outside the harbor by the San Juan and other rivers discharging their waters in the vicinity. In order to make a clear passage out to sea it is proposed to build long jetties through these bars, to serve as sand catchers. On the Pacific coast, at Brito, similar protection from sand is to be provided, but the bars are not nearly so extensive and troublesome as at Greytown. In the eighteen miles from Brito to Lake Nicaragua there will probably be four or five locks. The continental mountain range, represented in North America by the Rockies and in South America by the Andes, is here very low; it passes between Lake Nicaragua and the Pacific and the canal crosses it in the "West Divide," where the greatest depth of cut will be only 74 feet, or less than one-quarter as much as in the East Divide.

The total excavation for the whole canal, according to Mr. Noble, will be "approximately 102,000,000 cubic yards, of which 56,000,000 cubic yards is dredging; 27,000,000 cubic yards is earth above water; 1,000,000 cubic yards is mud below water requiring pumping; 16,000,000 cubic yards is rock which can be removed above water; and 2,000,000 cubic yards is rock which must be removed by sub-aqueous methods. . . . There will also be large expenditures for lock gates and equipment; sluice gates and machinery; weirs for the great controlling works and movable dams therefor; and the hundred other adjuncts of a great project."

In conclusion Mr. Noble says he does not doubt that a canal can be built and successfully maintained for any navigation by the Nicaragua route. Therefore, whether the particular line described is the best one or not, it seems evident that the Nicaragua Canal project is, at least, feasible. Whether the cost is $133,472,893 (highest official estimate, made by the Nicaragua Canal Commission) or $200,000,000 or even more, the best line ought to be promptly determined and operations begun upon a sound and permanent basis, financially and politically. The times are at last fully ripe for this epoch-marking achievement and it ought not to be longer delayed.

SCIENCE AND INDUSTRY NOTES

The impression that labor unions never accomplish anything to their own permanent benefit is once more dissipated in the case of the great Armour Packing Company dispute, which has been going on for the last two years. Recently a committee from the American Federation of Labor conferred with the Armour Company and an agreement was reached by which the company recognized the organization of its employees in trade unions, agreed to confer with them as such (a most important concession) and practically promised to grant a shorter working day in the near future. While all was not obtained that the laborers demanded, the agreement of a concern of such prominence as the Armour Packing Company to recognize and deal with its employees in organized bodies is a decided victory for the trade-union movement, and will undoubtedly help to induce similar action on the part of other employers.

A TRADE UNION VICTORY

Inspection of factories is a work in which women are fast acquiring peculiar skill and efficiency. There are nine women inspectors in New York state, seven in Illinois, five in Pennsylvania, two in Massachusetts, and one in Rhode Island. The prejudice of employers against any sort of official inspection of their establishments—a feeling which was particularly strong at first against women inspectors—is fast disappearing. Indeed, one of the first appointed women inspectors in this state, Miss Margaret Finn, in an interview in the New York *Tribune*, says: "Often, when I have finished an inspection and have ordered all the changes I think necessary, I am asked if there is nothing more I can suggest." This growing disposition to

WOMEN FACTORY INSPECTORS

comply with the state factory regulations and, in some cases, even to welcome visits of the inspectors, is an encouraging sign of progress. Such supervision of the conditions of work in factories and workshops is one of the most important and salutary features of the protective function of the state.

Last month we published an article entitled "Do the Railroads Rob the Government?" In this it was shown that even if the railroads do "PADDING THE MAILS" contrive to pad the mails somewhat during the quadrennial weighing period (upon the results of which compensation for carrying the mails for the ensuing four years is based) the government still comes out ahead because of the fact that this test makes no allowance for the normal increase of mail service required before the next weighing. We have received a letter from a postmaster in Iowa, calling our attention to another point of such manifest importance that we publish his communication herewith:

"I was considerably pleased with your article 'Do the Railroads Rob the Government?' and it is the first that has come to my notice that treats the subject fairly and intelligently.

"But there is one point that you have overlooked, probably because you have never been connected with the Post Office business. It is this: The weighing is always done in the spring and early summer, and this is the period of lightest mail. In the country offices there is usually a deficiency of fully thirty per cent. compared with the fall and winter. No system of padding could equalize this natural deficiency, and if the rate paid is not excessive, the government certainly has the best of the deal."

CURRENT LITERATURE

THE SPANIARD IN HISTORY*

This is the title of a very interesting and instructive as well as timely book. At this time, when Spain is making her last struggle for barbarism and brutality in this hemisphere, it is well that the English speaking people, and particularly citizens of the United States, should know the real position the Spaniard has occupied in history. In no other way can the Spanish policy of blood, greed and barbarity in Cuba be understood.

It is not difficult to understand that in a moment of exasperation awful acts may be perpetrated; but the systematic and continuous enforcement of a policy of devastation, ruin and deliberate starvation of whole communities, as exhibited in the corralling of the helpless reconcentrados within the military trochas of Cuba, is possible only to a people who by habit, character and tradition are steeped in the vices of intolerance, despotism and torture.

In reading the stories of the Weyler *regime*, people of civilized communities may naturally hesitate to give credence to the narrative. So repulsive and foreign to any people who have caught the spirit of nineteenth century civilization is this category of official crime that one very naturally seeks an explanation in exaggeration of statement, in the belief that in the last decade of the nineteenth century such things cannot be true of a nation counted within the pale of Christian civilization.

To understand how and why these accounts can be and are true it is necessary only to know the character of the Spaniard as revealed in his history for the last

---

* *The Spaniard in History.* By James C. Fernald. Funk & Wagnalls Company, New York and London. 1898. 144 pp.

five hundred years.   This is briefly but admirably told
in the little book under review.   It contains only one
hundred and forty-four pages, but it tells the story with
a clearness and force that leaves little to be desired.
Mr. Fernald writes with the attractiveness of a Fiske
and the eloquence of a Buckle.   The book contains
detail enough to bring out the leading facts, and is general enough to be fascinating.   The author has made
the history as attractive as a novel, without in the least
neglecting the historic character of the work.

After briefly tracing the origin of the Spanish race
and rise of the Spanish monarchy, the author describes
the Inquisition, the conquest of Granada and the expulsion of the Jews and Moors from Spain.   In these three
chapters, comprising thirty-six pages, is portrayed the
real character of the Spaniard in history.   The fiendish,
tiger-like qualities developed by their perpetual religious
war to exterminate the heretics, have characterized
their entire history.   Gibbon, Prescott, and in fact all
competent historians, testify to the unparalleled wanton
ferocity of the Spanish in dealing with everybody with
whom they come in contact.   Wherever they have gone,
whether in the name of religion or of government, their
policy has been to despoil, brutalize and oppress,—
never to expand, develop and improve.   As Mr. Fernald well says (p. 22) : "Spain has gone into every land
on which she has set foot, as her barons of the olden
time issued from their mountain fastnesses into the
domains of the Saracen, to ravage, plunder, and
despoil."

The Spanish Inquisition, which was instituted January 2nd, 1481, and continued its murderous policy for
three hundred years, is the greatest monument of
national ferocity, inhumanity and fiendish torture
human history contains.

It may be said that the Spanish Inquisition was an

institution of religious bigotry peculiar to the Middle Ages, and should not be cited in these days of religious freedom and political independence. Of Europe in general, this is true ; but with Spain the Inquisition is still the mirror that reflects her real character. While all Europe was then intolerant of all religious opinion differing from the doctrines of Rome, Spain was conspicuous in her unchristian brutality and in her really hypocritical purposes covered by religious fanaticism. It was not enough to appoint the Inquisition to inquire into the religious thoughts of every citizen and to apply all the tortures that the most fiendish mind could invent as punishment, but every vile inducement was offered to treachery and hypocrisy in the securing and convicting of heretics. Brothers, sisters, fathers, mothers, and neighbors were all made spies and detectives on each other. The evidence was secret, and the victim was never confronted either with his accuser or the evidence upon which the accusation rested. Moreover, evidence against a heretic by any kind of person was valid, no matter what his standing in the community ; even if excommunicated by the Church or convicted of the blackest crime known to the civil law, his word would be taken to convict a heretic.

There were different degrees of heresy. For some, the penalty was death without the shedding of blood, being the horrible formula for burning alive ; for degrees of doubt for which the fagot could hardly be brought into requisition, confiscation of property and commitment to the galleys ; but in all instances confiscation of property was a sure penalty. By this means the bloodthirstiness of the Church and the coffers of the King were both satisfied. It needed only a whisper to justify the punishment of a Jew for heresy, because that furnished an excuse for robbing him of his property. The nobility, or in fact any characterful person, if he was not a fawning follower of the king or of the butchers in the Church, could by this means be reduced to beggary, and the Church and king enriched by the process.

Hellish as was the act of the Church itself in instituting the Inquisition, the hypocrisy through which it was used to murder and plunder, purely for the purpose of wealth and political power, shows even a greater depth of depravity which has no parallel in the character of any other nation. It made treachery a virtue and gave religious sanctity to robbery, murder and political intrigue. Quoting the law, our author says :

" ' Every man, of whatever estate, loses all office, benefice, right, and dignity, as soon as he incurs inquisitorial punishment.' . . . It was further provided that the children and children's children of the condemned heretic could hold no office of honor or profit, nor wear silk, fine wool, gold, or other costly adornments."

After giving a vivid and eloquent account of the effort to conquer Granada, Mr. Fernald says : " After this it is needless to dwell on particular instances of cruelty ; as, for instance, to tell how Ferdinand and Isabella (Isabella being present in person) consigned the whole population of Malaga, some sixteen thousand persons, to slavery ; and how the hope of ransom was held out to the unfortunates with the assurance that their jewels and other personal effects would be accepted in part payment; and how, when these proved insufficient, the doom of slavery was carried into effect, the crafty Ferdinand thus securing both the persons and the property." * Thus by bald hypocrisy and cunning treachery the people were induced to give up all their wealth to save themselves from slavery,

* Page 68.

only to find that the word of the Spaniard is worthless, and that his love of cruelty alone can be relied upon.

By a very brief but vivid description of the Spanish in Mexico and Peru, Mr. Fernald shows that the fiendishness of the Inquisition characterized the Spaniard's conduct whithersoever he went. The treatment of the Netherlands by Philip II. is but another chapter of blood, plunder and treachery. The terrible Alva, Philip's *alter ego* for unconscionable ferocity, promised his master that he would silence all doubts in the Netherlands "by cutting off the heads of all the refractory nobles, and that from his confiscation of estates he would cause 'a stream of treasure a yard deep' to flow into Spain, and assure him [the king] an annual income of 500,000 ducats from confiscations."

The three leading nobles most to be feared in the Netherlands were the Prince of Orange and Counts Egmont and Horn. These three had been doomed to death by Philip before Alva left Spain. In order to make their capture easy, Philip wrote personal affectionate letters to them. The Prince of Orange, however, knew what to expect from Spanish diplomacy, and went to Germany, "but Egmont and Horn were flattered to their death. Alva himself, at his coming, effusively embraced Egmont, 'throwing his arm around the stately neck which he had already doomed to the block.' Then Alva invited both the Counts to a friendly little company at his own house, and there arrested them. All their estates were instantly confiscated, and after a protracted mockery of trial by written documents both were suddenly brought to the block.* . . .

"Alva boasted after his departure that he had executed 18,600 people in the Netherlands, besides all who perished by battle and massacre."

---

* Pages 108, 110.

Yet Philip II., whom Prescott and Motley agree
was "the most perfect type of the national character,"
was not savage enough in his efforts to exterminate the
heretics.   Buckle tells us * that in 1602 the Archbishop
of Valencia presented a memorial to Philip III. demanding sterner measures against the Moriscoes.   He
"assured the king that all the disasters which had be-
fallen the monarchy, had been caused by the presence of
these unbelievers. . . .   He declared that the Armada, which Philip II. sent against England in 1588,
had been destroyed because God would not allow even
that pious enterprise to succeed, while those who undertook it left heretics undisturbed at home. For the same
reason, the late expedition to Algiers had failed ; it
being evidently the will of Heaven that nothing should
prosper while Spain was inhabited by apostates. He,
therefore, exhorted the king to exile all the Moriscoes,
except some whom he might condemn to work in the
galleys, and others who could become slaves, and labor
in the mines of America. This, he added, would make
the race of Philip glorious to all posterity, and would
raise his fame far above that of his predecessors, who
in this matter had neglected their obvious duty."

This was so thoroughly representative of the spirit
of the Church that the Archbishop of Toledo, the then
Primate of Spain, thoroughly endorsed the scheme, with
one exception. "The Archbishop of Valencia thought
that children under seven years of age need not share
in the general banishment, but might, without danger to
the faith, be separated from their parents, and kept in
Spain. To this the Archbishop of Toledo strongly objected. He was unwilling, he said, to run the risk of
pure Christian blood being polluted by infidels ; and he
declared that sooner than leave one of these unbelievers

---

* *History of Civilisation.* Vol. II., pp. 46-50.

to corrupt the land, he would have the whole of them, men, women and children, at once put to the sword. . . . Bleda, the celebrated Dominican, one of the most influential men of his time, wished this to be done, and to be done thoroughly. He said that, for the sake of example, every Morisco in Spain should have his throat cut, because it was impossible to tell which of them were Christians at heart, and it was enough to leave the matter to God, who knew his own, and would reward in the next world those who were really Catholics."

By 1609 this demand of the Church for the expulsion of the Moriscoes became irresistible. Lerma, Philip's Minister, "announced to the king, that the expulsion of the Moriscoes had become necessary. 'The resolution,' replied Philip, 'is a great one; let it be executed.' And executed it was, with unflinching barbarity. About a million of the most industrious inhabitants of Spain were hunted out like wild beasts, because the sincerity of their religious opinions was doubtful. Many were slain, as they approached the coast; others were beaten and plundered; and the majority, in the most wretched plight, sailed for Africa. During the passage, the crew, in many of the ships, rose upon them, butchered the men, ravished the women, and threw the children into the sea."

It may be said that much of this religious and political persecution was done from honest motives. Yes, and so was the heartless corralling of the peaceful women and children of Cuba within the trochas, to die of starvation by thousands, and so was the treacherous blowing up of the Maine. Only a people who breathe cowardice and treachery can honestly act like demons. Such integrity is the integrity of the tiger in the sheepfold and of the fox in the hennery.

Weyler in Cuba was a typical Spaniard, and the blowing up of the Maine was characteristic of Spanish honor.   Spain is the only country in Europe on which modern civilization has had practically no effect.

The character of "The Spaniard in History" is correctly portrayed by Mr. Fernald in this little book. Every American citizen should read it—read it aloud— and it is so attractively written that whoever reads the first few pages will be sure to read it through.

ADDITIONAL REVIEWS

MARCHING WITH GOMEZ. By Grover Flint. His-
torical Introduction by John Fiske. 294 pp. Lamson,
Wolffe & Co., Boston, New York and London. 1898.
Illustrated. Price $1.50.

Mr. Flint, who is the son-in-law of John Fiske, in
1896 was correspondent of the New York *Journal*. In that
capacity he spent four months with the insurgent army
in Cuba, and in this volume he tells the story of what
he saw during that time. The story is attractively told,
in rather a journalistic style. It is chatty and bright
throughout, and profusely illustrated with sketches· of
the insurgents in camp life and some horrible specimens of the result of Weylerism. It gives an excellent
idea of how the Cuban revolution is prosecuted, the
methods and condition of the insurgent army, and also
of the itinerant insurgent government. The object of
the book is evidently not to tell a blood-curdling story
but rather to narrate in attractive form what actually
passed under the eyes of the writer while accompanying
the army of the revolution. It shows, without saying
so, that the revolutionists are in dead earnest; that the
insurgent movement is not a mere uprising of unscrupulous banditti but that it is a desperate, uncompromising struggle to throw off the yoke of Spanish rule.

From the remarks of General Gomez it is apparent
that the military leader of the revolution is not laboring
under any delusive optimism regarding the character of
the Cuban people or the experiment of self-government
after the Spaniards have been expelled. This is one of
the most wholesome features of the revolution. It too
often occurs in revolutionary movements that its leaders
have an inflated conception of the new government
which they are endeavoring to inaugurate. They too
frequently assume that disinterested patriotism will

everywhere prevail, that the best minds will volunteer in the service of organizing civil institutions: and that the people will of one accord co-operate in a universal endeavor to make the new government a model of political efficiency and personal freedom—all of which is often conspicuously lacking. At the close of a successful revolutionary undertaking, the new government is usually as much in danger of defeat from its previous friends as was the revolution from the enemy. To recognize this is to be prepared for it, and may go far to insure success in the organization of the new form of government when Cuban soil is rid of the Spaniard.

The narrative of Mr. Flint regarding the field operations of the revolutionary army and the life of the peasant sympathisers, and the justification of the revolution, finds great support in the introduction by John Fiske. This is a brief history of the Spaniards in Cuba and is told in Professor Fiske's always attractive and instructive style:

'"The first glimpse that we get of Cuba, after its discovery by Columbus, reveals to us with startling vividness the impression already entertained in the island with regard to Spaniards. It was not until 1511 that they began to occupy Cuba. The wrecking of Columbus' best ship on the coast of Hispaniola (Hayti) led to the founding of the first settlements upon that coast, and the discovery of gold in 1496 began bringing Spaniards by hundreds to the New World. How they behaved themselves in beautiful Hispaniola was long ago described for us by the good Las Casas, in his famous book, 'The Destruction of the Indies.' The story makes one of the most hideous chapters in the history of mankind. Rumors of what was going on from time to time reached the ears of a certain important chieftain in the neighboring island of Cuba, and he sent spies over to Hispaniola, who more than confirmed the worst things that had been reported.   One day, this chieftain, whose name was Hatuey, found a large ingot of gold and forthwith called together his tribal council. 'Know ye, my brethren,' said he, 'that this yellow thing is the god of the Spaniards; wherefore let us propitiate it with songs and dances, and pray it to turn the mind of those people away from coming to Cuba.'   So the Indians danced around the ingot until they grew weary, when their chief further observed, 'Let not this deity remain above ground and visible, lest if the Spaniards come peradventure he may prompt them to wickedness.' So the yellow idol was picked up and thrown into the river.   Thus did these cunning red men seek at once to cajole and to baffle the enemy.   But it was in vain. In the year 1511 came Diego Velasquez, and it was not long before poor Hatuey was tied to a stake and fagots piled about him.   While the flames were licking the flesh from his bones, a black-robed priest held up the crucifix and begged him to repent of his sins and secure a place in   heaven.   'Where is heaven?' cried Hatuey; 'are there any Spaniards there?'   'Yea, many,' quoth the priest.   'Then,' said the writhing victim, 'pray let me go somewhere else.'

"The dismal reputation thus won by the Spaniards, when they first took possession of the island of Cuba, has been maintained by them to the present day. . . .

"If we would properly understand the revolt of Spain's colonies, we shall do well to compare and contrast it with our own revolt against the government of George III.   The English colonies in America never suffered anything that could be called oppression, except for a brief moment under Berkeley in Virginia and under Andros in New England; but Berkeley's violence led to his removal, and the policy which Andros tried to enforce was quickly overthrown by a revolution in England, so that neither of these instances counts for much against the mother country. Our forefathers on this side of the Atlantic were not liable to arbitrary imprisonment or extortionate taxes, the privacy of their homes was not invaded, and they were free to speak and print their thoughts; when things went wrong they could scold and grumble to their hearts' content. They severed their political connection with England, not in order to gain new liberties, but to guard against the possible risk of losing old ones. Far different was it with the people of the Spanish colonies at the beginning of the present century. Their government, under viceroys and captains general sent out from Spain, was an absolute despotism. They were subject to arbitrary and oppressive taxation. The people of English America refused to submit to a very light stamp tax, imposed purely for American interests, to defend the frontier against Indian raids; the people of Spanish America saw vast amounts of treasure carried away year after year to be spent upon European enterprises in which they felt no interest whatever. They had no popular assemblies, no *habeas corpus* acts, no freedom of the press. Their houses were not their castles, for the minions of the civil and of the spiritual power could penetrate everywhere; a petty quarrel between neighbors might end in dragging some of them before the Inquisition, to be tortured or put to death for heresy. For that preeminently Spanish and Satanic institution survived in America until two decades of the nineteenth century had passed. . . .

"In such a political atmosphere corruption thrives. A planter's estate is entered upon the assessor's lists as worth $50,000; the collector comes along and demands a tax based upon the assumed value of $70,000; the planter demurs, but presently thinks it prudent to compromise upon a basis of $60,000. No change is made in the published lists, but the collector slips into his own

pocket the tax upon $10,000, and goes on his way re-
joicing.   Thus the planter is robbed while the Government is cheated.   And this is a fair specimen of what
goes on throughout all departments of administration.
From end to end the whole system is honeycombed
with fraud.

"The people of Cuba would not be worthy of our
respect if they were capable of submitting tamely to
such wholesale oppression and pillage.   They are to be
commended for the spirit of resistance which showed
itself in the Ten Years' War; and it is much to their
credit that, after repeated proof of the hopelessness of
any peaceful reform, they have once more risen in
rebellion. . . .

"For the sake of Cuba's best interests, it is to be
hoped that she will win her independence without receiving from any quarter, and especially from the
United States, any such favors as might hereafter put
her in a position of tutelage or in any wise hamper her
freedom of action.   All people liberated from the blight
of Spanish dominion need to learn the alphabet of free
government.   Cuba will have to learn it, as all the rest
of Spanish-America has had to learn it, and the fewer
the impediments in her way the better."

INDUSTRIES   AND   WEALTH   OF   NATIONS.   By
Michael G. Mulhall, F. R. S. S. 451 pp. Longmans,
Green & Co., London, New York and Bombay, 1896.

For a small volume of general industrial statistics
this is probably the most comprehensive in existence.
Perhaps the chief utility of statistics is for comparative
purposes, and this is the object most completely realized
in Mulhall's work.   The matter is arranged according
to countries, and covers population, working power of
nations, including the natural forces employed, agriculture, forestry, manufactures, transportation, com-

merce, banks and money, earnings—national and individual, wealth, taxation, etc. The facts extend back
for a period of about sixty years, in most cases, and
thus show the progress or decline of different nations as
well as their present relation to each other. It is not
pretended that absolute accuracy is obtained in all these
statistics, nor would such a thing be possible. Mr.
Mulhall, in fact, expressly quotes Leroy–Beaulieu on
this point: "We must avoid the absurdity of limiting
statistics to ascertained facts, for in many cases this
branch of science can reach only approximate results."
All that can be claimed for many classes of statistics is
that they show the general trend, and this claim is
usually just; for the proportion of errors is about the
same in the different items, so that comparison between
them is not vitiated. The condensation and massing
together of scattered and obscure data in such a way as
to render them practically useful and significant is the
distinctively good feature of Mulhall's statistics.

A STUDY OF ENGLISH WORDS. By Jessie M.
Anderson. 118 pp. American Book Company;. New
York, Cincinnati, and Chicago. 1897.

The student of rhetoric, orthography and accurate
use of language will find this small text-book helpful.
It discusses in a somewhat elementary way, but clearly
and pointedly, the general principles of language growth
and the illustrations of those principles in the development of the English language. The chapters on the
composition of our language, showing the proportion of
classic and Anglo-Saxon elements and methods of determining to which category different words belong,
are especially interesting. There are many important
suggestions, also, on the association of words and correct use of synonyms.

AMONG THE MAGAZINES

Mr. Walter Avenel argues, in the May *Forum*, that journalism as a profession is not "worthy the serious attention of educated young men" because it is not sufficiently stable and remunerative, etc. Precisely as bad a case could be made out regarding the law, or medicine, or the ministry, or engineering, or teaching, or any profession; but any such general statement would not necessarily be true in any of these instances. It is the man rather than the particular vocation that chiefly determines the question of success or failure in these lines. We have reached a point in our national development where there are large opportunities in all the professions, and in any of them energy, intelligence, and talent can win success. The question for a young man to decide, therefore, is not which profession is reputed to be the most remunerative regardless of the man's personal adaptability to it, but in which one can he most effectively employ his whole energy and develop his natural talents.

THE
FORUM

In an elaborate discussion of free public libraries, in the June *North American*, Mr. Herbert Putnam, President of the American Library Association, upholds the idea that library authorities should be permitted to select the kind of books that are purchased and circulated by the libraries. In this contention he is unquestionably right. It is urged by many that the business of a library should to furnish all the books that appear and let the public determine what is good and what is bad. This would be true if there were no other way for the public to get hold of books except through public libraries. Such, of course, is not the case; and since these libraries are maintained at public expense

NORTH
AMERICAN
REVIEW

for the sake of conferring a public benefit, the municipality or state becomes morally responsible for the character of reading furnished; it is its duty to see that the institutions *are* a public benefit and not the reverse. To buy all sorts of books and let the public determine which are worthy is no more reasonable than it would be to employ instructors in the public schools to teach all sorts of untruths and rubbish, as well as others to give genuine information, and then allow the scholars to decide for themselves what was true and what was false.

In the May number of this periodical Mr. W. F. Willoughby, of the United States Department of Labor, presents some statistics showing

THE YALE REVIEW

the concentration of industry in this country, and then discusses very sensibly the effect of this movement on the workingman. "The elimination of small employers" he very truly says, "is a minor question compared to the benefits or disadvantages that result to the workingmen employed in these enterprises." He believes that the effect on employees is decidedly beneficial because of the superior working conditions in large concerns, the greater ease of enforcing sanitary legislation in large establishments, the higher wages, the steadier employment, and the enlarged opportunities for efficient labor unions where great numbers of employees are massed together in large mills. One drawback, in Mr. Willoughby's opinion, is that while strikes will become less frequent in the era of large organizations they will become more violent and severe when they do occur. This very point, however, while true, will tend to compel both employers and employees to seek other means of adjusting their difficulties until finally the strike is entirely eliminated from our industrial relations.

INSTITUTE WORK

THE WAR PRICE BUGABOO

Great effort has been made in certain quarters to create an impression among the people that the war has caused a disastrous rise in prices. That is, disastrous to the general consumers, particularly the laboring classes. Some have even gone so far as to say that the money power entered into a conspiracy to bring on the war for the sole purpose of robbing the people by high prices. Of course it is true that war is a disturber of business conditions. Anything that suddenly disturbs industry will necessarily disturb business confidence. It is astonishing, when we examine the question closely, how much of business confidence and industrial stability we find depends on economic psychology.

Economic ignorance as to the general causes which affect prices has had much more to do with the recent price fluctuations than the war. There has been very little cause for any considerable change in retail prices. Much of the recent fluctuation in the retail market is due to an arbitrary effort to take advantage of the consumer. It is a traditional idea that war prices are necessarily high prices, and, in many cases, that is true. But it does not at all follow that it would be true in a country like this, with such a large proportion of the commodities used in social life produced at home. On the assumption, however, that wars must make high prices, unscrupulous dealers took advantage of war conditions and arbitrarily advanced prices of many articles.

The same thing is usually done before and after a change of the tariff. In 1891, the year after the McKinley tariff was adopted, a systematic effort was made by the free-trade press and politicians to create a high-tariff-price scare. They started the rumor that prices would bound upwards through the McKinley tariff, and this was said so much and so persistently that hosts of shop-keepers unscrupulously marked up their prices, which fact in turn was then cited by the press to frighten the people into endorsing a free-trade policy. In some states politicians went so far as to send peddlers throughout the country districts with tinware and other commodities, charging double the previous price, not so much in the hope of selling goods but with the specific object of convincing the house-wives of the country that they would soon have to pay nearly double prices unless their husbands and brothers voted for free trade.

Of course this form of cheating the public can only last a short time, as in the long run economic forces will prevail. But temporarily the public can be made to suffer by this psychologic disturbance regarding prices. It is always handy, and usually effective, for the shop-keeper to ascribe this rise in prices either to so-called class legislation, like "tariffs," or to monopolies like "trusts," with the assurance that the public prejudice created by socialists, populists and unscrupulous political editors can be relied upon to make this view acceptable to the masses. As a matter of fact, however, the prices of articles produced by the great trusts have been least susceptible to this shop-keeper, socialistic, war-price bugaboo.

The rise in wheat has been the principal cause of complaint. This is ascribed to the market perform-auces of young Mr. Leiter, yet his operations have really had very little effect on the price of wheat. Temporarily, for a few days, he created a disturbance, but in doing so if he made any money it was not out of the retail purchasers and final consumers of wheat products. Nor has the rise in the price of wheat been much affected by the war, for the obvious reason that the war could not alter the conditions which determine the price of wheat in this country. There has been a steady upward movement in the price of wheat during the entire years of 1896, 1897 and until the middle of 1898. On January 1, 1896, No. 2, red winter wheat, was 69 cents a bushel; January 1, 1897, it was $1.06¼ a bushel; January 1, 1898, it was 98¾ cents a bushel; June 1, 1898, it was $1.18 a bushel.

Mr. Leiter did not begin operations until April 2, 1897, and wheat had been steadily rising for a year and a half previous to that date, having risen during that time from 69 to 95½ cents, or 26½ cents a bushel, which was more than it rose from the time Leiter began his speculations to the time of his collapse, June 13, 1898. The truth is that Mr. Leiter did not control the price of wheat; he only took advantage of the rise by anticipating the upward tendency which was produced by causes absolutely independent of anything he or Armour or any other millionaires could do. The shortness of crops abroad was the cause of the rise in price, and Mr. Leiter undertook to get the benefit of that rise on a large portion of the American crop. As soon as he reached the point of trying to control the price instead of following it he began to lose, and finally, by June 13, he had done enough of this uneconomic purchasing to cause him a loss of three millions; thus clearly showing that he only made money by his dealing in wheat when he acted upon the economic movement of prices, and as soon as he began to take the management of prices in his own hands regardless of the economic causes, or miscalculating them, which is the same thing, he had to pay the penalty in heavy loss and finally in bankruptcy, as many another has done. This inflamed talk about Leiter making millions out of the bread of the working-man has no truth in it. The price of the laborer's bread was not perceptibly affected by anything Leiter did.

The same kind of bugaboo was raised in 1895 and 1896 on the silver question.   Mr. Bryan and his friends industriously circulated the theory that the price of wheat was governed by the price of silver, and 'great loads of literature were published to sustain this view. It happened that the price of wheat in 1895, and for some time previously, was very low.   Silver and wheat, like iron and numerous other commodities, had fallen in price.   To students of economics the reason for this was not at all difficult to understand; in fact, it was rather obvious.   But to suit the political theories of the New Democracy and enlist farmers in support of the Bryan free-silver campaign, it was asserted that the price of silver was reduced by the act of 1873, and the only way ever again to have reasonably high prices for wheat, or, as they loved to phrase it, "to bring back the day of dollar wheat," was to have free coinage of silver.   The managers of this movement knew very well that nothing would be more effective in getting the farmers' vote than to point an easy way to secure the return of dollar wheat.

Unfortunately for this doctrine economic causes began to operate, through diminished crops in Europe, to send the price of wheat up while the price of silver continued to go down.   By October 1, 1896, the price of wheat reached 78⅝ cents a bushel, and before election day passed the 80 cent mark.   While this did not convert the advocates and those who thought they had a strong interest in believing this doctrine (one fact seldom does convert fanatics) it had a very demoralizing effect upon the doctrine with a large number of farmers. The upward movement of wheat during 1897 and 1898 and the continued decline in silver has practically destroyed the validity of the theory that the price of wheat is governed by the price of silver with the entire American people.

All this only emphasizes the importance of correct public opinion regarding the general causes which influence and control prices. At bottom the great questions of protection, free trade, direct or indirect taxation, sound or inflated money, private or government banking and currency, long or short hours of labor, high or low wages and, in fact, nearly all politico-economic questions which affect the welfare of the masses and make issues for political parties turn upon how their adoption will finally affect prices and, through prices, profits.

Attention has often been called in these lectures to the fact that the foundation principle operating upon prices is the cost of production; that is to say, the cost of producing the dearest portion that can be continuously sold in the open market. This doctrine, which has been more or less recognized ever since competitive industry began, has become more and more clarified as the methods of industry have increased in precision and economic accuracy. Periodically new circumstances arise which produce a flutter and somewhat irregular movement in prices, which seems to invalidate the correctness of this cost of production principle. It is argued by more thoughtful critics that for a law of prices to have scientific validity it must not merely explain the movement of some prices, nor even of a large majority of prices, but it must account for the movement of all prices. This demand has a large element of reason in it. It is not scientifically true to say that a law which explains a given class of phenomena must necessarily account for all movements of those phenomena by the same process. What the true theory of prices must do is adequately to explain how all price movements are governed, not that they all move in accordance with identically the same process. A true theory of prices, as I have said, will explain how all price changes occur. If different processes obtain under different circumstances, then the true theory must explain what principle and process operates under each different set of circumstances. The cost of production theory does this, and it does it more completely than any other theory that has yet been suggested. It recognizes all the forces which operate upon prices, but it does not insist that all the forces operate equally under all circumstances.

It asserts first of all that in competitive society the general tendency is to establish uniformity of prices for the same commodity in the same market, and that this general or uniform price tends constantly to approximate the cost of producing the dearest portion that can continuously be sold. To be brief and explicit I may say that while it denies the old theory that prices are governed by the proportion between demand and supply, it does not ignore the fact that demand and supply are important factors. It affirms that demand is the first active force in price creation, that prices are created by demand, since without demand there would be no effort to produce and hence no price. Demand then is the fact that creates the first incentive to production, but the demand is wholly ineffective until it makes a price, and that price must be equivalent to the cost of supplying the article.

Thus, the price-creating force is wholly on the demand side. The cost of production belongs wholly to the supply side. It is an indispensable condition of supply. Without the equivalent of the cost of production nobody will continuously produce. Demand is the force then that furnishes the top line to which prices can rise, and cost of production the bottom line to which they can fall. Whenever demand has forced price above the cost of production line the profit element induces competition which forces the general or uniform

price down to the cost line of the dearest portion that
continues in the competition.

Under conditions of speculation, as in corners,
another element of the law is absent and hence a modification of its operation is revealed. Since cost of production exists only on the supply side it follows that it
can exercise influence on prices only when supply is
forthcoming. Any suspension of supply necessarily sus-
pends the operation of cost, except to the extent of
using a substitute. It is not difficult to see that when
two forces operate to produce a given result if one is
withdrawn or rendered *nil*, the other will exercise the
controlling force. If only demand is operating then
cost of production and all other forces which belong
exclusively to supply cease. Cost of production and
competition, therefore, cease to operate when, for whatever reason, supply is stopped.

Under those conditions only demand operates, and
the price will necessarily go up to the point not merely
of cost but to the point of full utility ; that is to say,
to the point where the consumer will go without or
substitute another article rather than pay the price; as,
for instance, with corner prices for wheat, rye, corn or
oats will at a certain point be substituted. When
that point is reached, supply again begins, this time in
the form of rye, oats or corn.

Briefly, then, it may be said that under conditions
of continuous supply the cost of the dearest portion
determines the price. Under conditions of suspended
supply (hence, suspended cost of production and competition) price is governed by the utility compared with
the cost of an inferior substitute for the same purpose.
Thus, the cost of production theory does explain the
movement of prices under all conditions, but it does
not ascribe all price movement to the same process,
and consequently answers all the conditions of a scientific or economic law.

ADAM SMITH
Author of "Wealth of Nations."

GUNTON'S MAGAZINE

ECONOMICS AND PUBLIC AFFAIRS

ARE WAGES REALLY FALLING?

The movement of wages, or the purchasing power of a day's work, is the true index of a nation's progress. If wages are generally tending upwards and the laboring class actually receiving a larger amount of the various necessaries and comforts of life for a day's work, real progress indicating an increase of social welfare among the people is indisputably taking place.

On the other hand, if wages are actually declining and the amount of commodities which enter into the habitual consumption of the people obtainable from a day's wages is declining, then material and social retrogression has set in. Wages then (real wages) are the true index finger on the dial of civilization.

During the last few years a great deal has been said by pessimists about the poor growing poorer and the rich growing richer. Some of the pessimistic expressions of Thorold Rogers in this direction have been made much of by the class of writers and speakers whose effort seems to be to prove that the condition of the laboring class is growing worse. The objective point of this is to buttress the claim that our present industrial system is inimical to justice and popular welfare and must be superseded by some kind of a socialistic regime.

We have frequently had occasion to correct the misapprehensions caused sometimes by partial statements and sometimes by misstatements of facts in support of this view. We have constantly held to the belief, which the great mass of available data seems to justify, that the general trend of industrial development is yielding through the movement of wages and prices an actual increased income for the laboring as well as the employing class; that the tendency of wages is upwards and that the price of the commodities upon which wages are expended is downwards. In short, that the rise of wages and fall of prices is the actual resultant of the modern industrial trend. Hitherto the facts have seemed to show that this was particularly true in this country during the last twenty-five years. The immense body of wage and price data collected by the United States Senate Finance Committee in 1892, covering a period of fifty years, 1840-91, taking 1860 as the datum line, conclusively indicated a marked progress shown by a general rise in wages, fall in prices, and increased purchasing power of the money in which wages are paid.

This investigation was so extensive and thorough, covering such a wide range of articles and conducted by the most expert statisticians in the country under the direction of a committee composed of critical representatives of the opposite political parties, that it seemed to insure a report as exhaustive and reliable as the present state of statistical science would permit. The fact that this Report shows a marked general rise in wages and net fall in prices would seem completely to sustain the hopeful conclusion that we are making *bona fide* progress, progress which carries with it a genuine observable improvement in the industrial, social, and political conditions of the whole people and conspicuously the laboring class.

Now comes the Massachusetts Labor Bureau with a Report on *Comparative Wages and Prices, 1860 to 1897*, which seems to indicate that wages generally are declining. The dates of comparison in this Report are 1860, 1872, 1881, and 1897. Care has been taken to reduce the wages for 1872 to gold, so that the basis of comparison will be the same in all the years.

Before considering the facts in this Report it may be well to note that the mere statement of the wages does not necessarily give the whole case, and though the facts as stated may be literally correct it does not follow either that they represent the entire conditions of the laborers in Massachusetts or that Massachusetts laborers represent the labor conditions of the entire United States.

In order to understand the real significance of this report it is necessary to ascertain (1) if the facts presented fairly represent the condition of labor in Massachusetts, (2) if Massachusetts industrial statistics are fairly representative of the whole country, (3) if the fall in wages has been more than offset by the fall in prices, (4) if the movement of wages during the sixteen years from 1881 to 1897 has been continuous, or whether any exceptional circumstances have occurred during that period which the Massachusetts tables do not indicate.

(1) First, then, as to the scope and representative character of the facts presented. The range of data included in the Massachusetts investigation is somewhat limited by the conditions of the work. This Bureau made extensive investigations of wages and prices for previous annual Reports for 1860, 1872, 1878, and 1881. Of course the investigation for each of these years covered a larger range of industries than that of the previous one, but in order to have a fair basis for comparing wages of 1897 with those of previous years only the industries which were investigated each year are included in the comparative statement.

For this reason 1872, 1881, and 1897 only are taken for the purposes of a general comparison, many of the important manufacturing industries having come into existence since 1860. For example, the glass, hosiery, metal and metallic industries, rubber goods, elastic fabrics, and straw goods have all come into existence since 1860; hence the investigation for that year gave no data for those industries. In 1872 even, the data for hosiery, metal and metallic goods, musical instruments, rubber goods, elastic fabrics, and woolen goods are either entirely missing or very meagre, so that eleven out of the twenty-two industries are not included in the general average for 1872.

The industries, the facts of which are complete for each of the three years, are represented in the following table:

TABLE I.

Industries.	Average Weekly Wages in Gold.			Inc + or Dec —	Inc + or Dec —	Inc + or Dec —
	1872	1881	1897	1872-1881	1881-1897	1872-1897
Blacksmiths	$16.44	$16.38	$16.00	$—0.06	$—0.38	$—0.44
Boots and Shoes	12.71	11.06	11.90	—1.65	+0.84	—0.81
Building Trades	15.66	11.00	15.83	—4.66	+4.83	+0.17
Cabinet Making	14.21	11.51	13.02	—2.70	+1.51	—1.19
Carpetings	4.89	5.94	8.26	+1.05	+2.32	+3.37
Clothing (Ready made)	9.71	10.90	9.01	+1.19	—1.89	—0.70
Machinery	13.84	16.48	10.80	+2.64	—5.68	—3.04
Metal Goods	6.06	13.42	9.51	+7.36	—3.91	+3.45
Paper	7.37	9.47	9.31	+2.10	—0.16	+1.94
Carriages	17.31	13.43	13.51	—3.88	+0.08	—3.80
Average	11.82	11.96	11.72	+0.14	—0.24	—0.10
Farm Labor with board	5.32	4.15	4.26	—1.17	+0.11	—1.06
Total Average	11.23	11.25	11.04	+0.02	—0.21	—0.19

It will be seen from the above table that exclusive of agriculture there was a slight general rise of fourteen cents a week from 1872 to 1881. Including agriculture, in which wages fell $1.17 a week during that period, the general average for all was a rise of two cents a week; or, in other words, wages were practically static. During the sixteen years from 1881 to 1897 the figures show that exclusive of agriculture there was a decline of twenty-four cents a week, and including agriculture a decline of twenty-one cents a week. In the whole twenty-five years, 1872 to 1897, exclusive of agriculture, there was a general decline in wages of ten cents a week, and including agriculture of nineteen cents a week.

Are these facts fairly representative of the conditions of labor in Massachusetts? They are fairly representative of agriculture, but hardly of manufacture, and they doubtless make a rather better showing than the real condition warrants. The reason for this, as already explained, is that for 1872 a large number of the industries were not reported, hence the facts for the whole table are limited to the industries reported for that year.

Thus, for instance, the wages of labor in cotton goods, glass, hosiery, leather, metal goods, musical instruments, printing, rubber goods, stone, straw goods and woolen goods are omitted from this table because the data were not sufficiently complete for these industries, some of which did not exist. In some of these omitted industries the decline of wages from 1872 to 1881 was quite marked, conspicuously the cotton industry* which was partly due to the substitution of cheaper immigrant labor from southern Europe and Canada. If the table for 1872 had been as complete as that for 1881, or had included the cotton industry, the result would have shown a slight decline in wages for the nine years (1872—1881). Additional evidence of this is suggested in the following table:

* There was one reduction, if not two, of 10 per cent. and one of 15 per cent. in cotton operatives' wages during this period.

TABLE II.

Industries.	Average Weekly Wages in Gold.		Increase or Decrease	
	1881.	1897.	Amounts	Per cent.
Farm Labor, with board	$4.15	$4.26	+$0.11	+2.73
" " without board	8.22	7.50	—0.72	—8.76
Blacksmiths	16.38	16.00	—0.38	—2.32
Boots and Shoes	11.06	11.90	+0.84	+7.59
Building Trades	11.00	15.83	+4.83	+43.91
Cabinet Making	11.51	13.02	+1.51	+13.12
Carpetings	5.94	8.26	+2.32	+39.06
Carriages	13.43	13.51	+0.08	+0.60
Clothing (ready-made)	10.90	9.01	—1.89	—17.34
Cotton Goods	7.59	7.71	+0.12	+1.58
Glass	10.68	12.03	+1.35	+12.64
Hosiery	10.22	8.97	—1.25	—12.23
Leather	11.05	10.54	—0.51	—4.62
Machines and Machinery	16.48	10.80	—5.68	—34.47
Metal Goods	13.42	9.51	—3.91	—29.14
" " (fine work)	10.07	11.59	+1.52	+15.09
Musical Instruments	15.81	18.06	+2.25	+14.23
Paper	9.47	9.31	—0.16	—1.69
Printing	14.95	19.59	+4.64	+31.04
Rubber Goods, Elastic Fabrics	7.56	9.96	+2.40	+31.75
Stone	13.25	13.87	+0.62	+4.68
Straw Goods	10.06	11.60	+1.54	+15.31
Woolen Goods	8.12	8.52	+0.40	+4.93
Average	$10.93	$11.36	+$0.43	+3.93

It will be observed that in the first table the average wages for 1881, in the eleven industries given, were $11.25 a week. In the second table, which includes the 12 industries omitted in 1872, the average wages for 1881 were only $10.93 a week, or 32 cents a week less than the average given in the first table for the same year (1881). A large part of this is accounted for by the fall in the cotton industry alone, which is one of the largest in the state. Had the facts been as complete in 1872 as in 1881, instead or showing a rise of two cents a week, as indicated by the first table, the figures would probably have indicated a decline of about 2.5 per cent.

(2) The second question to consider is: Are the industrial conditions of Massachusetts fairly representative of those of the whole country? The only way we know of ascertaining this fact is by comparing the statistics for Massachusetts with those of the Senate Report for the same periods, which includes all industries for the whole nation.

According to the elaborate tables in the Senate Report, Part I., p. 14, estimated by average according to relative importance of industries, 1872–1881, wages fell 1.6 per cent. The Massachusetts tables show a fall in wages in all industries for the same period of 2.5 per cent., indicating a close general similarity between the two investigations, or proving the approximate accuracy of both. It is clear, then, from both the Massachusetts Report and the Senate Report that from 1872 to 1881 there was a general decline in the average wages throughout the country of about 2 per cent.

(3) Whether this represents a real decline in the material condition and social welfare of the American workmen depends upon whether this fall in wages was fully offset by the general fall in the prices of commodities and conveniences on which these wages were expended. What, then, was the course of prices (in gold) from 1872 to 1881 ? An elaborate table showing the amount of commodities that a dollar would buy at retail in 1872, 1881 and 1897 and the increase or decrease in purchasing power is given on pages 26–29, Massachusetts Report, 1897. It includes 51 articles, as follows: 18 articles of groceries, 21 of provisions (including all kinds of meats, butter, eggs, etc.), 3 of fuel, 7 of dry goods and 2 classes of rents. This great mass of facts shows

that the purchasing power of a dollar in gold in a given quantity of these 51 articles, taken together, was 8.3 per cent. greater in 1881 than it was in 1872. That is to say, each dollar of wages would buy about 8.3 cents worth more in 1881 than it would in 1872, which is equivalent to about 8 per cent. rise in real wages. If we deduct the fall of 2.5 per cent. in wages from the 8.3 per cent. rise of purchasing power of money due to the fall of prices we have a net gain of 5.8 per cent. So that in Massachusetts, from 1872 to 1881, real wages rose nearly 6 per cent. instead of having fallen nearly 3 per cent., as the wage figures, taken alone, seem to show.

If we take the same facts for the whole nation we find the result even more encouraging than that shown in Massachusetts. On page 100, Part I., of the Senate Report on *Wholesale Prices and Wages*, the relative prices in gold for all articles are given, grouped by three different methods: (1) "Simple average;" (2) "All articles averaged according to importance, certain expenditures being considered uniform;" (3) "All articles averaged according to importance, comprising 68.6 per cent. of total expenditure."

The result of all these three methods is very similar. For instance, taking the whole period from 1860 to 1891, according to the first method, prices fell from 100 to 92.2; the second, to 96.2; the third, to 94.4.

To avoid tediousness of statement necessarily involved in frequent reference to three different methods of computation, which in the main are substantially the same, we shall for the purposes of comparison in this article use only one; viz., the computation by which all articles are averaged according to importance, comprising 68.6 per cent. of the total expenditure. The reason for taking this is that the price tables in the Massachusetts Report, with which we shall make frequent comparison, though computed by simple average include only fifty-one articles, comprising groceries, provisions, fuel, dry goods and rent.   Two of the computations in the Senate Report are for all articles, and hence include a large number which are not in the Massachusetts computation; but the method which takes only 68.6 per cent. of the total expenditure includes chiefly staple articles, hence the omitted 31.4 per cent. of total expenditure will necessarily consist largely of the articles not included in the Massachusetts computation.   For these reasons the results of this method are more nearly comparable with the Massachusetts tables.

According to this method of computation then (which is always represented in the Senate Report by the third right-hand column) the average price of commodities fell 10.7 per cent. between 1872 and 1881, giving an increased purchasing power of money of 11.9 per cent.

Deducting from this the 1.6 per cent. fall of wages gives a net rise of real wages of 10.3 per cent. for the nation, or 4.5 per cent. more than in Massachusetts. This difference of 4.5 per cent. may probably be accounted for by the fact that the computations in the Senate Report are based upon wholesale prices, while the figures for Massachusetts represent retail prices, which are necessarily much higher.   Obviously a fall of a given amount in the price of an article would show a smaller percentage on retail than on wholesale prices, since the basis of computation is much larger, often 20 per cent. and sometimes 50 per cent. larger, according to the increased cost involved in the retail trade.

Without attempting too much accuracy, therefore, where complete accuracy is unattainable, it is manifest that the Massachusetts showing is substantially in accord with the larger investigations of the Senate Committee.   Whether taken separately or jointly, they show that in all industries taken together from 1872 to

1881, real wages on an average increased not less than five per cent. and probably nearer ten per cent.

(4) It now remains to consider the movement of wages and prices from 1881 to 1897. It will be remembered that the figures for Massachusetts cover twenty-five years, 1872-1897, but give no facts for any dates between 1881 and 1897.

It will be recalled that the first table gave the facts for 1872, 1881, and 1897, but since it included data for only ten industries exclusive of agriculture (eleven in all) it could hardly be regarded as adequate fairly to represent the general condition of labor. This table shows that from 1872 to 1881 wages in gold rose on an average (without agriculture) fourteen cents a week; including agriculture, only two cents a week. From 1881 to 1897 it indicates an average decline of twenty-four cents a week for manufacturing industries and twenty-one cents for all industries, including agriculture, and for the whole twenty-five years, 1872-1897, it shows an average decline of ten cents a week for all industries exclusive of agriculture, and of nineteen cents a week including agriculture. It is this table that gives the idea that there has been a general fall of wages, both for the sixteen years, 1881-1897, and for the twenty-five years, 1872-1897. We have already seen that for the period preceding 1881 there was a net increase of real wages from five to ten per cent.

We will now consider the movement of wages and prices in Massachusetts during the sixteen years since 1881. According to the more complete presentation of data given in Table II., which we have found is in substantial accord with the exhaustive Report of the Senate Committee, it appears that the average wages, including agriculture, were in 1881 $10.93 a week, and in 1897 $11.36 per week, showing an actual increase of forty-three cents a week, or 3.9 per cent.

The question that arises in this connection is: Does the Massachusetts table fairly represent the wage movement during the whole of this sixteen years? That is to say, has there been a steady movement in wage conditions, which in sixteen years results in a rise of 3.9 per cent., or have there been conditions under which wages have risen in a more rapid degree and other conditions which have caused a sudden fall? If such is the case this table does not reveal the fact, and might be very misleading. The knowledge of this fact is very important in studying the wage question, because if conditions have existed under which a general though slow rise of wages occurred, then it is important that the public policy under which this took place be continued and efforts be made to emphasize the forces which promoted the rise of wages. On the other hand, if this meagre net result of 3.9 per cent. rise of wages for sixteen years is only part of a rise that has taken place, much of which has been destroyed by reverse conditions, it is of the utmost importance to economists and statesmen to know in what part of the period the rise took place, and in what part the fall, so as to be able to distinguish the policy under which the rise took place from that under which the fall occurred, that in the future the one which produced the fall may forever be avoided, and the other be continued and emphasized.

As the Massachusetts Report gives no figures for dates between 1881 and 1897, we must turn as before to the Senate Report* for data of the intermediate years, which show a general rise in wages of twelve per cent. from 1881 to 1891. It is well known that 1892 was the most prosperous year of the decade, and the data for

---

* *Wholesale Prices and Wages,* Part I., p. 14; Average according to relative importance of industries.

that year, if included, would show a still higher rise of wages.

Thus far, however, we have considered only the direct rise of wages in gold. In order to find the rise of real wages 1881–1891 we must now consider the movement of prices for that period. The data for this also will be found in the Senate Report already referred to.* From the facts there given it appears that prices fell 12.9 per cent. and the purchasing power of money rose 14.8 per cent. Thus the purchasing power of money increased about 2.8 per cent. more than wages rose, making nearly 27 per cent. increase of real wages during the ten years.

Had the industrial conditions which prevailed during the ten years prior to 1891 continued until 1897, gold wages would have risen 18 per cent. during the 16 years instead of 3.9 per cent. (as indicated by the 1897 Massachusetts Report) and real wages would have risen over 30 per cent. The fact that wages rose only 3.9 per cent. for the whole 16 years, during the first ten of which they rose 12 per cent., shows there must have been a net fall of at least 8 per cent. after 1891. This inference is fully sustained by wage data given in another form (yearly earnings) in the *Statistics of Manufactures* in Massachusetts. The data in these reports are very complete, though they do not include agriculture. The tables giving the yearly earnings of laborers in 75 manufacturing industries show a steady rise prior to 1892, and from 1892 to 1896 a marked yearly fall. The average yearly wages in these 75 industries in 1892 were $450.59.† In 1895 they were only $421.59,‡ a decline of $29.00. Since then wages of cotton operatives have been reduced 10 per cent. It is thus clear that

---

* *Wholesale Prices and Wages*, Part I., p. 100.

† Statistics of Manufactures, 1893, p. 53.

‡ Statistics of Manufactures, 1895, p. 89.

wages in gold, regardless of the fall of prices, went up and up, reaching the highest point in 1892, then they went down and down, reaching the lowest point in 1895. In 1896 they took a slight turn upwards, which was more marked in 1897.

Of course during this period prices also fell. The fall, 1881—1897, was equivalent to 30 per cent. increase in the purchasing power of money. About half of this may be accredited to the last six of the 16 years. But as the fall of wages since 1891 was over 8 per cent., the net increase of real wages was only about 7 per cent., as compared with about 27 per cent. for the previous ten years.

It should also be remembered that this period includes 1892, the banner year of the whole period, and 1897, which witnessed a marked rise of wages in nearly all industries. If these two years were eliminated and the four years 1893—1896 taken alone they would show an actual net decline in real wages. This means a real setback in the material and social condition of the wage class, a thing which has not before occurred in this country since the civil war.

Another feature of this situation which should not be overlooked is the marked difference in the character of the fall in prices in the two periods. In the period preceding 1891 the fall of prices was due to the introduction of new methods, of improved machinery, and superior industrial organization; it was the accompaniment and outcome of progress, profits and prosperity. On the contrary, during the period since 1891 (1893–1896) the fall of prices came from depression, bankruptcy, sheriff's sales, and losses. There is no evidence that in any industry new capital was invested, improved machinery applied, or more economic methods devised. Reduction of wages and curtailment of operations were about the only means employed to reduce

expenses.   In short, the fall of prices during this period represented the same retrogressive condition to
business men and employers that the fall of wages represented to laborers.

It is, therefore, not correct to regard the fall in
prices since 1891 as compensating the fall in wages; it
was not an advantage to the wage earners because, besides being accompanied by lower wages, it brought
with it what was even more disastrous, widespread
idleness.   So that, strictly speaking, the fall in prices
from 1892 to 1896 really represented loss to the community, instead of a gain as in the previous period.

For this sudden revolution in the industrial condition of the nation there is but one explanation—the
radical change of policy instituted in 1893 and continued
until 1897, the distinguishing feature of which was the
substitution of a non-protective for a protective revenue
policy. This period of disaster, fortunately for the nation,
was limited to a single presidential term.   It in no wise
represents the general industrial tendency of the country
or the economic spirit of the American people. It was a
temporary setback caused by a political accident which
it is fair to assume will not be repeated in this generation.   Despite this misfortune, the general industrial
tendency of the last twenty-five years shows a wholesome and (with this exception) a relatively steady
onward and upward movement, the unfailing sign of
which is a permanent rise of wages and a fall of prices,
or a net increase in the purchasing power of a day's
labor, coupled with a shortening of the working day.

The public policy under which this progress has taken
place should be continued and emphasized, especially
in the direction of lessening the hours of labor and improving the sanitary and social conditions under which
the masses have to labor and live.

SPAIN'S LAST OUTPOST—PORTO RICO

With the Philippines lost and Cuba within a few months of the same fate, Porto Rico remains the only important Spanish possession geographically remote from the home country. The Canary Islands are still under Spanish rule, but are comparatively near the Peninsula and hardly to be regarded as a distinctly foreign colony. Porto Rico is practically the last remnant of a once enormous colonial territory, and that remnant itself will undoubtedly have been lopped off before the present war is over, or its surrender made one of the conditions of peace.

Four hundred years ago Spain was on the threshold of a period of territorial expansion. Within a few decades after the voyages of Columbus Spain's dominion included—nominally at least, and in many cases actually—the greater part of South and Central America, the West Indies, Florida, Mexico, the gulf region and part of our Pacific coast. It was during this period also that the Philippines and the Canary Islands came under Spanish rule. For two centuries this wide empire remained practically intact, and then began the shrinkage which has since been steadily reducing Spain's territory towards its old peninsular limits. Jamaica, first, was wrested from Spain by the British in 1655; a part of Hayti was ceded to France in 1697, and the whole island became independent in the early part of the present century; the Bahama Islands came definitely under British authority about 1783. Between 1810 and 1820 Chili, Venezuela, Argentina and Paraguay achieved their independence, and during the next decade (1820–1830) Mexico, Ecuador, Guatemala, Nicaragua, Costa Rica, Colombia, Peru, Bolivia and Uruguay threw off the Spanish yoke. Florida was ceded by Spain to the United States in 1821.

After an interval of nearly three-quarters of a century this curtailment of Spanish colonial power is now about to be completed in the conquest of Cuba, the Philippine Islands, probably Porto Rico and perhaps even the Canaries, by the United States.

Cuba, Hayti and Porto Rico form a chain of islands having a general direction, from Cuba, of east by south, and separating the Caribbean Sea from the Atlantic Ocean. Porto Rico is the easternmost and smallest of these islands. It is traversed by the eighteenth parallel, north latitude; but, although wholly within the tropical zone, the temperature rarely rises above 97 degrees, owing to the prevailing northeast winds. The latitude is about the same as that of Bombay and of northern Luzon in the Philippine Islands. Porto Rico's longitude (sixty-six degrees west of Greenwich) brings the island about one degree further east than the extreme easternmost point on the Atlantic coast of the United States, i.e., Eastport, Maine. The distance from Porto Rico to Key West is about 1,000 miles; from the Cape Verde Islands, off the coast of Africa and almost directly east of Porto Rico, something over 2,000 miles. Cadiz, Spain, is considerably more than 3,000 miles to the northeast.

Porto Rico is rectangular in shape and almost three times as long as broad. East and west it measures 108 miles; north and south about thirty-seven. Its area is 3,530 square miles, or about one-twelfth that of Cuba, a little more than half that of the Hawaiian Islands and less than one-thirtieth of the area of the Philippines. The island is about two-thirds the size of Connecticut and nearly three times that of Rhode Island. An East and West mountain range forms the water shed for some 1,300 streams; forty-seven of these are rivers, but none navigable. Porto Rico is extremely fertile and is considered the most healthy island in the Antilles. The chief products are coffee and sugar; tobacco is extensively cultivated, and rice, maize and tropical fruits to a less extent. Dense forests cover the highlands and contain many valuable species of wood, and the excellent pasturage in other sections permits cattle raising on an extensive scale. Gold, iron, coal, copper and salt are found in Porto Rico, but only the salt mines are worked. The total exports of the island in 1895 amounted to about $14,600,000, imports $16,000,000. In the year ending June 30, 1897, the United States imported $2,181,024 worth of products from Porto Rico, and our exports thither amounted to $1,988,888. During the same period our imports from Cuba amounted to $18,407,211, exports to Cuba $8,259,776; imports from the Philippine Islands $4,383,740, exports thither $94,597; imports from Hawaii $13,687,799, exports to Hawaii $4,690,075.

According to recent statistics, the population of Porto Rico is 806,708, or about one-half that of Cuba, one-twelfth that of the Philippine Islands, and almost eight times that of Hawaii. On less than one-ninth the territory, Porto Rico supports 100,000 more people than the state of Maine. Of this population 480,267 are whites and 326,441 colored, the latter comprising 77,751 negroes and 248,690 mulattoes. This is a considerably better showing than in the Philippine Islands, where the bulk of the population is of the Malay and mixed races, but somewhat worse than in Cuba, where only about 31 per cent. of the people are colored, as against 40 per cent. in Porto Rico. In Hawaii 81 per cent. of the people are natives, Mongolians and of mixed races; only 19 per cent. are white. In South Carolina 59 per cent. of the population are colored, in Mississippi 58 per cent.; in Louisiana, 50 per cent. The white population in these southern states, however, is greatly superior to tho white element in either Cuba or Porto Rico; our southern white people are chiefly of English descent, while the Caucasians living in the West Indies are mostly of Spanish origin or immigrants from continental Europe. Eighty-six per cent. of the inhabitants of Porto Rico do not know how either to read or write. This is a much poorer showing than in Cuba, where 33 per cent. know at least how to read. In South Carolina the illiterates compose 45 per cent. of the whole population; in Mississippi 40 per cent.; in Louisiana 46 per cent.

San Juan is the capital of Porto Rico, and contains nearly 30,000 inhabitants. It is situated on a small island on the north coast, joined to the mainland by a bridge. There is a good harbor, protected by a Morro Castle near the harbor entrance, San Cristobal fortress on the land side, the fort of Caballero on an elevation, and several smaller fortifications. Ponce, on the south coast, is about half the size of San Juan, and there are numerous smaller towns and villages. Porto Rico is traversed by thirteen highways and fifteen side roads; it has less than one hundred miles of narrow gauge railroad, and only about 450 miles of telegraph lines. San Juan is connected with Jamaica and St. Thomas by cable.

Porto Rico was discovered by Columbus in November, 1493, on his second voyage to America. San Juan was founded by Ponce de Leon in 1511. The native inhabitants, as in Cuba, were enslaved and finally exterminated; negro slavery was then established and continued until 1873. Spain's sovereignty in Porto Rico has remained undisturbed except for attacks by the English in 1595, 1598, 1678 and 1797, none of which produced permanent results, and a revolution of the inhabitants themselves in 1820, which was suppressed in 1823. The system of government is like that in Cuba, and equally burdensome. The revenues are expended almost wholly for Spanish purposes; in a recent annual budget, for instance, pensions, interest on Spanish debt and salaries of colonial officers living in Spain consumed $735,928.80; the courts, and expenses of the established Catholic church, $378,740.50; increase of Spanish navy, $150,160.66; public works, $272,-214.02; civil government $719,315.26; while Porto Rico had to contribute $1,066,595.50 towards Spain's war expenses in Cuba and the Philippines.

Porto Rico is so much smaller than either Cuba or the Philippines that the social and political disadvantages of permanently attaching it to this country would not, perhaps, be serious, and might be overbalanced by the strategic value of the island as a coaling station and naval rendezvous. The Philippines might be disposed of to some European power, or to Japan, but with Porto Rico the case is different. When any American colony once passes out of European control it ought to remain out; either it should have an independent government of its own or come under the controlling influence of some already existing American republic.

The chief danger in annexing Porto Rico to the United States would be the impetus such a step would give to similar action in reference to other territory whose incorporation in the Union would be a positive detriment and menace to our social progress. Probably the best solution of the problem would be an American protectorate of the island, under which the machinery of an independent government should be set in motion and supervised until its operation became automatic and safe. In any event, if Porto Rico falls into the hands of the United States we should retain the permanent right to use the island as a coaling station and base of naval operations, whatever form of government may be established or whoever may acquire an interest in its affairs.

THE WAR TAXES

The new internal revenue law, part of which went into effect on June 14th and most of the rest on July 1st, is the first measure of the kind enacted in this country since the Civil War. It is important because it affects, directly or indirectly, almost our entire population, and because upon its proceeds the government depends very largely for the funds necessary to carry on the war with Spain. The law itself is long and wordy, and only those seriously affected are likely to pay much attention to its various provisions. In order to enable our readers to see at a glance just what these taxes are we have prepared a digest of the measure, leaving out the formal verbiage and summarizing details wherever possible. This digest (which can, of course, be kept permanently for reference) is as follows:

TAKING EFFECT JUNE 14TH.

TAXES ON LIQUORS—On all liquors, beer, ale, porter and other similar fermented liquors, $2.00 per barrel of 31 gallons, and at a like rate for fractional parts of a barrel. This is in lieu of the former tax of $1.00 per barrel. A discount of 7½ per cent. is allowed on all sales by collectors to brewers of the stamps provided for payment of this tax.

TOBACCO, CIGARS, etc.—On all manufactured tobacco and snuff, 12 cents per pound. On cigars and cigarettes weighing more than three pounds per 1,000, $3.60 per thousand. On cigars weighing not more than three pounds per 1,000, $1.00 per 1,000. On cigarettes weighing not more than three pounds per 1,000, $1.50 per 1,000. This is in lieu of the previous tax imposed by law.

SUGAR AND PETROLEUM REFINERS—All persons or corporations engaged in the business of refining petroleum or sugar, or owning or controlling any pipe line for transporting oil or other products, whose gross annual receipts exceed $250,000, are taxed ¼ of one per cent. on the gross amount of all such receipts in excess of said sum of $250,000.

LEGACIES—Taxes on legacies or distributive shares of personal property are levied according to the degree of relationship of the heirs to the testator. Where the whole amount of said personal property is more than $10,000, but does not exceed $25,000, the taxes are as follows: First, where the beneficiary is the lineal issue or a lineal brother or sister to the testator, 75 cents on each $100 of the legacy. Second, where beneficiary is a descendant of a brother or sister of the testator, $1.50 on each $100. Third, where beneficiary is the brother or sister of the father or mother, or a descendant of a brother or sister of the father or mother, $3.00 on each $100. Fourth, where the beneficiary is a brother or sister of the grandfather or grandmother, or a descendant of the brother or sister of the grandfather or grandmother, $4.00 on each $100. Fifth, where the beneficiary is in any other degree of relationship, or is a stranger in blood to the testator, or is a body politic or corporate, $5.00 on each $100. The legacy tax does not apply, however, to any property passing by will or by law to the husband or wife of the testator.

Where the amount or value of the legacy is between $25,000 and $100,000, all the above rates of tax are multiplied by 1½ ; between $100,000 and $500,000, multiplied by 2 ; between $500,000 and $1,000,000, multiplied by 2½ ; over $1,000,000, multiplied by 3.

TEA—On all teas imported from abroad, 10 cents per pound.

TAKING EFFECT JULY 1ST.

SPECIAL TAXES—(1) Bankers employing a capital

not exceeding $25,000, $50.00; where capital exceeds $25,000, a tax of $2.00 on every additional thousand dollars.

(2) Financial brokers, $50.00.

(3) Pawnbrokers, $20.00.

(4) Commercial brokers, $20.00.

(5) Custom-house brokers, $10.00.

(6) Proprietors of theatres, museums, and concert halls in cities having more than 25,000 population, $100. Where the edifice in which such entertainments are given is leased, the lessee pays the tax unless otherwise agreed between the parties.

(7) Proprietors of circuses, $100.

(8) Proprietors of all other public exhibitions or shows, $10.00.

(9) Proprietors of bowling alleys or billiard rooms, $5.00 for each alley or table.

TOBACCO DEALERS AND MANUFACTURERS — (1) Dealers in leaf tobacco whose annual sales do not exceed 50,000 pounds, $6.00; where sales are between 50,000 and 100,000 pounds, $12.00; exceeding 100,000 pounds, $24.00.

(2) Dealers in tobacco whose annual sales exceed 50,000, $12.00.

(3) Manufacturers of tobacco whose annual sales do not exceed 50,000 pounds, $6.00; sales between 50,-000 and 100,000 pounds, $12.00; exceeding 100,000 pounds, $24.00.

(4) Manufacturers of cigars whose annual sales do not exceed 100,000 cigars, $6.00; annual sales between 100,000 and 200,000 cigars, $12.00; more than 200,000 cigars, $24.00.

STAMP TAXES—The stamp taxes imposed by this law are very numerous and are arranged in two parts, Schedules A and B. Schedule A includes the following:

Bonds, debentures or certificates of indebtedness

issued by any association or corporation, 5 cents on each $100 of face value or fraction thereof.

Sales, agreements to sell, or transfers of shares or certificates of stock in any such company, 2 cents on each $100 of face value or fraction thereof.

Sales, agreements of sale, or agreements to sell any product or merchandise at any exchange or board of trade, 1 cent for each $100 of value of said sale or agreement, and for each additional $100 or fraction thereof, 1 cent.

Bank checks, drafts or certificates of deposit not drawing interest, or any order for payment of money drawn upon or by any bank, trust company or any persons, companies or corporations, at sight, 2 cents.

Inland bills of exchange, drafts, certificates of deposit drawing interest or any order for payment of money, otherwise than at sight or on demand ; also promissory notes, except bank-notes issued for circulation, and on each renewal of the same, 2 cents for sum not exceeding $100, and 2 cents on each additional fraction of $100. This tax will also apply to domestic money orders issued by the United States Government, and the price of such orders will be increased by a sum equal to the tax.

Foreign bills of exchange or letters of credit, if drawn singly or otherwise than in a set of three or more, 4 cents for sum not exceeding $100, and 2 cents on each additional fraction of $100. If drawn in sets of two or more, for every bill of each set 2 cents where the sum does not exceed $100, and 2 cents on each $100 or fraction thereof in excess of $100.

Bills of lading or receipts for goods exported from any United States port, 10 cents. This does not apply to vessels plying between United States ports and ports in British North America.

Bills of lading, or receipts issued by any railroad,

steamboat, carrier or express company for goods shipped over its line, 1 cent.

Telephone messages, for which the charge is or exceeds 15 cents, 1 cent; to be paid by the owner or operator of the telephone line.

Bonds, for indemnifying any person, firm or corporation who shall have become bound as security for the payment of money or performance of any given duty, 50 cents.

Certificates of profits and transfers thereof, 2 cents on each $100 of face value or fraction thereof.

Certificates of damage, and all other certificates issued by any port-warden or marine surveyor, 25 cents.

Certificates of any description required by law and not otherwise specified in this Act, 10 cents.

Charter party, for vessels not exceeding 300 tons burden, $3.00; between 300 and 600 tons, $5.00; exceeding 600 tons, $10.00.

Contract, broker's note or memorandum of sale of goods, stocks, real estate or property of any kind, issued by brokers, 10 cents.

Deeds, or any instruments conveying title to lands, houses, or other realty, when the consideration or value exceeds $100 but is less than $500, 50 cents; and for each additional $500 or fraction thereof, 50 cents.

Telegraphic messages, 1 cent.

Custom-house entry, for any goods or merchandise not exceeding $100 in value, 25 cents; between $100 and $500, 50 cents; exceeding $500, $1.00.

Entry for the withdrawal of goods or merchandise from customs bonded warehouse, 50 cents.

Life insurance policies, 8 cents on each $100 or fraction thereof; but on all policies issued on the weekly payment plan the tax is 40 per cent. of the amount of the first weekly premium.

Marine, inland and fire insurance policies, ½ of 1

cent on each dollar or fractional part thereof of the premium charged. This tax does not apply to purely co-operative or mutual fire insurance companies.

Casualty, fidelity and guarantee insurance policies, and indemnity bonds of any nature, ½ of 1 cent on each dollar or fractional part thereof of the premium charged.

Leases or agreements for rent of lands or buildings, 25 cents for a period not exceeding one year; 50 cents when between one and three years; $1.00 when for more than three years.

Manifest for custom-house entry or clearance of cargo for a foreign port, $1.00 for vessels not exceeding 300 tons burden; $3.00 for vessels of between 300 and 600 tons; $5.00 for vessels exceeding 600 tons. This does not apply to vessels plying between ports of the United States and British North America.

Mortgages on any kind of property, real or personal, where the amount is between $1,000 and $1,500, 25 cents; and on each $500 or fraction thereof in excess of $1,500, 25 cents. The same tax is levied on all assignments or renewals of such mortgages.

Passage tickets to any foreign port, where the price of ticket does not exceed $30, $1.00; price between $30 and $60, $3.00; price more than $60, $5.00. This does not apply to vessels plying between ports of the United States and British North America.

Power of attorney or proxy for voting at an election for officers of any industrial or commercial company, 10 cents.

Power of attorney to sell or lease real estate, collect rent, sell or transfer stocks, etc., 25 cents.

Protests of notes, bills of exchange, acceptances, checks, drafts, or any marine protest, 25 cents.

Warehouse receipts for property held in storage in any public or private warehouse, except receipts for farm produce deposited by actual growers thereof, 25 cents.

Schedule B includes the following:

On all proprietary medicines, whether patented or not, and on all perfumery, cosmetics, etc., a tax is imposed according to the value of the article; thus, where the retail price of the packet or bottle does not exceed 5 cents the tax is ⅛ of 1 cent; where price is between 5 cents and 10 cents, ¼ of 1 cent; between 10 and 15 cents, ⅜ of 1 cent; between 15 and 25 cents, ⅝ of 1 cent.

Chewing gum—On each package not exceeding $1.00 in value (retail), 4 cents. If exceeding $1.00 in value, on each additional $1.00 or fraction thereof, 4 cents.

Sparkling or other wines—1 cent on each pint bottle; 2 cents on larger bottles.

TAKING EFFECT AUGUST 14TH.

MIXED FLOUR—Manufacturers or packers of mixed flour, $12.00 per annum. This commodity is described as "the food product made from wheat mixed or blended in whole or in part with any other grain or other material, or the manufactured product of any other grain or other material than wheat."

In addition to the tax on manufacturers of this product there is a tax of 4 cents on each barrel or package of mixed flour containing between 98 and 196 pounds, 2 cents on every half-barrel or other package containing between 49 and 98 pounds, one cent on every quarter-barrel containing between 24½ and 49 pounds, and ½ cent on every one-eighth barrel containing 24½ pounds or less. This tax is to be paid by the makers or packers of the flour.

All imported mixed flours shall pay this internal revenue tax in addition to the customs duty.

GENERAL PROVISIONS

The law provides various modes of procedure in the case of taxes on manufacturers, corporations, etc., to prevent evasion of the tax. Thus, in certain cases it is required that regular reports be made to the internal revenue officers of the amount of business done, or goods handled, etc., in the departments of business to which a given tax applies.

It is required in connection with the stamp taxes that every person affixing a stamp to any document in accordance with law must write or stamp thereupon his initials and the date, so that the stamp may not be used again. Failure to do this involves a penalty of not less than $50 or more than $500 fine, or imprisonment for not more than six months, or both.

Numerous penalties are provided for infractions of this new revenue law, such as a fine of $10 for failure to put a stamp on telegraphic messages, $100 for failure to affix stamp to any document requiring same, $200 for intentional evasion of a stamp tax, $500 or six months' imprisonment, or both, for. failure to affix stamp to proprietary medicines, cosmetics, etc. and $1,000 or imprisonment and confinement at hard labor not exceeding five years, or both, for counterfeiting internal revenue stamps or attempting fraudulently to use same a second time.

DISTINGUISHED ECONOMISTS:—ADAM SMITH

It is always interesting for students of a science to be able to look upon the faces of the great men who have made the important contributions to the subject. It is our purpose during the coming year to publish the portraits of leading economists; those, at least, who have contributed the distinguishing features of the doctrines of the different schools of economic thought.

We begin with Adam Smith, whose great work, *Wealth of Nations*, is to the economic literature of modern times what Gibbon's *Decline and Fall of the Roman Empire* is to the history of mediæval Europe and Shakespeare is to English literature. While every subsequent writer of any account has ventured to differ with and criticise the *Wealth of Nations*, that work contains the elements of about everything that has since been published. The English School, of which Adam Smith is the father, may be said really to have furnished the foundation principles of the workable economic theories of the nineteenth century. Subsequent schools, which will hereafter be considered, have largely been modifications of the doctrines evolved by English economists, of whom Adam Smith was conspicuously leader.

The author of the *Wealth of Nations* was born at Kirkcaldy on June 5, 1723. His father, who was a person of some prominence in the locality, having held several political positions in the town, died when Adam Smith was only a few months old. At the age of three years he was kidnapped by some gypsies, who, had they been successful in keeping their prize, might have deprived the world of modern political economy.

He attended the public schools in his native place, and at the age of fourteen (1737) was sent to the University of Glasgow, where he remained three years. He then entered Balliol College, Oxford, where he remained seven years. At the age of thirty-two (1755) he entered the arena as an author by contributing anonymously two articles to the *Edinburgh Review*. Two years later he published his *Theory of Moral Sentiments*, by which he at once became famous. In 1762 the University of Glasgow conferred upon him the honorary degree of Doctor of Laws. Dr. Smith, as he was thenceforth known, was an intimate and devoted friend of Hume, and, indeed, of the most distinguished philosophers of the time. The following year he received an invitation to travel on the continent with the Duke of Buccleuch in an official capacity, whither they sailed in March, 1764, returning to England in October, 1766. The next ten years he spent in practical seclusion in the preparation of his great work, *Wealth of Nations*, published in 1776.

Whatever may be said to-day of the unsystematic or desultory character of the *Wealth of Nations*, it was the greatest work on political economy that had yet appeared and, really, the first treatise on economics from a truly industrial point of view. During his sojourn in France, Adam Smith closely studied the doctrines of the French physiocrats, a school of economists who treated only agricultural and extractive industries as truly productive, treating them as intermediary or middleman processes. Although Adam Smith owed much to the physiocrats, he differed completely from them on this point, effectively exposing the fallacy of this conception, and established for all time the doctrine that manufacture, trade and commerce are as truly productive industries as are agriculture or mining. In short, Adam Smith broadened the horizon of economic observation and included the economic interests and efforts of the manufacturing and mercantile classes in the purview of economics. In this way he brought the science down to later eighteenth century conditions, which included the great problems of wages, interest, profit, rent, free-trade

and protection, which have been the absorbing themes
of economic controversy during the nineteenth century.

In his *Theory of Moral Sentiments*, Adam Smith as-
cribes human actions entirely to sympathy. He there
lays down the principle that the rules of judging our
own conduct are arrived at solely by observing the conduct and interest of others. He says: " Our first moral
criticisms are exercised upon the character and conduct
of other people."

The whole reasoning in his *Wealth of Nations* is
based upon an opposite principle, *viz.:* self-interest. Not
sympathy with others, but interest in self. Perhaps the
most valid criticism upon his first book was that it
omitted self-interest in considering the motives of human conduct. The great defect in his second and
greater work, *Wealth of Nations*, was in omitting to
count with sympathy and the moral and psychical as-
peets of social life. Reasoning solely upon self-interest
he naturally reasoned only through the interests of the
class with which he was most intimately connected.
Though the class through whose interests he thought
and theorized was broader and more progressive than
the mere landed class through whose interests the physiocrats reasoned, it was too narrow to include the interests and welfare of the laboring class, which in his time
had scarcely evolved from the status of wardship. In
proportion, therefore, as this doctrine dominated public
policy, the interests of labor were neglected and those
of the employing class only were considered. As wage
conditions developed the defect in this theory became
more pronounced, and the doctrine declined in popular-
ity. It was to remedy the defects in this doctrine and
make economic theories conform more to the interests
of complex society, especially of the laboring class, that
the different schools of economics have since arisen.

EDITORIAL CRUCIBLE

SINCE WAR was declared the New York *Times* has in many respects made a commendable effort to be loyal and patriotic. The zeal with which it has defended our position against foreigners has sometimes gone far temporarily to justify the assumption that it is an American paper. It is, perhaps, too much to expect that the *Times* should all at once give up its mugwump habit of screeching about corrupt political motives governing all executive conduct. No more than a leopard can change its spots can a mugwump refrain from displaying his self-righteousness. But the *Times'* persistent and obviously malignant personal attack upon the Secretary of War has gone far past the patriotic point. It is manifest that its motive in this matter is either political or basely personal. In the midst of war constantly to berate the integrity and efficiency of the war department, like an attack upon the navy or the President himself, can serve only to shake the confidence of the people in those having the nation's honor and destiny in their charge. Sustain the government now and reckon with delinquents after the enemy is defeated, is the watchword of all loyal citizens.

PROFESSOR GOLDWIN SMITH is properly regarded as one of the best informed foreigners on American affairs, yet sometimes he talks like one who needs an introduction to us. Referring to the proposition to send Admiral Watson with a fleet to bombard Spanish coast cities, he says: " With the smoke of his first guns will vanish the Monroe Doctrine. If America will not let Europe alone she cannot expect to be let alone by Europe." So far as it relates to either the spirit or letter of the Monroe Doctrine this is supremely silly. From a Russian, French or Spanish editor such a remark might be attributed to pure ignorance; but from Goldwin Smith it must be ascribed to something quite different.

Our position in the present war is strictly in accordance with the spirit and letter of the Monroe Doctrine. Our object in this war is to rid this hemisphere of Spanish authority, because Spain has become a hindrance to free government and a menace to civilization. To pretend that the Monroe Doctrine forbids us invading the country of an enemy with which we are at war is simply childish. We want nothing of Spain except that she quit American territory. If it is necessary to bombard her coast cities to convince her of the necessity of this, then that is good Monroe Doctrine.

"If America will not let Europe alone," forsooth! When and where has America ever suggested interfering with Europe? If Spain will withdraw to Europe there is no danger of our molesting her; but if she has not the sense to do that it may be necessary for us to go there to teach her the obvious lesson of destiny. A little more of such empty juvenile talk and Goldwin Smith's utterances on American affairs will lose all claim to respect.

————

ALTHOUGH ADMIRAL CERVERA has not displayed any high fighting qualities, he at least shows the instincts of a gentleman and is entitled to genuine respect by the American people. Unlike the ordinary Spaniard, when Lieut. Hobson and his comrades surrendered to him after blowing up the Merrimac, he instantly recognized their bravery and suggested their exchange. In his report to his government about the destruction of his fleet he also frankly mentions the "noble generosity" with which he is treated as an American prisoner. Of course he attributes his defeat to the fact that he had to encounter forces three times as great as his own.

Perhaps he may be excused for a little exaggeration under the circumstances, although the disparity of forces is wholly inadequate to account for the overwhelming character of his defeat. It is not to be conceived for a moment that if the Americans had been on the Spanish ships and the Spaniards on the American that any such one-sided victory would have been possible. It is more than probable that if Spanish ships had been manned by Americans, some, if not a majority, of them would have escaped, and it is absolutely certain that more than one man on the attacking ships would have been killed. Oh, no, the victory was not won by superior force but by superior efficiency; not merely the difference in ships but the difference in the men. A nation whose navy can lose two whole squadrons in two battles and manage to kill only one man on the other side is inherently in-efficient. The personal quality of the men in the Span-ish navy, like the brutality of their soldiers and the in-humanity of their statesmanship, shows that Spain is rap-idly decaying from the dry-rot of impotent barbarism.

THE DISASTER which befell the French steamer La Bourgogne is one of the saddest events that has oc-curred in a generation. The number of lives lost has seldom been equalled in a single accident at sea. But it has another feature which makes it conspicuous as a horrible disaster, *viz.*, the conduct of the crew toward the helpless passengers. The savagery, for that it was, exhibited by the crew in stabbing, maltreating and in various ways murdering helpless women and children is distinctly a national disgrace. It is a disgrace to France that on an ocean steamer carrying the French flag such unrestrained savagery among the vessel's em-ployees could be possible. Making all allowance for the exciting circumstances, the affair is a marked reflec-tion upon French civilization. If the horrifying details survivors relate were all lacking, the mere fact that only one woman out of 100 or more was saved tells the story of the cowardly conduct of the ruffianly crew. Such a spectacle could never have occurred on an American or a British ship. It reflects on France because it shows a low tone of effective discipline and management as well as low grade of personal character. Wretches who would stab and club helpless women and children under such circumstances are always cowardly curs. If the discipline had been such as to mean death for such conduct, the very cowardice of such wretches would have put them on the side of decency. The conduct toward women, not merely in the drawing room but in critical positions, is a good criterion of the standard of civilization in any. country. Measured by this standard the Frenchman will still have to be accounted a barbarian.

COL. WATTERSON thinks we should "become a nation of warriors." In a recent interview he said:

"Look at the map of the West Indies. See where Cuba lies across our southern water front. Will any sane man say that we should ever permit it, once acquired, to pass out of our control? . . . . The United States from now on is destined to be a world power. Henceforth its foreign policy will need to be completely reconstructed. . . . . From a nation of shop-keepers we become a nation of warriors. We escape the menace and peril of socialism and agrarianism as England has escaped them, by a policy of colonization and conquest. From a provincial huddle of petty sovereignties held together by a rope of sand we rise to the dignity and prowess of an imperial republic, incomparably greater than Rome. It is true that we exchange domestic dangers for foreign dangers. . . . . We risk Cæsarism, certainly; but even Cæsarism is preferable to anarchism. We risk wars; but a man has but one time to die, and, either in peace or war he is not likely to die until his time comes."

Is this kind of verbiage to pass as argument in favor of a colonial policy? Think of the calibre of statesmanship that can suggest even that from a nation of shop-keepers we shall become a nation of warriors; that by a policy of colonization and conquest we are to escape the

menace and peril of socialism and agrarianism. Perish
the thought of such cowardice! By pursuing a policy of
war and conquest we might perhaps "escape the menace" of dealing with the new domestic problems our
highly complex industrial life has evolved, but we could
do so only by plunging the nation back into barbarism.
The man who wants this country to exchange domestic dangers for foreign dangers, to risk Cæsarism
and war, on the paltry ground that a man has but one
time to die and in either peace or war is not likely to
die until his time comes, is too shallow to be taken seriously and, despite his political professions, should be
counted among the enemies of free government and
democratic institutions.

Not the least surprising is his contemptuous reference to the United States as "a provincial huddle of
petty sovereignties." Has this predatory editor forgotten that he was a fire-eating Colonel in the rebellion to
disrupt the Republic, to maintain the sacred right of
"petty sovereignties" to "huddle" all alone in a confederacy in order to perpetuate slave labor?

It is encouraging to know that this loud-talking
Kentucky editor does not represent either Kentucky or
the South on this subject. The South is becoming
more and more industrial and less military; more of the
shop-keeper and less of the warrior, which means that
it is fast leaving the barbarism that this man Watterson
represents, and is ascending the scale of peaceful industrial civilization. Such rattle-headed talk as Watterson here reeled off is not representative of the sober
sentiment of any section or body of people in the United
States. It is the rant of a disappointed politician, whose
screech is the veritable voice of political anarchy.

CIVICS AND EDUCATION

RECENT MUNICIPAL EXPERIMENTS

The character and quantity of laws relating to cities, enacted during the last few years, show an increasing interest in problems of municipal government; which is a good sign, even though much of this experimental legislation may be in itself unwise. The bulk of these laws have had to do with the questions of municipal franchises and primary elections, and in both instances the tendency has been to safeguard popular rights more completely against possible aggressions of private interests. There has been a very decided trend, also, towards centralizing the executive functions in cities and increasing the power of the mayor. This is a conspicuous feature of the Greater New York charter, likewise of the new charter recently adopted in San Francisco.

The latter instrument provides for an interesting experiment in direct legislation; it practically introduces the initiative and referendum. A petition signed by legal voters to the number of 15 per cent. of the votes cast at the last preceding state or city election, will secure the submission of any desired ordinance to popular vote at the next election; and such ordinance, if adopted by a majority vote, cannot be repealed by the municipal legislature, but only by the people themselves. In the same way, any measure enacted by the municipal legislature may be referred to the people for final approval or rejection upon petition of 15 per cent. of the voters. This plan is in line with a law enacted by the California legislature in 1897, providing that upon petition of 50 per cent. of the voters of a county any desired measure must be submitted to the people of that county for acceptance or rejection, and, if approved by a majority, it becomes law. It will be interesting to watch the effect of this method of legislation in San Francisco. The proposition is distinctly more rational than the one sometimes advocated—that all laws enacted by legislative bodies be submitted to popular vote before going into effect. Such a scheme would be utterly impracticable, useless and positively dangerous, since the bulk of our legislation is on matters of minor importance and could not possibly be examined and intelligently passed upon by the voters at large. Under the present system, the thousands of bills annually introduced in our legislatures go through a sifting process in the various committees, and experienced lawmakers say that one of the most important services rendered by these committees is in killing bad bills. But for this sifting process a great mass of special legislation would be regularly enacted simply because of the utter inability of representative bodies to examine and discuss more than a small percentage of the bills that come before them. If this is true of small bodies of a hundred or so chosen men, it is plain enough that to submit all measures to popular vote would be a ridiculous farce and open the door to a continuous stream of vicious legislation. Those interested in securing special favors would always be on the alert to secure the passage of their bills, while on the side of the people there would almost never be any organized force in opposition. Laws would be either approved or voted down in bulk, good and bad together.

But the San Francisco plan is quite different and has its good side. Ordinary legislation is to be enacted by the municipal board of supervisors, but the power is reserved to the people of promptly bringing to popular vote any measure which such board may refuse to entertain or to approve. Whether much use is made of this privilege or not, it will undoubtedly create among San

Francisco's aldermen a livelier sense of the representative character of their office and a keener regard for the course of public opinion.

It is interesting to speculate on the possibilities of such a system here in New York City. Single-tax advocates, for instance, would probably have little difficulty in getting 15 per cent. of the voters to petition for submission of their scheme to popular judgment, even though less than 10 per cent. of such petitioners finally voted for it. This would give a clean-cut, popular decision on that one proposition, free from any political complications or confusion with other issues, such as free-silver, socialism or general anti-capitalism. The same test of popular opinion could be applied to socialism, and the exact strength of that movement revealed. The eight-hour day could be proposed by the workingmen of New York, and a vigorous campaign might result in its adoption, since a large majority of New York's population belong to the wage-earning and salary-receiving classes. Extension of educational facilities and various public improvements could either be voted directly, or a club held over the head of the administration and municipal assembly which would very materially stimulate progressive action on their part. Then, too, there would undoubtedly be fewer franchises granted for inadequate compensation and fewer contracts let to political favorites if it were known that all such ordinances could be promptly vetoed by a plebiscite.

Indeed, if the San Francisco plan were still further imitated the disposition of public franchises would be determined wholly by public vote. Street railway franchises in that city, however, are to be granted by the competitive bid system, the privilege to go to the company offering the largest percentage of gross receipts. After twenty-five years, moreover, the tracks and fixed plant of such street railway are to become city property.

This question of municipal franchises has been agitated with increasing earnestness during recent years. The Greater New York charter shows the effect of this agitation in the restrictions it places on the disposition of these public privileges. The board of estimate and apportionment must review very thoroughly all the conditions of a proposed franchise, its value and the compensation to be paid the city, and no franchise can be granted without the approval of this board and of three-fourths of the members of each house of the municipal assembly. The duration of all franchises is limited to twenty-five years.

Elsewhere similar restrictive action is being taken. In Kansas a radical law was enacted in 1897, with reference to light, heat, water and power plants. Of this measure Mr. E. D. Durand, in the March *Annals of the American Academy*, says: " This act requires the grantees of franchises to report in minute detail the exact cost of constructing their plant, and semi-annually thereafter the exact receipts and expenditures of every sort. A profit of six per cent. per annum is to be allowed on the actual investment shown by these statements, and the entire surplus of receipts is to go to the public treasury, unless a higher allowance be made to the holders of the franchise by consent of three-fifths of the taxpayers. No grant may be for more than twenty years, and after ten years the municipality may buy the plant at an appraised valuation."

The provision of this law requiring the entire surplus income to be paid into the city treasury will probably be entirely useless, since the companies can easily contrive to expend any such surplus in other ways or else will make no effort whatever to increase the efficiency and profitableness of the plants operated by them beyond the 6 per cent. limit. Much the better plan in all such cases is to grant the franchise to the company offering the largest fixed percentage of its gross receipts; then the profit incentive to improvements in plant and management remains in full force, and the city is assured of a definite return from the franchise during the given term of years.

Another matter to which considerable attention has lately been paid is primary elections. Though not strictly a municipal affair, it is in cities chiefly that the need of reform along this line has been felt. Mr. Durand, in the article from which we have just quoted, speaks of recent progress in primary reform in California and Wisconsin:

" The act adopted by the former state in 1895, for San Francisco only, has now been improved and extended throughout the state. It provides that all parties must hold their primary elections for choosing delegates to nominating conventions at the same time and place and under the joint supervision of officers elected by the county election commissioners from representations of the leading parties. The number of delegates is officially fixed, and official election registers are used to determine the qualification of voters. Each voter may cast his ballot for delegates to the convention of any one party he sees fit, on taking oath that he expects to support the party at the election. Rigid provisions are made to prevent fraud, 'packing' of primaries, etc.; while following the example set by Ohio last year, each candidate is required, after the convention and before election, to make a detailed statement of his expenses incurred for the purpose of securing the nomination, the total of such expenditures being limited on the same principle as are those of candidates for election. The Wisconsin law of 1897 is likewise based on one of 1895, which applied to Milwaukee city and county only. The present act is mandatory in all cities of over 10,000 population, and may be adopted by any town, village or city on popular vote. Each party has a separate primary and chooses its own officers. Preliminary meetings are, however, called a few days before the primary, at which any person may, at will, propose names of delegates to the party convention. The names are all placed, in an order to be determined by drawing at random, on a blanket ballot. The voter, at the primary, in secret, marks a cross opposite those whom he wishes for delegates, up to the number to which the precinct is entitled. Any voter duly qualified, as shown by the official election registry lists, must be allowed to take part in the primary, provided that, in case he is challenged, he swears that he voted for the party at the last election. Missouri also adopts, for St. Louis only, a primary election law with some improved features, and Delaware enacts somewhat similar provisions for New Castle county, the seat of the city of Wilmington."

The New York legislature, last winter, enacted a primary election law for all cities of 50,000 and over which has attracted wide attention because of the radical departure from previous methods for which it provides. It puts the conduct of party primaries on practically the same basis as that of general elections. Voters, when registering to vote at the general elections, may, if they want to take part in the primaries, declare their party allegiance and thus become entitled to vote at the primaries of that party. There are to be two annual primary days; one on the first Tuesday in June to elect delegates to state conventions, the other on the seventh Tuesday before the November election to elect delegates to local conventions. These primaries are conducted by the regular election inspectors and the voting for all parties is done at the same polling places in each district. Different colored ballots are used for each party, and anyone may prepare and furnish to the inspectors ballots for any candidate, provided only that such ballots are of a specified size, weight and texture, and of the color assigned to the candidate's party.   Every voter is given one each of all the ballots that may have been thus provided for his party, retires to a booth and makes his choice.   He must return all the ballots, folded so as to conceal the names, to the inspectors, delivering first the one he means to vote; the others are placed in a separate box and subsequently destroyed.

Whenever, upon enrolling himself with a given party, a voter is challenged, he may compel his registration by declaring that he is in general sympathy with the principles of that party, that he means to support its nominees generally at the next election, and that he has not taken part in the primary or conventions of any other party since the first day of the preceding year. The expense of these primaries is to be a public charge, and the system may be adopted, if desired, by any town or city of over 5,000 inhabitants.

The first test of this system took place in June last in New York City.   The "organization" candidates in both parties were quite as successful as formerly, showing either that the charges of corruption under the old system were greatly exaggerated or that the reform element is comparatively inactive and makes the fatal mistake of supposing that political victories can be won without organization or effort if only a fair law is obtained.   If once this delusion is abandoned the better element in all parties can easily control the primaries and nominate the candidates.   This was probably true, also, to a very large extent under the old system of primary elections, but with a law providing safeguards as ample as does the present the blame for any future triumphs of spoils politicians in our city primary elections must rest wholly upon the well-intentioned citizens who, by their neglect and indifference, permit such victories to be won.

Mrs. Humphry Ward is not only a novelist of rare talent and power, but an effective worker for practical

Mrs. Humphry Ward's Work in London social reform. Passmore Edwards House, a beautiful building recently completed for social settlement work in the north of London, is the outcome of years of effort on her part to realize some of the ideals developed in Robert Elsmere. Though located in a poor district it is not especially designed to get hold of those in abject poverty. Passmore Edwards House reaches the middle class of laborers and artisans, by means of lectures, concerts, classes for general instruction, industrial education for the young, boys' clubs, debates, sociological societies, etc., and is becoming a powerful factor of social improvement. The very poor are, of course, not quite within reach of an institution of this sort, but it undoubtedly affects them in one of the very important ways in which those classes can be affected, *viz.*, through the indirect influence of that portion of the laboring class which does come in contact with uplifting and progressive forces.

———

According to statistics collected about a year ago, there were in the whole city of London at that time

Growth of London 767,679 inhabited houses, which was nearly one-sixth of all the houses in England and Wales together. The increase during the preceding year had been 14,591 houses. Birmingham had at the same time 85,624 inhabited houses, Liverpool 91,484, and Manchester 100,249. The twin cities of Manchester and Salford had altogether 139,412 inhabited houses, which is the largest number in any one group in England, outside of the metropolis, but, as the London *Daily News* says, the capital city within ten years, at the present rate of growth, would add more houses than the total number in Manchester and Salford together. London continually annexes large towns on all sides, but none of these contains nearly so many houses as are added to the city every year in the normal process of growth.

This is the movement that is going on in all modern countries and, so far from its being a menace to civilization, as is feared by many, it is in fact one of the chief signs of civilization and of social progress.

The *Locomotive Firemen's Magazine* for July contains an editorial attack on American colleges for their unpatriotism in the present war. The charge is that the rich men whose sons attend these colleges are opposed to the war, and, by their patronage, control the attitude of the faculty. This simply shows the ease of proving that the whole world is decaying whenever something rotten is discovered in a corner of Denmark. True, there has been a lukewarmness in our large colleges during the present crisis, but that is chargeable, not to any improper capitalistic influence, but to the ultra-scholastic, *laissez 'faire* attitude of mind that largely dominates higher educational institutions as a legacy from the English School economics and metaphysical philosophy of a half-century ago. Rich men's sons form only a small percentage of the total number of college students, and moreover the rich men of the country themselves have, as a class, been supporters of the war, many of them offering their personal services even, and others granting leave of absence on pay to employees, etc. Of course the eye blinded with prejudice cannot see this. Verily it is easier for a camel to pass through the eye of a needle than for a rich man to escape damnation, even for his virtues.

Colleges, Rich Men and War

SCIENCE AND INDUSTRY

RAILROADS AND THE GOVERNMENT.

B. W. ARNOLD, JR.

For the purely American principle that whatever can be done without the government should so be done, has been substituted of late years by many of our citizens the Continental idea that whatever can be done by the government should be done by it; and, along with other claims occasioned by this change in sentiment, the demand has been made that our government should purchase and operate the steam railways. The main reason given for such action is that the evils of our present system will be remedied, though just how is not always shown. In addition, the facts are cited that our postal service has proved exceedingly satisfactory and that the experiment of government ownership has been successfully made in certain foreign countries. A full summary of all arguments advanced in support of this scheme would be about as follows:

(1) The costly law suits between different roads would be avoided. (2) Investors in railroad stocks would no longer suffer from the dishonest speculations of railroad directors. (3) Transportation being a social function demands, especially in joint traffic, uniform methods and unified instruments like the mail service, and the power and prestige of the state is necessary to secure them. (4) This plan of railroading has been successful in Prussia and Belgium and therefore we could safely employ it. (5) The profit in railroading would go into the United States Treasury. (6) Rates would be lowered. (7) No discrimination would be practised. (8) The waste of money occasioned by cut rate wars between competing roads would be saved.

Let us examine these claims. In the nature of the

case the first two would be true, for lawsuits would not arise between roads under common ownership and the government itself would be in this instance both investor and manager. In answer to the third it may be said that, while a certain analogy does exist between the railroading business and delivery of mail, the problems of conducting those two businesses are not at all the same, the transportation problem being far more complex. Where one fact could be named in the interchange of freight and passengers from one road to another, or from one state to another, that demands constant uniform methods of federal control, a dozen matters of detail arising in the handling and development of traffic can be cited that require quick, elastic, varying methods, which can only be properly furnished as necessity arises through the good judgment of able, experienced men, doing business on the spot and thoroughly acquainted with all industrial conditions present. The number of papers and letters carried from year to year is a more or less fixed quantity and can be fairly approximated at a given time; if unexpected demands arise from any quarter the new needs are met at once by extension of old methods and by only a small outlay of either capital or labor; the employment is simply a distributive process in which the charge for delivery is not based at all on cost of service and little special effort is made to build up and enlarge the business.

Not so with railroads; they must continually seek to develop new traffic, to populate new districts and establish new towns; they must constantly increase and extend their work, having an eye to the increased production of goods as well as to their distribution. The amount of transportation is therefore quite variable, being constantly affected by the industrial conditions of every community, and of course any enlargement or contraction of railway facilities must involve large investment of money and employment of much time and labor. The mail service theory of charges would shortly bankrupt every railroad in the country. The political evils apparent in our system of mail delivery, in spite of civil service reform, would be multiplied a thousand times in our transportation system in case of government ownership. About one-twelfth of the adult male population of the United States is employed in connection with our railroads, and to have all these offices at the disposal of the political party in power, to be changed if desired with the changes in administration, is not a safe condition for the independence of individual voters or the interest of the country.

The fourth claim, that the United States would do well to take charge of the railroads because Prussia and Belgium have succeeded, fails to recognize any differences between their forms of government and ours, or between the railroad problems presented there and here. Prussia has about 13,000 miles of railroad, the United States has over 180,000 miles; their system has 80,000 employees, ours at present would require over 800,000; the inclination of the German mind is bureaucratic and ours is just the opposite; the area of Prussia and Belgium together is 145,840 square miles, that of the United States is 3,602,990 square miles. Their system has been constructed under the supervision of the state and there are practically no competing lines; our system has been built entirely independent of the government and competing lines are numerous. Their trade and country are fully developed and no new lines are being constructed; our business is steadily expanding in volume and roads are constantly being laid to build up new sections. Germany (and the same can be said of France) has a perfected civil service of long standing and their governments are decidedly execu-

tive and administrative in form; the United States has
a crude, imperfect civil service and the government is
parliamentary and legislative in form.*   These important differences must be taken into account before safe
conclusions can be arrived at and, when they are carefully considered, the fact will appear that operation of
our roads by political machinery would in all probability be fraught with far more disastrous evils than are
sustained at present under private management.   Nor
has state ownership in these countries been altogether
without its faults, for, since Belgium has purchased the
rival lines that competed with the state lines (now owning about three-fourths of all the mileage in the State)
some healthful and proper competition has been
stopped.   In consequence, a certain diminution of activity and some tendency toward slackness of management have occurred, and there has been a lowering of
profits without corresponding lowering of rates; there
has been a multiplication of unnecessary forms and offices with no actual business, and a serious manipula-
tion of accounts to make a favorable showing for the
government.   Great complaint is made of the lack of accommodation, cars, etc., all of which evils arise from the
connection of the railroads with the government.†

Italy has tried private management of roads, mixed
ownership, (*i.e.*, government roads competing with roads
of private citizens,) and also exclusive state ownership.
Not satisfied, it afterwards appointed a Parliamentary
Commission to make a most thorough investigation of
the matter and report facts to enable the government to
see the best policy for it to pursue with reference to its
roads.   The Committee reported that the Italian

---

* C. F. Adams: "Railroads: Their Origin and Problems."

† Arthur T. Hadley's "Railroad Transportation: Its History and
Its Laws," p. 217.

government ought to get rid of its roads at once and charter large private companies to manage them. They claimed (1) that state management had proved more costly than private management; (2) that political dangers were very great and (3) that the State was prone to tax industry and not to foster it.*

The fifth claim is that the profit of the business will go into the United States Treasury. If the business is as economically administered as at present and a profit is made, of course it will, but strict economy is not generally a marked characteristic of work conducted by the government. If the business is run for profit will it not be on virtually the same basis as at present, and will not the same methods be employed unless charges are raised? If this profit be money that could have remained in the pockets of the people, this method of collecting money would be simply a form of taxation. It could be run for the single purpose of collecting taxes, but this surely is not desirable, because the change is advocated for the benefit of the people and not to make money out of them.

The last three claims have special reference to railroad rates and, being closely related, can be considered together. Since cut-rate wars between different roads will not arise under government ownership, competition, which always tends to lower rates, will be removed and charges will probably be increased. In fact, the most unfair discriminations found in railroading are made in attempting to meet the cut-throat competition of ill-placed bankrupt roads which are doing business at such low rates that running expenses are barely covered, much less net profits yielded on the fixed capital invested.

The fact that the principle of unrestricted competi-

* A. T. Hadley's "Railroad Transportation: Its History and Its Laws," p. 253.

tion has been employed in the conduct of our transportation business accounts in large measure for the gravest evils of our present system. The freedom of each road making rate sheets at will is what renders our charges discriminating, unreasonable, and unsteady; and if government ownership is the only remedy for this evil the sooner had the better. However, (note the fact) rates would be raised instead of lowered, for it is the profitless basis on which insolvent, ill-conceived roads are conducting their business in order to get traffic that is at present playing havoc in railroad affairs and forcing all to questionable methods in developing trade. The statement that our railroads are making exorbitant profits is not borne out by facts, and freight rates in the United States are lower than anywhere else in the world. Freight charges here average but .85 of a cent per ton per mile; in 1896 they fell to .806 cent.

Discrimination unquestionably exists at present, but it is more than possible that under government ownership we should have federal legislation on rates that would favor one section of our country at the expense of another. On the other hand, is it not true that justice both to roads and the public demands that certain discriminations be made, both between different localities and also in classification of goods? Surely charges cannot be made for coal and cattle on the same basis as for chinaware, for the former will not bear the higher rates of the latter though it may cost more to handle; nor can through freight be charged as local for a reason somewhat similar. The public ought to have the benefit of the best utilization of the natural resources of different localities, and the present condition and future development of manufacturing and commercial industries should count for something in determining transportation charges. The theory of making fair rates to all is a complex one, and no doubt the practice meets with obstacles still greater.*   That absolute equity has not governed rate sheets in the past history of our railways goes without saying, but this does not argue the necessity of government ownership nor show that government appointees would do more satisfactory work than officers who at present own and operate the roads. A railroad thrives as its patrons thrive, and railroad corporations must seek the building up of the communities they serve, for it is their own interest so to do. Short-sighted policies which destroy the business life of a community are recognized as hostile to the permanent interest of the roads themselves, and are not in general employed except when necessitated by an unlimited destructive competition. Of course there are localities of whose support the roads are independent, and their interests suffer.

Two reforms, however, must be secured; first, the evils of unlimited competition must be got rid of, and second, the railroad corporations in their engagements with each other and treatment of the public must be made amenable to law.†   Several different proposals besides government ownership have been offered to gain these points. One theory presented is that the government should fix the schedule of rates, allowing private ownership and management, and employ summary means to enforce them. This is a foolish and impracticable scheme, as no one would be willing to do business under such conditions. Another is that the railroads should be managed through courts by receivers; this has been tried repeatedly and with little satisfaction, since the roads here generally only run further in debt. A third theory is to legalize pooling; *i.e.*, make all agreements between competing roads as to

---

* C. H. Cooley's "Theory of Transportation."
† C. F. Adams: "Railroads: Their Origin and Problems."

maintenance of rates or division of territory, traffic or earnings, binding in the courts. Could the government have some supervision and knowledge of the contracts in the making, or were the engagements made both public and legal, requiring settlement in case they were broken, this plan might be advisable. Voluntary pooling, not legalized, will do no good for it has been tried and a sad lack of commercial honor has been found, so that open breach and total disregard of such engagements has been tolerated.

The fourth plan suggests a combination of the government's authority with the exercise of responsible power by the roads themselves, acting conjointly instead of independently. This last appears most practicable and desirable, for undoubtedly the true methods of railroad management are to be found in the proper co-ordination of the powers and a just balancing of the interests, of both railroad and government representatives. The complaint cannot be made by the railroads that all interference in their business on the part of the government is unwarranted and unconstitutional, for the powers of railway corporations are only delegated powers and may be limited or revoked. The effort to bring about a better co-operation between the government and railroads is recognized by the existence of a Board of Arbitration and State Board of Control in France, in the Railway Commissions and Board of Trade in England, and finally in our own State Railway Commissions and Inter-State Commerce Commission. This last named Commission has done a considerable amount of good work since its creation in 1887, notwithstanding the numerous criticisms made upon it. The Inter-State Commerce Commission Act may have some serious defects but the spirit of the law is right, and by co-operation on the part of the roads these faults may be removed. The Commission had considerable trouble in enforcing the law at all on the start, owing to the popular belief (sustained by the decision of the courts, Dartmouth College Case) that corporate privileges were irrevocable powers delegated from the State, and to the general contempt of railroad corporations for all law; but nevertheless it has labored on and aecomplished many beneficial results. It has made the railroads regard law; it has gained publicity of accounts, which is good for the investor; stated clearly and made the public see in what the railroad problem consists; harmonized the railroads and the public by settling amicably and satisfactorily hundreds of difficulties that have arisen.

SCIENCE AND INDUSTRY NOTES

It is understood that the Argentine Republic is about to abandon its experiment in state ownership of rail-
Failure of State Management roads. The government's lines show large deficits, and the Minister of Finance has submitted a proposition for leasing them all to private companies, on the ground that under private management no such waste and loss would occur. It is to be hoped that we may not, in this country, be forced into a similar costly experiment, merely to learn a lesson already sufficiently clear.

Mr. Arnold's article, published in this department this month, is an interesting discussion of the railroad
Government and Railroads problem but contains very little in the way of practical suggestion. He seems to look towards an increase of governmental authority over railroads; in this we have very little confidence. Certain regulations must exist and be enforced; indeed, the roads themselves undoubtedly welcome an authoritative enforcement of uniformity on certain points. Nevertheless, the most effective remedy for discrimination and rate-wars would be to legalize pooling. If necessary the government might be invoked to enforce maintenance of pooling contracts, but as a general rule state interference in matters of rates and service should be kept at a minimum. The state may properly create opportunities for industry, and prescribe such general conditions thereof as public health, morals and education demand, but ought to take no part in industry itself, nor should it attempt to substitute statutory laws for the economic laws governing prices and wages.

A report from United States Consul Goodnow, at Shanghai, to our State Department, on the firecracker
Chinese
Firecracker-
makers industry in China, reveals once more the miserable condition of labor in that country. During 1897 nearly 27,000,000 pounds of firecrackers were exported from China (chiefly to the United States) and these represent only a small proportion of the total number manufactured. They are used in China at all sorts of ceremonials, festivities, weddings, funerals, etc. The crackers are made in the same shops where they are sold, and in the homes of the workmen themselves. Generally the entire family help; practically the whole work is done by hand. In Canton the export price of 10,000 of the ordinary small crackers is sixty-two cents. At Shanghai 5,000 cost sixty-two cents, and 1,000 of the largest kind sell for five dollars. The hours of labor are from 6 A.M. to 11 P.M., and the laborers work seven days in the week. Thirty women and ten men, it is said, can make 100,000 crackers per day, and for such a day's work a man is paid seven cents, a woman five cents. Apprentices in the firecracker business are bound out for a term of four years, during which they receive only their board. Expert workmen receive ten cents per day, but that is the maximum. The five and seven cent per day rate, says our consul, represents about the average wages paid in Shanghai for common labor. This, of course, will buy enough rice to sustain life, and some sort of shelter at night, but that is all. Is it any wonder that, with the quality of citizenship such a wage rate must give, China has social degradation, paganism and political despotism?

CURRENT LITERATURE

AMERICA AND EUROPE*

This little volume contains three distinct discussions; first, an article on "The United States and Great Britain," by David A. Wells, reprinted from the *North American Review* of April, 1896 ; second, an address on "The Monroe Doctrine," given by Edward J. Phelps before the Brooklyn Institute of Arts and Sciences, March 30th, 1896 ; third, an address on "Arbitration in International Disputes," given by Carl Schurz at the Arbitration Conference in Washington, April 22nd, 1896 ;—all growing out of the Venezuelan problem which was prominent at that time.

To take up such a book as this seems like dipping into ancient history, yet it is surprising how many points brought out in the Venezuelan controversy have a direct bearing upon our present struggle with Spain. The proposition for an Anglo-American alliance has been so warmly received in this country during the last few months that it is difficult to realize how bitter was the feeling against England only two and a half years ago. So far as that feeling expressed itself in the demand that Great Britain should arbitrate the Venezuelan matter, it was justified, but when it went to the extent of putting this country in a position of permanent antagonism to England in all great questions of commerce and future destiny, it was wholly on the wrong track.

Prof. Wells' statement of England's contributions to civilization and her present attitude and influence among the nations, while weakened by his constant unfavorable references to the United States and cynical

* *America and Europe.* A Study of International Relations. 128 pp. 1896. G. P. Putnam's Sons. New York and London.

comments on our policies, is nevertheless in the main just. What he terms the "enlightened selfishness" of England has indeed been the means of reclaiming a very large portion of the human race from barbarism and establishing order, justice, and humane civilization. The methods by which her empire has been extended have not always been just and merciful, but there is no savage tribe or barbarous nation upon which her rule has been imposed that has not in consequence been lifted out of the mire of degradation and put upon the highway of progress.

England's magnificent contributions to the industrial, social, intellectual, political and moral progress of the race render it of first importance that our attitude towards her should·be one not of jealous antagonism but of friendliness and co-operation. Fortunately, the hostile spirit against which Mr. Wells protested in this article has been practically supplanted by a truer conception of the common destiny of these two great nations as leaders of human progress.

Mr. Phelps's address on the Monroe Doctrine is not only far less philosophic but in most respects is so offensively anti-American as to be keenly exasperating. England herself would now unquestionably allow a much broader interpretation to the Monroe Doctrine than Mr. Phelps is willing to ascribe to it. He took the narrowest possible view of our attitude towards the republics of this hemisphere and insisted that we are justified in interfering only when our own interests or safety are definitely threatened. Not satisfied with denouncing our position in the Venezuelan matter, he branched off into a tirade against the then remote suggestion even of interference on our part with Spain's policy in Cuba. Needless to say, in the light of recent experience no audience could now be found in this country that would tolerate such a deliverance as the following:

"Spain! An ancient nation long celebrated in history, once the chief seat of that fine learning which institutes like yours are built to foster, whence and under the patronage of whose enlightened queen, Columbus came to open this continent to our ancestors. And now there has broken out in her province a rebellion, which, so far as I can learn, is a rebellion of banditti; a rebellion of pillage, and arson, and murder, with no attempt at an organized government, no capital, no centre, no recognized head. It has nothing to stand on but crime. And it is proposed that we shall attack Spain since she has become less powerful than we are, and set up that class of people in the independent government of Cuba. Upon what ground is this proposal justified? Again it is the 'Monroe Doctrine.'"

That this is still Mr. Phelps's opinion on the subject is shown by his fine-spun argument against American interference in Cuba, published shortly before hostilities broke out. "An ancient nation long celebrated in history," indeed!—celebrated for what? Misrule, tyranny, awful religious persecutions, intolerable cruelty, and systematic plunder and enslavement of colonies and subjugated tribes. One cannot read such a grossly misapplied eulogy as this of Mr. Phelps's upon Spain without a flush of strong indignation, but is it some satisfaction to reflect that utterances like this merely hasten the day when the Phelps type of political doctrine and statesmanship will be permanently discredited with the American people, and, in fact, with any people in whom a spark of patriotism or of genuine interest in the promotion of human progress remains.

ADDITIONAL REVIEWS

THE WORKERS: AN EXPERIMENT IN REALITY. By Walter A. Wyckoff. Cloth. 270 pages. Charles Scribner's Sons, New York. 1897. $1.25.

This book consists of a series of articles first printed in *Scribner's Magazine*. It purports to relate the literal experiences of the author in donning the garb of an actual tramp. Mr. Wyckoff went out and actually earned his living in the ranks of manual labor. He appears to have engaged to do anything and everything from a respectable occupation to sawing wood for his supper and sleeping in a deserted barn. At one time he was a day laborer at West Point, another a hotel porter, another a hired man in an asylum, another a farm hand, and another working in a logging camp, and so on.

The experiences he went through in each of these new occupations he relates in a very interesting and readable manner. Incidentally the story reflects the condition and social life of the laborer. The writer usually makes the laborers tell something of their story in their own broken fashion, which adds something of interest to the narrative. Besides making it seem more like a literal, non-formal statement, this gives a touch of romance to it, which adds to the attractiveness of the reading if not to the seriousness of the story. As a study of the labor question, however, it has much less merit. The facts related are told in such a way as not to furnish any reliable representative data. Each experience related may be literally true and yet the book fail to represent the condition of any class or group of workers the author entered. It may have been an interesting experience for the writer, and it is attractively presented to the reader. It is suggestive and may serve to enlist the interest of a certain class of readers in the labor question, and as such may be a helpful addition to the tons of books published on labor themes.

In view of the fact that the author is a lecturer on sociology one is struck with the rawness with which the subject is left for the reader's digestion and assimilation. As a narrative relating one's experience in tramping and trying to work at anything and everything for which he had no natural or trained fitness, it is an interesting book. As an addition to the discussion of the labor problem, it is worth very little.

BANKING SYSTEMS OF THE WORLD. By William Matthews Handy. Cloth, 190 pp. Chas. H. Kerr & Co., Publishers, Chicago, Ill. 1897.

It is very seldom that we are able to speak favorably of any monetary publication issued by Charles H. Kerr & Co. Nearly everything on that subject coming from that source is in the interest of some form of fiat or government money. This little book is an exception; it is a brief, concise and attractively written account of the salient features of the banking systems of different countries. As to theory, it is practically colorless. Whether the author is a free-silverite or a greenbacker, he is evidently familiar with the actual character and history of modern banking. His statement of the two banks of the United States and the banks of England, Canada and continental Europe, though brief, is clear and comprehensive enough at least to contain the salient facts. It would be well if the readers of the free-silver literature issued by these publishers could be acquainted with the contents of Mr. Handy's little book. It might not convert the followers of Coin and Bryan to sensible ideas on money, but if they would familiarize themselves with it they would at least escape some of the crude errors with which free-silver literature is so overloaded.

Mr. W. T. Stead, in the July *Review of Reviews*, quotes this amusing (and apt) comment of Carlyle's on Gladstone's conscience : "There never was such a conscience as his . . . . But, eh, sir, he has the most marvelous faculty in the world for making that conscience say exactly what he wants."

Gladstone's Conscience

———

Mr. Henry E. Foster, in the June *Arena*, writes on the "Decadence of Patriotism," and in citing the causes for this supposed decadence says that: "We are drifting away from old-time landmarks, from old-time theology, from old-time simplicity, from old-time morality, from old-time statesmanship and old-time conditions of material and social equality." All of which is true. We are, indeed, drifting away from old-time theology—which was little more than superstitious fear of torment; from old-time simplicity—which was the simplicity of narrow lives, meagre education and inferior social conditions; from old-time morality—when it was the regular thing to engineer all sorts of special legislation through Congress and the legislatures by out-and-out bribery or dividing up the spoils; from old-time statesmanship—which had to deal with entirely different problems from those which now confront us; and from old-time conditions of material and social equality—which was the equality of relative poverty, when but few were better off than the rest because all were about equally poor. We are drifting away from all these things, and in proportion as we do so we shall approach higher conditions of civilization and human welfare. What effect this progress has had on the national spirit the experience of the last few months has amply demonstrated. Mr. Foster should open his eyes and look about him.

"The Ancient Landmarks"

INSTITUTE WORK

AFTER THE WAR—WHAT?

On being asked on a certain momentous occasion what he intended to do next, Napoleon is accredited with saying: "My concern is always with what I will do if I lose. I can do anything if I win." Our case is just the reverse. We are not concerned at all about what we shall do if we lose, since ultimate victory was from the first a foregone conclusion. Our concern is what we shall do when we have won. Just three months have elapsed since the war began, and the end is clear to everybody. Our purpose in entering upon the war was specific and clear. Spain's excuse was to save her national honor. We have no "national honor" in the Spanish sense to save. With Spain, national honor appears to mean assurance to the world of her love of gore; to prove that she is not afraid to face war. We have no such honor to vindicate and no such feeling about which to concern ourselves. Our mission even in war is peace. It is the promotion of the possibilities of peaceful government and industrial progress.

We needed, perhaps, an introduction to Europe. It is now a long while since the old world was really acquainted with us, except in the slimmest official sense. We are strangers to Continental Europe. Russia knows nothing of us. France can think of us only as "American pigs." Germany has a little better acquaintance, but even Germany has but a slight notion of what America means in national power, political development and civilization. Austria, Italy and the rest of Europe are practically strangers to us. England is a little better acquainted. She knew us rather intimately more than a hundred years ago, and has never thoroughly dismissed us from her acquaintance.

This conflict has already served as something of a surprising introduction of the United States to Continental Europe. Instead of a green, dollar-chasing, headstrong, long-haired people, known chiefly as cowboys and cattle-herders, they have realized that the United States is a strong, somewhat symmetrically developed nation; that while we have made more progress in industry than any other country in the world has made in many times the same length of time, we have concurrently developed political strength, scientific knowledge, social refinement and general intelligence, all of which seems to be a revelation to the conceited nations of the old world.

For a considerable time the press of Russia, which always pretends to be friendly, and of France, which boasts of being a republic, and of Germany, which prides itself on its military nerve and superiority—the tone of the press in all these countries was that of belittling and sneering at the rashness and unreadiness, and unacquaintance with military affairs, of the United States. While they all admitted that we were rich, they thought that we were crude, rough and ignorant.

Three months' war, however, has disabused them and all the rest of the world of that notion. We began as no other nation ever began a foreign war, *viz.*, with an army made up mainly of volunteers. For a few weeks at first, of course, in the hurried effort to organize the volunteer army, many mistakes were made, but it is now clear to everybody that the volunteer army of the United States is organized and is developing an efficiency equal to that of a regular army. The work already done before Santiago shows that our volunteer army lacks nothing of the grit, discipline, energy and effectiveness that was expected of the regular army.

This has been more than a surprise to foreigners. The greenness expected was not there. The insubordination and lack of discipline were not there; but the concerted, orderly efficiency that were not expected were surprisingly there, and a dash and heroism excelled nowhere except in a few exceptional instances in the history of warfare. All this shows, not only to us but to the world, that two things have occurred in this country under the industrial *regime*, with more than a half century of non-militant policy, *viz.*, that the wealth development of the country has produced a citizenship that has intelligence and energy never developed by a mere military policy. A life of militarism gives obedience and discipline, but it does not give the background of intelligence and patriotism that characterizes a well-fed, progressive, prosperous and intelligent citizenship.

It is this fact that is at once surprising to the world and gratifying to us. It is a demonstration to all mankind that civilization unarmed is stronger than armed barbarism; that the nation's real strength lies not in the mere use of arms but in the development of prosperous, intelligent citizenship, whose patriotism is always more reliable, whose nerve is always stronger, whose will is always more determined, and whose purpose is always more enduring than any force bought by ten-cent-a-day rations in a life of militarism.

The other side of our exhibition, the navy, has also convinced the world of our unsuspected power. It was a byword that we had no navy, and nearly all Europe had believed that we were such a nation of purchasable politicians that corruption to the point of putrefaction pervaded our political life. The constant yawping of our mugwump press against the integrity of our public men and political machinery was such that political pestilence was assumed to pervade every department of our public life. Our ships were thought to have been built by corrupt contracts, and hence were

only shoddy structures; and it was charged that jobbery
so pervaded the navy yards, and especially building contracts, that our warships were little more than imposing structures of papier mache.   Any European power
which had a navy was supposed to be able to march up
and either frighten or demolish the American navy in
short order.

All this has disappeared.   The world has been
disabused of this whole line of flippant assumption
regarding American public life and the integrity of its
official conduct.   Instead of this effete and impotent
exhibition our navy has shown a scientific perfection,
our ships a structure and endurance and efficiency,
equalled in no other country.   The Oregon, which was
built on honor by the United States government, has
shown an endurance and perfection and efficiency that
no battleship in the world ever before revealed.   It is
not in the history of naval achievements that a ship of
anything like her dimensions should steam at a high
rate of speed thirteen thousand miles without an
accident, without a stoppage for any sort of repairs or
adjustment of machinery, and land home ready for
battle the moment her bunkers were refilled with
coal.   In this war our navy has performed feats such
as no country can boast of.   The engagement at Manila, in which the entire Spanish fleet was destroyed
and not a single man in the American fleet killed, has
no equal in the history of naval warfare.   Nor was this
an accident.   All investigation has shown that it was
the result of sheer superiority.   The engagement of
our fleet with the cream of the Spanish navy in Santiago was practically a repetition of the same superior
skill and naval efficiency.   Another entire Spanish
fleet was destroyed, only one man killed on the American side, and no American ship disabled.

This is an introduction of the United States to

Europe which will forever prove that, whether we have a large standing army or not, we are a nation to be reckoned with; that while we are not seeking conflict it is unsafe for any other power to merely trifle with us on the assumption that we are inexperienced in warfare and therefore may easily be defeated. It also shows to the world that the quality about which Spain has said so much, and which seems to be the one great point of her national honor, *viz.*, her capacity to fight, is largely a myth; it shows that she has neither real fighting grit nor capacity. Every performance thus far on her part has been a running away. To be sure, Cervera did not surrender without an effort, but his effort was to run, and he lost because he could not run fast enough. The peculiar inefficiency even of Cervera's fleet is shown in the fact that only one man was killed on the American side.

All this, I say, has served completely the purpose of introducing the United States to Europe, not as a military nation, but as a strong industrial nation that can fight when it is necessary. So completely has this been demonstrated that now all the nations which began with sneering, described our crudeness, predicted that our coast cities would be bombarded, that although Spain was a second-rate nation she would soon lay Boston and New York under tribute, and that although in the long run by our superior wealth we might finally succeed it would be an expensive experiment, and that Spain would make it cost us dearly, all because of our unpreparedness and military inefficiency—the nations, I say, which predicted all this, have already changed their tone. They are now frankly telling Spain that her end is in sight, that there is but one outcome, that the proper thing for her to do is to seek peace, of course with honor.

So that in reality the question now is not so much

a question of war as a question of peace. There is no person in the world competent to form an opinion who does not admit frankly that peace is now the consideration. What the conditions shall be, and how they shall be brought about, is the next problem.

To have brought the war to this status, and revolutionized the opinion of Europe regarding the American nation in the short space of three months, without having endured a single defeat or even a single retreat, is not only creditable to the army and navy but it is creditable to the Administration and to the American people.

The question now is, will peace be concluded with the same credit? Shall we conduct the terms and conditions of peace with as much credit as we are conducting the war? There seems to be abroad an idea that Spain's sensitive nerves must be shielded from the humiliation of direct negotiation for peace, and that there must be some mediation by the neutral powers of Europe. It is encouraging to see the firm and sensible tone of the Administration on this point. If reports can be credited, the Administration has discouraged the idea that third party negotiations will be effectual, and intimated that the negotiations must be conducted directly with Spain. This is as it should be. There is no reason whatever for any third party interference. The advice of France ought not to be entertained in the least; she is not needed for any reason whatever. There is nothing in this conflict which can not be properly discussed and adjusted by Spain and the United States. So far as we are concerned it is an American affair. The main proposition was to compel Spain to quit this hemisphere; the outcome must be none other than her effectual and permanent departure. The opinion of France or Austria is of no avail on this point. They are known to be in reality partisans

of Spain. In dealing with France or Austria we are
not dealing with neutral nations but with Spanish partisans. It is much better—it will have a better effect
upon Europe, a better effect upon Spain, a better moral
effect in the United States, and altogether a better
effect upon Cuba to have the peace negotiations conducted by the United States directly with Spain. Spain
had all the opportunity that could be desired to retire
gracefully. She did not do it; perhaps she could not.
Then she must do the next best thing, and retire now
with less grace.

Another disadvantage to the unnecessary interference or intercession of European powers is the tacit
admission of Europe's right to intervene in American
affairs. That is the one thing which the Monroe
Doctrine most pronouncedly rejects. It is the one
feature of the national policy of the United States upon
which our people are most sensitive, and properly so,
because we are in the most complete political and
geographical segregation from Europe. Our political
policy is unlike Europe's, our form of government and
spirit of institutions is a new departure in civilization,
established against the opposition and with the universal
distrust and political enmity of official Europe. We
have a right, therefore, to suspect the motive of any
continental nation in participating in American affairs;
moreover, once to permit their intervention would be a
dangerous precedent for future interference. And
there is really no need of it. There is no danger of an
unlimited prolongation of the war because of the
evenness of the combatants which calls for any interference of third parties. The defeat of Spain is obvious
and will be absolute. Our disposition is not in any
sense to take undue advantage or have anything like
revenge. On the contrary, the whole spirit of our
government and of our army and navy officers has been

to show the utmost leniency, courtesy and humane treatment of Spain whenever any of the Spanish soldiers or sailors have fallen into our hands.   At Manila the Spaniards were awestruck at the magnanimity of Admiral Dewey.   They expected to be treated as they would have treated Americans, and did not know how to understand the courtesy and generous treatment Admiral Dewey extended to them.   The same spirit is pervading the conduct of General Shafter and Admiral Sampson at Santiago.   I say there is no disposition, therefore, either in the government, army, navy, or the American people, to do anything to Spain in the way of revenge, and since there is absolutely no doubt as to the outcome there is no need of any third party intervention, and none should be tolerated, and I believe none will be.

As to the conditions of peace; it is the experience of all great bodies, and even of individuals, that conduct is governed largely by circumstances.   It is doubtful if the policy of a single nation, except temporarily in a few rare instances, was ever governed by foresight and political philosophy or principle.   It is very largely determined by accidental or unforeseen circumstances.   Nearly all the great political achievements in domestic reform have been accomplished by compromises arising out of unforeseen circumstances. The history of almost every great measure is the history of compromises, radical modifications of plans, and highly mixed motives; so that the peace that will have to be concluded is sure to be unlike what was expected at the beginning of the war.

The first fact which was not looked for was the extraordinary victory at Manila, which practically put into our hands the Philippine Islands.   It was thought that we would first take Havana and capture Cuba.   Instead, the test of battle is to be in Santiago, and probably

Porto Rico will be taken before the conquest of Cuba is attempted. All this is something of a change from the original program. Thirdly, the idea was scarcely entertained of going to Spain, but with the annihilation of the Spanish fleet and the seeming mixed cowardice and procrastination of the Spanish ministry, the fleet may descend on Spain and so the seat of warfare be transferred to Spanish waters. So the war has taken an unpremeditated or unforeseen course, and peace may involve or bring about unexpected conditions.

It has been intimated, however, that the policy of our government in peace negotiations is to demand the absolute freedom of Cuba, possession of Porto Rico, and the occupation of the Philippines pending the payment of the indemnity decided upon. This is a highly rational and consistently American policy. If this proves to be the program of the Administration it should receive the unqualified support of the American people. Of course this policy will be objected to by a certain class who are anxious for what is called the "new foreign policy." There will be those who would like to convert the United States into something of a military nation, a colonial or conquest-seeking republic. This idea was voiced a few days ago in an interview by Colonel Watterson, editor of the Louisville *Courier-Journal*. In this interview Col. Watterson said in effect—and there are a few papers, like the New York *Sun*, which voice the same spirit—that everything falling into our hands as prize of war should be kept as the result of our destiny, even though we did not expect it.

In considering the effect of this policy Col. Watterson suggested the benefits, one of which was that it would convert the United States from a nation of shopkeepers to a nation of warriors; that by this means we should avoid the menace of socialism and agrarianism at home. He admitted that it might bring us Cæsarism, but it would enable us to avoid anarchism. In other words, he frankly asserted that the outcome of this war should be made a pretext for instituting a belligerent military policy, and exchanging what he called our domestic dangers for foreign dangers. This means, if it means anything, the cowardly policy of trying to evade the solution of social problems at home by creating military problems abroad, and so treat the social discontent, which for the most part is the legitimate demands of the laboring people at home, by a military policy.

This is exactly what might be feared from the hot-headed, pro-jingo spirit which sometimes is in danger of being created by too much success. If such a policy should result it would make victory over Spain a calamity to the United States. Better, I would even say, that Dewey had been defeated and Sampson's ships driven ashore, and Shafter's men taken prisoners, than that such a result should come with victory over Spain. Seriously, however, this is not to be anticipated. The Wattersons and the purely belligerent jingoes do not represent the United States. The promptness with which the call to arms was responded to, the calm, deliberate efficiency and courage that has been displayed by the recruiting army, the soberness of the whole people with the news of unparalleled success, the lack of a single great meeting of rejoicing anywhere in the country under victories like those of Manila and Santiago, is extraordinary. Probably in no other country could an army and navy have met with such overwhelming success without a domestic inflammation taking place throughout the country. In any other country meetings would probably have been held and boisterous demonstrations, fireworks and glorifications been indulged in as a demonstration of the national spirit. Spain even went into ecstasies over the first report that Cervera had run away. No such thing has occurred, I say, in this

country. Not even in a single one of the large cities
has a big demonstration taken place, and this shows
more conservative reserve and level-headedness among
the mass of citizens than might reasonably have been
expected. It shows that, after all, victory is not likely
to turn the heads of the American people, and there is
every reason to believe this will continue, for the industrial interests of this country have become dominant.
A century of persistent industrialism has developed in
the people a thoroughly social and industrial character,
not love of war for war's sake, nor for victory's sake, nor
glory's sake, nor even for so-called national honor's
sake. Victory is only sought for the political and industrial results which we would gladly have secured,
if possible, by diplomacy.

   If this spirit is maintained, and as I have said there
is every reason to believe that it will be, then we may
properly expect that the conservative American spirit
and not the jingo spirit of the Wattersons will prevail
in the peace negotiations and future policy. What
America needs is development of our domestic civilization, not extension of territory or political responsibility. The war, if conducted to a close in this spirit,
will be a real advantage—an advantage to us and an
advantage to the world. It will be an advantage to us,
first, in creating and cementing a strong, national patriotic spirit. We did not know what good Americans
we were until we were confronted by a foreign foe.
There were great differences of opinion as to the wisdom of beginning hostilities, but the moment they were
begun, with the exception of a single New York paper,
there was but one voice in the country, which was:
"Support the government. Sustain the action of the
United States." There was no longer any discrimination. This was the first evidence of a homogeneous
national spirit, and this is the more surprising because,

more than any other nation in the world, the United
States is composed of heterogeneous population. The
people of every nation in Europe are citizens of the
United States. Hundreds of thousands of Germans,
Englishmen, Irishmen, Frenchmen, Italians, even
Spaniards and Austrians, make up the population of
this country. They are citizens; they have made this
country their adopted land, but nevertheless it was only
to be expected that when we assumed hostilities toward
an European power, in which any or all of these countries might participate, there would be some dissensions,
some conflict of sentiment, some lingering of patriotism
for the mother country among these foreign groups of
our population. But no! In some cases we have whole
cities and sections practically dominated by certain
alien nationalities, but not a single expression has gone
forth from any of these groups dissenting in the least
from the policy of the United States. The sentiment,
so far as known, stands a complete solidarity. This, as
I said, will do much towards cementing and intensifying and bringing into active, conscious expression, a
patriotic national feeling which we are so much in need
of in this country.

, The second benefit of the war is what I have called
the introduction of the United States to the old world.
It will serve completely to show Europe that, though
peaceful and industrial, we are decisive, patriotic,
heroic and efficient in war as well as in industry.

Third, it will teach the world that after all the
strength of nations does not consist in compulsory military service but in the industrial development and
social welfare of the people; that intelligent, prosperous
citizens make better defenders of the nation, as volunteers, than all the enforced soldiery of low paid populations.

These three things are really worth something to

have discovered. It is worth a great deal, not only to Europe but to the Orient, to know that poverty is weakness and wealth is strength; that strength does not consist in the unrelenting orders of a Kaiser but in the patriotic impulse and characterful determination of well-fed citizens. This also is worth something to our own country. Our millionaires and employers have not sufficiently realized that their safety and ultimate prosperity depends on the welfare of the mass of our people. In fact, as a lesson of this war, every American millionaire, every employer, great or small, ought to learn that not only his personal safety and safety of his property, but the safety of the nation, the respect of the republic, the honor of our institutions, depends not on his wealth but on the social status and industrial condition of the great mass of the laborers.

The real interest, then, of the nation, is not to change its policy but to continue it—continue the policy that has made it great. If it is recognized as keeping the front place among the greatest nations from now on it will not be due to its army or its navy; it will be due to the industrial policy under which the nation has been developed and its military and naval success made possible. It is continuance, then, of this policy, which will make the republic great. It will be greater still if it can turn from this military digression and resume its previous industrial policy. Its previous industrial policy has given us our wealth and prosperity; it has given the laborers of this country something to fight for, something to esteem; as Carl Schurz said in his recent article in a German paper correcting the misconceptions of the Germans regarding America, all Germans who have made their home in this country will fight as readily for their new fatherland as they ever would for their old fatherland. Nothing has made this possible, I say, but the industrial policy under which the mater-

ial prosperity of the people has undergone a progress
not witnessed in any other country.

That policy gave us a marked increase in wages,
a cheapening of wealth, and an enlargement of the
social opportunities of the people. For twenty years
prior to 1892 that progress was unbroken and unparalleled, and since the digression of four years' effort to
introduce a new policy, which proved so disastrous, we
have re-entered upon the same policy under which our
great success and progress was accomplished. This
has been temporarily interrupted by the war. The objects of this war—freedom of Cuba and expulsion of
Spain from this hemisphere—having been accomplished,
our duty to ourselves, our duty to the welfare of our
citizens, our duty to our national character, our interest
in civilization, our influence over the political and social
destinies of mankind, all demand that we should resume that policy, return to the industrial and social
statesmanship by which our greatness thus far has been
accomplished, and show the world—demonstrate to history—that a successful, prosperous and free people can
be industrial and at the same time, when occasion demands, be more military than the military. In short,
demonstrate that the strength of national defense and
national influence and national leadership consists, not
in the maintaining of standing armies and in forced
military service of the citizens, but in the material and
social welfare, political freedom and individuality of
the common people of the nation.

QUESTIONS AND ANSWERS .

Question.—As a part of the terms of peace, you say
that we ought to retain Porto Rico. Why do you advocate this, when opposed to the annexation of Hawaii?
Porto Rico has nine times the population of Hawaii.
Nearly half of them are colored and 90 per cent. illiterate.

Answer.—It is not necessary to annex Porto Rico

because Spain is dispossessed, but there are many reasons why Porto Rico might better be under American authority than Hawaii. Porto Rico is not quite half the distance of Hawaii and is dangerous territory for such an enemy as Spain to occupy. Having nearly a million population it is probably equal to an experiment of self-government on some modified plan of responsibility to the United States. The possibility of having in some way to assume the responsibility of Porto Rico is one of the doubtful outcomes of the war, which has undoubtedly hastened the annexation of Hawaii, but in no case ought Spain to be permitted longer to own Porto Rico.

Question.—Serious as might be the results of an imperialistic policy on our part, how can you say that such a thing would be worse for the progress of civilization, both of the United States and of the world, than such a tremendous calamity as the victory of Spain and degradation of the United States, with the destruction of our progressive spirit and world influence? Would it have been better for England to have been conquered by the Great Armada than that she should have entered upon the colonial policy along with which she has developed the highest civilization in the world?

Answer.—Oh no; the cases are quite different. The colonial policy of England did not imply a setback to her domestic policy, although for a long time it did largely obscure English domestic social problems and had much to do with establishing a cheap-labor theory of wages. But England's colonial policy began before her domestic manufactures were developed and, for a time at least, it did furnish an extension of markets for her factory products. With us the case is the reverse. We have a population rapidly marching towards a hundred millions, with territory capable of supporting a thousand millions. Our future development depends not on increasing our territory, but on extending the proportion of our manufacturing and urbanizing industries. This is especially important with us because we represent a different type of political institutions. What I intended to say, and think I did say, was that if the present war should cause us to institute a policy of war and conquest that should exchange the treatment of domestic problems for foreign controversies, thus compelling us practically to ignore the industrial and social questions that our own progress has properly created and solution of which the welfare of our people imperatively demands, such a result would be a greater calamity to the people of this country, and indirectly to civilization, than would the retention of Cuba by Spain; because our defeat in this war would at least compel our statesmen to devote their attention to domestic problems. To neglect the domestic problems of the United States for foreign diplomacy and war would be a check to the progress of the republic which would be a calamity to free institutions everywhere.

QUESTION BOX

The questions intended for this department must be accompanied by the full name and address of the writer. This is not required for publication, but as an evidence of good faith. Anonymous correspondents will be ignored.

Editor GUNTON'S MAGAZINE: In your lecture on Gladstone in the June magazine you mention the fact that the English Tories, at the time of the repeal of the corn laws, were protectionists. How does it happen that the Tories, who have been wrong on nearly all the great questions of the century, should have been, according to your idea, right on the tariff question?

M. S., Providence, R. I.

The English Tories, like a great many other people, thought through their interests, and their interests
were in favor of protection.   In the true economic sense,
the Tories were not right.   They were in favor of protection, to be sure, but it was protection only to the
landed interests of agriculture.   In their idea of protection the Tories had no idea of expanding the national
life through diversification of industry.   On the contrary they would gladly have kept England an agricultural country.   They were even socially as well as
economically hostile to the progress of the mercantile
manufacturing class, and to a large extent they are so
yet.   The sound economic idea at the bottom of a protective policy, that is, industrial expansion for the
social and political development of the people, was no
part of the Tory doctrine of protection, nor, in truth, of
the Liberals, who were free traders and manufacturers.
Their policy of free trade was in the interest of manufacturing and diversified industries and, to the extent
that it developed that, it was the real progressive idea for
England.   But it led to the development of an abstract
laissez faire economic doctrine that denounced protection under all circumstances.   It was as narrow and as
a theory as unsound as the Tory doctrine, and as a policy of universal practice more so.

The Tories, it should not be forgotten, were on the
side of factory legislation, but here again their attitude
was not from any recognition of a political policy in
favor of improving the condition of the laborers, but
simply to spite the Liberals for having repealed the corn
laws.   They believed, like the Liberals, that reducing
the hours of labor would injure the manufacturers and
as landed Tories that was what they wanted; so that
the laborers really got most important aid from the
Tories through the accident of a desire to injure the
manufacturers.

Editor Gunton's Magazine: Dear Sir:—In the April number of Gunton's Magazine on page 272 you stated, in answer to an inquiry, that the Standard Oil Company never opposed the pipe line system. I beg to call your attention to the history of the Standard Oil Company as given in *Wealth against Commonwealth* by H. D. Lloyd, published by Harper Brothers. Mr. Lloyd supports his statements by referring to official and other records, and it does not seem to be consistent with the off-hand and perhaps not well considered answer given by you as above. The tone of your magazine indicates a desire to disseminate truth and not to defend interests. The inquiry of the "Fall River Student" may require further answer.

Truly, F. S. R., Auburn, Indiana.

Our answer to "Fall River Student," in the April number, may have seemed to our friend somewhat off-hand. The reason for that, however, was that we have discussed the subject many times before and at great length. He is correct in thinking our answer to be inconsistent with Lloyd's *Wealth Against Commonwealth,* because Mr. Lloyd's book is very inconsistent with the facts. Our issue for July, 1895, contained an article entitled *Integrity of Economic Literature,* which was an exhaustive review of *Wealth Against Commonwealth.* For our estimate of the character and fairness of this book, we recommend our correspondent to read that article; also a three column review in the *Boston Herald,* December 16, 1895.

It is doubtful if there is any one topic upon which greater liberty is taken with the facts than on the doings of the Standard Oil Company. That seems to be regarded as a matter not merely for loose statements but for general misstatements. Anything against the Standard Oil Company appears to be accepted regardless

of the character of the evidence in support of it or the
authority making it. The presumption is that it is a
wicked institution and therefore anything bad may be
charged against it, with the assurance that the half can
never be told. This is the spirit of *Wealth Against
Commonwealth* and of much else that is said and written
on this subject. It is not to be assumed that the Standard Oil Company is an organization of angels, nor that
it has never transcended the moral law in its economic
development, but it is to be assumed, and ought to be
insisted upon, that when statements are made against
it they should be as fair and as fully supported by as
good evidence as if they were made against any other
company or individual.

———

TO LOCAL SECRETARIES

The Gunton Institute desires to have full and accurate information about the work of its Local Centers,
and requests the secretary or other proper officer of each
of such centers to send in a report for file and reference
in this office. Such report should state the membership of the center, what proportion of women members,
names of officers, the number of active students and
candidates for a diploma, total number of meetings during the season and average attendance, character of
meetings, place of meetings, prospects for next year's
work, and any other general information that might be
of use to the Institute. We shall then be in a position
to make suggestions and render any assistance that may
be possible in the work of extending or reorganizing
these centers for another season's campaign. It is
earnestly hoped that every local secretary or organizer
will take pains to send us this report; even one omission
would make our list incomplete.

THOMAS ROBERT MALTHUS

Author of "Essay on the Principle of Population."

GUNTON'S MAGAZINE

ECONOMICS AND PUBLIC AFFAIRS
RESULTS OF THE WAR

The war is over. Hostilities have ceased and negotiations for a final treaty of peace, of which the protocols have already been signed, are under way. Spain has relinquished her sovereignty over Cuba and ceded Porto Rico to the United States; the Madrid government agreed to surrender the city, bay and harbor of Manila, before the capture by our forces, pending subsequent determination of the future of the Philippines.

This war, though of minor importance compared with such a struggle as the Southern Rebellion or the American Revolution, will nevertheless take rank as one of the most remarkable in history. Remarkable, it was, not merely because of the brilliancy and completeness of the victory won in so short a time, but chiefly because of the unusual motives which induced the war and the far-reaching results which will flow from it. This struggle was undertaken in the cause of humanity and freedom for a small group of relatively inferior population; out of it will come forces which, if wisely directed, will irresistibly bear forward the standard of humanity and freedom throughout the world.

The proof of this is found in results already apparent. These results radiate, as it were, in widening circles from a center of disturbance, like water from the spot where a stone has fallen. The center of disturbance in this case was the island of Cuba. Under Spanish dominion barbarous cruelty, despotism and revolution prevailed everywhere ; the United States protested, threatened, and finally took up arms to end a state of affairs that had become intolerable in the eyes of civilization. This course was denounced by some as wickedly inhumane, but the instinctive conviction of the people overruled false logic. It is a fact of universal experience that no great good is ever accomplished without some loss. The possible sacrifices of war weighed less in the balance than the outraging of moral sentiment which Spanish brutalities at our very doors involved.

In Cuba, then, first of all, the cause of humanity and freedom has been advanced. The next and larger circle of influence proceeding from this war affects the whole western hemisphere. Spanish dominion has been absolutely removed from this part of the world ; Cuba is to be free, and Porto Rico becomes a part of the United States. This means that no American country is any longer to be hampered in the growth of democratic institutions by foreign interference. The Monroe Doctrine has been positively asserted by arms, and tacitly recognized by the world. Canada is practically self-governing, and all America may now be considered firmly grounded on a basis of free political institutions. This will give an immensely increased prestige to the democratic principle of government everywhere; it will mean a long step forward for the cause of political freedom in monarchical Europe.

The next circle of results is even wider yet, and has to do with the permanent peace of Christendom. Out of this war has grown a friendship and close understanding between the two great nations which are leading the civilization of the world. England and America represent the highest steps yet taken in human progress. Their whole trend of influence is for peaceful industrial evolution and continual advance in political and religious freedom, wealth, intelligence and development of individual character. Though always united by ties of blood, never until now have they stood side by side in mutual recognition of a common mission and duty and with a sincere disposition on both sides to exert a united influence on world problems. The moral effect of England's friendship in restraining continental Europe from assisting Spain shows what a guarantee of permanent peace would lie in a definite Anglo-American understanding. No nation or group of nations is ever likely to risk a conflict with the united Anglo-Saxon race, nor even to disturb the peace in any quarter where English and American industrial interests are involved. War is cruelty, peace is humanity; and our war with Spain has actually served the cause of humanity at large just because out of it has grown this effective strengthening of the bonds of world peace.

Finally, the broadest circle of all is one that concerns the guiding influence of this nation in civilization. This is of far greater moment than the salvation of Cuba or extension of democracy throughout this hemisphere; it is more significant even than the guaranteeing of future peace through an Anglo-American union. This war has demonstrated the inherent soundness of American civilization and institutions. During recent years there had been a growing conviction both at home and abroad that the republic was coming under the yoke of evil influences and was slipping back from the high standards of its founders; that we were given over to sordid materialism; that the American spirit was dead; that our military and naval establishments were ineffective bungles, and that the will of the people no longer controlled public policies. In three short months these voices have become silent, and now others are heard, frankly admitting what true American patriots have steadfastly maintained, that underneath many surface disturbances the current of national life **has** all the time been running deep, strong and true. English criticism **has** changed to respect and warm admiration, while the dislike of continental Europe is at least no longer expressed in sneers. This war has shown to the world that instead of having sunk into gross materialism we are capable of making vast sacrifices purely for the sake of a moral ideal; that our citizen soldiery is as safe a reliance as the standing armies of Europe; that our navy is only excelled by two others, perhaps, in the world; that public opinion does control American policies, even to the great issues of war and peace. The American spirit has vindicated itself alike in heroic valor and magnanimous courtesy to the conquered, and in a series of naval victories unparalleled for dash and brilliancy in history.

All this, besides vindicating American institutions, teaches a lesson that much of the world has yet to learn—namely, that peaceful industrialism is the surest basis of national greatness, national spirit, and advanced civilization. For generations the example of the United States has been undermining old ideals of national supremacy; this war will serve to hasten that process many fold. Within the nation it has renewed our confidence in ourselves, reunited sections once hostile, and prepared the way for a new era of national progress. If the problems growing out of the war are wisely and conservatively treated, and domestic issues not subordinated to foreign-colony chasing, the United States will more strongly than ever exert its stimulating influence upon civilization and lead the way onward. No longer in the spirit of egotism but with an increasing sense of great responsibility this nation believes itself the leader of world progress in the present epoch of history. The war with Spain has confirmed our right to that belief; it ought to strengthen our determination ever to safeguard and develop the social, intellectual and moral quality of American citizenship, which is the primary source of our leadership and power.

THE OUTLOOK IN DOMESTIC POLITICS.

Now that the war with Spain is ended, military problems will cease to be the all-absorbing topics of public interest. Peace will bring with it many serious and vexatious questions of foreign policy, and domestic problems of equal moment will again demand attention. Although the war has done much to weld the national sentiment into a single patriotic voice, it has not abolished political parties. When the pleasant days of October arrive the machinery of political campaigns will begin to operate, and on the eighth of November a new Congress will be elected.

It is one of the misfortunes of war that it always absorbs public attention and, for the time being, submerges domestic questions of perhaps great and vital importance. It is for this reason that a colonial policy, or a policy of any kind which involves the anxieties and excitements of military operations abroad, is seriously inimical to social and industrial interests at home. As pointed out in our last issue, anything which tends to attract the attention of statesmen or to direct political forces away from domestic interests is equivalent to sidetracking the various important industrial movements with which business men and laborers are vitally concerned. It is true that nothing quite so successfully heads off domestic discontent as a foreign war. It is now conceded that, the Franco-Prussian war, so disastrous to France, was chiefly brought about by Napoleon III. as a means of escape from internal discontent.

In a country like ours, anything which centers public opinion and public interest on a foreign object operates by just so much to defeat home demands. For this reason the war just ended, and the policies arising out of it, will necessarily occupy considerable prominence in the issues of the coming election. The questions of protection, finance, labor, in fact of all measures bearing directly on the business interests and social welfare of the American people at home, will be largely subordinated to problems growing out of the war. Already the idea seems to be gaining force that a radical change in our national policy should be introduced. For some reason or other it is urged that we ought to cease being a purely industrial nation and become a military power, with a policy of foreign conquest and colonial possessions.

How the two parties will divide on this is a little problematical, although the parting of the ways is beginning to be visible. Logically, the party of *laissez faire* and minimum government might be expected to be the party of territorial expansion and a colonial policy. The central idea behind the political thinking represented by this *laissez 'faire* doctrine is free trade or unlimited competition. This always carries with it an economic eagerness for possession of foreign markets, rather than development or extension of home markets. It is born of the notion that it is better to sell abroad than at home. The supreme importance of foreign trade, however meagre or far removed the market, is indefinitely magnified in looking through the lenses of this doctrine. It carries with it also that superficial platitude that foreign markets and free trade are the precursors and handmaids of personal freedom and universal brotherhood. To overawe less civilized people into buying our wares is a part of the non-intervention policy implied in this doctrine. It is legitimate to coerce and oppress in order to compel inferior people to let us sell in their market, but it is wicked paternalism—vicious favoritism alike inimical to personal freedom and civilization—to protect our own markets from the onslaught of inferior civilization.

The political party most imbued with this idea is

the Democratic.   So far as the Democratic party represents any political principle at all it stands for the idea
of minimum government, free trade, antagonism to all
forms of state encouragement to domestic industry,
and the maximum effort to obtain foreign markets.
Consequently, the Democratic party is the logical advocate of a colonial policy and territorial expansion.
Nothing could more completely carry out the Democratic idea of political neglect of industrial conditions
at home.   A colonial policy would furnish a complete
excuse for ignoring demands for legislation on the domestic issues which affect the lives and interests of the
masses.   It would, more effectively than anything else,
carry the idea into practice that unlimited competition
is the sole and sufficient solvent for all industrial and
social ills.   We might naturally expect, therefore, that
the opportunity created by the war to advocate a colonial
foreign market policy would be eagerly seized upon by
the leaders of the Democratic party, and that in the
coming election they would make it their chief political
issue.   Nothing could give more plausibility to the
political vapor about "untrammelled freedom" in the
right to trade in Timbuctoo than would the advocacy of
this foreign market colonial policy.

The Republicans, on the other hand, might logically be expected to array themselves against this new
policy.   If the Republican party stands for any one
political idea more pronouncedly than another it is the
idea of directing the influence and authority of government to protect, encourage and promote the industrial,
social and political interests of the American people at
home.   From Hamilton down, the distinguishing element in the political doctrine of the Republican party
has been protection to American interests and aversion
to sacrificing or in any way remotely exchanging
domestic markets for foreign glory.   The political theory

of the Republican party, so far as it has any, is the theory of protecting and developing the political interests, industrial welfare and social civilization of this nation. Its tenacious adherence to and persistent application of this doctrine is what has contributed so much to the growth of this country in wealth, freedom, intelligence and national power during a marvellously short period.

At the opening of the war this principle was frankly declared. It was proclaimed by the Administration, by the public press, and by representatives of both parties throughout the country. Not conquest, was the cry, but liberation of a neighboring country from the oppression, torture and plunder of a European monarchy.

But the signs of the times, so far as they can now be read, indicate that neither party is likely consistently to stand for its principles in the campaign upon which we are about to enter. The Democratic party, though somewhat divided upon the subject, appears to be drifting towards an anti-colonial policy. Curiously enough, that portion of the Democratic party most thoroughly committed to the free-trade and foreign-market idea, represented by such men as Cleveland and Bryan and the negative professors in our eastern universities, backed by mugwump journals like the New York *Evening Post* and *Boston Herald*, are strongly opposed to the new colonial policy. Contrary to every political and economic tenet they hold so dear they are pointing out the dire evils of a conquest and expansion policy.

Judging from the attitude of the party in Congress, the party press, and with one or two exceptions the party leaders, the Republicans appear to be drifting in an opposite direction. Thomas B. Reed, who is individually the strongest man in the Republican party, has become a butt of attack by the Republican press because he has not thrown his influence in with the annexation idea but rather has discouraged it. So that,

like the Democrats, the Republicans seem to have dis-
regarded political principle and tradition and turned to
the worship of new gods.   It now seems probable that
in the coming campaign the Republican party will turn
its back upon the pronounced domestic, internal, American line of policy by which it has become great and
been associated with the most extraordinary period of
the nation's progress.

Why have the two great political parties thus
almost reversed their respective positions, the Democrats advocating what is essentially the policy of the
Republican party and the Republicans espousing what
heretofore has been Democratic gospel? It is difficult
to explain this radical departure in the policy of
the Democratic party except on the ground of political
expediency.   Perhaps the controlling motive of the
party leaders is opposition to the other party.   The
attitude of Bailey and Bryan and their ill-mated mugwump associates is probably governed by the motive of
" Oppose the Republicans."   In other words, as a party
the Democrats will oppose the new policy because the
Republicans are for it.   But then, the question of no
less importance arises: Why are the Republicans for it?
There is nothing in their party traditions to warrant it,
and nothing in experience to justify it, yet they seem
to have gone over almost bodily to the idea of a colonial
policy. Why should the war with Spain and the success
of Dewey, Shafter and Schley have created this change
in the political policy of the Republican party? All
this success was expected, except perhaps that the
victories were greater than anticipated.   Everybody
expected that the Spanish would ultimately be beaten,
and we knew that Spain would have to leave Cuba.
The war was begun for that purpose.   Then why should
realization of this purpose revolutionize the political
ideas and policy of the Republican party?

As already stated, it is not due to any political principle or previous experience. The only reason seems to be that the Republican party is governed more by impulse than by principle ; that military success has given it political swell-head. Because our army and navy were manifestly superior to those of Spain and we can take from Spain her colonies, are we to make conquest of territory part of our national policy ?

Of course there are numerous political interests which would arise in connection with such a policy. To establish colonial governments is to create a large number of lucrative political and military positions which would be at the disposal of the Administration and, of course, of the party in power. This multiplication of the political fleshpots is naturally very tempting to a large number of people in both parties. To keep the territory acquired in war, therefore, and establish colonial governments in Hawaii, Cuba, Porto Rico and the Philippine Islands, is to open up new and almost unlimited political resources. The Governors-General and staffs, political agents and trading rights which would be directly and indirectly at the disposal of the party would almost double federal patronage. As an immediate party advantage this seems of course very important, and may be expected to influence the thinking of empiric political philosophers. Unfortunately, such motives of temporary political expediency sometimes outweigh the influence of principle and true statesmanship.

If in the coming campaign the two political parties thus practically exchange positions on an important phase of national policy, it may create a great change in the political fortunes of these parties in 1900. If the Republican party so far loses its head as practically to ignore its own history and professed principles and adopt a strange, and what is logically a Democratic, foreign policy it will abandon its distinctive position as the stanch friend and protector of domestic industry. It may then be expected to indulge in the foreign-market economic lingo, and gradually ignore and even oppose the interests of home labor. It will become more and more influenced by the idea that cheap labor at home helps effective competition abroad, and thus in spite of itself become alienated from the economic doctrines and political policy by which it has always proclaimed high wages for American labor to be a cardinal feature of sound national policy. If the Republican party becomes committed to this new foreign policy it may expect very soon to lose the confidence of those whose economic interests are at home. It will soon lose the right even to expect the confidence and support of the wage and business classes. It will become an importers', rather than a domestic-industry, party. Such a policy may give it temporary success while the flush of military victory is on, but when this subsides, as it will in a few months, the nation will return to the interests and problems which affect the prosperity and welfare of the great masses of our people at home. Then the very impulse and spirit and political theory which made the Republican party the party of high wages, of encouragement to American industry, and national prosperity, and gave it national support on these grounds, will serve to deprive it of popular support among the industrial interests of the nation.

This war has not sufficiently changed economic conditions to warrant any reversal of public policy in this country. If the leaders of the Republican party are not wise enough to see that the constructive, home-development policy which gave the party its great success in leading the nation to prosperity is the policy the country will still demand, and is the one our immediate and future development must have, but are carried by the mere jingle of military victory to adopt a policy of militarism and conquest, it may expect soon to meet its political Waterloo. This country is an industrial country, and any party which shall seriously undertake to make it into a military nation and exchange our domestic welfare for foreign prestige will find itself heading for the pastures of political defeat.

A WISE WORD OF CAUTION

No ENGLISHMAN has ever written more discerningly regarding American affairs than James Bryce. The keenness of his insight into the spirit of our institutions and our real mission in the world was fully confirmed by his memorable address before the American Society in London on the Fourth of July last. Said Mr. Bryce: "Her [America's] highest claim to the admiration and gratitude of mankind will continue to be this—that she was the first country to try the great experiment of popular government, and that she has gone on trying it upon the grandest scale. Upon the success of that experiment, upon the peaceful and orderly development of her democratic institutions, the future of the world very largely depends. Many nations have had a career of conquest and of civilizing dominion. But to make an immense people prosperous, happy and free is a nobler and a grander achievement than the most brilliant conquests and the widest dominion."

To-day this nation stands at the parting of ways, and there is imminent danger that the policy of home development by which our greatness has been achieved will henceforth be subordinated to a new territorial expansion idea and chasing of foreign colonies. Mr. Bryce fittingly re-voices the word of caution uttered by the Fathers of the Republic and never perhaps more seriously needed than just at this moment.

TRUSTS *VS.* THE TOWN

C. D. CHAMBERLIN

The unequivocal industrial tendency to-day is toward the so-called trust. Newspaper notices give almost daily evidence of this fact, and the sharp competition for the world's markets by American manufacturers makes a closer division of labor and a larger investment of capital of first necessity. The most natural thing to do is to form a trust and thereby secure both. That the trust idea is commercially successful needs no demonstration. In fact, where feasible at all, it is the only way open to large success. There is no gainsaying the fact that it is based on the true economic principle and has therefore come to stay and is the legitimate outcome of its predecessor, the factory system. It is also peculiarly American, and is more nearly an industrial democracy than any other form of commercial institutions.

It is American because of the youthfulness of American industries as compared with the old, long established and immensely wealthy houses of the older nations, which represent the accumulations of a long line of ancestry engaged in the same business and transmitted as a hereditament from father to son. The trust is American because it represents a union of wealth and effort. It is American because it represents progress in the rapid unfolding of this nation's industrial resources. It is democratic because it represents the investments of many, and the many elect the officers who are in control and who for inefficiency or malfeasance may be removed from office. It is democratic because it does not promise any hereditary descent in the control of affairs.

But while we may not ignore this tendency nor fail to admit the logic of this trend, we must look with apprehension on its effect upon the many manufacturing

173

hamlets with which this country is dotted and which so greatly aid the agricultural interests of our eastern and middle states. The trust necessarily seeks a commercial and financial center, a large and wealthy city where it is daily in touch with the pulse of trade and finance. It means, then, abandonment of the smaller factories in the rural towns and withdrawal of the employees who are the tenants of the houses of which the town is built, patrons of the local stores, and consumers of the products of the local farms, leaving the thrifty manufacturing village an empty distributing point for rural necessities which are obviously sold to the farmers at a higher price, while their product is bought at a much lower price on account of the transportation charges anticipated to get it to the consumer.

That this is appreciated by the people is evident from the fact that much investigation into and legislation against trusts is engaging their representatives in the legislatures of the various states, but the immediate effect will not be fully appreciated by those most interested until too late. The trust not only produces an article for less cost than the small manufacturer but it goes farther. It seeks to reduce the cost of distribution by omitting the jobber and in many instances the retail dealer, and selling through its own channels directly to the consumer wherever possible, thus saving to itself the profits of both. By the change then not only the farmer but the country merchant, the country bank, and the village property holder are all alike menaced. Farmers of the eastern and middle states have known something of the reduction in land values produced by the opening and operating of large tracts of farm lands in a large way in the West and South-West, and the cheapened product therefrom, aided by the improved and cheapened transportation, but such reduction is only a fraction of what is to come with the industrial changes

now in progress. Those towns which are the happy
possessors of from six to twenty thriving manufactories
employing from 50 to 200 or 300 hands each should
guard them jealously, and the farmers who have derived
thrift therefrom should lend their aid so far as may be
to their maintenance. These factories not only make a
profitable home market, give value to real estate and
thrift and population to a town, but they also pay a
large percentage of the taxes, which would not be notably lessened by their loss but would have to be added
to the burdens of others. How far-reaching the change
will be time will tell, but its effect cannot be doubted.
The Town has a fight for self-preservation against the
Trust, and should be fully awake to the menace of what
will come if it loses in the contest.

[EDITORIAL NOTE.] Mr. Chamberlin raises a good
point and one that deserves serious consideration. What
he says in regard to the inevitable industrial tendency
towards trusts, and the advantages to come from that
movement, is quite in accord with the views of this magazine; nevertheless, it is of great importance that the
growth of towns and cities all through the country, particularly in the great rural sections, shall steadily proceed,
because it is from these centers that the moving forces of
progressive civilization radiate. Consequently, if it
were true, as Mr. Chamberlin thinks, that the smaller
towns and cities are being killed off by the growth of
trusts, a serious problem would be presented and some
legislative restriction of the trust movement might be
justifiable. The question should be looked into thoroughly and discussed with entire fairness.

There is no doubt that the last two decades have
witnessed the relative decline of a certain class of small
towns in the old-settled portions of the country, chiefly
the East. Neither is there any doubt that much of this

is chargeable to the modern tendency towards concentration. The beginning of this change was wrought
by the railroads. Wherever and as fast as steam
transportation took the place of wagons or stages in
any given section of the country, the fate of all manufacturing towns not on the line of the road was sealed.
Manufacturing, therefore, tended more and more to
localize itself along the railways and the non-railroad
towns relapsed into agricultural communities. The next
step was a natural continuation of the same movement.
Certain kinds of industries can be conducted much
more economically and profitably in large establishments than in small; hence, many of the small concerns of this class, even though located on railway
lines, found it difficult to compete with the more extensive plants that had naturally grown up in the larger
towns and cities, and thus were gradually compelled
either to withdraw from business or consolidate and go
to larger towns themselves. It is quite true, therefore,
that certain lines of industry have been steadily center-
ing in the large towns and cities, at the expense of
country villages.

But is this movement chargeable especially to the
trust? Not at all. It is due to the general concentrat-
ing tendency of which trusts are merely one phase. In
fact, the trust integration seldom takes place until after
the industries affected by it have already migrated from
the villages to the large towns. The railroads and competition of larger concerns were and are responsible for
that movement, while the trust is simply an organization of already established concerns and often does not
involve changing the location of factories at all. In
some cases of course it means closing up the smaller
and extending the larger plants, but clearly this is
simply a continuation of the earlier movement and is
chargeable, not specifically to the trust, but to the entire

general trend to which we have referred. The problem therefore becomes a much broader one than that merely of "Trusts *versus* the Town." It expands into the larger question of whether or not the whole modern trend of industry is hindering the multiplication and growth of towns and cities throughout the country.

So far from that being true, the facts show that the trend is exactly the other way. According to the Eleventh Census, the number of cities in the United States increased from 141 in 1860 to 448 in 1890, and of these new communities 187, or 60 per cent., were places of between 8,000 and 20,000 population—hardly more than large towns. The greatest gain of all was in towns of between 8,000 and 12,000 population ; these increased from 62 to 176 in the three decades. Cities of from 12,000 to 20,000 population increased from 34 to 107 ; 20,000 to 40,000, from 23 to 91, and so on. There was only one city of between 500,000 and 1,000,000 population in 1860, and one in 1890. Not until 1880 were there any cities of over 1,000,000; there was one of that class in 1880, three in 1890.

It is clear, therefore, that the growth in the number of small towns and cities has been pronounced, and that, instead of the small localities being killed off by the larger it is among these very towns of from 8,000 to 12,000 inhabitants that the principal gain has taken place. The total increase of 307 consisted, of course, of small places which passed from below to above the 8,000 mark during the three decades. All this occurred, it should be remembered, during the period of most marked concentration in industry.

If, however, the growth of railroads and concentration of industry has resulted in the decline of a certain class of small towns, how can this general increase be explained? Chiefly, we believe, by the fact that practically all decline has been in the case of towns of insignificant population—say of less than 3,000 or 4,000—and this has been much more than offset by the multiplication and growth of towns of 5,000 to 10,000 and upwards.   Thus if the little industries of a group of small villages should gradually center in one of those villages, the latter would soon become a large town and be included in the census list, while before none of these places would have been recorded either as towns or cities. Thus, in the older sections of the country, for each new town added to the list of places exceeding 8,000 inhabitants there may be two or three or more smaller places left in a static or declining condition.   The census statistics for places of from 1,000 to 2,500 population confirm the statement as to the stagnation or decline of very small towns throughout the eastern states.

Throughout the West the case is different.   There small towns and large (except the "boom towns" of a few years ago) are steadily growing.   Most of these places have come into existence since the new conditions of concentrated industry were established and hence are making use of instead of suffering by these conditions.   Only such industries as are capable of success in relatively small places are being located in the towns of the West, and that region is not being built up with thousands of little agricultural communities, as was done in the East before the modern industrial era came in.   Thus, while some of the small towns of the West may, hereafter, recede before their stronger neighbors, the movement cannot possibly be so widespread and significant as it has been throughout the old states of New England and the Atlantic seaboard.

There is every indication, however, that towns of 5,000 to 10,000 and upwards will continue to thrive and increase in number.   In the first place, while many lines of industry must be carried on, now-a-days, in large establishments, it does not follow that such concerns will tend to locate themselves in very large cities; indeed, to avoid heavy taxation they are tending more and more to seek towns and cities of moderate size. Good railroad facilities make this possible, and thus we see that while railroads were at first the means of drawing village industries into larger towns, they are now becoming the strongest force to keep such industries from going into the great cities. Moreover, the economic tendency is and will be more and more for manufacturing industries to locate themselves near the sources of raw material, because transportation of finished commodities is relatively much more economical than of bulky raw products containing a great amount of waste. This means that manufacturing will steadily diffuse itself throughout the country, according to the geographical distribution of natural resources; while the very large cities will become more exclusively mercantile, commercial, financial and general distributive centers.

Look wherever we will the facts confirm this theory. Most of the manufacturing in New England, of cotton and woolen goods, boots and shoes, paper, cutlery, bicycles, etc., except in Massachusetts and Rhode Island, is carried on in towns of from 5,000 to 25,000 inhabitants ; and, in the two excepted states even, in places of less than 50,000 or 75,000. The cotton industry is going South, near the raw cotton ; woolen manufacture will eventually move westward, near the raw wool; in both cases establishing industrial communities in those sections. Iron is manufactured near the iron mines, furniture (very much of it) near the forests of Michigan, flour near the wheatfields of Minnesota, raw sugar on the plantations. In time, most of the refining of sugar will undoubtedly be done near the sources of its production.

Another important fact. New industries are con-

tinually coming into existence, and the vast majority of
these establish themselves in relatively small towns or
cities, because they cannot begin on a sufficiently large
scale to command success in a large city. Some of these
may finally move to the cities but, with the progress of
invention, new enterprises are continually being established, and may be counted upon as a permanent reliance of the small town.

Thus from every point of view the steady multiplication and prosperity of most towns and cities of
from 5,000 and 10,000 population upwards, seems to be
assured. Villages, especially in the East, which have not
reached that point and cannot reach it will probably remain static or decline. Since their places are being taken
by an increasing number of larger centers, this decline of
small villages need not necessarily be considered a calamity. From a sentimental or a local standpoint it may
perhaps be deplored, but the nation's interest is not in
the mere preservation of little cross-roads hamlets but in
the increase and distribution of communities sufficiently
large and complex to exert a genuine socializing influence on its inhabitants and the surrounding country.
It is hardly possible to get much of this influence in a
place of less than 10,000 inhabitants; with a smaller
number there is not enough complexity of interests,
variety of ideas and social intercourse, nor a sufficient
basis for first-class educational facilities and public improvements. The drawing together of industries,
therefore, in such a way as to increase the number
of moderately large towns and small cities is an advantage to the whole country, even if the small villages do
cease to be centers of industry and trade.

But it is not to be assumed that the small villages
will be entirely wiped out, even though many of them
may lose a part of their population. Certain kinds of
industries will always be found in these small villages,

such as lumber and planing mills, grist mills, barrel
factories, cheese and fruit-canning factories, creameries,
carriage shops, and repairing establishments of various
kinds. Many of these villages, also, will probably be
transformed into residence places, educational centers
and summer resorts,—witness the fine old towns of
New England. Others will form the *nuclei* of future
agricultural towns, in which the farmers will live and
and go out to their work every day. Improvement of
country roads and more general use of farm machinery,
permitting shorter hours of labor, will contribute to
this result ; eventually, the trolley will probably be
used for this purpose, just as it is now employed to
take city workers into suburban districts at night.

The modern trend of industry is producing two
distinct results—cheaper wealth and higher wages ; in
other words, increased consuming power of the masses
of the people. This increased consuming power means a
larger effective demand for the products of industry—
hence more factories and more factory towns. Trusts
do not affect new industries at first, and many kinds of
manufacturing are never reached by the trust at all,
because no economy would result. These combinations
occur in certain kinds of long-established industries,
but the factories themselves, even when consolidated
in a few great plants, are not necessarily located in
large cities. High taxes and remoteness from raw materials operate against that movement. We do not
believe there is any ground for supposing that trusts
are proving or will prove inimical to the small towns
and cities of the country. On the contrary, the concentration tendency, with the natural balancing checks
we have mentioned, is directly contributing to the increase of that class of communities whose influence is
a powerful stimulative factor in the social progress of
the nation.

OPPORTUNITIES FOR SOUTHERN WOMEN
JEROME DOWD

It must be evident to the most casual observer that the absence of diversified industries in the South limits the field of employment for both sexes. In Massachusetts there are about ninety occupations in which women freely engage. Hardly half so many occupations are open to women in any one state in the South. In the North about half of the female workers are employed in domestic service, but in the South this large field is occupied almost exclusively by negro women. Almost all of the unskilled labor, such as laundrying, scrubbing, hoeing and picking cotton, done by women of the South is confined to the negro race. The opportunities for white women, especially for those who are poor, are very much circumscribed. Their chief means of support is found in cotton factories and in needlework. In the mills of the South they work 11½ or 12 hours a day, many of them having begun their mill careers when only 7 or 8 years old. They have poor educational advantages and in some places none at all. The hardships they endure often render them mentally indisposed toward education or culture of any sort, and at the same time render them physically unfit for the responsibilities of motherhood which they assume too readily in order to escape the hardships of factory life. It is to be doubted whether, upon the whole, the employment of women (and children) in the factories of the South is a real contribution to the economic, moral or physical well-being of the people.

New York city is said to "beat the world" for cheap clothing, its supremacy in that business being due to the sweater system. But in fact the South is about to lead New York in that branch of trade. The clothing business is a growing and a prosperous one in many southern towns and cities, and the goods are now shipped to New York and sold in competition with the sweater product of that city.

In pants manufacturing the difference in wages of women in New York city and in North Carolina is as follows : *

Basters in New York	average $6.00 per week.	
" " North Carolina	" 3.00	"
Pressers in New York	" 13.10	"
" " North Carolina	" 6.50	"
Machine operators in New York	" 9.25	"
" " " N. Carolina	" 4.07	"

The miserable wages paid southern women for sewing is not due to a grinding spirit on the part of the manufacturers, but to the restricted field for the employment of white women, which occasions over-crowding in the few occupations open to them and makes labor and life cheap.

The most pitiable class in the South are the white women in the country, especially in those sections where agriculture is on the decline. The young men of the farm do not fare half so badly. They are attracted to the city, get into the currents of trade, or enter a profession and become the " plutocrats," " gold bugs," leaders at the bar in politics and in social circles. But the women not finding an opportunity for a livelihood in the city are compelled to remain at home. The few who are educated find opportunity in the country here and there to teach school, but a majority of them have only a rudimentary education. The public schools in some of the states run only three months; not long enough to do much good to the pupils nor to justify a good teacher in undertaking the work. Within the past few years the prospect for the women of the country has been somewhat brightened by the establishment ·of

---

* 11th Annual Report U. S. Com. Labor, pp. 153-4.

normal and industrial schools in several of the states, where tuition and other expenses are comparatively light. Still, few of the women of the country have the means to pay their board at such schools, and it is to be hoped that the policy of establishing free scholarships, which has been almost overdone at male colleges, will be made to prevail at colleges for the other sex. The "Female Colleges" of the South have in the past largely excluded the poor girl by the high rates for board and the multiplicity of extra expenses. While male colleges in the South cannot run without outside help, some of the female colleges are real money-making institutions.

Our statistics of the insane show that the largest proportion of female victims comes from the rural districts, and it is not improbable that one of the causes is absence of opportunities to use the faculties with which God has endowed them. Thoughtful people should be awake to the importance of placing education within the reach of this class of women.

While there are not one-half so many occupations open to women in the South as in the North, there are as many women in the former section dependent through loss of their husbands, poverty or other causes, as in any other portion of the Union. If so, the conclusion is that, opportunities for work being less, the suffering is greater. If some novelist could but picture the lives led by this large class of unfortunate women it would be a reproachful and humiliating revelation. Nothing is more astounding than the halo with which Southern chivalry surrounds young women in the days of courtship and the insensibility with which are viewed those who depend on daily toil for their daily bread.

It remains to suggest in what way the opportunities of white women in the South may be improved. There is no section of the country more favorably situated than the South for literary achievements.   Here exists the purest Anglo-Saxon blood.   The people are fine specimens of physical manhood and womanhood.   They have strong natural intellects especially marked by glowing imaginations.   The women are quick-witted, vivacious, abounding in originality and bubbling over with the richest humor.   All that is needed is some stimulus in the way of sober serious purpose, some systematic study and incentive in order to bring these natural gifts into useful service.   Fame and fortune await the coming of writers who shall portray the life of our mothers and grandmothers in colors that are native and natural.   Our novelistic aspirants too often make the mistake of laying plots in foreign countries or seeking to attract the reader by startling situations or pleasing phraseology.

Journalism is another inviting field for women. They are already entering it and some of them stand at the very top as reporters and contributors.   Women are good news-gatherers by nature, and there is no reason why their natural propensity should not be put to profitable use.

The practice of medicine offers some opportunities to women in large cities.   There are quite a number of lady physicians in Baltimore and a few may be found in every southern state.   Women do not succeed well as general practitioners, but as specialists they succeed admirably.   As our cities enlarge the demand for lady physicians will increase.

Our women have already taken to stenography and typewriting and it is not necessary to urge them along that line.   It is a singular fact that so many women take up stenography and typewriting and so few acquire the art of bookkeeping.   The experience of the writer has enabled him to observe the work of quite a number of women accountants and he believes that they are immeasurably superior to men in speed, accuracy and neatness. With the exception of a few lines of business, bookkeeping is in every respect congenial and appropriate work for the gentle sex.

In this connection the government service offers employment for a large number of women. However, very few southern women have positions in the service, except as postmistresses, of whom there are a great many. The opportunity is open to them through civil service examinations to fill many governmental positions.

Very few women, comparatively, are employed as saleswomen in stores. There is a false pride which keeps many women from this sort of work. They prefer the hardest labor with the needle at home, where their poverty and dependence are somewhat hidden, to the more remunerative work in stores where they must expose the fact to everybody that they are bread-winners. If there is any one thing the South could dispense with to more advantage than another, it is the false pride which dominates many of our men and women, a pride which makes them choose a life of idleness or systematic "sponging" on their friends rather than to be seen at work with the commonalty.

Enlarged opportunities for the white women of the South will come gradually through the growth of large cities and the development of diversified industries. Along with this evolution there must be a gradual relaxation of prejudice against women's entrance upon new fields of work.

In conclusion, a word must be said in behalf of opportunities for women in the South who do not have to labor for their daily bread. There is a serious work to be done in the world by each individual, high and low, and it is no longer to anybody's credit to belong to a leisure class. Idleness is not good for rich or poor, or man or woman, and nothing is more dangerous to civilization than a large class of people without duties or responsibilities.   In former times the ideal gentleman or lady was one who could live without work or care, but, thanks to the progress of morals, that ideal is now discounted by the best religious and literary teachers of our age.   The ideal hero or heroine in modern times, as expressed in our literature and art, is one that renders some useful service to society or does faithfully some humble duty.   The writer is afraid that southern women are a little slow in getting away from the old ideal.   Too many of them make amusement their chief business.   Too many still refuse to take life seriously or feel any obligation to utilize the splendid resources within them.   It is a deplorable thing when one can watch the sun rise and feel no sense of obligation to render a day's service, or to see the sun set and feel no sense of duty performed.   It is time all people were learning that idleness can never bring rest and that freedom from responsibility can never bring joy.   It is not necessary for women to hire out for wages in order to be useful.   The best work done in the world is done without wages.   There is an immense field of usefulness for all the women of the South if they have but the will to find it and cultivate it.

DISTINGUISHED ECONOMISTS:—MALTHUS

This month we present the second number in our series of portraits of distinguished economists. We began in August with Adam Smith, the founder of English-School political economy ; in the present issue we give an excellent and very rare portrait of Malthus, the second famous contributor to that great body of economic doctrine.

Thomas Robert Malthus was born in 1766 on his father's estate in the county of Surrey, England. At eighteen years of age he was sent to Cambridge, and at thirty-one became a fellow of one of the colleges of that university. In the same year (1797) he received clerical orders and was placed in charge of a parish in Surrey. He inherited a strong interest in social and political problems, and out of discussions with his father on the possibility of realizing the Utopian social ideals held up by the optimistic French liberalist, Condorcet, and the English radical, Godwin, grew his famous *Essay on the Principle of Population*. This work was published in 1798 ; a second and much larger edition appeared in 1803. About 1805 Malthus was appointed professor of modern history and political economy in the East India Company's College at Haileybury, and during his twenty-nine years of service there he produced several works on economic topics, notably *An Inquiry into the Nature and Progress of Rent* and *Principles of Political Economy*. The *Essay on Population*, however, is practically the sole basis of Malthus' fame. He died in 1834, at the age of 68.

The name of Malthus is popularly associated with cold-blooded indifference and pessimistic disbelief in the possibility of social progress ; yet this is a serious injustice to the man, however aptly it may apply to his philosophy. Malthus was an amiable and warmly sympathetic man, and his great argument on the necessity of restricting increase of population was based upon a sincere desire to prevent human suffering. The defects in his work were due, not to the man or his motives, but to the narrow limitations of the age in which he wrote.

Briefly, his theory was that population tends constantly to outrun the means of subsistence. He argued that, if unchecked, population would naturally double itself every twenty-five years, that is, would increase in geometrical ratio, while means of subsistence can be increased in arithmetical ratio only. Hence, from his standpoint, disease, pestilence, excessive labor, wars and famine are all necessary, however painful, means of checking what would be a ruinous increase of population. He recommends late marriages and moral self-restraint as the only preventives of the other and more severe checks provided by nature.

Doubtless, in view of the conditions prevalent in Malthus' time and before, there was strong justification for his doctrine ; but modern industrial progress has rendered it as obsolete as Ptolemaic astronomy. The wheatfields of America, Australia, Argentina and Russia alone are capable of sustaining enormous populations, and vast tracts of land have gone into disuse because of the cheapness of production elsewhere. Steam transportation by land and sea, and the factory system, have so revolutionized the conditions of a century ago that the real problem now is to stimulate social demands and raise the standard of living sufficiently to make consumption keep pace with possible production. A " glut " instead of a famine is the modern economic bugbear. Malthus deserves to be read, however, because of the marked influence which he exercised upon subsequent economic thought. That influence has now disappeared, but it was largely responsible for some of the most serious errors in English-School reasoning.

EDITORIAL CRUCIBLE

OVERWHELMING VICTORY on land and sea is followed now by the protocols of a peace treaty conceding all the American demands to the utmost. This result, while expected all along, is cause for profound satisfacfaction. The vigorous conduct of this war and its swift conclusion reflect high credit on the Administration at Washington, and it is pleasing to note that the President's course is warmly approved by the press of all parties. The peace negotiations, too, appear to have been conducted with a gratifying promptness and decision thoroughly in accord with the temper of the American people at this time. The objects of the war have been accomplished and a new era of progress opens before the Republic. The peace of the world has been restored; may it be long before it is again broken.

THE EARLY ending of the war makes it entirely probable that this fall will witness a great expansion of business prosperity. The signs of this are already seen in many quarters, and business men unite in predicting a large and increasing domestic and foreign trade. Even the *Atlanta Constitution*, a rabid free silver organ, says : " The outlook is wonderfully bright. . . . . There will be a jubilee winter ahead of us. Hats off to our welcome visitor, Prosperity!" Bryanism will decline along with this renewal of industrial progress, but it will not do to assume that the labor and financial problems can be neglected merely because of good times. Now is the time to settle the currency question, establish a shorter hour system for factory operatives, restrict immigration, provide national labor insurance, and push vigorously the work of municipal reform, so that the coming prosperity may not again be interrupted by socialistic discontent and threatened revolution.

DESPITE THE friction with Germany in the Philippines, it is probable that in any decisive lining-up of the nations Germany would be found siding with England and the United States.   More than any other continental nation her interests are industrial, like ours. The commercial ties which unite her to the later branches of the Teutonic race are rapidly growing stronger, and will more and more affect the political attitude of her government. The very large and growing German population in America, too, constitutes a bond of union of increasing strength, so that war between the two countries would have many elements of a fratricidal struggle.   German offishness in the war just ended was due chiefly to jealousy regarding the future of the Philippines and not, as in France, to racial and political sympathy with Spain.   Conflicting interests may often divide the Teutonic nations, but their fundamental tendency is the same, and they will more and more exercise a united stimulative influence on the progress of civilization.

THE BOSTON HERALD says that the Louisiana sugar planters may be expected to show ''determined antagonism to any policy that threatens them with the industrial disaster which would inevitably follow the letting down of the customs barriers that now guard them from the competition of sugar raised in Cuba and the Philippines." This is surprising indeed ! A part of the *Herald's* economic creed has always been that no interest could possibly suffer '' industrial disaster " by letting down the bars of protection. The impending dangers of imperialism will not be wholly without advantage if they serve to awaken a mugwump journal like the *Boston Herald* to the fact that domestic industrial interests are really of enough importance to be worth protecting from destruction. To be thoroughly consistent, these papers ought to welcome annexation of any kind of foreign territory as a means of extending the area of free trade and enabling the oppressed American consumer to buy his sugar, *et cetera*, "in the cheapest markets."

———

THE CHICAGO CHRONICLE does not like the article on *Industrial Dangers in England* in our July number; in fact, we are seldom honored with the approval of free trade and free silver newspapers. The *Chronicle* declares that British manufacturers will only laugh at our suggestion that England must be prepared to adopt a protective policy or face socialistic disturbances among her laboring classes. Well, it happens that Joseph Chamberlain, perhaps the most prominent statesman in England to-day, is an ardent champion of a colonial customs union, and in this position has the implied support of the Salisbury administration. This scheme is distinctly protective. It contemplates discriminatory duties in favor of British colonies against all outside competitors in the English home market, and free trade between England and the colonies, just as the United States has free trade between the states and protection against all outsiders. The *Chronicle* says that England needs no protection because more than half of her products are sold abroad; but it is just these foreign markets that she is certain to lose unless the customs union is adopted, which would save at least her own colonial markets. Not even her home market is proof any longer against competition from continental Europe. It may be a long time before England adopts a protective policy, but eventually it will have to come, as some of England's own brightest statesmen already foresee.

HAWAII HAS become a part of the United States; Porto Rico will soon follow; Cuba and the Philippines will doubtless remain under American control for a considerable time. The problem of how to govern these new possessions becomes, therefore, at once extremely serious, more so than would be the case with any other power; because from the very nature of our institutions these populations are likely at almost any time to be incorporated in our political system. If these foreign islands are given a territorial form of government they may be admitted as states whenever partisan necessity seems to demand it.

Porto Rico and Hawaii should be governed as colonies, with an increasing measure of self-government but without representation in Congress. Cuba should be given a military government until such time as its capacity for stable self-government is fully proven; and Manila, if retained for the present as a commercial and naval basis, should be administered by a colonial governor. This might seem like violation of the spirit of American institutions, but that is just what must come if the United States is to undertake the government of grossly inferior populations. Ultimately Hawaii and Porto Rico may become states, but for a long time to come their relation to our political fabric ought not to be any closer than that of colonies. Universal democracy is the essence of the American idea of government, but without self-preservation first of all we cannot maintain even what democracy we already have.

CIVICS AND EDUCATION

EAST SIDE LIVING CONDITIONS

Municipal Affairs for June last contains a symposium on "The City's Health." Mr. Henry White, garment-cutter and General Secretary of the United Garment Workers of America, contributes the first monograph, on "Working Conditions." Dr. Annie Sturgis Daniel, Physician in Charge of Tenement-House Practice at the New York Infirmary for Women and Children, writes on "Living Conditions." Mr. Charles F. Wingate, journalist and civil engineer, discusses "Sanitary Construction." Mr. Homer Folks, Citizens' Union Alderman from the 29th District of New York City and Secretary of the State Charities Aid Association of New York, writes on "Public Hospitals." Dr. J. H. White, of the Medical Division of the United States Immigration Service at New York, takes up the question of "Contagion and Quarantine," and Stoyan Vasil Tsanoff, of the Culture Extension League of Philadelphia, tells of the advantages of "Children's Playgrounds."

Our attention has been especially attracted to Dr. Daniel's article on "Living Conditions," since it contains many very suggestive points which throw light on social problems of wide scope. Dr. Daniel's investigations were made among the East Side tenement-house population, between Fourteenth and Bayard Streets and from Elizabeth Street to the East River. This is distinctly a foreign section. "Indeed, in this region, in half an hour's walk, one will find signs in the Hebrew, Greek, German, Russian, Hungarian and Italian languages more frequently than in the English, and in some parts of this district one may spend a day and not hear one word of English." The following is particularly interesting: "To know the Russian or

Polish Jew does not in the least give one an idea of the Italian, the German or the Russian. Each nationality is as distinct as in its own native home over the sea. Each requires to be studied entirely apart from the others. Persons of one nationality will occupy a tenement-house to the exclusion of all other nationalities. Occasionally, one will see the entire front house occupied by one nationality and the rear by an entirely different country, as in a block in Elizabeth Street. A front house is peopled by Irish, the rear by Italians. There is no trouble between the two, because each holds the other in contempt as belonging to a lower order of the human family."

This well-known fact seems to us conclusive evidence of the impossibility of amalgamating the lower grade of immigrants with the native or higher-class population upon whom the quality of our civilization rests. We are often told that it is a part of the mission of this nation to take in the unfortunate of all lands, amalgamate them with our own people, and raise the whole to a higher level. The thing cannot be done, at least not until after a long period of time in each individual case and usually not until several generations have passed through a refining process under American conditions. The Jew remains a Jew, the Hungarian a Hungarian, the Russian a Russian, the Italian an Italian, and long before the descendants have passed up into a state of civilization anywhere near the American type their places have been taken by others of the same inferior grade from the slums of Europe. Thus we have a perpetual element of low-grade immigrant population, no matter how the second or third generations improve, and the effect of this is continuously to retard the progress of the others and to lower the general social life.

This stereotyping and perpetuating of national

types in the manner revealed anew by Dr. Daniel's investigations constitutes one of the very strongest arguments for restriction of immigration.   In fact, the necessity of that policy becomes more and more evident as our study of municipal life and political conditions in this country becomes more careful and widespread. That is the first broad, general remedy which must be applied before any specific treatment of slum conditions can be undertaken with prospect of permanent success.

Dr. Daniel also investigated the questions of incomes and rent.   For a given group of families in 1891 the average income was found to be $5.99 per week, the average rent $8.62 per month; this for families consisting on an average of four people.   In 1897 the average income was found to be $5.23 per week (or a decline of 76 cents), and the average rent $9.75 per month, or an increase of about 25 cents per week.   This decline in wages is not explained, but undoubtedly is chargeable in part to the general falling off during the severe depression of 1893-4-5, from which we have not yet fully recovered.   Furthermore, it is probable that there was a deterioration in the quality of the population, cheaper laborers having taken the place of dearer ones employed in 1891;—another commentary upon the effect of practically unrestricted immigration.   In fact, it is well known that during recent years the quality of immigration has been distinctly poorer than at any previous time in our history.   The increase in rent may possibly be due somewhat to improvements in the quality of the tenements, but is more than likely chargeable to the imposition of landlords, due to the ignorance and timidity of their alien tenants.

In her medical work in this district Dr. Daniel had exceptional opportunities for studying the details of domestic life among the extremely poor.   What she found out with reference to the food consumed by different grades of East Side foreigners is as significant of the effect of previous social and industrial environments as it is revolting as a condition permanently existing in the metropolis of the western world.   Says Dr. Daniel: '' The amount of meat eaten varies with nationality and the length of residence in America.   It is also regulated by the traditions which are brought to this country.   The Italian, having eaten little meat in his own country, requires at least a few months' residence here before buying meat.   At first it is only eaten once or twice a week.   Among the Germans soup is usually made daily.   If nothing else can be obtained the lungs of animals are boiled, and the resulting fluid is not altogether unpalatable, but I do not know just how much nourishment can be obtained from it.   Breakfast usually consists either of tea or coffee and bread.   Among these people milk or cocoa is an unknown thing as a drink— another relic of their distant homes.   Eggs and fish are much eaten among the Jews, while vegetables, cheese and macaroni are the staple articles among the Italians.   Food can be obtained in any quantity and at any time.   A half egg, a leg of chicken, five cents' worth of soup meat, a loaf of bread or a quarter of a loaf, or even a solitary potato, may be bought.   From April to November the food is cooked upon a kerosene stove.   It is cheaper than coal.   The table is never spread, the hours of eating are never certain, and the family rarely eat a meal together.   One symptom of improvement in social condition is when the family begin to eat their food on plates (that is, the uncooked food), instead of taking it directly from the paper in which it was purchased.   The cooked food is kept on the stove in the vessel in which it was cooked, each person helping himself."

The amount expended for food, says Dr. Daniel, cannot be estimated with any precision, though it has

been stated to be from 9 to 11 cents per day. She
mentions families within her knowledge that have existed for weeks on five cents a day for food. " Women
(among the Hebrews) tell me that they can give a
morning and evening meal, the latter consisting of
soup, bread, coffee and a vegetable, for $3.00 per
month per person and make money."

The expenditure for clothing has been estimated
at about $10.00 per annum for each adult, but Dr.
Daniel thinks it often falls far short of this amount.
Household furniture is extremely meagre and consists
(in addition to the bedding, which the immigrants
usually bring with them,) of three or four chairs, a
table, stove, bed, mirror and usually one or two pictures
all "bought on the installment plan, at a price two
or three times greater than its real value."

Irregularity of employment is rightly considered
by Dr. Daniel one of the greatest evils in the life of the
laboring class. Of 12,519 wage-earners connected with
families who applied for help to the New York Infirmary for Women and Children during the past five years,
only 2,830 worked regularly throughout the year. Of
course the period of idleness in many of the other cases
may not have been long, but probably was sufficient to
appreciably reduce the annual income. It should be
remembered in this connection that these people are
chiefly employed by small concerns, clothing contractors, tobacconists, etc., and it is in this kind of industry
that irregularity of employment is most common. Concentration of industry in large establishments, and
thorough organization permitting constant adjustment
of supply to the demand, is the one great movement
that will reduce and finally abolish this evil in all classes
of productive industry as it has already done in many
of the more advanced grades.

It may be safely predicted that regularity of employment will increase almost in a direct ratio as the thousands of little, stuffy, precarious establishments that now compete with each other all through the East Side are combined in large factories under centralized management, capable of maintaining stable conditions.

Overcrowding is another grave evil and is charged by Dr. Daniel to the " small or irregular earnings of the man." This compels two or more families often to live in the same apartment and divide the rent. Among 726 families whose cases she investigated, 505 had only two rooms each, 41 had only one room each, and 144 three rooms. It is customary in many cases for families already overcrowded to take lodgers to help pay the rent.

In conclusion, Dr. Daniel discusses the question of what can be done to remedy these conditions. " I know of no way," she says, " to increase the man's wages when all that he can sell his labor for is $1.25 to $2.00 per day. The men complain that other men underbid them. But it is human nature, however much we may despise it, for a man to pay his laborers as little as he can get them to work for. There are so many men out of employment that many a man is compelled to underbid others and sell his labor for less than it is worth rather than to steal, starve or beg. . . . . Some think that if the women and children would not work, the wages would go up. Very likely, but what man would sit two hours and finish a pair of trousers for 2 cents ? I believe that women and children under fourteen years should be withdrawn from work, but not entirely with the idea of raising a man's wages. If there is a demand for only a certain number of men to work only that number can be employed."

The trouble with these pessimistic conclusions is that they assume certain things to be inevitable which are not at all so. There is no law of nature that a man cannot get more than $1.25 to $2.00 per day for his labor. What he can get is a social question and the conditions which determine his income are capable of being acted upon in such a way as to increase it. Low wages are due not merely to a surplus of laborers but to the fact that so many of them are cheap foreigners, who are willing to work for a sum which will maintain them as they were accustomed to live at home, but which is below the grade of social decency here. If this class were restricted in number it would become absolutely necessary for employers to hire a certain portion of laborers of a higher social standing, and what these received could be insisted upon by all laborers employed for similar work, since wages under modern conditions are determined not by individuals but by groups.

Again, a legal limitation of the hours of labor, say to eight hours, would necessitate the employment of many more to do the same work that is now performed; and the increase of expenses which this would involve would force employers to combine their plants in large establishments and introduce more efficient machine methods of production to avoid an increase in the price of their product. Of course no man would sit two hours and finish a pair of trousers for 2 cents; but the work would have to be done and, if the women and children were withdrawn from work, employers would have to pay a man for this service what would be necessary to maintain him according to the social standard which his class insisted upon maintaining.

The demand for labor is not a fixed, unchanging quantity, but under normal conditions steadily increases. Therefore, if immigration were restricted and child labor absolutely and effectively prohibited, the ordinary increase of population would not necessarily tend to produce any over-supply of workers. Under such conditions a gradual rise of wages might be possible among these people, such as has been gained by almost every other class of wage receivers throughout the country, and thus after a time it would no longer be necessary for the women in the families to work at all. Improvement in the social environment of the East Side population, quality of the tenements, streets, and educational opportunities are the means which should be used to stimulate this movement towards increasing wages by raising the standard of social tastes, habits and demands. These measures, combined with restriction of immigration, limitation of hours of labor, and prohibition of sweat-shops and child labor, compose the general public policy which ought to and must be applied to this problem before it can ever be permanently solved.

Dr. Daniel recognizes the importance of prohibiting tenement-house work. She thinks that our present factory laws, if there were a sufficient number of inspectors, could reduce the sweat-shop evil to practically nothing, provided also that children under 14 years were compelled to attend school throughout the school year. If the factory laws were enforced there would be no opportunity for these children to work at home after school hours as at present. The fact is, however, that even with very rigid inspection it has been found difficult to stop tenement-house work without infringing on certain domestic rights. The most effective way of stopping this evil would be to tax every landlord the full amount of the rent for any building in which sweat-shops existed. This would force the workers into the factories and aid the process of concentration which is absolutely necessary before there can be regularity either of employment or of hours of labor, or decency of working conditions, or fair wages.

As to overcrowding, Dr. Daniel thinks that the present laws of the Board of Health, if strictly enforced, would diminish if not entirely suppress the evil, "but a much larger force of sanitary inspectors would be necessary." If this is the case, then we ought to have a much larger force, and it is to secure just such service as this that progressive and liberal municipal administrations are so necessary and the opposite type such a menace to general social progress. Taxation for such a purpose as this ought to be hailed as a blessing instead of continually decried as a necessary evil to be kept to the lowest possible limits.

As to the matter of reducing the exorbitant rents now charged for inferior accommodations, Dr. Daniel can think of no remedy except cheaper rapid transit to the suburbs. This will doubtless have some effect, but growth of intelligence among the tenants themselves will be a still more important factor, since a considerable part of the rents charged in the East Side districts represents pure imposition. As Dr. Daniel herself says, these people "can easily be made to believe that the rent all over the city is equally high." The higher grades of skilled laborers are not troubled by the rent question. They obtain decent quarters and at prices commensurate with the accommodations received.

A general arbitrary reduction of rents, however, would probably accomplish little, since if it were spread over a large area it would doubtless be followed by a corresponding reduction of wages. The real remedy is to increase the intelligence of the people themselves so that they cannot be imposed upon by the landlords, and next, to so act upon social and industrial conditions that their wages will steadily rise, thus rendering the rent item one of proportionately less and less importance. While rent is of course increasing in some parts of New York City it is declining in other parts, and with the increase in rapid transit facilities there is no reason to suppose that this item of expenditure will anywhere keep pace with the rise of wages in the future any more than it has in the past.   Not to abolish rents but to increase wages is the real solution of this particular problem.

Dr. Daniel gives some examples of what has been done abroad in the way of erecting model tenements. " Glasgow was the first to begin the movement, and has erected seven large lodging-houses with accommodations for 2,000 persons, separate houses being provided for men and women.   The expense has been $400,000, but a profitable return is yielded.   Tenements, public baths and laundry-houses have also been provided upon a large scale.   Liverpool has demolished about 5,000 unsanitary buildings and erected in their place dwellings having all the sanitary appliances."   Other instances are cited, and Dr. Daniel warmly approves the idea of having such buildings constructed by the municipality. It seems to us that as the profitableness of these superior tenements is demonstrated private capital will tend more and more to invest in them, instead of in the miserable rookeries of former periods, and thus solve the question of proper housing by making decency profitable and barbarism costly.   The city might well aid in making barbarism costly by continually increasing the number of its requirements as to the quality of tenement houses, and if it develops that private capital will not go into the erection of model tenements fast enough then it would be better that the city erect them than not to have them at all.   Nevertheless, present experience seems to show that the movement for better housing will steadily and permanently proceed without the necessity of the city itself going into the landlord business.

CIVIC AND EDUCATIONAL NOTES

Clinton Rogers Woodruff, in discussing the work of the National Municipal League, in the *Yale Review* The Root of for August, says that the primary cause Municipal of inefficiency and corruption in city gov-Corruption ernment is public indifference to municipal questions. This is unquestionably true. Once create a strong, permanent public demand for good municipal government and the methods of securing such government will be promptly forthcoming. Partisanship or non-partisanship would cease to be an issue, because the parties themselves, to succeed at all, would have to reflect and execute the public will on these matters. Agitation and education on municipal problems and responsibilities is one of the first duties not only of the social reformer but of every patriotic citizen.

Principal Booker T. Washington, of the Tuskegee Normal and Industrial Institute, suggests that much Educating can be done toward raising the standard Cuban of life and political capacity among the Negroes Cuban negroes by educating numbers of them at the Tuskegee Institute and returning them to Cuba to become centers of intelligent, progressive influence. There is merit in this suggestion, and the possibility of good results has been demonstrated in numerous instances throughout the South since the Tuskegee Institute began its work. The cost of bringing one student from Cuba and giving him a year's education, in which industrial training forms a large part, is only one hundred and fifty dollars. Education of this sort is one of the right ways, even if limited in its practical scope, of introducing forces into Cuba which will raise her population to higher capacity for self-government.

Boston is becoming exercised on the question of slums. There has been a somewhat general impres-

Boston's
Slums

sion that the chief city of Massachusetts was comparatively free from the slum evil; at least that it had nothing compar-able for vileness to the tenement-house districts of New York and London. In the *Charities Review* for July, however, Mr. H. K. Estabrook presents detailed evi-dence of disgraceful living conditions in considerable sections of Boston territory, and suggests that public opinion in the Bay State has been too long lulled into a sense of security on this subject. "Because Boston has never had any slums like those of old Mulberry bend in New York, or those of Bethnal green in London," says Mr. Estabrook, "very few persons in the city have felt the need of improving the houses of the poor." Doubt-less there is a good deal of truth in this statement, but public interest is evidently becoming aroused on the sub-ject at last. During 1897 a law was passed by the Massachusetts legislature authorizing the Boston Board of Health to order the inhabitants of buildings unfit, for various reasons, for human habitation to vacate the same, and further, to order the removal of any such buildings unfit for habitation or which constitute a menace to the health of adjacent districts. Already the Board has exercised these new powers in several cases, and if vigorous agitation is kept up Boston will probably stamp out the slum evil before it ever ap-proaches such conditions as once existed in, and still re-main in some portions of, the East Side in New York City.

SCIENCE AND INDUSTRY

NAVAL LESSONS FROM SANTIAGO

Whatever new departure in our foreign policy may grow out of the war with Spain, we shall certainly discard from henceforth all remnants of the idea that safety lies in unpreparedness for war. It has long been a favorite theory in many quarters that our geographical position practically insured us against all danger of warlike foreign complications, and further, that if we refrained from building a navy or keeping a standing army or fortifying the coasts, permanent peace would be assured, since we should be literally compelled to arbitrate or compromise all foreign disputes. This anæmic doctrine placed peace above national honor, or, what is still more important, above the maintenance even of those principles and policies upon which the very integrity of the nation and performance of its great mission in civilization depend. The war, however, has put iron into the nation's blood and, while it may lead us into serious errors in the line of attempted territorial expansion, it will have the one good effect at least of preparing us vigorously to maintain the Monroe Doctrine and hold democracy safe from external assault throughout this entire hemisphere.

It is not probable that we shall have any considerable increase in our standing army, because, with Spain finally dislodged from American territory any future struggles we may have with foreign powers will necessarily be chiefly naval. War with England·is almost inconceivable, and she is the only European power that will henceforth possess any important foothold on this continent. Furthermore, the performances of our volunteer troops before Santiago showed a marvellously rapid adaptability of American citizen soldiery to actual service ; indeed, there is probably no country in the world where such a transformation of inexperienced militia-men and raw recruits into trained, persistent, deter-mined fighters could have taken place in anything like so short a time. It is at once a tribute to the alert, in-telligent, self-reliant quality of American citizenship and a proof of reserve fighting strength in our popula-tion so great that a large standing army would be superfluous and a useless burden.

Not so with the navy, nor with coast defences. As Colonel (then Assistant Secretary of the Navy) Roose-velt said in this magazine last January : "If a nation desires any weight in foreign policy of any kind—that is, even if it desires only a guarantee that no foreign nation will adopt towards it a hostile policy—then it must possess the means to make its words good by deeds," and, since we have little either to fear from or accomplish by land operations, " if the United States is to have any foreign policy whatsoever it must possess a thoroughly efficient navy." That this truth is now fully appreciated is seen in the recent action of Congress on the matter of naval appropriations. The sum voted for naval purposes during the fiscal year ending June 30th, 1899, exceeded $56,000,000, almost double that appropriated in recent years ; more than $20,000,000 of this amount is to be expended on new war vessels, in-cluding three coastline battleships, four harbor-defence monitors, sixteen torpedo-boat destroyers and twelve torpedo boats. Between $9,000,000 and $10,000,000 was appropriated, also, for the erection or strengthen-ing of forty coast fortifications and providing same with armament.

It seems certain, therefore, that our future policy will be directed towards making the United States a first-class naval power. It is important to remember, how-ever, that naval greatness consists not merely in quantity

of ships but chiefly in their adaptability to conditions
of modern sea fighting. Just what features are of great
and what of minor importance must be determined by
experience ; this is why the battle of the Yalu River in
the Chino-Japanese war aroused, and the Santiago conflict of last July is arousing, the keenest interest of
naval experts the world over. These are the only really
significant tests that have been had of the fighting and
resisting qualities of battleships and cruisers of strictly
modern type, and in both cases the demonstrated points
of strength and weakness were strikingly similar.
After the battle of Santiago our Board of Survey examined the wrecked Spanish cruisers and made several
suggestions in regard to construction of warships, of
which the most important are :

(1) That no wood be used in the construction of
battleships.

(2) That fire mains be placed entirely below the
protective deck.

(3) That if torpedoes are carried on fighting ships,
they should be below the water line.

(4) That rapid-fire batteries are of supreme importance.

The *Scientific American* points out that all these
recommendations, drawn from the Santiago fight,
simply confirm what had already been taught by the
Yalu River battle, and ought to be promptly heeded.
Thus : "The fact that each of these recommendations has
been persistently urged of late years by naval construct-
ors goes to prove that the art of warship building is by
no means so tentative and theoretical as is commonly
supposed. It is also noteworthy that the lessons of this
fight as here given are the very same that were taught
by the battle of the Yalu between the Chinese and
Japanese fleets, and emphasized only a few weeks ago
in the destruction of the Manila fleet.

" Of the four suggestions of the Board, the abolition of wood is undoubtedly the first in importance.
Anyone who understands how fierce is the heat engen-
dered by the explosion of a shell will realize that the
presence of wood, or indeed of any inflammable material in the proximity of the explosion, is more than
likely to start a fire of greater or less intensity. If the
ten pounds of powder were taken out of an 8-inch shell
and burnt in the open, comparatively little heat would
be noticeable ; but when the charge is burnt in the
closed chamber of a shell, the temperature increases
with the increase of pressure until at the instant of
rupture the heat is terrific — sufficient to cause any combustible material, such as wood, to burst instantly into
flames.

" Wooden decks, wooden partitions between staterooms, wooden furniture, should be absolutely barred
from the interior of a ship which is intended to become
the target for bursting shells, and particularly so if the
shells contain high explosives. . . . There is absolutely
no excuse for the presence of wooden bulkheads and partitions on a modern warship. In our reconstructed
' Chicago,' the staterooms are divided by partitions of
corrugated iron; and if considerations of comfort in peace-
time cruisers demand that wooden decks shall be laid,
the planking should all be treated by some satisfactory
fire-proof process. From Commander McGiffen's memorable account of the Yalu, it is evident that the Chinese
spent as much time fighting fire as they did in fighting
the enemy, and it was the same terrible foe that finally
caused the Spanish captains to up-helm and run for the
beach.

" The wisdom of the second recommendation is
evident from the experience of the ' Maria Teresa.'
Soon after she came out of the harbor, a shell set fire
to her after cabins, and according to one of Admiral

Cervera's staff, when a signal was sent to the engine-room to start the pumps, it was found that the fire mains had been broken by a shell. Fire mains are as much out of place above the protective deck as steam pipes; the hydrants alone should be exposed.

"The third recommendation of the Board, that no torpedo tubes should be carried above the water line, is, no doubt, prompted by the fact that the bow of the 'Vizcaya' was torn asunder by her own bow torpedoes, which were exploded either by being struck by our shells, or by the heavy concussions, or the heat of the conflagration to which they were exposed during the fight. The great risk to the ship itself in carrying tor-pedoes above the water line had already been shown at the Yalu, when a Chinese cruiser which attempted to ram was sunk by the explosion of her bow torpedoes, due to a hit by a Japanese shell. So greatly did the Chinese dread the risk, that in many ships they threw the tor-pedo warheads overboard before the fight. The more advanced of our experts advocated the installation of submerged tubes on the 'Alabama,' 'Wisconsin' and 'Illinois,' but for some inscrutable reason were over-ruled. We are glad to know that they will be fitted on all of our new ships. The submerged tube is placed below the protective deck, and therefore below the water line; hence the torpedoes are never brought above the water line, and they are as completely sheltered from shell fire as are the engines, magazines, or boilers.

. . . .

"The supreme importance of the rapid-fire gun is once more attested. It was the 4.7-inch guns of this type on the Japanese cruisers that enabled them to crush the more heavily armed and armored ships of the Chinese fleet; and we have it on the word of the Span-ish officers that it was the storm of well-aimed shells from our secondary batteries that drove the Spanish crews from the guns. The big 12 and 13-inch guns did not prove to be so effective as the secondary batteries. The ships appear to have been hulled by the 8, 6, and 4-inch weapons, while the superstructures were riddled by our 6-pounders, which are very effective at the close ranges at which the fight was carried on. If the report that the Spanish ships were rarely struck by our heaviest guns is correct, the fact furnishes another parallel to the Yalu engagement. Four of the Japanese vessels carried a 12½-inch Canet gun of 66 tons weight, which was, and is, one of the most powerful weapons in existence. Theoretically, they should have sunk every ship in the Chinese fleet; as a matter of fact, they did very little damage.

"We know of no reason why a 13-inch gun should not reach the mark as certainly as an 8 or 6-inch weapon, unless it be that its slowness of fire, coupled with the enormous percentage of misses that occurs in the heat of an engagement, reduces its chances of scoring a hit to a very low figure. It is here that the incalculable value of rapid fire comes in ; out of the storm of rapid-fire shells which poured upon the doomed Spanish ships a large number were certain to land, even if only one in ten found the mark.

"Finally," says the *Scientific American*, "we would draw attention to the great value of armor protection for the gun crews. The rapid-fire batteries of the 'Vizcaya,' 'Teresa,' and 'Oquendo' were very inadequately protected, as the searching fire of our 'pounder' guns soon demonstrated. The value of a gun is multiplied four-fold if it carries a stout shield and the sides of the ship in the wake of it are plated with a fair thickness of armor. It is contended by the English designers that if their ships do not carry so many rapid-fire guns as other ships of an equal or less displacement, the protection of the guns by 6 inches of steel

more than offsets their numerical inferiority. One excellent feature of our latest battleships is the splendid
protection afforded the 6-inch rapid-fire batteries. The
murderous fire that drove the Spaniards from their guns
would much of it be ineffectual against the secondary
battery of the ' Kearsarge ' or ' Alabama.' "

With reference to rapid-fire ordnance, shown at
Santiago to be so vitally important, *The Engineer* (London) points out that the battleships of the United States
navy are almost wholly deficient in this style of armament. The Indiana, Iowa and Oregon have no quick-
fire guns of over 3.9-inch calibre ; the Iowa has only
six, and these of only 4-inch bore, delivering a blow
of less than one-third the force of a 6-inch gun. Germany, on five battleships mounts 46 rapid-fire guns of
calibre exceeding 3.9 inches; Russia, on six battleships
has 62 ; France, on nine battleships has 88 ; England,
on nineteen battleships has 206. The greater part of
the damage to Cervera's fleet turns out to have been
done by the Brooklyn's 5-inch rapid-fire guns, of which
she has twelve, and by the secondary batteries of all of
our vessels that took part in the fight. Only two shells
larger than 8-inch took effect at all, both on the Maria
Teresa. The New York has twelve 4-inch quick-firing
guns ; most of the smaller cruisers, monitors and gun-
boats are equipped with rapid-fire ordnance ; and there
is no good reason why our great battleships should be
deficient in this respect. The vessels now under construction are, indeed, to be provided with rapid-fire
guns ; the Alabama and Wisconsin will each have fourteen 6-inch, the Kearsarge and Kentucky each fourteen
of 5-inch calibre.

Another lesson of the Santiago battle, indeed of
the whole naval experience of the war, is the relative
insignificance of torpedo boats. Practically nothing was
accomplished by these craft on either side. The

Spanish Temerario, which was expected to make serious trouble for the Oregon and Marietta, ran up a South American river 2,000 miles to escape them ; while the two destroyers (Furor and Pluton) accompanying Admiral Cervera's fleet were pounded to pieces by an armed pleasure-yacht, the Gloucester.

Finally, the question of speed is a very serious one, especially as we are about to enter upon the construction of so many first-class battleships. It seems perfectly clear that but for the speed and prompt manœuvring of the Brooklyn and Oregon, two and perhaps others of Cervera's fleet would have escaped. The Cristobal Colon covered some fifty miles before she was finally overtaken and run ashore. The other and slower vessels in our blockading squadron could have taken comparatively little part in the fight had not the Spanish cruisers been compelled to pass directly in front of them. As it was, their fire was really effective only on two of the enemy's ships. Naturally, therefore, the Navy Department's offer to accept, even at reduced price, a speed of 15 knots in the new battleships created the greatest surprise and almost universal protest. It is felt, and justly, that the original limit of 16 knots should be raised to 17 or 18 instead of lowered to 15, even if this would involve certain modifications in other respects. The latest vessels of European navies have an 18 and perhaps 19-knot speed, with greater displacement than our heaviest battleships. In fact, what experience we have all tends to confirm the theory that speed and rapid-fire ordnance are of even greater importance in modern war vessels than enormous size of ship or thickness of armor.

SCIENCE AND INDUSTRY NOTES

The *American Federationist* calls attention to one important fact about labor strikes which almost univer-

A Point About Strikes

sally escapes public notice, *viz:* that in very many strikes, regarded as failures, at the time, the thing demanded is granted within a short time afterwards, without friction, but as an outcome of the agitation which the strike set in motion. Thus, the great iron manufacturing concern of Jones & Laughlin, at Pittsburg, has just granted the eight-hour day and five per cent. increase of wages to a large additional group of employees, while last year a strike by these same men for eight hours completely failed. Twenty years ago the engineers of Great Britain struck for nine hours and failed, but two years afterwards the nine-hour system was conceded without any renewal of the struggle. The same thing occurred in many cases after the great strikes of 1886 in this country; and it is a point to remember in discussing the effect of trade-unionism on wages and conditions of labor.

The completion of the Congo Railroad and its official inauguration on July 1st last is an interesting sequel

New Congo Railroad

to the great work of Livingstone and Stanley in the heart of the Dark Continent. Only ten years ago the world was for many months utterly ignorant of the fate of Stanley's expedition, then cutting its way from the upper Congo along the Aruwimi towards the headwaters of the Nile. Already a railroad has followed his course as far as Stanley Pool on the lower Congo, some 370 miles from the ocean. Steamboats can ascend the river to Matadi, about 110 miles; the railroad then covers the 260 miles to Stanley Pool, and from there on steamboats can go fully a thousand miles into the very heart of Africa. Other important lines are projected to connect the navigable portions of tributaries of the Congo, and in a few years the resources of that immense region will be easily accessible to the outside world. The new railroad is entirely a Belgian affair, built with Belgian capital and by Belgian engineers.

———

In a recent interview in the New York *Tribune*, on the future of the bicycle trade, a prominent manufac-
Cost the   turer expressed some fundamental facts
Real   very clearly and forcibly as follows:
Factor   "The public can rest assured that bicycles will be cheap in the future, but it must not con-
found the meaning of the word cheapness with that of some other word. Because bicycles will be cheap it does not necessarily follow by any means that they will be sold below the cost of production and the expense of placing them on the market. When I say that bicycles will be cheap, I mean that the keen competition between the large manufacturers will necessarily compel the latter to be content with small profits. As a couse-
quence of this the great facilities which these manufac-
turers have for turning out bicycles in large numbers will cause them to be sold cheaply. But the public should remember that bicycles will not be sold for any great length of time below the cost of production, any more than any other article of trade, and $100 wheels will not be sold for $50, or $50 wheels for $25." This simply expresses what every practical business man and manufacturer knows, that neither supply and demand nor "marginal utility" but cost of production is the final determinant of value. This is one of the most significant facts in the whole range of economic science.

CURRENT LITERATURE

SOCIAL FACTS AND FORCES*

Like a great many books that are published now-adays, especially on economic themes, this is a series of lectures delivered by Mr. Gladden in Chicago and repeated for the students of Iowa College. Mr. Gladden is a minister, with an active, usually wholesome, and sometimes practical bent of mind. He takes hold of social questions with an enthusiasm that might well be imitated by other clergymen. As is natural to the preacher mind he is somewhat sentimental and in danger of running off into quasi-socialism. At any rate he is predisposed to underrate the efficiency of economic forces and individual enterprise and overrate the efficiency of the collective action of society.

In this little book his themes are the factory, the labor union, the corporation, the railway, the city and the clergy. He is altogether more at home and says the best things with the fewest errors on the first and last topics—the factory and the clergy. His chapter on the clergy should be read and digested, and if any doubts arise, re-read by every clergyman in the country who has not learned that it is his duty as a minister, as well as a citizen, not merely to familiarize himself with economic and social questions but to make the study of these subjects, in their theoretical and practical aspects, a part of organized church effort.

On corporations, particularly railroads, Mr. Gladden is a little afflicted with the public-ownership idea. Trusts and monopolies inspire in Mr. Gladden the full quota of fear for the future of society. His economics

---

* *Social Facts and Forces*. By Washington Gladden. G. P. Putnam's Sons, Publishers, New York and London. Cloth, 227 pp.

are a little too much of the dabbling order to enable him fully to comprehend the economic and social significance to the community of the large corporate form of industrial organization.

On labor unions he is fair and wholesome. He recognizes the shortcomings that ignorance and inexperience among labor leaders entail upon the union movement, but he does not let this force him to the irrational attitude of condemning labor unions as tyrannous, un-American and something to be got rid of. On the contrary, he recognizes labor organizations as a part of modern society which has come to stay.

His lecture on the factory goes far to atone for the shortcomings of the other lectures. In this he has grasped the true significance and inwardness of the factory system and its influence upon the social condition of labor and the duty of society in the premises. He sees that the factory system is economically an improvement on all previous methods, and therefore its disadvantages must be dealt with, not by overthrowing the system, but by social regulation of the conditions under which the factory operates. On this subject it is is pleasing to note that Mr. Gladden does not look to any form of socialism for reform. It is not to public ownership of the factories that Mr. Gladden looks for this, but to society regulating the conditions under which the factory system shall be conducted ; and conspicuously among the reforms that he sees are most needed, and from which most may be expected, is reduction of the hours of labor. Here we cannot do better than let Mr. Gladden speak for himself (p. 39) :

"One reform must come soon — that is, a reduction in the hours of labor. The marvellous improvements in machinery, and in the utilization of natural forces, will compel us to shorten the working day. The productive power of the machinery in use is said to be doubled by invention and discovery every seven years. In fourteen years it would be quadrupled ; in twenty-eight years it would be multiplied eight-fold. I do not vouch for this estimate ; but something like it is true. Now the population doubles only once in thirty years ; so if this were true, the productive power of our machinery increases more than four times as fast as the population. It is manifest that the machinery cannot be kept running all the time ; if it were, the production would be disproportionate, and stagnation would ensue. As a matter of fact, much of the existing machinery is idle a good part of the time. It can be demonstrated, I think, that all the goods now produced by machinery could be produced if the customary hours of daily labor were diminished by one or perhaps by two. And it would be vastly better for the health, the morals, and the thrift of the working-classes to work eight hours a day all the year round, than to work ten hours a day for ten months, and be idle for two months in the year.

" How shall this change be brought about ? It ought to come as the result of amicable agreements between masters and men; possibly, however, the greed of some employers would make it necessary to restrict by law the hours of labor. Therefore it is a question upon which we may be called to act, and on which we ought to have an intelligent opinion.

" The question of child-labor is far more urgent. In ten years, we are told, child-labor increased 58 per cent.—more than twice as fast as the population. These children are crowding their own fathers out of employment ; strong men stand idle in the market-place because no man hath hired them, while their children are toiling in the mills and the factories. Thus the health of many of them is injured, the minds are dwarfed, their lives are blasted. And this is an evil that will not cure itself. It grows by what it feeds on. The economic laws will not remove it ; they only aggravate it. Nothing in the world will cure it except the intervention of the conscience and good-will of the nation, by stringent laws, sternly enforced. We must shut young children out of these mills by law. There are men enough in this country to do the work of the country, to till the fields and to tend the machines; and they must do it. It may cost a little more ; very good ; it ought to cost a little more ; that is exactly what we want — to put a little more money into the pockets of the working-classes. Then we must have compulsory education, thoroughly enforced, gathering the children that we have shut out of the factories into the school-houses and training them for usefulness.

" The American people will not suffer that terrible oppression and degradation of the children of the poor which the economic forces now at work are threatening. The strength of the nation is in the vigor and hopefulness of its working-classes ; we are not, I think, such fools as to suffer them, in their very childhood, to be enfeebled and crippled for life before our very faces. And I trust that higher motives than these would hold us back from such a fatal policy. It stirs my blood, I own, to hear that in this rich country, this land that boasts so much of liberty, child-labor in the factories is increasing twice as fast as the population. Can you understand what that means ? Listen :

> " Do you hear the children weeping, O my brothers,
>   Ere the sorrow comes with years ?
> They are leaning their young heads against their mothers,
>   And *that* cannot stop their tears.
> The young lambs are bleating in the meadows;
>   The young birds are chirping in the nest;
> The young fawns are playing with the shadows;
>   The young flowers are blowing toward the west:
> But the young, young children, O my brothers!
>   They are weeping bitterly;

They are weeping in the playtime of the others,
 In the country of the free.

  * * * * *

" They look up with their pale and sunken faces,
 And their look is dread to see;
For they mind you of their angels in high places,
 With eyes turned on Deity.
' How long,' they say, ' how long, O cruel nation,
 Will you stand, to move the world on a child's heart—
Stifle down with a mailed heel its palpitation,
 And tread onward to your throne amid the mart ?
Our blood splashes upward, O gold-heaper!
 And your purple shows your path;
But the child's sob in the silence curses deeper
 Than the strong man in his wrath!' "

" We shall not suffer this curse, I know ; for law, with flaming sword but kindly mien, will turn the little children of the poor from the portals of mill and mine and factory ; and liberty, with gentle hand, will lead them into the ways of hope and happiness."*

---

*Mr. Gladden calls attention, in a footnote, to the fact that while the above was in the press census reports were received "showing a reduction during the last decade in the number of children employed in factories, the result, no doubt, of wise legislation and efficient factory inspection."

AMONG THE MAGAZINES

Harper's for August contains a very readable chapter of "Reminiscences, Anecdotes, and an Estimate" of

Mr. Gladstone, by George W. Smalley.

Harper's An interesting illustration of Gladstone's oratorical power is given in a remark made to Mr. Smalley by Ashton Dilke, an extreme Radical, after hearing a speech by Mr. Gladstone at Woolwich. Said Mr. Dilke: "You know that I am no friend of Mr. Gladstone, and am out of all political sympathy with him. But so long as he spoke I was his disciple. If he had told us to go out and set fire to the town, I should have gone."

In the *Forum* for August Mr. Brooks Adams, author of "The Law of Civilization and Decay," writing

The on *The Spanish War and the Equilibrium*

Forum *of the World*, traces in detail the westward movement of commercial and political empire and shows the growing dependence of England upon the United States for future safety and progress. Very suggestively he says that Great Britain may "be not inaptly described as a fortified outpost of the Anglo-Saxon race, overlooking the eastern continent and resting upon America."

In the same number, Prof. Brander Matthews has an interesting and very sensible article on "New Trials for Old Favorites," in which he protests against the "superstitious veneration paid to the minor [literary] masterpieces of the past." He pleads for a greater self-reliance in judging literary products, and less exaggeration of the merits of older at the expense of contemporaneous work. "For us to advance in the right path," says Prof. Matthews, "we must look at literature, as we look at life, with our own eyes, and not through the spectacles of our grandfathers."

INSTITUTE WORK

This month the Institute Work Department contains the prospectus of the GUNTON INSTITUTE for 1898–99, and curriculum of studies both for the ensuing season and for 1899–1900. For convenience of arrangement the Question Box is placed first in the Department this month, instead of in its usual place at the end.

QUESTION BOX

The questions intended for this department must be accompanied by the full name and address of the writer. This is not required for publication, but as an evidence of good faith. Anonymous correspondents will be ignored.

Editor GUNTON'S MAGAZINE: A friend of mine and myself are in difference as to the answer to a certain question concerning wages. Regarding you as an authority on economics, I respectfully appeal to your decision as to which of the two answers is correct. The question is: How are wages affected by an increase or a decrease in the capital of a country? The first answer is as follows: If there is an increase of capital wages will increase, if a decrease of capital wages will decrease. (This is the general tendency). The reason for this, briefly, is that if there is a prosperous year and capital increases more rapidly than the number of laborers, the capitalist, in order to invest, will necessarily pay out of the total value of his product a relatively greater share to labor in wages. The demand for labor will be greater than the supply and inevitably wages will increase. The greater the demand the more valuable is the supply, and vice versa. Where the demand for labor is small and the supply of laborers is great, the value of labor decreases.

The second answer is as follows: The wages of a laborer do not increase or decrease with an increase of capital, and they do not increase or decrease with a decrease of capital. There may be a decrease of capital and wages still be high. There may be a decrease of capital and still wages be low. Your answer will be very much appreciated.

R. K., 29 Broadway, New York.

While the first answer has some truth in it, it.is essentially incorrect. It assumes that wages rise and fall directly as the capital invested in industry increases or decreases. This is an old assumption that has long ago been rejected by careful economists. It is the doctrine of the wage fund, which nobody now accepts. Yet there is a certain amount of truth in this answer. For instance, it is true that wages tend to increase in times of prosperity; that, however, is not because there is more capital invested in industry but because the people, for some reason or other, are consuming more wealth. That is the basis of the prosperity itself. The investment of capital is the consequence of prosperity, not the cause of it. In brief, the first answer, *viz.*, that wages rise and fall directly as the investment of capital increases or diminishes, is essentially wrong.

The second answer is more nearly correct, although negative. It is true, as stated, that wages may be high where capital is very small and wages may be low where the investment of capital is very large. For instance, take Australia or California when first settled; the investment of capital was abnormally small, but wages were exceptionally high. The investment of capital in England is exceptionally large, though wages are much lower there than in Australia, and less than half what they were in California when the investment of capital was very small.

Then again, in Asia the investment of capital is very small and wages are very low; and the investment of capital is very large in the eastern states of America and wages are very high. So that wages may be high with large per capita investment of capital, or they may be high with a small investment of capital, and vice versa. The reason for this is that the wages are not governed by the capital at all, but by the conditions governing the social life of the laborers. The reason wages were high in California with small investment of capital was that the cost of living of the laborers who went to California was very high, and hence their wages were correspondingly so. The same was true of Australia. In Asia, with a very small investment of capital, wages are very low. The reason is that the cost of living of the laborers in Asia is only ten or twelve cents a day. If our correspondent will compare the wages of different localities and countries he will find that in general they are high or low according to the cost of living of the laboring class, and not according to the amount of capital invested. They may sometimes seem to accompany capital, being high where capital is abundant and low where capital is scarce, but they will frequently be found quite contrary to that. They will always be found to correspond to the cost of living, being high where the cost is great and low where the cost is small.

GUNTON INSTITUTE
ANNOUNCEMENT
1898-99

The GUNTON INSTITUTE is the product of more than twenty years' unremitting effort on the part of its founder and President. Throughout all this period the ultimate object has been the establishment of an institution of national scope and influence, for popular education in the principles of social economics and their practical application to American industrial and social conditions. This object is at last being realized. The success of last year's work especially has demonstrated that the institution has within it the elements of solid and permanent growth, that it supplies a genuine need of the American people, and that its future is to be one of wide significance and usefulness.

The distinguishing feature of Professor Gunton's work in economic and political science has been the substitution of positive, optimistic principles, upon which a whole system of progressive, helpful public policies can be logically and scientifically based, for the negative, disheartening, barren doctrines of the old school. As the exponent of this new point of view the GUNTON INSTITUTE has before it a work second in importance to none other in this country.

DEVELOPMENT OF THE INSTITUTE

Thirteen years ago, in the Rev. Dr. R. Heber Newton's church, then on Forty-eighth Street, New York, Professor Gunton began a series of annual lecture courses, from which developed, first the School of Social Economics, and later the GUNTON INSTITUTE. The School was established in 1890 on East 23rd Street. Its purpose was to prepare young persons for college and at the same time give a thorough course of instruction in social economics, political

225

science, and the duties of good citizenship. In 1891 it was.
found necessary to enlarge the scope of the work still further
and to provide more roomy quarters for lectures and recita-
tions; and the six-story building at the corner of Sixteenth
Street and Union Square East was leased. At the same
time a monthly magazine, the SOCIAL ECONOMIST (now
GUNTON'S MAGAZINE), was established. In 1897 the institution found a new home at 41 Union Square, in the ten-story
building at the corner of Seventeenth Street and Broadway,
right in the heart of the metropolis, the center of business.
and of educational work.

OUR WORK IN 1897

This last step was preparatory to the long anticipated
plan of establishing an Institute on a much broader scale.
than the School of Social Economics, and extending its.
work throughout the whole country, thus giving it a truly
national significance and influence. A plan of home study
and organization of local clubs or "centers" was adopted as.
best calculated to reach the largest number of people, especially that class who are able to devote only a limited
amount of time to study of any sort, and that only during
occasional leisure hours.

Two annual courses were mapped out, one on social
economics and the other on political science. Each course.
was divided into topics, so arranged as to give a progressive
and logical development of the subject from the rudiments.
up, and each month complete lessons were given in the
Magazine on the curriculum topics for that month. These.
lessons consisted, first of a lecture by Professor Gunton,
then an outline of the reading required for the month in.
each of the three books prescribed, suggestions for collateral.
reading, a large number of aids and notes on both required.
and suggested readings, hints to students, and suggestions
for the organization and conduct of local centers, with programmes for meetings. A question box was also introduced, in which queries of students regarding unclear
points in the course of study were taken up and fully answered. In addition to this, complete reports of Professor

Gunton's Wednesday evening popular lectures in New York City were sent to all students in the form of a weekly Bulletin.

The 1897-98 course was on social economics, and appropriate reading was mapped out each month in Professor Gunton's *Principles of Social Economics* and *Wealth and Progress*; also in *Economics of Industry* by Professor Alfred Marshall, of the University of Cambridge, England. Selected readings in all the great economists from Adam Smith down were suggested, with critical comments and explanatory notes on same; reference was also constantly made to numerous authentic sources of statistical information. At the end of the year a thesis was required from students on some phase of the winter's work.

The plan proved strikingly successful. Hundreds of students were enrolled within a short time, numerous thriving local clubs were formed, and the ground prepared for organization of other centers in scores of places all over the country. Men and women entered into this course of study with equal interest and enthusiasm, and in many cases it developed that working people having the minimum amount of leisure were the very ones who took hold of the proposition most heartily and achieved the best results. Thousands of people were at least made familiar with the work and aims of the GUNTON INSTITUTE who never heard of it before. Reports from both individual readers and local centers already formed show that the outlook for the coming season is most encouraging.

IMPORTANCE OF THE WORK

A knowledge of economic and politico-economic questions and of their practical bearing upon American conditions is more important to American citizens to-day than the scholarship implied in a college degree. Republican institutions hang in the balance, and their permanence and prosperity will depend upon the education and good sense of the people upon these subjects, especially the questions of Money, Protection, Labor, and, at the present time particularly, of Foreign Policy.

To this educational work the Gunton Institute is especially devoted. It is strictly scientific in method and American in sentiment, and aims to give that comprehensive familiarity with sound principles of public policy which intelligent citizenship demands. Especially is a thorough and practical education in this class of subjects indispensable to professional men, who are naturally regarded as students and leaders of thought and whose opinions are sought and respected. The great influence exerted in every community by its clergymen, lawyers, physicians and teachers carries with it a grave responsibility; hence their attitude on the great questions affecting the social progress of the nation should be sound, wholesome, helpful and well-grounded in a broad accquaintance with economic principles and data. America to-day is solving for the world some of the most serious problems of civilization, and she can afford to have no "blind leaders of the blind."

WHAT THE INSTITUTE STANDS FOR

The Gunton Institute stands for a rational, orderly and thoroughly harmonious system of constructive social philosophy. This system of philosophy not only successfully harmonizes and explains economic and social phenomena from a central viewpoint of progressive development, but suggests in every instance some practical line of action leading to an ultimate solution of these problems, and to a sound, constructive public policy.

It is a philosophy of virile, positive action, emphatically distinguished from the negative, hopeless pessimism of what has heretofore been justly called the "dismal science." It denies the utility of any system of sociological theory which does not throw some light on the great problem of what to do and how to do it. It is the antithesis of *laissez faire.*

It is conservative as well as progressive. It analyzes the facts and principles of social evolution with a view to suggesting a broader and more intelligent application of the forces by which progress always has been and always can be achieved; and thus it leads directly away from the doctrines of social revolution and reversal of established economic tendencies demanded by socialism, anarchism, and, under a thin disguise, by the single-tax.

It offers a practical and scientific treatment of the labor question. It deals with the trades-union movement and the modern concentration of capital as complementary phases of a great general tendency which, properly understood and treated, is capable of yielding the largest benefits to the wage-workers and to society at large. It finds in the principle of national development something far deeper and more essential to the progress of civilization than mere "jingo" pride or territorial expansion, towards which so many are now turning with mistaken zeal.

It finds in the general policy of protection, whether against crime, or ignorance, or disease, or degrading euvironments, or low-wage labor or the products of such labor, something broader and more fundamental than mere governmental favoritism.

It is the finger of science, pointing the path along which the progress of the human race from barbarism towards the highest civilization has been and is to be accomplished.

FOR WOMEN AS WELL AS MEN

The projectors and promoters of the Institute realize that the true American educator and citizen fail of their fullest usefulness to society if they neglect in any regard to encourage women to know so far as may be what men know. In the arena of public affairs, of a better social economy, of a broader and purer citizenship, of a happier home life throughout the republic, is a broader field for women's endeavor, not necessarily in such a participation in affairs as seems, in these later days, to have brought many good exertions into disrepute, but rather in the knowledge on the part of women of what is good and what is bad in a community of which their own homes are the basis, and in the resolution to influence these present conditions as forcefully as possible with this added loyalty and information.

The Institute desires, then, not only the attendance of women upon its lectures, but the interest, from no matter what distance, of women everywhere in the publications and courses of the Institute, and equally with men in the competition for honors. A fair proportion of lectures and reading matter of special interest to women is given, and just as these features of the work will appeal none the less to men, so the work which might be thought especially appropriate to men will be found of interest to women students also. It is hoped that women will enter freely into the work of the Institute, joining the mixed clubs or organizing clubs exclusively for women, as circumstances may suggest.

PLAN OF WORK

The plan of instruction is very simple. All that is necessary is to register as a student of the GUNTON INSTITUTE, procure the required literature and enter upon the work, following the directions, aids and suggestions which will appear from month to month in GUNTON'S MAGAZINE, and, at the end of the year, writing a thesis. Students are expected to communicate with Institute officers regarding any points in the course of study upon which further instruction or explanation may be desired. All such communications will be carefully considered and answered either through the medium of the magazine or by direct correspondence. In this way every enrolled student is brought into immediate connection with the Institute.

TIME REQUIRED

The full course of study embraced in the curriculum covers a period of two years. The courses are so arranged, however, that the work of the second year does not necessarily depend upon that of the year preceding. Each year's course is essentially independent; which makes it practicable for all students in any one year to enjoy the same course.

Thus the students who enrolled in the winter of 1897-98 took the course in Social Economics; those who enroll this fall and winter will take the course in Political Science; in the fall and winter of 1899-1900 the course in Social Economics will be given again, though its scope will doubtless be somewhat extended. This arrangement enables students to take either course first without any disadvantage to the logi-

cal order of studies.   Students may enter and begin study
any time during the year and the Institute will furnish the
necessary back literature.   It is estimated that the outline
of study given in the curriculum will require about five
hours' work each week.   Each course covers a period of
eight months.

THESES AND CERTIFICATES

During the last month of the year students of the Institute will be required to write theses upon topics chosen by
the faculty as best filling the requirements of various groups
of students, according to their experience, ambition, etc.
These theses will all be examined carefully and students
will be rated according to their merit.   The offices of the
Institute reserve the right to publish any of these productions, and the award of certificates at the end of the ac-
ademic year will thus be determined according to the deserts
of each undergraduate.

LECTURE REPORTS BY BULLETIN

The advantage of the lecture course given in New York
City under the auspices of the Institute is extended to all
enrolled students by a series of Weekly Bulletins containing
reports of such lectures and of the discussions following
them.   Where local centers exist these reports can be read
and discussed in the meetings.

GUNTON'S MAGAZINE

In addition to the required reading in each number of
GUNTON'S MAGAZINE an entire department is exclusively devoted to the work of the Institute.   Each month during the
school year an outline of the reading and study intended for
that month is given; also suggested programmes for meetings of local centers, explanatory notes and aids on the required reading; a department of Answers to Questions received from students, besides items of news regarding the
progress of the movement.

LOCAL CENTERS

In addition to individual home study the GUNTON INSTI-
TUTE plan contemplates the formation of Local Centers or
Study Clubs, holding regular meetings for discussion and
mutual assistance. Even if the club numbers not more
than five or six members, good results can be obtained and
the interest of the work materially increased. There are
few communities where at least this small number of people
of both sexes cannot be interested in the formation of a local
center for the study of practical social economics and political science under the direction of the Institute. Clergymen,
lawyers, political leaders, editors and school teachers will
naturally take the lead in the organization of such clubs.
Meetings can be held at the homes of members, thus introducing a pleasant social element, or in churches or public
halls, where the center is sufficiently large. In the latter
case the public can often be invited to attend the meetings
and many new students interested in that way. The plan of
organization of a local center should be as informal as possible, and in most cases a president and a secretary will be
the only necessary officers. Secretaries of local centers
should notify the GUNTON INSTITUTE promptly of the formation of such centers and thereafter keep the Institute informed as to the growth of the club and progress of the work.

LOCAL CENTER LIBRARIES

By the local center plan it becomes possible, also, to reduce expenses and enlarge the range of reading. Thus, in
a club of twelve persons, if each member were to obtain
only one volume, chosen from the list of books recommended
for collateral reading during the course, a library of a dozen
selected works, available to all the members, would be secured.

New York state clubs are especially fortunate in being
able to utilize the traveling library plan of the University of
the State of New York. Libraries of from 25 to 100 books,
including duplicate volumes if desired, can be selected by
local centers, and upon formal application and payment of
the required fee to the library department of the University
the books will be sent in a neat oak case with card index and

full instructions. The rental charge, covering six month periods, is $2 for 25 volumes, $3 for 50, $4 for 75 and $5 for 100. At these rates the library must be accessible to the general public in the community where located; when the use of the library is restricted to the members of the local center, double rates are charged. Full information regarding this excellent opportunity may be obtained by addressing the Traveling Library Department of the University of the State of New York, Albany,N. Y., and libraries may be ordered direct from Albany or through the GUNTON INSTITUTE. A few other states have library systems similar in in some respects to that in New York. These states, and the officers to whom application for information should be made, are as follows:

Michigan, Mrs. Mary C. Spencer, State Library, Lansing, Mich.

Iowa, Mrs. L. H. Cope, State Library, Des Moines, Ia.

Montana, Mr. F. C. Patten, Public Library, Helena, Mont.

In Wisconsin and Massachusetts libraries are circulated by private philanthropy. For details address, respectively, Mr. F. A. Hutchins, Free Library Commission, Madison, Wis., or Miss Mary Morison, Peterborough, N. H.

Philadelphia has a municipal system of traveling libraries, information regarding which may be obtained of Mr. John Thompson, Free Public Library, Philadelphia, Pa.

A classified list of standard works, many of which will be recommended for collateral reading during the course, will be sent to all enrolled students, for the guidance of local centers in selecting libraries or of individual readers desiring to purchase economic literature.

THE COURSE FOR 1898-99

The course of study for the coming season is of peculiar importance because of its direct bearing upon the great new problems growing out of the war with Spain. It takes up the theory of national or group development, the meaning and requirements of patriotism, theory of statesmanship, the Monroe Doctrine, and the principles which should govern our foreign policy, particularly with reference to colonization and annexation. Having shown the true position and mission of this republic with reference to the progress of civilization, the course takes up in detail the various domestic problems to which wise and vigorous statesmanship should be applied; such as taxation, protection and free trade, money, banking, trusts, factory legislation, trades-unions, hours of labor, labor insurance, political parties, public education, charity, and municipal reform. The lessons begin in the October number of the Magazine.

EXPENSES

The only necessary expense is for the literature required in carrying on the work of instruction, which, for 1898-99, is as follows: Gunton's *Principles of Social Economics* ($1.75), and *Wealth and Progress* ($1.00); GUNTON'S MAGAZINE ($2.00 per year), and the GUNTON INSTITUTE BULLETIN ($1.00 per year). Both books, Magazine and Bulletin will be furnished to Institute students for $5.00. To those who purchased the books last year the only expense during the coming season will be the subscription to the Magazine and Bulletin; the two are sent for $2.50.

SPECIAL TO LOCAL ORGANIZERS

Any person who will take the initiative and organize a local center of six or more members will receive a complete outfit free, consisting of the Magazine and Bulletin for one year, Gunton's *Principles of Social Economics* and *Wealth and Progress*.

APPLICATION SLIPS

A blank form for convenience of students and subscribers will be found among the advertising pages in this number, perforated so to be easily detachable. Any one desiring to enter the courses of the Institute is requested to fill out a blank and mail it to the Secretary, 41 Union Square. Additional slips in any number will be furnished on request; and friends of the Institute and the Magazine everywhere are respectfully urged to send for them for distribution where they will do the most good.

CURRICULUM

The courses of study have been prepared with especial reference to affording the maximum amount of useful information. The subjects covered are so arranged as to render the greatest possible aid to a clear understanding of present day questions. While they include the history and theory of most of the subjects, yet in every case they are intended to lead to constructive, practical suggestions for intelligent, helpful citizenship.

COURSE FOR 1898-99—POLITICAL SCIENCE

I. THEORY OF NATIONAL DEVELOPMENT.

   a Importance of group development.

   b Influence of diversified industry on national welfare.

   c Influence of patriotism.

II. NATURE AND FUNCTIONS OF GOVERNMENT.

   a Paternal *vs.* protective aid.

   b Individual and the State.

III. THEORY OF STATESMANSHIP.

   a The business man's *vs.* statesman's point of view.

   b The laborer's position in national welfare.

   c The viewpoint of public policy.

IV. FOREIGN POLICY.

   a Territorial policy.

      1 The doctrine of colonization.

      2 The doctrine of annexation.

      3 The Monroe Doctrine.

      4 The position of the Republic.

   b Protection.

      1 History of protection.

      2 Theory of protection.

      3 Practical effect of protection.

      4 Export bounties.

    5 Restriction of immigration.

c Free Trade.

    1 History of free trade.

    2 Theory of free trade.

    3 Practical effect of free trade.

    4 The reverse interest of England and the United States.

V.   THEORY AND PRACTICE OF TAXATION.

    a Tariff taxes.

    b How and when they affect prices, and when not.

    c Direct and indirect taxes.

    d Personal property tax.

    e Income and legacy taxes.

    f Influence of taxes upon wages.

VI.   MONEY.

    a Metallic money.

    b Paper money.

    c History and theory of Bimetallism.

    d History and theory of Monometallism.

    e Free coinage of silver.

    f Fiat paper money; (Greenbacks).

VII.   BANKING.

    a Banking experience in United States.

    1 New England Banks (The Suffolk).

    2 First and Second Banks of United States.

    3 State Banking system.

    4 Sub-treasury system.

    5 National Banking system.

    b English Banking system.

    c Canadian Banking system.

    d Banking in France and Germany.

    e Banking reform.

VIII.   THE STATE AND CAPITAL.

   a Corporations and the public.

   b Corporations and individuals.

   c Character and influence of trusts.

IX.   THE STATE AND LABOR.

   a Factory legislation.

   b Legal rights of trade unions.

   c Legal restriction of strikes.

   d Injunctions against strikers.

   e The rights of non-union workers.

   f Mutual labor and capitalist unions.

   g Labor insurance.

X.   MUNICIPAL GOVERNMENT.

   a National parties and local politics.

   b Public education.

   c Public improvements.

   d Municipalization of franchises.

   e Housing of the poor.

   f Tenement-house problem.

   g Public and private charity.

COURSE FOR 1899–1900—SOCIAL ECONOMICS

I.   FIELD AND FUNCTION OF SOCIAL ECONOMICS.

   a Limits of the field of study.

   b Man in his social life.

   c Definition of progress.

   d Point of view.

II.   INFLUENCE OF INDUSTRIAL LIFE ON SOCIAL AND POLITI-
        CAL INSTITUTIONS.

   a Pastoral industry (theocracy).

   b Agriculture (autocracy).

   c Simple manufacture and trade (monarchy).

   d Capitalistic manufacture and commerce (democracy).

III.   EVOLUTION OF WAGE AND CAPITALIST CLASSES.

   a Feudalism.

      1 Town Life.

      2 Magna Charta.

      3 Free cities.

      4 The Church.

   b Wage and capitalist classes.

      1 Rise of tenant farmers.

      2 Capitalist artisans.

      3 Industrial guilds.

      4 Apprentice system.

      5 Factory system.

IV.   WEALTH.

   a Meaning and nature of wealth.

   b Different kinds of wealth. Capital. Commodities.

   c Distinction between man, service and wealth.

V.   PRODUCTION.

   a Former theories of production.

     1 Physiocrats.

     2 Adam Smith, etc.

   b Hand production.

   c Capitalistic production.

     1 Effect of machinery on labor.

     2 Effect of high wages on production.

VI.   CONSUMPTION.

   a Desire and demand—initial forces.

     1 Influence of psychic forces.

     2 Influence of education.

     3 Influence of sanitation, etc.

     4 Effect of consumption on production.

VII.   VALUE AND PRICE.

   a Supply and demand.

   b Cost of production.

   c Elements of cost.

   d Effect of competition.

VIII.   DISTRIBUTION.

   a Wages.

     1 Definition of wages.

     2 Influences that affect wages.

     3 Effect of charity.

     4 Day work wages.

     5 Piece work wages.

     6 Woman's wages.

     7 Country and city wages.

     8 Forces that increase wages.

   b Rent.

     1 Different kinds of rent.

     2 Economic difference between rent and wages.

     3 Popular fallacies regarding effect of rent on wages.

c Interest.

     1 Economic character of interest.

     2 How it differs from wages, rent and profits.

     3 Its effect on prices.

     4 Who pays the interest?

d Profits.

     1 What constitutes profits?

     2 Effect on prices.

     3 Effect on wages.

     4 Why large in some industries and small in others.

     5 Are large profits a burden on the wage-earners and consumers?

     6 Whence do profits come?

IX. SOCIAL REFORMS.

a Socialism.

     1 Its history.

     2 Its theory.

     3 Its practical effect.

b Single tax.

     1 What it means.

     2 Its probable effect.

     3 Its literature.

c Populism.

     1 Its rise.

     2 Its history.

     3 Its methods.

d Labor organizations.

     1 Knights of Labor.

     2 Federation of Labor.

     3 Trade unions.

DAVID RICARDO

Author of "Principles of Political Economy and Taxation"

GUNTON'S MAGAZINE

Economics and Public Affairs
GROWING POLITICAL SENSE

Like all human characteristics, political sense is a matter of slow development; so slow, indeed, that we often get impatient with the tardiness of its oncoming. Experience with blunder, failure and defeat seems to be the only effective means of educating the public mind.

New York has been having a long and vigorous course in this kind of education. In no state in the Union have the political parties been divided so obviously on the lines of decency and degradation as in New York, particularly New York City. Tammany, which is now the Democracy of New York, stands publicly labelled before the civilization of the world as the party of political chicanery and social dishonor, against which decency should unite. The Republican party in New York, on the other hand, may be said generally to embrace the elements of social decency and high-minded public policy. Yet the Republican party, especially in the metropolis, is so torn asunder by internal factions that Tammany reigns supreme. Last year this political folly reached its climax. After having had for four years a fairly progressive municipal administration, whose election was secured by the wholesale exposure of Tammany rottenness, the government of the metropolis was again handed over to that organization. The people of New York did not want Tammany, yet the campaign was so conducted as to put Tammany in power by an overwhelming majority. The election of Van Wyck as the first Mayor of Greater New York is a monument to the political folly of New York Republicans.

It is encouraging, however, to note that this costly lesson has not been without good effect. It impressed, temporarily at least, the fact that victories are not won by factional strife and disintegration but only by organization and some degree of harmonious action. Both the so-called machine and the reformers have evidently learned something of this lesson. . The vigorous tirade against " Plattism " and the machine has taught the organization leaders that public sentiment, outside of the enrolled membership of political organizations, must be counted with in the selection of candidates for public office ; and the reformers have learned that merely to denounce party organization and hurl epithets at party leaders does not insure political success. The lesson taught by the disastrous failure of this go-it-alone policy, as the grand culmination of previous lessons of the same kind, is evidently bearing fruit. The machine is showing no disposition to force into nomination a one-man candidate, and the reformers are at least hesitating to venture again to " go it alone." Mr. Low, the leader and candidate of the reformers, has definitely refused to aid in any independent movement, which, in a recent letter to a member of the Citizens' Union, he characterizes as " unreasonable and unprofitable, and similar to the attitude of the Prohibitionists, who sacrifice all practical results year after year for the sake of a theory." The letter is as follows :

"I have your letter of September 13. I am not very well acquainted with the details of the situation, but so far as I can base an opinion on the surface of things I should think that the proposed action of the Independents in this State is the one thing that can cause the defeat of Colonel Roosevelt and the possible loss of a sound-money Senator from New York, as well as sound-money representatives in Congress.

"On the other hand, I can see absolutely no benefit to accrue from the course which has been taken and which is proposed. It seems to me to be unreasonable and unprofitable, and similar to the attitude of the Prohibitionists, who sacrifice all practical results year after year for the sake of a theory. I regret to differ so radically from one whose opinion I value so highly as yours, but under the circumstances you can perceive that I can take no part in an independent movement this year. Yours sincerely,   SETH LOW."

This letter is highly gratifying because it shows that experience counts, and that enough of it will really develop political wisdom. The result of all this is that in the gubernatorial election in New York this year, on the Republican side, the people are sure to have an opportunity of voting for a high-minded, efficient public man for Governor. The plane of the contest has been raised, and the futility of third parties fully recognized.

Before this reaches our readers, the Republican convention will have met at Saratoga and nominated a candidate for Governor. The candidate will be either Governor Black or Colonel Theodore Roosevelt. The peculiarity of the situation is that Colonel Roosevelt, who is conspicuously a reformer of the advanced type, appears to be the candidate of the machine. Nothing could more conclusively demonstrate that the Republican organization is not attempting to select a candidate for Governor who can be made the instrument of Mr. Platt or any other political magnate. If there is a person in the United States who is proof against that sort of thing it is Colonel Roosevelt.

Governor Black and Colonel Roosevelt are very unlike individualities. Governor Black is a man of great political regularity. He is in no sense a kicker, but he is a man of political breadth of view. He is a party man, but his partisanship is patriotic. He is not merely a politician, he is a statesman. Few men in public life to-day have a clearer conception of the fundamental principles of political philosophy than has Governor Black. His speeches are masterpieces of political thought and comprehension of public policy. As Governor he has been dignified, efficient, straightforward and true to his party principles and public utterances. The one exception to this was his appointment of Lou Payn as Insurance Commissioner. No satisfactory reason has ever been given for this, and probably never will be. Governor Black has shown a favorable disposition to wholesome industrial, municipal and educational legislation. He has doubtless given offense by some of his vetoes, yet they too have been in the right direction.

In short, as Governor Mr. Black has been a success, and there are no special reasons why he should not have a second term. Yet there are many circumstances which seem to conspire against it. The war with Spain is an overshadowing and all-absorbing national event. Mr. Roosevelt, by his service in the Navy Department and later in the Army, and his exceptional position in the decisive battle of the war, has unconsciously, as it were, come to the front in public regard and esteem and become conspicuously a public favorite.

If this were all there was to Mr. Roosevelt, there would be no reason for electing him Governor. To elect merely successful soldiers to prominent political offices is poor policy; born and trained soldiers are seldom broadly progressive statesmen. But Mr. Roosevelt is not the popular candidate for Governor solely because he is the hero of Santiago. That was but a climactic incident. Colonel Roosevelt is conspicuously an active personality in political life. In this respect he is really extraordinary. He is one of the few men in this country who is at once a loyal partisan and an indefatigable fighting reformer; but he is a reformer who shows political sense. He has many times demonstrated that he has as much courage in politics as he has in war. He has held many important public offices, and it is notorious that he always worked harder and did more than any of his subordinates. He is a man of action. As president of the Civil Service Commission he was a marked success. He did much to take the glittering nonsense out of that machine and put into it a streak of practical hard sense. As Police Commissioner in the City of New York he did what everybody had regarded as impossible—enforced the law. His attitude toward the police was so frank, fair and manly that during the short time he held that office he made the entire force his friends, because for the first time every policeman came to realize that he was sure of a fair hearing and fair treatment at the hands of the head of the department, no matter what his politics or what the "pull" against him. As Assistant Secretary of the Navy Mr. Roosevelt was equally conspicuous for the same active, efficient, executive qualities.

It is true that Mr. Roosevelt, whether as soldier or civilian, is essentially a fighter, but he is a fair fighter and he always fights *for something*. He is liberal and broad-minded in the best sense of the term. He recognizes, as few public men do, the growing significance of social problems, and few public men are more alive to the importance of making a liberal, rational recognition of the labor question a part of our public policy. Moreover, Colonel Roosevelt is actively interested in broadening the social, educational and economic aspect of municipal policy, which is one of the most important spheres of public improvement in this country.

While Colonel Roosevelt is vigorous, positive and aggressive, he is also scholarly and eminently dignified. To be sure, at times he seems a little more impulsive and will act quicker than most men, but he will *do* more. It is these qualities that make him popular. If the public does not always agree with a man it always admires a person who has courage, actions, ideas, sense and patriotism. If Mr. Roosevelt receives the nomination at Saratoga there will be little doubt as to his election. Political enthusiasm will run high, and New

York will be sure of an active, efficient, progressive Governor.

If Mr. Black should get the nomination, he might not inspire so much enthusiasm but, as we have said, he has already demonstrated his capacities as an efficient Governor. The high statesmanlike qualities and broad political gauge of Governor Black were indicated in a recent interview in which he said: "After the Republican State convention is over, we should all take off our coats and go to work for the candidate who is nominated for Governor, no matter who he is. We are Republicans, and we stand by our party under all circumstances. I certainly shall do all in my power to elect Colonel Roosevelt if he should happen to be the Republican candidate for Governor, by speaking and working for him, and I have no doubt he would do the same work for myself if I should receive the nomination." That breathes the true spirit of political harmony, without sacrifice of political freedom and competition. What Governor Black said of Colonel Roosevelt is undoubtedly true. He is not the kind to sulk in his tent. He couldn't stand it.

This is really a great advance over the condition of a year ago. It shows that both the machine and the reformers have learned something, and that political sense is really dawning in New York; that neither personal dictatorship nor political self-righteousness can longer be permitted to destroy a natural political unity which ought to and can give New York State and New York City high-minded, clean-handed, public-spirited administrations. If the lesson of last year is as well learned by Mr. Low's followers as it appears to have been by Mr. Low himself, the early emancipation of the metropolis from Tammany rule is an assured fact.

SOUND MONEY MISREPRESENTATION

It is not an uncommon experience for important public movements to suffer serious injury from the over-zeal, exaggeration, and ill-digested statements of its friends. The sound currency movement is not without friends of this character. The Sound Currency Committee, located at 52 William Street, New York City, has been doing some very important work in the line of monetary education. It has probably published more good literature on sound currency and banking than any, if not all, other sources of sound money propaganda. It publishes a bi-weekly tract, every issue of which contains a special discussion of some phase of the money question. These publications have from time to time contained some of the best contributions to the subject that have appeared anywhere, both as to the history of coin, currency and banking in different countries and the theory of sound currency and banking principles and practice.

One of these issues recently contained a monograph by Mr. Edward Atkinson on the "Cost of Producing Silver." A more misleading discussion of the subject has not appeared in the literature of the New Democracy. Of course it would be difficult for a Sound Curreney Committee of the Reform Club to avoid having something from Mr. Atkinson, since the Reform Club is the mother of the free trade movement, of which Mr. Atkinson is a high priest. The soundness of most of the literature issued by this Committee would lead one to suppose that Mr. Atkinson's document was one which courtesy rather than merit compelled it to accept; its whole reasoning and handling of facts is so contrary to any economic method of discussing the subject.

If the people of this country are really to be educated into sound ideas on currency and banking, which is the

most important domestic question now demanding consideration, the discussion must be fair and scientific;
that is, based upon sound economic principles. Of the
question of the cost of mining silver the people in the
East are utterly ignorant from practical experience, and
they depend for their ideas on the impartial literature
of the subject. In the West, particularly in the mountain states, a great many people have a practical knowledge of the subject. If the sound money movement is
to command the confidence and respect of the whole
nation, it must so state the facts that those who are
acquainted with them cannot object to the fairness and
accuracy of the presentation. Otherwise its literature
simply serves to mislead the people of the East, who
have no experience on the subject, and disgust the people of the West, who have an every-day acquaintance
with the facts, and thus create a false public opinion in
one part of the country and a sectional bias in the other.

Now this is exactly what Mr. Atkinson's formal and
very pretentious discussion of the subject is well calculated to do.

Sound money advocates are generally disposed to
create the impression that the free silver movement is a
dishonest movement; that in reality it is the result of a
conspiracy on the part of the mine owners by a trick of
legislation to cheat the rest of the community out of
hundreds of millions every year. Mr. Atkinson makes
bold to affirm, and insists that he proves, this proposition. On page 3 he says:

"I am now prepared to prove, from the published accounts rendered
to the stockholders of the Broken Hill Proprietary Company and other
mining companies of New South Wales represented in London, that the
cost of placing fine silver upon the Londen market for five years, from
May 31, 1891, to May 31, 1896, inclusive, computed according to the customary method of crediting the by-products to the cost of the principal
product, namely, silver, has been less than 25 cents or 12½ pence, per
ounce. Also, that the copper production of the Anaconda mine in Montana, in the last fiscal year, ending June 30th, 1897, yielded a profit over

and above all charges of every name and nature, without regard to the silver production. Also, that in that year of low prices the sales of the largest silver product ever made at that mine in one year—namely, 6,057,067 ounces fine—yielded $3,881,551.75 in gold; the whole of this sum received for silver being in addition to the profits upon copper."

After making a considerable display of figures, which we will consider later, he closes his paper with the following declaration:

"I charge, on circumstantial evidence, without absolute proof, that the representatives of British silver, probably covering three-quarters of the world's product, have been endeavoring, in collusion with a similar class of men in this country, to promote what is called bimetallism abroad and free coinage here. Their purpose is to induce the farmers and cotton growers of this country to exchange the food, the fibres and the fabrics of this country, which the world cannot spare but must have, even at high gold prices, especially this year, for their silver, which is produced at a cost of from 25 cents an ounce down to nothing at the rate of 16 to 1, or $1.29½ an ounce, under an act of force or legal tender."

If this statement means anything, it means that the silver with which the world's market is supplied does not cost more than twenty-five cents an ounce. That is to say, that twenty-five cents is the maximum cost, and that the cost varies, or, to use Mr. Atkinson's own words, silver "is produced at the cost of from twenty-five cents an ounce down to nothing." The boldness with which Mr. Atkinson makes this statement seems to have so impressed the Sound Currency Committee that it printed the first of the above quoted paragraphs on the title page in italics, thus evidently regarding it as a conclusive statement of the case.

With this seeming endorsement by the Sound Currency Committee, Mr. Atkinson's statement will be very naturally accepted through the eastern and non-silver-producing states as well founded and incontrovertible, because the people of the eastern states are practically unacquainted with the facts except as they get them from sound money sources.

We may, therefore, expect to see this repeated by

the eastern press and echoed by political speakers as a
well authenticated statement of the facts regarding the
cost of silver. But when this statement of the case is
sent into the West, particularly into the silver-producing
states—as it will be,—we may expect to see it denounced
as either an utterly ignorant assertion or a wilful misrepresentation of the facts. No amount of respectability
can make the people of Park City, Utah, for instance,
have any respect for the authority of such a statement
when they daily gaze upon whole streets of houses
with the windows and doors nailed up and see miners
loafing about the streets or moving away, because
mines cannot produce silver even at fifty or sixty cents
an ounce, to say nothing of twenty-five. People who
know anything about the facts of silver production
know that Mr. Atkinson's statement does not correctly
represent the case. To publish such statements with
the endorsement of the Sound Currency Committee,
then, must tend ultimately to throw discredit on the
whole sound money literature which emanates from
eastern sources. To be sure, Mr. Atkinson in this, as
in most other cases, presents a considerable array of
facts in support of his statement, of which he says: ''I
challenge disproof.''

The error in Mr. Atkinson's statement is not in the
actual misquotation of the figures he presents but in
the utter misapplication of their relation to the general
cost of producing the market supply of silver. He
quotes the figures of two mines, one the Broken Hill
Proprietary Company, in New South Wales, and the
other the Anaconda Mining Company, of Butte, Montana. These are confessedly the two best mining
properties in the world. Mr. Atkinson takes from the
official reports of these two companies the cost of producing silver. In one he finds it costs something less
than twenty-five cents an ounce and in the other that it

costs nothing, being a by-product of copper; and concludes from that that the cost of producing the world's
supply of silver is from twenty-five cents to nothing
per ounce.   It does not need an expert in economics—
just a little business sense is sufficient—to show that this
is an utterly fallacious way of arriving at the truth on
this matter.   It would be just as true to say that because a few of the best concerns in New England can
manufacture cotton cloth of a given grade at two cents
a yard, that two cents a yard is the cost of producing
the market supply of cotton cloth, and that any price of
over two cents a yard represents net profit to the manufacturer.

Mr. Atkinson knows, as every cotton manufacturer
knows, that such is not the truth; that such a statement
would violently misrepresent the facts of the cotton industry.   While there are a few of the very best
equipped manufacturing establishments that can make
cotton cloth at two cents, there are many more who cannot make it for less than two and one-eighth and two
and one-fourth cents a yard, and hence, when cotton
cloth is selling at two and one-fourth cents a yard, it
does not represent a quarter of a cent a yard profit;
and with a considerable portion it represents bare cost,
no profit at all.   In that case, instead of saying that the
cost of producing cotton cloth is two cents a yard, the
economic and practical truth is that it costs two and
one-fourth cents a yard, because that is the cost upon
which the market price is really made and must rest so
long as the needs of the market will take the two and
one-fourth-cent cloth.

The case of silver is exactly parallel.   It is undoubtedly true that the Broken Hill mine in New
South Wales can produce silver at a cost of twenty-five
cents an ounce.   It is equally true that the Anaconda
mine in Montana gets a large quantity of silver, and

also gold, as by-products with copper. The copper mined by this company pays the entire cost of the concern; the silver and gold are by-products, and as such are a part of its profit. Charging, as Mr. Atkinson properly does, the cost of all production to the major product of the mines, *i. e.*, copper, the silver and the gold cost nothing. But would anybody in his senses be expected to take seriously a theory which should base an estimate of the cost of supplying the market with gold and silver on these costless increments of gold and silver production?

The theory upon which Mr. Atkinson appears to proceed is that the cost of supplying the market with a product is to be estimated upon the cost of furnishing the least expensive portion of the general supply. The logic of this would be that since the Anaconda mines produce both silver and gold as costless by-products, therefore silver and gold have no cost of production. And this is practically what Mr. Atkinson has done, for he takes the Anaconda mine, with its no-cost product, and the Broken Hill Company mine, with 25 cents cost, and declares that the cost of producing silver is from "25 cents an ounce down to nothing."

There have been some mines in Cripple Creek in which the cost of digging gold has averaged less than $1.00 an ounce. Why not, therefore, say that the cost of producing gold is less than $1.00 an ounce? Or, to be consistent, take the minimum case, the Anaconda mine, where both silver and gold cost nothing as by-products, and say that since both silver and gold are produced for nothing, therefore the whole price of both metals is profit to all the mine owners.

But to keep to Mr. Atkinson's own statements: if the cost of producing silver is only from 25 cents an ounce down to nothing, will Mr. Atkinson explain how it is that the price of silver still remains at 61 cents an ounce? If the miners can produce silver at from 25 cents to nothing per ounce, by what economic principle can they keep the price up to 61 cents an ounce? If the price of an article can be kept up to over 60 cents an ounce, regardless of its cost, why cannot it be kept at $1.00 an ounce? And if $1.00, why not $1.29, which for so many years was the prevailing price of silver? Now there is some reason why the price of silver fell from $1.29 in 1872-73 to 61 cents to-day.

Mr. Atkinson and the Sound Money Committee ought to know what that reason is. In his multitude of explanations given for the general fall of prices, particularly of cotton fabrics, iron, steel, *etc.*, Mr. Atkinson has over and over again shown that it was due to the great economies created in the manufacture of these products by the use of modern inventions in improved machinery. Nobody has made it clearer that the fall in the price of cotton cloth from 15 to 2¼ cents a yard was due exclusively to that fact. When the Bessemer process was introduced in the manufacture of steel, and the cost of production reduced from over $100 a ton to $25, why did not the steel rail manufacturers keep the price of rails up at $100 a ton? The obvious answer is that they could not. Why? Because the margin of profit was so great that producers went into competition with each other and kept lowering the price as long as their margin of profit would permit, until the price reached the no-profit point with some of the competitors. With these the cost of production prevented any further cut and so long as they could stay in the market their necessary cost held up the price, and those who could produce at a smaller cost received the difference in profits. No other reason prevented cotton cloth from remaining at 15 cents a yard, where it was in 1830. .

The same reason has prevented silver producers from keeping the price of silver up to $1.29. Improved

methods of mining and extracting the metal from the
ore, as illustrated by the colossal machinery of the Anaconda Smelting Company in Anaconda, Montana, and
the appliances by which small increments of silver and
gold can be extracted from lead and copper ores as by-
products, together with the discovery of rich veins, have
lessened the cost of producing silver.   Competition between the various producers equipped with improved
processes of various degrees of efficiency, during the
last twenty-five years, has reduced the market price from
$1.29 to 61 cents an ounce.

Why has the price stopped at 61 cents? Why did
it not follow the cost of the Broken Hill Company's silver to 25 cents, or the cost of the Anaconda Mining
Company to nothing? For the same reason that the
price of steel rails has not dropped to the cost of the
Carnegie Company's product, nor of cotton cloth to the
cost of production in the best equipped and managed
mill in the country. But the price has dropped to the
cost of production of the most expensive competitors of
these best concerns. If the price of steel rails had
dropped to the Carnegie cost of production, neither the
Carnegie Company nor any other steel rail concern
would ever have $1.00 of profit. Carnegie would be
without profit, and all the others would be producing at
a loss. The price of steel rails is held up to the present
point, not by the small cost of the Carnegie Company,
but by the higher cost of his less efficient competitors.
So it is with silver. The price of silver is not and cannot be governed by the cost of producing it under conditions of greatest advantage, as in the Anaconda mines,
but by the cost of that portion of the required supply
which is produced under the greatest disadvantage.
Everybody acquainted with silver mining knows that
while there are some mines that produce silver at a very
low cost, like the Broken Hill mine, and some that get

it at no cost as by-product, there are many mines being worked in which it costs over 60 cents an ounce, and some that are worked at an actual loss, because the loss would be greater to let the mine stand idle.

For instance, the Ontario Mine, in Park City, Utah, cannot produce silver at sixty cents an ounce. It can only work in chambers that yield a certain amount of lead, which furnishes a by-product and makes the production of silver barely feasible. Yet in the same locality, if not in the same mountain-side, is the "Silver King" mine, which can produce silver at so much less cost that it can distribute about $40,000 a month in dividends.

The cost of production of the Broken Hill companies and the "Silver Kings" has practically nothing to do with fixing the market price of silver. The price is fixed necessarily by the cost of working the poorer mines whose products are needed to supply the general demand, and these bonanza mines reap fabulous profits to the extent that their cost of production is less than that of their dearest competitors.

Mr. Atkinson's elaborate and somewhat pretentious analysis of the cost of producing silver by the Broken Hill and Anaconda mining companies is utterly worthless as throwing any light whatever upon the cost of production as affecting the market price of silver, because the companies whose facts he presents are not those which exercise the controlling influence upon the price of the product. It is for that reason that his statements, quoted earlier in this article, though plausible to the uninitiated, really amount to flagrant misrepresentation to those at all familiar with the every-day facts of silver production.

It is only because the Broken Hill and Anaconda mining companies exercise practically no influence in keeping up the price that they are receiving the greatest bonanza profits. The workers of the smaller or less profitable mines, who are making no profit at all and much of the time struggling with a margin of loss, are the ones whose cost of production keeps the price of silver at sixty-one cents an ounce and permits the Broken Hills and Anacondas to reap colossal profits by virtue of their minimum cost.

Maximum cost and no-profit mines are being worked in every mining state in the West, alongside of highly profitable mining properties. These facts are familiar to the ordinary observer in every mining community. Therefore, Mr. Atkinson's conclusions, which are made regardless if not in ignorance of these facts, can only have the effect of creating in those communities disgust at his presentation as worthless, if not malignant, misrepresentation of the subject.

Mr. Atkinson's blunder in this matter is an example of what economic confusion and error come from mistaken notions or loose reasoning on the all-important subject of prices and values. If his presentation of the subject had been governed by the principle of differential cost, recognizing price movements as governed by the cost of the dearest increment of required supply, he would never have made the offensive blunder of dogmatically asserting that the cost of silver is from twenty-five cents to nothing an ounce, when the sustained price is sixty-one cents an ounce,—a blunder which is offensive in that all who know of the existence of mines in which the cost is over sixty cents an ounce cannot do other than regard his statement as a worthless misrepresentation, because it is manifestly contrary to what they know to be an every-day experience.

In the light, however, of the theory that the general price of any staple product is held up by the cost of producing the dearest portion of the supply the market will take, these facts presented by Mr. Atkinson, and those so familiar to the depressed miners who are working profitless property, become intelligible to everybody. From this viewpoint all the facts—maximum profits and declining profits, as well as profitless mining undertakings,—can be presented rationally and interpreted without offence to anybody. To the extent that Mr. Atkinson's presentation of this subject is understood to be the eastern view, will the West properly regard the East as misunderstanding and misinterpreting, not merely the silver question, but western interests in general.

The propagation of sound ideas on money and banking is the most important feature of industrial education for the immediate future. This country, more than any other, is open to grave dangers from misinformed and misdirected public sentiment upon this subject. Nothing can prevent the progress of much needed economic education more effectually than such uneconomic discussion of important industrial questions as is presented in Edward Atkinson's monograph on the cost of producing silver.

DISTINGUISHED ECONOMISTS :—RICARDO

David Ricardo is in many respects one of the most distinguished economists of the century. Of the permanent principles in economic science which experience and criticism have confirmed, Ricardo probably contributed more than any other economist. Unlike most economists since his time, Ricardo was not a professional economist. He not only did not teach or lecture in any college or university, but did not even receive a college education. His father was a Jewish merchant from Holland who settled in England early in life. His third son, David Ricardo, was born April 19th, 1772. The elder Ricardo was a successful member of the London Stock Exchange, and his son's education was directed with reference to following the same business.

His most distinguished disciple, McCulloch, says: "Classical learning formed no part of his early instruction; and it has been questioned, with how much justice we shall not undertake to decide, whether its acquisition would have done him service." Be that as it may, Ricardo was not a product of the college class-room but of the business mart, and his economic thinking, which was always virile, direct, and affirmative, dealt with the problems of real life which were confronting the public and perplexing the statesmen of his own time, and his economic doctrines were evolved from the discussion of these very questions.

His first appearance as an economic writer was in 1809, when he published a series of letters in the London *Morning Chronicle*. During the next two years he figured conspicuously in the discussion of the money question, which was then the topic of great national concern in England.

But it was in 1817 that Ricardo published his great

work (*Principles of Political Economy and Taxation*) which put him permanently at the head of the classical economists of the century. In this work he did more to clarify and establish the foundation principles of economic science than any writer before or since. Perhaps the chief criticism to be made on Ricardo is that in considering economic principles he was content to trace their application to the particular problem in hand, assuming that what would apply to the simple industrial conditions of England in the first quarter of the century would apply to the most complex conditions of all time.

In this way he left some of the most important and far-reaching truths of economic science in a partially developed state. Hence, much that he presented which was fundamentally true has since been the subject of confusing controversy. Prominent among these points is the doctrine of differential cost, which is the essential feature of the Ricardian law of rent. While Ricardo was not the first to state this principle, he was the first to elaborate it and command for it public recognition. This doctrine was that the market price of corn (wheat) was determined by the cost of raising corn on the poorest land in use.

Here we have the statement of the foundation principle of all price making and profit yielding enterprises. The difficulty with Ricardo, however, was that he was seeking to explain rent rather than prices and, while stating the principle that governed both, he elaborated only that which governed rent. By the statement of the law that the price of corn was governed by the cost of production on the dearest land in use, he found the principle which explained rent. Since the corn raised on the dearest or least productive land in use fixed the market price, manifestly that land could yield no rent, as the price of the product covered only the cost of working the land and marketing the crop. Recognizing what all experience taught, that in the open market prices tend to uniformity, he saw that whatever land would yield more for the same outlay would furnish a margin of profit, a part of which the landlord could demand as rent. From this he deduced the general principle that rent arises from the different degrees of productiveness of different land contributing to the same market, increasing as the cost of production falls below that on the least productive land in use.

This Ricardian law of rent has been almost universally accepted by economists of all countries. It thoroughly explained the principle of rent. It will be observed, however, that the very principle of rent, thus so clearly deduced as to receive universal approval, is a deduction from the law of prices, *viz.*, that prices are governed by the cost of producing that portion of the supply which is continuously produced at the greatest cost. All other portions of the general supply which are produced at a less cost yield a surplus, part of which may go as rent to the landlord, part to the capitalist in interest, and part to the entrepreneur as profits.

Although Ricardo incidentally stated this law in relation to prices, he elaborated and emphasized it only in relation to rent; so that his doctrine in regard to rent was accepted and its relation to prices was ignored. Ricardo was the one economist of his time who did not unconditionally accept the supply and demand theory of prices. Though he did not elaborate the theory of cost of production, except as just stated in relation to rent, the essential principle is there, and it is only in the expansion and application of that principle to all forms of prices, including wages, that a consistent scientific body of economic doctrine will ever be evolved.

EDITORIAL CRUCIBLE

LAST OCTOBER we greviously offended some very good people by doubting the wisdom and questioning the integrity of the management of the Citizens' Union movement in New York. The official announcement of this body that it now intends to nominate an independent state ticket for the purpose of defeating Colonel Roosevelt, if he receives the Republican nomination, more than sustains the worst we said. It is highly gratifying to see that Mr. Low himself has found the masqueraders out, and repudiates them.

AS WE PREDICTED would be the case, the free traders have begun to use the policy of expansion as an argument for establishing free trade. The *Boston Herald* has seriously laid itself out in a constitutional argument, showing that if we take the Philippines and Porto Rico we must have free trade between those islands and the United States. The *Philadelphia Record* admits it will be a costly undertaking to hold all the Philippines, and exclaims: "But if as a result trade shall be emancipated, who shall say the nation will not be the gainer?" This is true free trade doctrine. No sacrifice is too great to secure free trade.

THE DOLEFUL predictions so freely indulged in by the Chicago *Inter-Ocean* and other ultra-annexationist journals, forecasting the defeat of Thomas B. Reed for Congress, have all turned out to be mere empty talk, clearly indicating that the wish was father to the thought. The immense majority given Mr. Reed, putting him considerably ahead of his ticket, shows that the people of his district, reflecting the sentiment of the people of Maine, not merely sustain but believe in his anti-annexation attitude. Mr. Reed is too straight-

261

forward and strong a public man to be shouted out of court by mere noisy sentimentalists. His virile patriotism, strength of character, and comprehensive view put him clearly to the front as a statesman. In short, he is a better representative of the true American policy and statesmanship than any of those who have endeavored to detract from his power or compass his retirement from public life, in the interest of military conquest and a belligerent foreign policy.

So RARELY are we able to agree with the position of Carl Schurz on important national questions, that it is a pleasure to find a public utterance of his which has the true American ring. In a recently published letter he voices the sound American idea on annexation of Cuba and the Philippines:

" I heartily agree with my friend, ex-Senator Edmunds, in maintaining that the solemn declaration of Congress ' that the situation in Cuba and not the expansion of territory was the sole cause of the war ' forbids us to take and hold any territory by conquest, and that if we do that declaration will be dishonored.

" I am also convinced that the annexation of those territories would not yield us any commercial or other advantages to compensate us for the heavy burdens it would impose upon us, for the political demoralization it would bring in its train, or for the impairment of their national character the American people would suffer by it. I believe that we can get as many coaling stations or naval depots as we need without annexing populous territories with them, and that we can open new markets for our exports by suitable agreements connected with the peace settlement without violating our plighted faith, without burdening our people with costly armaments, and without entangling the republic with dangerous political responsibilities in. distant and tropical regions in which our political institutions can never prosper. I believe that such annexations will create in this republic a political atmosphere in which the government of the people, by the people, and for the people, will be in grave peril."

If national honor is to be anything of a distinguishing characteristic of our public policy, we are bound to live up to the spirit of our public declaration at the commencement of the war, *viz.*,—that freedom of Cuba and not expansion of territory was the cause and purpose of the war. It will be remembered that Spain denied that such was our object, and declared that we meant conquest. This view was reasserted by many of the journals and public men of France, Germany and other European countries. They clearly impugned the sincerity of our declaration, and predicted that American success would prove that it was an empty pretence.

To the extent that we now annex islands previously belonging to Spain, particularly Cuba and the Philippines, we shall demonstrate that their suspicions regarding our sincerity were well founded, and that our promise not to take is valuable only so long as we have not the power to take, and that, after all, our real policy is based upon

> The good old rule, the simple plan,
> That those should take who have the power,
> And those should keep who can.

COLONEL ROOSEVELT has won a permanent place, and a warm one too, in the regard of the American people. He is a man of positive peculiarities, constantly springing surprises by doing the irregular, if not the unexpected; but his surprises are nearly always in the right direction,—in the direction of honest, vigorous, wholesome, patriotic action. He always does something. Like the rest of the human race he makes some mistakes, but they are never the mistakes of indolence and indifference. Pharisaical neutrality has no place in Mr. Roosevelt's makeup. His errors are the errors of action; the errors of doing something. Colonel Roosevelt is not built on the plan that everything comes to him who waits, but rather on the plan that everything comes to him who works. It is doing that accomplishes, and that is why Mr. Roosevelt has such a warm place in the hearts of the American people to-day. He is by birth an aristocrat and by nature a democrat. He has the strength of character and good sense to be a reformer without being a mugwump. He can oppose boss dictatorship without denouncing party organization as mere corrupt machinery. Besides being a ranchman and a scholar, a reformer and a partisan, a rich man and a social student, he is a thorough-going, warm-blooded American patriot. All this has been demonstrated by his public action in different positions as legislator, Chairman of the Civil Service Commission, President of the New York Police Board, Assistant Secretary of the Navy, and Colonel of the Rough Riders in the Spanish War.

Much praise has been given to Colonel Roosevelt for the way he led his regiment up the hill at Santiago under the withering fire of the enemy. Referring to this in his farewell address to his regiment at Montauk Point, he said: "It was not so much bravery on my part. I had to run like hell to keep the boys from running over me." This remark shows the sterling quality of the man. In the case of most people the streams of compliment that have been poured out upon Colonel Roosevelt would have created an incurable state of swelled-head—a sort of Nebuchadnezzar estimate of his abilities,—but, whether he felt the swelled-head or not, he had the good sense to attribute the cause of his running to the enthusiasm of his comrades, so as to give them a full share in the compliment. Nobody will charge Mr. Roosevelt with being particularly modest; he is not unaware of his own abilities and ambitions and success, but he has what is so often lacking—the good sense not to let it spoil him.

This is shown also in the following advice he gave his regiment in the farewell speech referred to:

" Now here's a thing I want to warn you against: Don't get gay and pose as heroes.   Don't go back and lie on your laurels; they'll wither.   The world will be kind to you for about ten days, and then it will say: ' He's spoiled by the fame of the regiment in Cuba.' Don't think you've got to have the best of everything, and don't consider yourselves as martyrs in the past tense.   What I want of all of you is to get right out and fight your battles in the world as bravely as you fought the nation's battles in Cuba."

Whether Colonel Roosevelt is elected Governor of New York State or is called to serve the public in some other capacity, or is permitted to rejoin the ranks of useful, progressive citizens, he will always be known as one of America's distinguished characters and one of the best products of American institutions.

—————

It so seldom happens that a paper, and particularly a paper devoted to any special line of industry, talks sensibly on so-called monopolies, that we cannot resist the temptation to clip and reprint the following editorial from a recent issue of the *Shoe and Leather Reporter:*

" The Carnegie Company secured from the Rocke-fellers, on payment of a royalty of twenty-five cents a ton, the privilege of taking out of the ground not less than 1,200,000 tons of Mesaba ore a year.   They ac-quired in addition the control of the great Norrie mine on the Gogebic range.   This was all the hard and soft ore they could use for thirty years or more.   They made arrangements to transport it from the head of fifty cents a ton. In 1887 the transportation cost $2.25 a ton. As one and two-third tons of ore are used in the making of one ton of pig iron, there is a saving of $2.91 per ton. They built a railway by which the ore is carried from Lake Erie to Pittsburg at much less expense than formerly. These economies enable the Carnegie Company to obtain a profit on their iron and steel, and yet to sell them at lower prices than they were ever sold at before. Andrew Carnegie is characterized as a monopolist by men who hate the successful. The appellation of benefactor would be much more suitable to apply to him. It is the same with the great corporations which have grown up under modern economic conditions and have acquired wealth by cheapening production, at the same time lessening the cost of the products to consumers."

Of course, the Carnegies and Rockefellers are not to be regarded as philanthropists in contributing to the economic prosperity of the country. Fortunately for the public, their contributions to public welfare are an inseparable part of their own success. If they could succeed in making their millions without ministering to the public benefit, the public might be forgotten; but the economic construction of society is such that this is impossible,—their very efforts to make large fortunes necessitate the improvements which inevitably give the public a part of the benefits they create in cheaper and better products. Every book that is written and every paper published and every speech delivered which decries the idea of large enterprises, is a real enemy to public welfare.

There is no feature of public education which so much needs attention as the cultivation of wholesome ideas on this subject. It is, therefore, encouraging to see even a paragraph in a public print which aims at correcting the effect of the economic prejudice with which the social atmos here is fast etting surchar ed.

CIVICS AND EDUCATION

EDUCATION AND THE STATE

Not all that is entitled to the name education is to be found within school doors. Indeed, the little learning that is dispensed from the desks of pedagogues holds but a small place in the sum of knowledge acquired by the average man or woman through social contact and daily experience in the world of work and achievement. Emerson says: "You send your child to the schoolmaster, but 'tis the school-boys who educate him. You send him to the Latin class, but much of his tuition comes, on his way to school, from the shop-windows."

Education is commonly spoken and thought of as if it were something that applied only to the childhood and youth of life; the adult becoming a giver of instruction and ceasing to be a learner also. This is a part of the same fallacy that looks upon learning in general as a product of text-book-cramming, school discipline, and examinations. Every experience of life that adds anything to an individual's store of knowledge is an education; every social neighborhood is a school room, and every man is a center of educative influence, be it great or small, uplifting or degrading, to all who know him or whom he knows. Environment is the greatest molder and educator in the world, and the school is never out, nor the teachers off duty.

It is because this very simple but fundamental truth is little appreciated that so much false and narrow sentiment exists with regard to the limits of the educational function of the state. Almost without exception the best thought of civilization accepts the theory that school education for the young should be a public undertaking, conducted and supported by the community at

large. This policy has easily justified itself to the
reason. Childhood is ignorant and helpless. It does not
know what influences to admit and what to avoid. If
not given, in his youth, the benefit of the experience
and learning that have preceded him, man would consume the richest portion of his life in getting wisdom
by the hard road of guesswork, experimentation and
mistakes. He would exhaust his energies and capacity
for new achievement, in battling with crude difficulties
that the race has long since overcome and gone on to
the solution of the higher and more finely drawn questions of intellectual and ethical life and of social organization. So important is it, indeed, that every man and
woman should be started in life with this preliminary
equipment that the matter must not be left to the choice
of the children themselves, nor even to the will of the
parents, but some universal system must be provided
which shall not only put educational opportunities within the reach of all, but shall guarantee to these future
men and women the sound quality and usefulness of
the instruction given them. Private enterprise can
neither furnish this universal opportunity nor guarantee
and enforce this necessary standard of educational work.
The community must do it collectively, and do it, if
necessary, even against the will of the minority;—this
for the sake of social progress, and hence ultimately of
the survival of civilization.

Unlike very many of the lines of action carried on
by modern governments, the providing of free public
education has had the hearty endorsement of almost
every school of political and social philosophers. Herbert Spencer stands almost alone among this class in his
contention that all education should be left to private
enterprise. This position, however, is not so much the
result of any evidence of serious injury wrought by
the public school system as of a desire on Spencer's part

to be logical and thorough-going in his opposition to all kinds of state activity except preservation of order and administration of justice.

In the United States the public school system has always been one of the most popular features of our institutions; it has even become the center of a great deal of genuine sentiment, and is generally described as one of the foundation stones of the republic. As a result of this almost universal public sentiment on the subject, the public school system of the United States has made rapid and steady progress, both in the quality and efficiency of the work done by it, and in practical results. In the twenty-six years between 1870–71 and 1896–97, the number of public school-houses in the United States increased from 132,119 to 246,828, and the value of school property from $143,818,703 to $469,069,086. The total expenses connected with the construction and operation of these schools, including teachers' salaries, *etc.*, amounted to $1.75 per capita in 1870–71 and $2.62 per capita in 1896–97, almost all of this being raised by public taxation, state and local.

During this time also many compulsory education laws have been enacted, and child labor in manufacturing establishments prohibited in numerous states of the Union; the intention being to secure the practically universal attendance of children in the public schools. No protest against the increasing expense of providing this education has arisen anywhere, nor has the growing importance of the public school system in our national life been hailed with anything but satisfaction by political scientists and students of social institutions. Private initiative has had full sway in the one department of this work which the state could not occupy, *viz.*, development of improved educational methods. The new ideas in pedagogy proceeding from German, English and American universities have been and are being tested and adopted in our public schools, until the whole system of education in the United States is now as different from that of twenty-five years ago as are the many of our industrial methods from those of the 40's and 50's.

As we have said, all this has been readily accepted as in accord with sound principles of social and political science. It is nothing less than astonishing, therefore, that almost every other proposed line of state educational effort should have been, and even now be, so bitterly opposed, in the name of "economics," as unwarrantable interference with private rights. The primitive idea that education is purely a matter of schoolhouses and pedagogues seems wonderfully tenacious, and the *laissez faire* economists as a class rarely exhibit the least capacity to take any broader view of the subject. It is one of the unexplained mysteries why this school of doctrinaires, while admitting the propriety of public school education for children, should utterly fail to see that environment, which is the educator of both child and adult, as much as the pedagogue is of his pupil, is also a proper subject for the attention of the state. Yet they have fought step by step every reduction in hours of labor of factory operatives—a reform of a distinctly educative character in that it provides opportunity for broader social and intellectual life. They have opposed every attempt to restrict the foreign immigration which is furnishing, on such matters as standards of living, social conditions and ideas of government, a type of education full of danger to the progress and even safety of the republic. They have sneered at the trades-union movement and, until very recently at least, thrown their influence against it in practically every contest between capital and organized labor; although this movement, in its educative influence upon workingmen and in its possibilities along this

line, is one of the most important features of modern
society. Most persistent of all, perhaps, have been the
attacks of the *laissez faireists* upon tariff protection to
domestic industries,—a policy whose chief ultimate
effect is the creation of towns and cities, which are the
nurseries of practically all that civilization ever develops in education, science, literature, art and social refinement.

There are a few evidences of a broader attitude of
mind on certain kinds of state educational effort, even
among those who still rigidly adhere to the free-trade
doctrine. This broader attitude has come chiefly on
questions of municipal reform. The urgent necessity
of dealing with the pitiable and dangerous conditions
in the slums in our great cities has modified and even
reversed the no-government-interference prejudices of
a considerable class, and they have become the principal
advocates, not only of more and better public schools,
but of compulsory education, clean streets, prohibition
of child labor in factories, suppression of sweat-shops,
sanitary inspection, and creation of new parks, public
baths, recreation piers, and public libraries. They have
fought for legal enforcement of healthful conditions in
the department stores, as well as for limitation of the
hours of labor of shop girls. Some of them, particularly those interested in the university settlement
movement, have even come to the point of joining
hands with the trades unions in various efforts to improve the conditions of labor. Indeed, most of the
active municipal reform workers of this class have gone
so far as to demand out-and-out socialism in certain
directions, such as municipal ownership and operation
of gas and electric light plants, and of street railways.

Probably no more curious—even amusing—spectacle of philosophical inconsistency was ever presented.
The identical people who continually protest against

tariff protection as unjust interference of government
in private affairs and gross violation of the great principle of *laissez faire* are at the same time the organizers,
spokesmen and financial backers of all sorts of civic
leagues and political movements designed to compel
city governments to condemn private property to get
space for parks, raze old tenements owned by private
individuals, build municipal lodging houses, prevent
women and children from working even in their own
homes, and even assume the ownership and operation
of several important lines of private industry.

The truth is that on most of these municipal problems the old-school free traders have simply been
compelled, by virtue of their own practical common
sense, to ignore their political theories entirely and use
the means at hand to bring about manifestly necessary
and desirable results. If their sharing in municipal
reform movements were based on any logical doctrine
of state promotion of social and educational progress, instead of on a sort of sympathetic empiricism, they could
not possibly bring forward any general principle of no-
government-interference as an argument against tariff
protection. Once admit that it is the proper and scientific province of the state to act upon the social environments of the people, so that the educative influence of
those environments upon individual character shall be
progressive, stimulative and uplifting, instead of degrading and deadening,—once admit this, and the
methods of obtaining these results cease to be questions of general principle and become matters of practical feasibility. Tariff protection at once takes rank as
a scientifically correct policy, because of its indirect but
most far-reaching and effective educational influence in
diversifying industries and creating centers of civilizing
influence. To the practical objection that this policy
involves public taxation, the answer becomes: so do

public schools, so do clean streets, so do public libraries
and parks, so do effective systems of water supply, sanitation and drainage.   If the one is a system of robbery
of the many for the benefit of a class, then so is each
and every one of these other objects of public expenditure.   School children are a class no less than manufacturers; so are tenement-house dwellers, so are users
of public libraries and parks, so are the ''sweaters,'' so
are factory operatives.   Indeed, the complaint that tariff
protection means extortion from the many for the benefit of a class, if it had any point at all, would apply with
much greater force to almost all these other lines of
public action, for this reason: the tariff, by equalizing
the difference between the native and foreign cost of
production, merely establishes the possibility of an industry being conducted in the home country.   It does
not confer abnormal profits upon those particular industries, but simply seeks to give them approximate
equality of opportunity.   If its effect were really to
give exceptional profits there would be at once an
abnormal rush of capital into the protected industries—
a thing which has almost never taken place, and where
anything like it has occurred the result has been to
create such a competition that the temporary ''bonanza''
disappeared about as promptly as it came.   Thus, whatever indirect taxation results from a protective tariff
policy is not a special contribution to the pockets of
favored manufacturers, but is simply an investment of
the people in one very important form of educational
influence, *viz.*, the progressive urban centers that grow
up with the diversification of manufacturing industries.

On the other hand, the funds spent on public
schools, clean streets, sanitation, condemnation of old
tenements, *etc.*, are direct contributions by the community for the special benefit of particular classes.
Yet when do we ever hear taxation for these purposes

termed "Robbery of the many for the benefit of the few"?

The time is coming when a broader theory of the educational and protective functions of the state must be adopted. The predicament of those who are trying to retain some vestige of the minimum-government theory, and at the same time accomplish a whole series of social reforms by means of legislation, can only be avoided by abandoning the *laissez faire* doctrine and viewing the whole question of the state's functions from a new standpoint. In the let-alone doctrine there was at least this one very large grain of truth, that personal character is best promoted by self-reliance, and that whatever the individual can do best for himself alone he should be permitted so to do. Experience has proved, however, that there are very many lines of effort in which, were the individual to rely wholly upon himself, he would have no time or energy left for the higher duties and opportunities of life; also, that these selfsame tasks, as a rule, can be performed far more effectively and cheaply by the collective action of the community than by the divided efforts of each citizen. About all these lines of action are found to group themselves under a few general heads, such as preservation of order and security, administration of justice, supplying of educational opportunities and the right sort of educational influences, protection of higher against lower standards of social life, and the carrying on of a few simple enterprises of a public nature, wherein uniformity of service is the chief requirement, and highly expert managerial talent is not demanded, such as the building of public roads and furnishing of water supply and good drainage. To go much beyond these limits makes government a paternalistic hindrance and takes away the necessity of self-reliance and private initiative; but when the state confines itself to creating

and safeguarding *opportunities*, it does not do *for* the
individual, but simply enables him to do for himself,
on a broader and higher scale than would otherwise be
possible.

The natural tendency of the mind is to go to an
extreme—either believing enthusiastically in no-government (anarchy) or in all-government (socialism).
The rational social philosopher will recognize the serious dangers of either course in practical experience and
seek to follow in the line of sound reason, neither
ignoring the state nor erecting it into a god, but using
it simply as an instrument for securing to everyone
those general opportunities and environments which
the individual, unaided, cannot obtain for himself.   It
is no more rational to refrain from so using the state
because we cannot absolutely know just what environments will produce a good effect than it would be to
abolish public schools because all that is taught in them
is not true wisdom.   It is the function of the economist
and social scientist to study social conditions and learn
from experience what environments make for the progress and happiness of the race, just as it is the function
of the physical scientist to study the facts of the physical
universe and learn its laws.   It is then the business of
the statesman and of the pedagogue, in their respective
fields, to apply what has thus been discovered or learned.
Mistakes are made and can never be wholly avoided,
but if nothing were ever undertaken in public or
private life save that which could be guaranteed free
from error the world would come to a standstill to-
morrow.

H. HAYES ROBBINS.

CIVIC AND EDUCATIONAL NOTES

The Report of the U. S. Commissioner of Education for 1896–97 contains translations of the text-books
Teaching of Civics in Europe used for teaching civics in Switzerland and France. Though of a somewhat elementary nature, these little books give a very concise and definite statement of the working details of government in these two countries, and the Swiss text-book has also a brief history of the development of Swiss political institutions. In a future number we shall give a summary of this portion of the Commissioner's Report. Information of this sort is difficult of access to the general reader, and is seldom found in a form so concise and understandable.

Although it is now stated that room has been provided for all children who may apply for enrollment in
Overcrowded Schools Again the public schools of New York City, it appears that this is made possible only by a considerable extension of the half-time system. Inasmuch as about 3,500 children were turned away on the opening day some such arrangement of course had to be made, to avoid an odious reproach to the metropolis of America. But the half-time system, except for certain kinds of instruction, is not creditable and ought not to be continued a day longer than is necessary to complete the school buildings which were so long delayed by the exasperating debt limit controversy.

For a time after the inauguration of the present Tammany administration in New York City, Col.
Neglected Streets Waring's effective system of street cleaning was seemingly maintained, and there was little cause for serious complaint. Such, however, is no longer the case.

There is a distinct deterioration in the quality of service rendered, and the streets are not kept up to the former standard of cleanliness. A walk through the lower east side reveals a condition of dirtiness and neglect which, while not so bad as under the old Tammany system, is far worse than it ought to be or would be under a competent and progressive civic administration.

In Brooklyn the street pavements are being seriously neglected. Only 2½ miles of pavement of all kinds were laid in Brooklyn during the first six months of the present year, while during 1897, under the predecessor of the present Tammany Commissioner of City Works, twenty-five miles of street were paved or repaved. Moreover, practically all of the work now being done is simply the carrying out of contracts for asphalt and other first-class paving, left over from the previous administration. During 1896, under Mayor Wurster, about twenty-four miles of pavement were laid, and in 1895, under Mayor Schieren, more than twenty-eight miles. During the last year of Mayor Boody's administration (1893) only 2 miles of granite and one of asphalt pavement were laid.

It is the same old story. Tammany put forth, last fall, the usual hypocritical cry about "reform extravagance," and the people responded by voting for "economy and low taxes." As a result they are getting dirty streets, neglected pavements and arrest of additional street improvements. Every such experience merely confirms the truth, which certainly ought to be recognized in this day and age, that civilization not only costs something but is worth every penny of the expense.

SCIENCE AND INDUSTRY

IRRIGATION AS A CIVILIZER

Prosperity and social progress in the West is chiefly a question of diversification of industries and urbanizing of population. The latter is the real force ; indeed, the main reason why it is important to have a larger number and variety of industries throughout the agricultural ·West is that around these industries towns will grow up and cities ultimately be developed. Nevertheless, there is no reason to suppose that the gathering together of the population, which is to do away with the isolating, stagnating features of rural life, will come exclusively by means of manufacturing industries. The effect of these will be to bring progressive city influences and permanent city markets nearer and nearer to the farms, but other forces will have to contribute to any very direct alteration of the status of farm population itself. Undoubtedly the West will always be one of the great food producing sections of the earth. Agriculture will remain the principal industry and, therefore, something is needed, from a social standpoint, to draw a denser population into those sparsely settled regions and thus make it possible for the farmers themselves to live in village and town communities within easy reach, every day, of the lands they cultivate. In addition to the growth of factory towns, one of the greatest promoters of a complex population in the West, with opportunities for an increasing urban life and hence decreasing rural isolation, will be scientific irrigation.

There are enormous tracts of land in the West which, with proper irrigation, would support here in the United States probably the densest population in the world. This is the ultimate fact, of interest now chiefly in setting at rest any bugaboo scare about population outrunning the means of subsistence. The immediate interest of the West in irrigation lies, as we have suggested, more in its social consequences. This view of the subject is well set forth by Prof. F. W. Blackmar, of Kansas University, in a paper contributed to the *Kansas University Quarterly.* It seems to us a noteworthy and very encouraging thing that one of the clearest analyses of the needs of the West, from a broad scientific standpoint, that has recently appeared, should come out of the West itself. There is a sense, however, in which this is not surprising. Probably there is more real, serious thinking and study on social and economic questions among the rank and file of the population in the West than in any other section of the country ; which is merely another way of saying that despite all the mistaken notions and crazes that have come so far, and will come, the West is in a more hopeful condition as regards the final correct solution of these problems than is the East. It is more than probable that when the first emotional impulses for any kind of social reform have spent their force, and a broader knowledge takes the place of the superficial trash that has been vended throughout the West as economics and sociology during the last dozen or fifteen years, some great and far-reaching movements of genuine social reform will come out of that wonderful empire beyond the Mississippi, and carry the whole nation up to higher standards of economic, social and civic life. Scattered indications of that saner attitude of the western mind are important just because they denote the trend ; such an indication (for it is little more, perhaps) is this article by Prof. Blackmar.

Its interest does not lie so much in any discussion of the scientific features of irrigation itself as in the character of the writer's arguments. He bases his plea for a thorough-going system of irrigation in the arid regions of the West almost entirely upon social considerations, —chiefly, the need of large and complex population. We give a few extracts to illustrate this ::

"Modern irrigation, while it increases the means of the support of life, also has acted as a distributor of population. Nearly all irrigated lands have been divided into small tracts which by the use of water yield as great a return as larger farms without irrigation. This has made denser population in agricultural districts and thus relieved the congested districts. More than twenty years ago the writer rode over the plains of Fresno, California, where no house was to be seen, where a few sheep and cattle roved over land which furnished a scant pasture. Now, by the aid of water, densely populated rural districts with their schools and churches cover the land; villages and towns have sprung up and the land yields luxuriantly of nearly every fruit and vegetable product.

"*Other things being equal, the progress and activity of society depend upon the density of population.*

"Of course this must be within limits, for an overcrowded population will be as detrimental to progress as a sparsely settled population if the means of food supply is limited. But next to land, people are important for progress.

"Educational facilities are not good in sparsely settled communities for it takes accumulation of wealth to furnish the means of education. The possibilities of higher education are only guaranteed in densely populated countries. The possibilities of a modern Yale, Harvard, Johns Hopkins, Chicago, and Leland Stanford and other educational centers are possible only to wealthy countries filled with people. Indeed, the progress of state universities goes forward only with the increase of wealth and population.

"Our public school system varies greatly with the population. It is found to be poorest in outlying sparsely settled districts. It is best in densely populated districts that are not overcrowded. The point taken by our Superintendent of Public Instruction that it would be better to have fewer schools and better schools simply means that good schools cannot be well maintained in a sparsely settled district. Wherever the lands of New England have been partially depopulated the first signs of decay are noticed in the decline of the school house and the church. . . . .

"Among the evils of farm life is that of its isolation. There is a craving for social life. This craving is natural and in the line of all social development. The isolated condition of farm life is neither conducive to intellectual and moral growth nor to contentment and happiness. It certainly is not altogether the hard labor of farm life which causes so many young men to leave it for the towns and cities. Could they feel that there was something of interest and elevation taking place in the farm communities as there is in cities and towns, there would be a greater inclination for them to remain upon the farm. And the fact that so many of our best young men leave farming communities for other pursuits is indeed a detriment to farm life and to farming communities in general. Nor is this the worst feature of isolation. A careful observer must have noticed the growth of crime and suicide in farming communities during recent years. It cannot be owing entirely to agricultural depression, for indeed people of the cities have suffered as bad business reverses as those of the farm. We can only attribute this rapid increase of crime and suicide to the lonely monotony of the isolated farm life without means of interest or elevation nor indeed common association. The best development of modern life must be accorded to social contact. Indeed our language, our religion, our education and all higher forms of culture come. about through the association with our fellows. And if a denser population can be brought about by irrigation it will be a vast contribution to social advancement. The effect of a wider association is seen in the Grange movement which spread almost universally throughout the farming communities. In summing up the various influences of this movement it can readily be affirmed that its social influence is the greatest of all. So likewise might it be said for the Farmers' Alliance in its beginning. And I consider it very unfortunate that these two great organizations should have gone into politics and been subjected to the fortunes of political warfare. . . . .

"A highly developed political life is found only in a relatively dense population. The perpetuation of liberty means a discussion of the affairs of local as well as the affairs of the national government. And it is only through the discussion by men of varied interests looking from different standpoints that right ideas of popular government can be understood and maintained. The isolated conditions of farm life have been detrimental to every popular movement for the improvement of government that has ever sprung up in our Republic. It is strange to relate that all genuine movements for popular freedom have sprung up in towns and not in country places. The condition of political government in the South prior to the war was owing largely to sparsely settled communities. And so much were they wanting in means of education and political development that a large portion of the youth were sent to the North to be educated. Even now the South is scarcely recovered from antiquated political, social and economic usages. In local government and in economic organization it is still far behind the northern and western sections of the country. But we have

an illustration of the difficulties of local and state government when we turn our attention to the vast sparsely
settled portions of the western part of the state of Kansas.   Give those sparsely settled counties a relatively
dense population and they will teem with new life.
Political power will increase, better ideas of government will prevail, schools,'colleges, churches, newspapers, publishing houses, libraries, museums, will flour-
ish where now to-day it is with difficulty that a government is maintained in good form and the public school
system supported."

With reference to the economic effect of opening
up new agricultural territories by means of irrigation,
Prof. Blackmar makes a curious statement.   Starting
with the assertion that prices are determined by supply
and demand, he proceeds in the same paragraph to
prove, unconsciously perhaps, but very thoroughly and
exactly, that they are determined not by supply and
demand but by the marginal cost of production.
Thus :

" Prices are regulated according to the law of
supply and demand, and if a large amount of agricultural produce is thrown upon the market it will have a
tendency to lower prices until through the development
of other industries it should be absorbed.   But a small
amount of irrigable land in the United States could
scarcely be the controlling element in the establishment of prices.   Should Kansas develop the arid lands
of the West, she would be able to throw agricultural products into eastern markets and the markets of
the world more cheaply than could be done by agriculture in eastern Kansas, Missouri, or any other territory
where irrigation is not resorted to.   The products of
the irrigable lands would receive the same price regardless of cost of production as those of other lands
where the cost of production is greater.   The result

would be that larger profits would come to the irrigated land, or else prices would fall. Should irrigation be carried to such an extent that the farm produce should be increased sufficiently to cause a fall in prices, the poorer classes of farms would go out of use while still the irrigated lands would continue to be cultivated at a profit. Whichever result might occur, the irrigated lands would profit at the expense of other territory less favorably situated."

Prof. Blackmar could scarcely have given a clearer illustration of the true law of prices and its practical operation. What he observes in the case of produce raised on irrigated lands and on poorer lands, respectively, is exactly what also occurs all the time in the case of certain portions of the supply of every commodity regularly offered in the market. The reason why the more cheaply raised grain from irrigated lands would, as he says, get the same price in the market as that from lands on which the cost of production is greater, is simply that the price is determined by the cost of producing the dearest portion of the necessary supply. Competition will continuously operate to keep the price down to that point, but, so long as the dearest portion of the supply at any given time is needed, the price must cover the cost of producing that portion or the producers will withdraw from the field. If a new supply of more cheaply produced wheat, or cloth, or shoes, or hats, or beef, or iron, or coal or whatever comes into the field, competition soon forces out entirely what had been the dearest and price-determining portion of the whole supply, and the price falls to the level of the next dearest portion and so on. The cause of the fall in price, however, is not merely the increase of supply but the fact that the new increment is more cheaply produced than some portion of the previous supply. If the new increment were not produced any more cheaply than the dearest portion of the supply already being regularly offered, there could be no permanent fall in price. If the market did not need the newcomer's product, he would simply have to sacrifice his stock and perhaps go into bankruptcy; prices, after a temporary disturbance, would remain as before.

It is in just this way that the world price of wheat is determined. If the European crop is a failure, that portion of the whole supply becomes the dearest, and the price of wheat must be high enough to cover the European cost of production; then the American producer, with an abundant and more cheaply raised crop, of course gets the difference as profit. When our crop is small the American supply becomes the dearest, and the price will only cover our cost of production; Europe, if its crops are large, then gets the margin between its own cost of production and the price determined by our dearer supply. The same process would take place within the United States with reference to particular portions of the domestic crop. New increments of wheat from irrigated lands would drive the dearest competing lands in Russia or Argentina, or wherever, out of use, and, in years when the American supply was dearest in the world market, would even cause our own dearest wheatfields to be abandoned. The net result would be merely to transfer the point of profitableness in wheat raising from one section to another, not to injure the industry as a whole; while the consumers would get the benefit in cheaper bread.

In conclusion, Prof. Blackmar prophesies that the ultimate result of scientific and thorough irrigation would be so to improve the social status of farming, **as** an occupation, that the tendency of young men to leave the farms for the cities would **be** materially checked. He says:

" Thus we shall find that irrigation may become a

means of developing a permanent industrial life ; of reducing uncertainty of agriculture to certainty ; of removing restlessness and discontent. It will furnish a means of development of a higher industrial organization including a division of labor which shall furnish a means of the rapid accumulation of wealth. It will insure better educational facilities and a higher educational standard. It will develop better social conditions. It will elevate the religious life and develop the religious nature. It will furnish an opportunity for a higher political development which shall be conducive to good government and the administration of justice. Therefore with better schools and churches, with better means of social enjoyment, with a more perfect and satisfactory government, with good roads for rapid communication, with the use of the telephone and the electric light, with a better water supply and a more perfect sanitation, with a daily mail, carrying the news to every farm house, all of which are dependent upon a relatively dense population, farm life will be made the most attractive and wholesome life of the land. And these conditions brought about by irrigation may be extended to the fertile districts receiving sufficient natural rainfall until we shall find that farm life, so uncertain and unattractive in the past, shall become the most attractive of all occupations on account of its freedom and its social and political conditions. Then let us hope that the young man shall return from the college to the farm and help his fellow in building up the most free, enlightened and attractive communities found anywhere in this broad land. It is dangerous to prophesy but I will venture the conjecture that within fifty years in the United States there will be a change in the attitude of young men of good ability. Instead of seeking the law and medicine, and commercial and educational positions, they will return to the farm where they will find full scope for their educated abilities in the industrial, social, economic and political life which it offers."

It is useless to expect that the urban trend of population will ever entirely cease. Nevertheless, with greater density and concentration of rural population, one of the chief motives for deserting the farms will be diminished and a better quality of business talent will remain in agricultural pursuits. This would be an important and welcome result, and one that could easily come about alongside with the other fact that the more highly specialized, exacting and remunerative enterprises conducted in and from the cities will always continue to absorb the best skill and genius of the nation.

Many of the most important laws of social economics are merely formal statements of the simple common-
Demand, the Primary Force places of business experience, and because of this very commonplaceness their significance is often overlooked. For instance, the inventor Edison expressed, perhaps unconsciously, a fundamental economic truth when in a recent article he said that the first rule of success in invention is to "find out if there is a real need for the thing which you want to invent." This rule, as Mr. Edison also remarked, "will do for any other business in which you might wish to engage." In other words, demand is the real motive force behind all industrial and social progress, and the moral of this is that the first effective step in promoting business prosperity, good wages and social elevation of the lower grades of society is to stimulate and diversify the tastes and wants and standard of living of the people with whose conditions we are dealing.

———

The report of the New York State Bureau of Labor Statistics for 1897 contains some interesting data regard-
Labor Unions in New York State ing trades unions and wages during the first three quarters of that year. Thus, on March 31st, 927 labor organizations were reported; on June 30th, 976; on September 30th, 1,009. The total membership of these unions was, on March 31st, 142,570; on June 30th, 151,206; on September 30th, 168,454. These organizations covered 23 different industries, besides several classed as miscellaneous. The report as to wages also shows a steady gain, the average earnings of male members of these unions during the first quarter of 1897 being $155.06 each; during the second quarter, $159.12; during the

third quarter, $174.40. We are unable to determine from the report itself what method of averaging was employed to obtain these results, but since the same system was undoubtedly used in each case the figures given may fairly be considered as indicating at least the general trend of wages and of the trades-union movement. The showing is encouraging, because steady improvement in the conditions of labor is no less a forerunner than a consequence of business prosperity.

Prof. Frank L. McVey, of the University of Minnesota, has an interesting note in a recent number of the *Journal of Political Economy* on "Co-operation by Farmers." He describes the plan by which farmers of Steele County, Minnesota, in groups of 500 or more each, have erected and are now operating some nineteen creameries, dividends being declared on the basis of the amount of milk furnished by each farmer. One of these creameries costs from $3,000 to $5,000 to build, and the annual expense of operation is about $2,400. The aggregate receipts of all these creameries would permit a net return of $210 to each farmer interested, if all contributed equally. This system not only removes the drudgery of butter-making from the homes of the farmers, but insures them a prompt cash return for their dairy products, in place of the unsatisfactory "credits" allowed for butter by local stores.

Prof. McVey calls this a "co-operative" system, but it is so only in exactly the same sense that a railroad company or manufacturing corporation is co-operative. Enterprises of this sort are worthy of imitation among farmers everywhere, because they are in the direct line of industrial evolution; but they are strictly corporate concerns, and do not embody socialistic features, as the term co-operation, in its popularly accepted

Farmers' Corporations

v

CURRENT LITERATURE

A HISTORY OF CANADA *

This volume gives a very readable and interesting account of the history of Canada. With the laudable effort to make his country as important as possible in the arena of civilization, Mr. Roberts writes in such a way that one might imagine Canada soon to be, if it is not already, one of the greatest countries in the world. Yet this feeling does not prevent the writer from giving a rather clear and concise account of Canada's history despite his anti-American bias, which is constantly observable. He divides the history of Canada into three periods: (1) The period of French dominion, (2) The period of English dominion, (3) The period of confederation.

The history of the French period, which he regards as dating to the fall of Montreal in 1760, he gives at considerable length. He has great praise for the statesmanship of Talon, whose memory, he says, "should be honored from Ontario to the Gulf." This statesman evidently thought bachelors were very poor citizens. Mr. Roberts tells us (page 80) that, in order to promote the rapid and natural increase of the population of Canada,

"Talon exerted himself to procure in France suitable wives for the colonists, and as many as twelve hundred girls were shipped to Canada between 1665 and 1670. The girls, as a rule, were selected with great care, and usually from the country rather than the city, country girls being found best adapted to the rough life of a new land. Each girl on her marriage—and the weddings took place in batches of thirties as soon as possible after the coming of each ship-load—received a generous dowry from the King, with which to begin her housekeeping. Young men refusing to marry were made to feel the royal displeasure, and were not allowed to hunt, fish or trade. Under these conditions,

---

* A History of Canada. By Charles G. D. Roberts. 493 pp. Lamson, Wolffe & Company; Boston, New York and London. 1897.

290

bachelorhood became inconvenient in Canada, and presently uncommon."

Despite all this effort, however, to punish bachelorhood and put a premium on marriage, at the end of the French period, ninety years later, the population had only reached 60,000. The struggle for supremacy between the French and the English, which soon after the middle of the century became very fierce, grew with varying fortunes until the final triumph of Wolfe at the "Plains of Abraham." The success of the British over the French involved more for Canada than the mere transfer of authority. It involved a radical change of laws and customs. Up to this time Canada knew only French law and institutions, which in many respects were wholly unlike the English, especially with reference to the principle of trial by juries. The English, of course, insisted upon the introduction of English law. To the new conquerors the principle of trial by jury was insisted upon as the supreme safeguard of their liberty. The French did not seem to object to this in criminal cases. Indeed, they were glad of the new security from imprisonment without trial which this principle of the Magna Charta insured to them, but they were strongly opposed to having civil cases tried by jury. To their notion it was too tedious and expensive. They insisted that trained judges were more competent to try civil suits.

To the English, certain phases of French law were very obnoxious, especially those relating to the purchase of land, and to mortgage and marriage. Mr. Roberts says (page 177):

"By the seigneurial tenure the purchaser of land in a seigneury was compelled to pay to the seigneur the *lods et vents*, already referred to, which were an amount equal to a twelfth of the purchase-money, besides the full sum paid to the seller. As this tax was chargeable not only on the value of the land, but also on all buildings and improvement, which, while costing the seigneur nothing, were often far more valuable than the land itself, it was considered by the English settlers an intolerable handicap.

"The French law of mortgage exposed the new-comer to still greater hardships. By this law, when a man mortgaged his land in security for a loan the transaction was a secret one. Thus a man might mortgage his farm many times over, and then quietly sell it. The unhappy purchaser would presently see his property taken from him and sold to satisfy the claims of those holding the mortgages. Instances of this sort were not numerous, indeed; but very few were needed to make the 'old subjects' cry out, and demand a public registration of all mortgages.

"In regard to the property-rights conferred on the wife at marriage, there were provisions in the French law which English settlers, marrying in ignorance of them, found peculiarly exasperating. The wife, by French law, had two claims upon her husband's property, the one of 'dower' and the other of 'partnership.' The former gave her, in case of her husband's death, half of all his real estate; the latter gave her, even during his lifetime, half of all his personal property. It was in regard to this claim of partnership that the difficulty arose, for if the wife died before the husband, this share of hers went at once to her children, or, children failing, to her nearest relatives. Thus a man might find half of his personal property suddenly taken from him and handed over to strangers. Such a contingency could be guarded against only by a formal contract made before the marriage."

Despite these differences we are told that, during the ten years immediately following the conquest, "the country increased in wealth and population more rapidly than it had ever done before." The French, however, chafed severely under the working of the English law, and as a compromise the Quebec Act was passed by the French Parliament in 1774. One of the peculiar features of this Act was the restoration in that province of the French civil law and establishment of the Roman Catholic church as the state church. This practically made Quebec into a French colony, which it has ever since remained. This feature of the Quebec Act will prove a serious impediment to annexation of Canada to the United States, whenever the time for that arrives, unless in the meantime the separation of church and state in Quebec is voluntarily accomplished, since a state religion is definitely forbidden by the con-

stitution of this country. Clearly this part of the Quebec Act would have to be abolished before that province
could become a part of the United States.

But it is when our author reaches the period of the
American Revolution that his anti-American bias appears. Speaking of the American colonists, whom he
sometimes calls rebels, he says (pages 182-183):

"When the bugbear of French invasion no longer terrified them,
they clung no longer to the mother's skirt. No longer occupied in
fighting the enemy at their gates, they turned their turbulent energies
to fighting the officers of the King, the regulations of Parliament. That
they had bitter grievances the most hostile historian must allow. But
that these grievances were sufficient to justify them in setting their
swords to the throat of the motherland,—this is what no fair critic can
grant. That motherland had just been fighting their battles, pouring
out her blood and treasure lavishly to rid them of their foes. The
Seven Years' War, as far as England was concerned, was purely a war
for the colonies. In this imperial cause she burdened herself with a
debt that was in those days held appalling. It was not to be wondered
at that she should expect the colonies to contribute something toward
the payment of this debt. The only way in which they could be called
on to contribute seemed to be through the medium of taxes."

In describing the refusal of the thirteen colonies to
submit to taxation without representation, he adds:

"Their smouldering wrath, fanned by agitators and demagogues
who now strut as patriots across the page of history, flamed out at last
in open rebellion."

Speaking of the throwing the tea in the Boston
Harbor, he says (page 185):

"Boston was the center of the popular indignation. A revenue
cutter was attacked and burned. A merchant caught selling English
goods was stoned in the streets. The very preachers from their pulpits
stirred up the people to insurrection. Then came the childish farce of
the 'Boston Tea Party' (1773), when a band of Boston citizens, dis-
guised as savages, boarded a British ship and emptied her cargo of tea
into the waters. This, of course, was a deliberate felony, none the less
criminal because ridiculous; but it is sometimes held up to admiration
as a dignified and patriotic protest against unjust taxation."

It is in pleading the cause of the American Tories,
or "loyalists" as he calls them, that our author rises to
his greatest heights of eloquence. He charges England

with ingratitude and cowardice in neglecting to provide
for the loyalists in the treaty of peace.   He says: "She
was so bent on being generous to her triumphant enemies, that she failed in common justice to the friends
who had staked their all upon her fidelity and prowess."
But the optimistic temperament of our author finds a
way of seeing that this cruel injustice to the King's
faithful was in reality but a providential way of conferring an everlasting benefit upon Canada.   The cruel
neglect of the loyalists by England and their ostracism
by the American colonists drove them across the bor-
ders into Canada, and thus by a process of natural or
providential selection, sent the pick of the earth into
Canada to lay the foundation of her future greatness.
He exclaims (page 195):

"But the destiny that governs nations was working to great ends.
It was decreed that of stern and well-tried stuff should be built a
nation to inherit the northern half of this continent.   The migration of
the loyalists will some day come to be recognized as one of those movements which have changed the course of history.   It will be acknowl-
edged as not less significant and far-reaching in its results than the
landing of the Pilgrim Fathers.   For, without detracting from the
achievement of our French fellow-citizens, who have moulded a great
province, it is but truth to say that the United Empire loyalists were
the makers of Canada.   They brought to our making about thirty
thousand people, of the choicest stock the colonies could boast.   They
were an army of leaders, for it was the loftiest heads which attracted
the hate of the revolutionists.   The most influential judges, the most
distinguished lawyers, the most capable and prominent physicians, the
most highly educated of the clergy, the members of council of the
various colonies, the Crown officials, people of culture and social distinction,—these, with the faithful few whose fortunes followed theirs,
were the loyalists.   Many of them would never have consented to
dwell under the flag of the new republic.   Many others, accepting the
decision of the war, would have forced themselves to accept also the
new government; but for having remained true to their allegiance
they were hounded to the death as traitors.   Canada owes deep gratitude indeed to her southern kinsmen, who thus, from Maine to
Georgia, picked out their choicest spirits and sent them forth to people
our northern wilds."

With this choicest blood of the colonies and the

continuance of loyalist institutions, Canada ought properly to have forged ahead and left the United States far behind in the race of national growth. Yet for some reason, not quite clear to Mr. Roberts, this republic has not merely marched but galloped ahead, in population, wealth, freedom and everything that counts for a high civilization,ᐟwhile Canada, with loyalist stock and royalist government, remains a colony with an almost static population of less than five millions.

Notwithstanding this anti-American spirit, this severe criticism of the Revolution and the Revolutionists, and laudation of the loyalists, a modicum of which is true, Mr. Roberts takes on a more impartial spirit in tracing the subsequent history of Canada. In discussing the third period, the period of confederation, his tone is fair and his statements moderate, discriminating and interesting. Of course he is a free-trader, and whenever touching the national policy in relation to the United States, which he frequently does, the flavor of that doctrine always appears, and frequently to the disadvantage of the discussion.

His account of the Riel Rebellion and the Pacific Scandal, and the recent political history of Canada, is all that could be desired. Despite his bias against the United States, the historic trend of events has forced our author to note the possibility of final absorption of Canada by the United States. In forecasting the future of Canada, he says (page 439):

"The future presents to us three possible alternatives,—absorption by the United States, Independence, or a federal union with the rest of the British Empire. The first of these is the fate which, as we know, has long been planned for us by our kinsfolk of the great republic. The Monroe doctrine, already referred to, seems to anticipate it; for in the eyes of some American statesmen and historians it is the manifest destiny of the United States to occupy the North American continent."

Of course he enters his protest against this, and

disparages national independence. Therefore as the only means of escaping from ultimate annexation and absorption by the United States he concludes with the following almost pathetic plea for imperial federation (pages 440, 441):

" Meanwhile there is rising into view a grander idea, which appeals to a higher and broader patriotism. The project of Imperial Federation fits at least as logically upon our career as Independence. Indeed, it gives a fuller meaning to our whole past,—to our birth from the disruption of 1776,—to our almost miraculous preservation from seizure by the United States while we were yet but a handful of scattered settlements,—to our struggle for unity,—to our daring and splendid expansion,—and to the cost at which we have secured it. Independence, moreover, is selfish in its aims, while Imperial Federation considers not our own interests only, but those of the mother country, and the growing debt of loyalty which we owe her. It is possible to conceive of a form of Imperial Federation which would so guard the autonomy of each federating nation and so strictly limit the powers of the central government as to satisfy even those who desire absolute independence. The practical independence enjoyed under such a federation would be secured by the force of the whole empire. . . . . Imperial Federation would admit us to full political manhood without the dishonor of annexation, or the risk and the ingratitude of Independence. It would build up such a power as would secure the peace of the world. It would gain for our race a glory beside which the most dazzling pages of earth's history would grow pale. It is a less daring dream than that which Canada brought to pass when she united the shores of three oceans under the sway of one poor and scattered colony. It is Canada who has taught feeble provinces how to federate, how to form a mighty commonwealth while remaining within the empire. It may be her beneficent mission, also, to lead the way toward the realization of the vaster and more glorious dream."

THE COMING REVOLUTION. By Frederick L. King.
F. L. King, Publisher, Chicago, Ill. 1898. Paper
covers, 124 pp.

Like many thousand earnest but somewhat vision-
ary enthusiasts, Mr. King thinks he has a " message to
the workers of the world," capable, in his opinion, of
solving all industrial and social ills. He proposes to
abolish all middleman's profits by getting the people to
invest their savings in co-operative concerns, thus returning the entire profits of industry to the employees
and consumers. He wants to start a large colony out
West, somewhat on the Debs plan, and meanwhile to
get the movement under way by organizing co-operative
stores, *etc.*, right in the large cities of the East. He
does not propose any political action, and hence his
scheme has at least the merit of comparative harmless-
ness, although we should be sorry to see any considerable number of wage-workers put their savings into a
scheme that has been tried and proved practically worthless hundreds of times. Indeed, just why Mr. King
should imagine that this very old and often tested proposition is a brand new message to the world, we cannot
understand.

A sample of the free and easy way of handling
facts, common to most literature of this sort, might be
given. Throughout his book Mr. King refers to the
dense poverty of the workingmen, and often in the
same paragraph speaks of the vast accumulated savings
of these same people as a fund sufficient to start enough
co-operative enterprises to revolutionize the country.
On page 20, for instance, he declares that "the masses
are constantly getting poorer" and on the opposite page
(21) says that the annual earnings of the ten million
wage-workers of the United States " cannot *average* less

than about $500 each," and hence that "the *workers* of the country *are* the real capitalists."

Statistics show that the average per annum wages of workingmen employed in manufacturing industries in this country were only about $248 in 1850, $272 in 1860, $335 in 1870, $355 in 1880, and $446 in 1890. Mr. King may not be far from right, therefore, in placing the present average wages at about $500 per year, which is more than double what they received in 1850. We certainly hope that the workingmen of the country will continue to get poorer in this direction just as fast as possible; indeed, the faster the better.

——————

THE ARITHMACHINIST. A Practical Self-Instructor in Mechanical Arithmetic. By Henry Goldman. The Office Men's Record Co., Chicago. 1898. 128 pp.

This is a detailed exposition of the theory of mechanical computation and description of a clever machine invented by Mr. Goldman for relieving the mental strain on bookkeepers and accountants and reducing the liability of errors in addition, multiplication, *etc.*, to a minimum. For this instrument, which is of relatively small compass, he claims exceptional merits of simplicity and ease of operation. Whether the Goldman invention is thoroughly practical or not, there are evidently possibilities in this line; indeed, it seems as if there were almost no branch of industrial effort in which some sort of mechanical aid to human labor cannot be invoked.

AMONG THE MAGAZINES

In the course of an eulogy of Bellamy, in the August *Arena*, Editor Ridpath says that practically "all of Bellamy has been accepted *except* his remedial agencies and his prophetic indications." If this is true, then Bellamy has proved a more useful contributor to social progress than we had ever imagined. Many of his criticisms of existing social institutions were utterly unwarranted, but unquestionably they set people to thinking more seriously than ever before about numerous societary defeets that ought to be remedied. If, therefore, Bellamy's readers have accepted him to the extent of becoming interested in social reform, but have rejected his crude and impossible schemes of *presto, change!* regeneration, then his work was of genuine benefit to the world. Such an outcome would be a tribute both to Bellamy and to the good sense and judgment of the American people.

The
Arena

In the issue of this magazine for August 13th there is a striking article signed "Diplomaticus," quoted from the *Fortnightly Review*, London. The writer asks the question, "Is there an Anglo-American Understanding?" and argues that the logic of Mr. Chamberlain's famous Birmingham speech of May 13th last strongly indicates that there is such an understanding already in force. He bases the probable grounds for such a tentative alliance upon community of industrial and political interests in the new era of international developments opening before us. Several incidents have occurred to support this view that an understanding of some sort already exists between the two countries, and if this should prove to be the case it ought to be welcomed on

Littell's
Living
Age

this side of the Atlantic, provided it does not obligate us to become directly embroiled in England's territorial problems in the Orient. With these she is no less capable of dealing effectively and successfully now than heretofore.

————

An article of exceptional interest, as coming from a gentleman prominently connected with the organized Sociology and Philanthropy charity movement, is that on "Sociology and Philanthropy" in the *Annals of the American Academy* for July last, by Frederick Howard Wines, Associate Editor of the *Charities Review*. We call this article exceptionally interesting because it shows a trend of thought regarding charitable movements which is as wholesome as it is unusual among those directly concerned in them. In the first place Mr. Wines rejects the idea (very popular in some quarters, since it has the sanction of Herbert Spencer, who, indeed, employs it throughout his entire work) that sociological phenomena can be treated by the same rules that apply in the realm of biology. The basic proposition of this theory, *viz.*, that society is an organism, lays a logical foundation for state socialism, and makes the state superior to, instead of merely an instrument for carrying out the will of, the individual. On this point Mr. Wines says:

"I have long since discarded for myself my early prepossession in favor of certain once popular trends of sociological thought. I no longer believe in the preponderating value of the biological method of approaching the study of sociology. The biological analogies between the life of a plant or an animal and that of society do not appeal to me as once they did. Interesting and suggestive as they are, they are after all but analogies, not identities of relation or mode of action, and metaphor is not argument. They are worth something as illustrations, and may cast a sidelight upon truth, but, if followed too fast or too far, they are more apt to prove misleading will-of-the-wisps than torches to the patient seeker after truth. Society, if it is an organism at all, is not an organism of the same kind as a plant or an animal, and it is of more importance to point out the differences than the resemblances between them."

Coming directly to the question of applied sociology, he says, correctly, that the philanthropist, in his practical efforts, requires the knowledge and intelligent direction which only the broader studies of the sociologist can give. This broader study reveals the fact that charity is only a temporary expedient for relieving conditions that ought to be abolished entirely. Thus: "Charity is a fine thing, no doubt; but justice is a finer. Justice is fundamental, charity supplemental. Charity steps in to relieve the situation where justice has partially failed."

One of the best lines in which beneficial philanthropic efforts can be exerted is in the encouragement and extension of sociological and economic teaching as to the real causes of poverty and the lines of public policy and private action necessary progressively to remove it. The trouble lies not so much in unjust distribution of wealth, as Mr. Wines seems to imply, as in lack of opportunities, of incentive, of stimulus, of education, on the part of the poor. It is to the raising of these lower social levels, not by mistakenly pulling down the top of the structure but by definitely applying pressure at the bottom where it is needed, that public effort should be directed; and the promotion of public education in this direction is one of the highest and greatest opportunities of philanthropists to-day. A contribution to this end is a positive step towards abolishing poverty; the same benefaction if applied to purely charitable effort may be a means simply of perpetuating the evil it seeks to relieve.

Institute Work

THEORY OF NATIONAL DEVELOPMENT

In the evolution of society the nation is the political formation through which alone civilization, with all that implies, is developed. It is the highest type of the group principle through which the differentiating influences of social forces operate. Recognition of the principle of group development is of prime importance in the study of political science. This is in reality the distinguishing feature of modern civilization. The general characteristic of ancient, particularly Roman, civilization was universal government. The aim and object of Roman policy was to bring all the known world under the political government of Rome ; in short, to establish a universal empire.

This type of government is incompatible with a high, complex civilization. Universal uniformity, or even conformity, necessarily involves universal simplicity. High complexity of life and great variety of tastes, habits and aspirations, necessarily beget a great variety of demands and policies. Consequently, as civilization advanced, industrial, social, religious and political interests and points of view multiplied, and segregation into groups having some common purpose and social and political affinity became inevitable. People can only progress by making new experiments, and this can only occur where some general consensus of opinion and desire prevail. Thus we find that universal government is compatible only with low civilization and simple industrial and social habits, and that it is superseded by group formation and national development as the industrial and social life increases in complexity. Compare China and Russia with England and the United States.

The group is the background of social opportunity. It furnishes social influences and education to the individual units. Through the natural affinity between the members of the group, the conduct and ideas of each operate upon those of all. This is impossible where the class chasm is so great that intercourse is impossible. For instance, the inhabitants of Mott Street would learn little by associating with the " Four Hundred " of Fifth Avenue. They are in every way too far apart directly to influence each other. They must each draw their inspiration, criticism and general cultivation from the influences that operate through the group to which they belong.

Now this is true throughout the whole gamut of social life. The more complex the civilization the greater will be the number of group formations. The greatest group feasible is the nation. The nation is the grand aggregate in which all the smaller groups, industrial, social and political, have a common purpose and general affinity, and it must be sufficiently homogeneous for the top and bottom to touch in some of the phases and forms of life. It is through the nation as a political entity that the general influences and type of civilization are evolved. Thus, for instance, the nation whose laborers are mostly slaves cannot have as high a type of civilization and political institutions as one whose laborers are free, well-paid wage earners.

The nation, therefore, may properly be regarded as the nursery, kindergarten and common school of civilization. Without it, high types of complex civilization and free institutions would be absolutely impossible. The prime duty of statesmen, then, is so to direct public policy as constantly to promote the conditions, influences and opportunities that make for national develo m n because it is only through the institutions and influences of life within the nation that society can advance.

It is as true of nations as of individuals that their highest duty is to make the most of their own possibilities. It is only by making the most of one's self that one can contribute the maximum aid to others. The nation which develops the highest type of social life and political institutions contributes the most to general civilization, because it solves the largest number of economic and social problems. It furnishes the greatest leadership in civilization, and the best methods of promoting social welfare.

Recognizing, then, the importance of national development, the student of political science is concerned at the very outset with the principles and methods which promote the growth and expansion of national life. There is no principle truer in social life than that the type of society is mainly formed by the type of industries by which the people earn a living. If the industries of the nation are simple and uniform, any considerable degree of social diversification and national development becomes practically impossible. For instance, take a nation in which the industries are principally agriculture, mining and forestry. The industrial habits of the people will be so simple and uniform that their social life will be almost static. China is an illustration of this uniform simplicity, or non-diversification of industry. Russia is another illustration, though not of such long standing and hence not quite so stereotyped.

With diversification of industry we necessarily have diversification of interests and growth of new and competitive ideas. This is the yeast of social evolution. The introduction of new interests is the life of progress. Without it, social advance can never occur. Clearly, then, the mainspring of national development is the diversification of industry, because out of that only can come the social and olitical differentiation and activit

which shall make for new and higher forms of civilization. If one type of industry, therefore, will contribute
more to the national welfare and social development
than another, that type should be encouraged. This
necessarily involves application of the protective principle in society. Wherever diversification of industry
and social life requires the aid of collective social action,
it is for the interest of society that the protective influence of the nation be given. This may be exercised
in a hundred ways. Compulsory education is one form
of protection. All the machinery of the judiciary and
police functions are of a protective character. Indeed,
government itself came into existence as a social necessity to fill various protective functions.

In the simplest form of primitive society there
were practically no political institutions. With every
step in the growth of new interests and new ideas came
some innovation of political institutions. Each step in
the development of modern government, from its very
earliest stages, has been the result of society's effort to
institute collective authority for the better protection
and promotion of individual and social interests. Every
modification of existing laws, every radical change in
form of government, is brought about for that purpose
and that purpose only. In reality, therefore, every
political institution directly or indirectly fills some protective function. It is for that purpose such institutions
came into existence, and when they cease to fill that
function " reform " is demanded, and a modification or
a radical change is brought about, which will supply
the new kind of need. We may say, therefore, in the
broadest and most philosophic sense, that government
is essentially a protective institution; but we must not
here confuse protection with paternalism.

There is a marked difference between a paternal
government and a protective government. Paternalism
protection means guarding

the opportunity for the people to do for themselves. These two forms of government are frequently confounded, and those who are opposed to protection *per se* (usually because they do not understand it) make a special effort to create the impression in the public mind that the two are identical; that protection is only another name for paternalism, and that paternalism is necessarily bad. Both of these statements are wrong. Protection is as different from paternalism as democracy is from despotism. But it is not true that paternalism is always bad. Whether protection or paternalism is the better policy for a nation depends entirely upon the state of civilization.

In the early stages of society, where social simplicity, political ignorance and industrial impotence prevail, a merely protective government would be as futile as democracy. In that crude state of society, paternalism is the more efficient and hence the superior form. For instance, in Russia to-day and in many other countries where political despotism, industrial monotony and social simplicity generally prevail, industrial progress might be greatly hastened by a thoroughly paternal public policy. For instance, if Russia waits for individual initiative in the building of railroads and introduction of diversified industries, she may linger in her present agricultural and practically mediæval state for an indefinite period. If, on the other hand, the government would build factories and conduct manufactures, as it has built what railroads there are in Russia, and simultaneously give the maximum encouragement for individual investment in similar directions, Russia's industrial progress towards nineteenth century conditions might be hastened by several generations. In a low simple state of society there are neither capital, energy nor ideas that can create industrial initiative except by the slowest process of evolution, and any innovation of ca italism must come from without.

Under these conditions the government is the most effective power in the community in industrial enterprise as well as political control.   Clearly, therefore, paternalism is not necessarily an evil under all conditions.   It is an efficient form of collective action in a simple state of civilization.

On the other hand, when society has passed the primitive stages of industrial and social life and reached a period of individual initiative, popular representation and capitalistic enterprise, then paternalism becomes a coddling hindrance and protection becomes the true form of political policy.   In other words, when the era of individual initiative, capitalistic enterprise and popular government is reached, the highest function of government is not to do for the individuals, but to limit itself strictly to protecting opportunities for individuals to do for themselves.   In short to furnish *opportunity*.

This is entirely consistent with the universal principle of progress.   The advancement of society from theocracy to democracy consists of a series of industrial, social and political changes which tend ultimately to increase the sovereignty of the individual and diminish the authority and arbitrary power of the government.   This is as true of society as it is of the individual.   In the early years of childhood it is the manifest duty of the parents not merely to give opportunity for the children to do as they please, but to do certain essential things for them.   The next stage is to encourage the idea of the child beginning to do for himself and, after the period of individual initiative is reached, parental authority diminishes and individual responsibility increases.   So with the childhood of society, paternalism is the more efficient form of governmental activity, but true statesmanship and political philosophy will so use the paternal function of government as ultimately to render it unnecessary, so that
omes onl protective.

The function of government under representative institutions, or in the protective era, is manifestly, then, to use the collective influence of political institutions to protect and promote the industrial and social opportunities. To repeat what has often been emphasized in these pages (because it is so fundamental to a correct comprehension of the principles of political science) all social and political unfoldment and progress arise directly or indirectly out of the habits established by the modes of industrial life under which the people live. People live as they work. Speaking particularly, therefore, the character of their employments shapes the character of their social life, and the social life shapes the character of political institutions. Diversity of industrial occupation means diversity of social life and ideas, and this is the key to political advance. The prime function of government, therefore, in modern society, is first and foremost to insure, so far as possible, protection and encouragement to all the opportunities and conditions for diversifying the industries of the people. Public policy and domestic legislation, peace or war, expansion or contraction of territory, should all be subordinated to this one great fact, because this is the source and mainspring of the differentiating forces and progressive inspirations which make for broader national life and higher civilization. With this, all else will come ; without it, nothing worth having will come. It is not extension of territory but expansion of civilization that makes for national greatness. It is not to utilize our natural resources, but to civilize our population, that government should be used.

Briefly, then, the theory of national development is the theory of broadening the social life and increasing the individual freedom and sovereignty of the citizen. To aid and promote all the opportunities and forces which make for this end is the true function of overnment.

WORK FOR OCTOBER

OUTLINE OF STUDY

The Gunton Institute Course in Political Science is divided into eleven general sub-heads, shown in the curriculum published in the GUNTON INSTITUTE BULLETIN of September 24th. This curriculum was also published in GUNTON'S MAGAZINE for September, but since that time two or three additions have been made which materially extend the scope and increase the value and interest of the course. Thus, an entirely new topic has been inserted, as Number III, on "Evolution of Political Institutions," with five sub-divisions; also, under the topic "Theory of Statesmanship," two sub-divisions have been added, *viz.*, "Political Parties" and "Civil service; spoils *vs.* merit system." Then, in the section "The State and Labor," a sub-division on "Hours of Labor" has been inserted, under which will be treated the very important question of legal restriction of working hours in manufacturing establishments, looking forward to the general eight-hour day.

The eleven topics in this course will be covered in monthly lessons in the magazine, from October to May inclusive, consisting of a lecture by Professor Gunton on the topic for the month, an outline of required and suggested reading in certain standard works, with notes and suggestions on the readings, a question box, and suggestions to local centers, with programmes for meetings. The work for October covers Topics I and II of the curriculum, as follows:

I. THEORY OF NATIONAL DEVELOPMENT.
   (*a*) Importance of group development.
   (*b*) Influence of diversified industry in national welfare.
   (*c*) Influence of patriotism.

II. NATURE AND FUNCTION OF GOVERNMENT.
   (*a*) Paternal vs. protective aid.
   (*b*) Individual and the State.

REQUIRED READING

In "Principles of Social Economics," Chapters I
and II of Part IV. In GUNTON'S MAGAZINE for October,
the class lecture on "Theory of National Development." In GUNTON INSTITUTE BULLETIN No. 3 (Sept.
24th,) lecture on "Need of Political Education."

SUGGESTED READING *

In Burgess's "Political Science and Constitutional
Law," Chapter I of Book I, Part I; Chapters I and IV
of Book II, Part I; Chapter I of Book II, Part II. In
Spencer's "Illustrations of Universal Progress," Chap-
ter X. In Willoughby's "The Nature of the State,"
Chapters VI and XII. In GUNTON'S MAGAZINE for Oc-
tober, article on "Education and the State." In GUN-
TON INSTITUTE BULLETIN for Sept. 10th, lecture on
"Our Country."

NOTES AND SUGGESTIONS

Required Reading. The first chapter assigned in
Professor Gunton's "Principles of Social Economics" is
on "Laissez faire as a Guiding Principle in Public Policy;" it may be called a justification of the state as an
instrument of authority in human society,—a demonstration that the best government is not necessarily that
which governs *least*, as the popular saying has it, but
that which governs best, whether much or little. The
only strictly scientific statement on this point is that the
best government is the one that most nearly fits the
needs of the people; in a low civilization this generally
means autocracy of practically a despotic type; in a
highly complex and enlightened society it means restricted governmental authority and almost complete

---

* Books here suggested may be obtained of publishers as follows, if not available in
local or traveling libraries : *Political Science and Constitutional Law*, by John W. Burgess, Ph.D., LL.D., of Columbia University ; Ginn & Co., Boston ; 1891 ; 2 vols., 337-404
pp. $5. *Illustrations of Universal Progress*, by Herbert Spencer ; Appleton & Co.
New York, 451 pp. $2.00. *The Nature of the State*, by Westel Woodbury Willoughby
Ph.D., of Johns Hopkins University ; Macmillan & Co., New York ; 1896 ; 448 pp. $3.00

individual liberty.   In either case it is the character of
the people that determines the character of the government.

The second chapter discusses "The State; or, the
Nature and Function of Government."   In this, the idea
just developed is carried still further and it is shown
that all governments, whether despotisms or democra-
cies, are, in a broad sense, representative of the people
living under them.   The moral of this is, of course, that
the first step in reforming and liberalizing a government is to raise the industrial, social and intellectual
status of its subjects.   In the next place it is shown that
while the no-government idea is entirely unsound, the
government should always be treated and thought of
only as an *instrument* for accomplishing certain desired
things that can be done better by the joint action of the
community than by individual efforts; it is only a means
and never an end in itself; improvement of the individual is the end.   In other words, to go into the matter
more technically, the state is a voluntary *organization* of
individuals, not, as Herbert Spencer and others have
tried to show, an involuntary *organism*, of which each
individual is merely a functional part.   That theory
logically makes the state the supreme end of all human
exertions, and leads directly to socialism, with the community owning and managing all forms of business and
productive industry, as the proper form of government.
This "social organism" idea is analyzed in detail in the
chapter under consideration.

Having shown the fallacy of the no-government
doctrine, which means simply social neglect and indifference to societary evils, and likewise of the social organism or all-government theory of the state. which
means abolition of personal independence and self-reliance and deadening of all the competitive incentives
to progress, Professor Gunton proceeds to outline the

true scientific functions of the state, describing them as the *protective* and the *educational*. These terms carry a very much broader meaning than they at first suggest; so far from referring alone to tariffs and public schools, they embrace every phase of wholesome legislative effort designed, on the one hand, to stimulate social progress and give *opportunities* for self-improvement, and, on the other, to guard each great societary group against dangerous and retarding influences, whether from within or without. What these proper educational efforts are will be considered in detail when we reach the topics "The State and Labor" and "Municipal Government;" the protective functions of the state are to be treated under "Protection," in the January lesson. Both will be touched upon indirectly under the topic "Theory of Statesmanship."

In the class lecture on "Theory of National Development" which appears at the head of this department this month, Professor Gunton brings out a point not fully covered in his book, namely, the theory of *group* development, as the great, essential condition of social progress. It is this primary natural law that at bottom makes necessary and justifies the separation of the human race into nations, and lays a solid and enduring foundation for patriotism. Indeed, when it is recognized that the world progresses to higher and truer civilization only as its various national groups progress, and that through and by means of the complex, yet harmonious, development of such groups the greatest contributions to civilization are made, patriotism becomes one of the noblest of all human sentiments.

In the Bulletin lecture on "Need of Political Education," which we have included in the required reading this month, Professor Gunton points out the importance of accurate and comprehensive knowledge of the principles of political science, as a necessary basis of intelligent citizenship. Most important of all is it to obtain a definite *point of view*, from which one can determine the correctness or error of the various lines of proposed public policy, and shape his action accordingly. The present course is intended, primarily, to give just that clear, intelligent and definite point of view.

NOTES ON SUGGESTED READING

It is not probable that Professor Burgess's " Political Science and Constitutional Law " will be found in the average local library, and, unless state traveling libraries are available, the only way students can avail themselves of these volumes is by purchase. In some cases the members of local centers may desire to club together and purchase a few standard works of this character. The reading suggested in Burgess's " Political Science " this month is all to be found in volume I, and is strongly recommended. The first chapter mentioned is on " The Idea of the Nation," and defines the nation as a population of ethnic and geographic unity; clearly distinguishing this from the *state*, which is the political organization of a nation. In the next chapter (No. 1 of Book II), Professor Burgess treats " The Idea and the Conception of the State," showing, in a very logical discussion, that the state is and must be, first, all-comprehensive, embracing all persons living under it; second, exclusive, allowing no rival authority within the same limits of organization; third, permanent, since the sentiments and necessities from which the state springs are inherent in human nature; fourth, the state is sovereign, and must be considered as possessing absolute ultimate power. This view of course makes it necessary at once to distinguish between the state and *government*. The state, being the whole organized population, can set up any form of government and limit or extend its powers; so that, while the government may be greatly restricted, the state is absolute, simply because there is no higher source of human authority. This absoluteness, moreover, as Professor Burgess shows, instead of being inconsistent with individual liberty is its source and support. He well brings out this point in the next chapter suggested, *viz.*, "The Ends of the State." Thus: "There never was, and there never can be, any liberty upon this earth and among human beings outside of state organization. Barbarie self-help produces tyranny and slavery, and has nothing in common with the self-help created by the state and controlled by law. Mankind does not begin with liberty. Mankind acquires liberty through civilization. Liberty is as truly a creation of the state as is government; and the higher the people of the state rise in civilization, the more will the state expand the domain of private rights, and through them accomplish the more spiritual as well as the more material ends of civilization; until, at last, law and liberty will be seen to be harmonious, both in principles and practice."

The ultimate end of the state is described as "the perfection of humanity; the civilization of the world; the perfect development of the human reason, and its attainment to universal command over individualism; the apotheosis of man." The steps by which the state attains this end are, first, the establishment of government and liberty,—that is, determining in what directions the individual's conduct must be controlled and in what left free; second, the promotion, by means of government and liberty, of the highest *national* civilization. The final purpose—world-civilization—will be achieved only through perfection of the national types.

The last chapter suggested is on "The Idea, the Source, the Content, and the Guaranty of Individual Liberty." In this the ideas just developed are carried out more in detail with reference to one of the steps, namely, establishment of liberty, by which the state works towards its final purpose. It is shown how the methods of establishing liberty, as well as the amount and kind of liberty, vary in different states and under different degrees of civilization. The United States, according to Prof. Burgess, is the only great nation in which the state itself does actually establish and guarantee liberty as well as government ; this it does by means of the Constitution. In other countries the line of distinction between the state and the government is, as yet, quite unclear, and the state, instead of establishing both government and liberty establishes government only, leaving to government the privilege of granting or withholding liberty. This is best illustrated in the case of England, which has no written Constitution ; practically all the popular liberties being secured only by Parliamentary enactment.

The chapter suggested in Spencer's "Illustrations of Universal Progress," is on "The Social Organism." This is the chapter analyzed by Professor Gunton in the reading given in "Principles of Social Economics," and requires no special comment here.

In Doctor Willoughby's book, "The Nature of the State," we have recommended the reading of two chapters, one on "The True Origin of the State," the other on "The Aims of the State." The author goes quite deeply into the psychological aspect of the question in discussing the origin of the state. He finds it to proceed originally out of "a sentiment of community of feeling and mutuality of interest." The political organization which we term the state, however, is not formed as the result of a sum of individual wills, but of a *general* will which consists only of "certain sentiments and inclinations that concern general interests." Doctor Willoughby, it is important to note, entirely rejects the Spencerian idea that the state is an organism.

The other chapter suggested in this work, *i.e.*, on
" The Aims of the State " is important and significant.
It is a logical and wholesome discussion of the proper
extent and limits of the state's control over private action, from the standpoint of the highest expediency.
The author first dissects the anarchistic theory, that the
state has no proper functions at all and should be non-
existent; and then takes up more at length the individ-
ualist idea that the state should only apply itself to
maintaining order, and that, as morality and knowledge
increase, the state's activity will diminish and ultimately cease entirely.   Spencer is the most prominent representative of this view.   Its four essential postulates
are; first, that self-interest is a universal principle in
human nature; second, that each individual knows his
own interests best and, if unrestrained, will surely follow them; third, that in the absence of external restraint free competition will exist and, fourth, that this
free competition always develops the highest human
possibilities.   Admitting, for the time being, the first
point, Doctor Willoughby emphatically denies the second, showing how, in such cases as compulsory education, sanitation, *etc.*, large groups of people do *not* know
their own interests best, and require coercion.   Even
the third point " is also not necessarily true.   Genuine
competition is possible only where the contesting parties possess comparative equality of strength.   Where
there is not this equality a contest means·not competition, with any of the resulting benefits that the fourth
postulate predicates, but simply a destruction of the
weaker party. . . . Furthermore, as Professor H. C.
Adams has shown in his excellent monograph, *The State
in Relation to Industrial Action*, law may often serve not
so much to check competition as to raise its moral
plane."

The fourth proposition is likewise refuted very

thoroughly. Following Lester F. Ward's line of argument, Doctor Willoughby shows that unrestrained competition is at once the most wasteful and most cruel means of bringing about the "survival of the fittest," and also that "the whole upward struggle of rational man" has been to substitute more humane, scientific and rational means of natural selection for mere unreasoning struggle between individuals. Such struggle prevents the opportunity for development along higher lines and, as Huxley says, "the creature that survives a free fight only demonstrates his superior fitness for coping with free fighters—and not any other kind of superiority."

The other two theories regarding the aims of the state are ; first, that it should be used to promote the general welfare, wherever that end can be attained more effectively by joint than by individual action ; and, second, that the state should itself conduct all departments of productive industry. The latter of course is socialism. There would be no fundamental theoretical objection to socialism, provided it could be shown that productive industry could be conducted with better results to the community at large by the state than by private enterprise. But this is exactly what cannot be shown ; in fact, all experience and all impartial interpretation of human nature show that the best results come when the state confines itself to creating and protecting industrial *opportunities*, leaving it to private initiative and enterprise to take advantage of those opportunities and conduct the industries. Doctor Willoughby does not definitely advance this idea of the state as a creator of opportunities, but lays a logical foundation for it , when he shows that the state's true function is to promote the general welfare by whatever efforts require joint rather than individual action. Finally, he makes the point—and very justly—that while the state's activities in this direction may even increase rather than diminish, such increase does not necessarily imply a tendency towards socialism, for the reason that the state only becomes socialistic when it assumes duties that could and would be performed as well or better by the people if left to their private resources. Making this distinction, it is clear that the state may act in very many important directions without being in the least socialistic. What these directions are will be pointed out in detail throughout the course. It is because we have rejected both the no-government and the all-government theories that it becomes necessary to consider so carefully in just what ways the state should and should not act, to promote the general welfare. This is Political Science ; and it is the necessary basis both of wise statesmanship and of sound, intelligent citizenship.

The article on " Education and the State," in the October magazine, is suggested, as showing the wide range of wholesome legislation that can be scientifically justified as parts of the educational function of the state.

Local Center Work

The Gunton Institute courses are especially adapted for individual home study. Often, however, where several persons in the same locality are reading the course, it will be found a decided help to meet together from time to time and discuss points of interest. No formal organization is necessary for this; nevertheless, it is perfectly feasible, if desired, to have a regular club, with officers, stated meetings and programmes. Material for two or three programmes can probably be found among the following suggestions:

Reading of President Gunton's Bulletin lecture on "Need of Political Education." Explanation, by organizer of the club, or other member, of the educational purpose and methods of work of the Gunton Institute.

Question Box; queries on any part of the work to be brought in and either discussed in the meeting or forwarded to the Institute for answer, either directly or in GUNTON'S MAGAZINE. Informal discussion of interesting or unclear points in the readings for the month. Papers on: The Golden Mean between Anarchy and Socialism; Why We Have Nations; Is Patriotism Narrow or Broad?; What Good Citizenship Demands; Is Despotism Ever Justifiable?; Paternalism *versus* Education and Protection; Is the State the Enemy or the Safeguard of Liberty? Debate: *Resolved*, that government has helped human progress more than it has hindered it. Debate: *Resolved*, that perfect liberty requires abolition of all government. Debate: *Resolved*, that patriotism is, finally, the broadest altruism.

QUESTION BOX

The questions intended for this department must be accompanied by the full name and address of the writer. This is not required for publication, but as an evidence of good faith. Anonymous correspondents will be ignored.

Editor GUNTON'S MAGAZINE: Dear Sir:—Title and trust companies seem to be encroaching on the business of the national banks, both apparently doing the same business. Where is the difference? National banks I understand pay nothing on deposits; title and trust companies pay interest.

S. W. H., West Phil'a, Pa.

The function of title and trust companies is quite different from that of national banks. Title and trust companies are more like savings banks. They receive money for relatively permanent investments. National banks, on the contrary, are commercial institutions whose chief function is short-time accommodation to business men. Deposits in national banks are all subject to instantaneous withdrawal. Trust companies and savings banks in no wise furnish this business accommodation, through which over ninety per cent. of the business of the country is transacted. The difference between trust companies and savings institutions, and national banks, is that the former are institutions for the investment of savings and the latter are institutions for furnishing credit accommodation, which is the greatest instrument of trade that modern civilization has developed. Scientific banking is really the organization of loanable credit; this is the most important feature of a sound national monetary system.

A free-trade and single-tax correspondent writing from Atlanta, Georgia, in commenting upon our attitude with reference to the late war, says:

"All war seems to me wrong and I am unable to justify the recent conflict. My point of view is, tariff produces war and the cost of war must be met by increased tariff."

The application of this last remark is equally vague whether as against war or tariffs. Of course the tariff had absolutely nothing to do with producing the Spanish war, and, in the next place, the cost of the war is being met by internal taxation and not increase of tariff at all. Furthermore, no war was ever caused by a tariff anywhere in the history of the world.

JOHN STUART MILL

ECONOMICS ,AND PUBLIC AFFAIRS
DISREPUTABLE JOURNALISM

The question has often been asked, is journalism deteriorating in America? If we compare the daily papers of a quarter of a century ago with those of to-day there are many aspects in which a marked improvement is manifest. The great dailies to-day furnish very much more and an infinitely greater variety of reading than did the dailies of a generation ago. There are many literary features of the modern journal which are real additions to current literature; this is especially true of certain Sunday papers, some of which are veritable magazines. The possibility of much of this is due to the great improvements in the art of printing, such as the development of the Hoe presses, which print both sides and fold the paper without touch of human hands.

But with these improvements have come features which look like positive deterioration. One is the almost extinction, in the case of many newspapers, of the art of reporting. The reporter who can report was once a conspicuous feature of a daily newspaper, especially in large cities. In Europe, particularly in England, this is so still. In this country, however, we have developed a type of journals which are not newspapers but scandal mongers. Instead of informing the public of occurrences in the community that are of legitimate public concern, and commenting upon them editorially so as to aid in creating an intelligent public opinion regarding them, the object seems to be rather to appeal to the lowest passions and inflame a feeling of enmity, suspicion and distrust, every class in the community against every other, particularly the laborers against the well-to-do. There are more people who will give a cent for twelve pages of scandal, abuse, caricature and venal misrepresentation than will give two cents for clean, wholesome news and an intelligent discussion of public affairs. Consequently, the representative papers of this new journalism have become little more than scurrilous sheets filled with slander and abuse of almost everything reputable and useful in society. No public man can expect measurably fair treatment at their hands, unless perchance he is able to purchase their good will by paid "write-ups" or a liberal expenditure in the advertising columns. Nearly every successful public man is traduced, lampooned, and directly or indirectly charged with dishonesty and corruption, whenever the sensational purpose of these journals can be served by so doing.

In the discussion of economic questions, this scandalous feature of journalism runs riot. They appeal to the suspicions, passions and ignorance of the laborers by constantly practicing their art of vilification upon rich men or conspicuously successful corporations. With the growth of socialism, populism, and anti-wealth public sentiment this class of journals has directed its most venomous arrows towards a few of the most successful corporations which they are unable to bleed through the advertising departments.

A most scandalous illustration of the methods of this new type of journalism was recently perpetrated by the New York *World* in connection with recent litigation against the Standard Oil Company. Regardless of the merits of the hearing, it furnished an opportunity for a sensation. A man by the name of Rice, from Marietta, Ohio, who has all along been a moving spirit in anti-trust agitation, especially against the Standard Oil Company, was present, anxious to "serve the cause." This was evidently too good an opportunity to be lost, so the New York *World* got this Mr. Rice to tell, in the form of an interview, the most sensational story he could put together of how the Standard Oil Company had ruined him and other independent refiners, and to give the full effect it was accompanied by a twelve-inch picture of Rice and Rockefeller facing each other, and representing Rice as saying: "You know well that by the power of your great wealth you have ruined my business, and you cannot deny it."

In this interview Mr. Rice makes a series of statements going to show that the Standard Oil Company practically owns the railroads, tampers with the traffic, and by various devices gets flagrant discriminations by which it obtains an advantage over all independent shippers, and by these unjust discriminations is enabled practically to monopolize the oil business. Wherever the statements seemed especially bitter they were printed in large black-faced type. This story with its pictorial setting was hurled broadcast throughout the country, as if the allegations contained in it were verified and indisputable facts, and to insure that it shall have its full influence among its uninformed readers the *World* refuses to publish anything on the other side.

Fairness, and the integrity of economic discussion, to say nothing of the necessity of wholesome public opinion upon this important question, demands that at least some of the truth shall be told on this matter.

In order to understand the true inwardness of this situation, it is necessary to know who and what Mr. George Rice is. He has been heralded forth as an innocent emigrant from the Green Mountains of Vermont, who has been a martyr to the machinations of the Standard Oil Company. Briefly, the facts of the case are as follows: Mr. Rice entered the oil business about thirty years ago. During the first ten years he

attended to his business and developed a fairly prosperous plant, worth somewhere between $20,000 and $30,-
000. About this time, in the late '70's and early '80's, great improvements were introduced into the oil business by the Standard Oil Company and other energetic concerns, not alone in the process of refining but also in the methods of transporting, such as owning their own tank cars, *etc*. Mr. Rice failed to recognize the significance of this economic change, adhered to the old methods, and necessarily began to get left in the competition for business. Instead of turning his energies to the employment of the superior methods, he conceived the idea of compelling the Standard Oil Company to buy up his plant at a fabulous price. His property, which was steadily becoming *passe* as we have said, was worth something under $30,000; he endeavored to sell to the Standard Oil Company for a half a million. It refused to buy the property at any such price and Mr. Rice threatened to compel them to give that or make it cost them twice as much in annoyance and litigation. In various ways he has pursued the Standard Oil Company all these years to make good his threat and "stand it up for a round half million." The Standard has persistently refused and Mr. Rice has as persistently pursued it with charges before the Inter-State Commerce Commission, in litigations, and through sensational articles in the press, all in order to make it cost Mr. Rockefeller's company a high price for refusing his proposition, which was literally a demand for black-mail.

The facts of this case have been made public in the court records and in other ways which do not reach the general public, but, having the ear of the sensational press, he keeps playing the role of a martyr in the hope of ultimately securing his half million. In an interview published in the *Boston Herald*,* the editor of this

*Dec. 24, 1895.

magazine exposed the facts of this blackmailing effort. Since then Mr. Rice has renewed his efforts through his agents (sometimes irresponsible brokers and sometimes reputable lawyers) repeating the offer to stop all litigation, head off adverse and injurious legislation in Ohio and other states and actually prevent certain decisions of the Inter-State Commerce Commission adverse to the Standard Oil Company, if it would pay the half million demanded. But the company has persistently refused to pay this blackmail, and consequently Rice has continued to carry out his threat to harass and if possible to make it cost the Standard more than the blood money would have amounted to. By the aid of anti-trust sentiment and sensational journalism he has been enabled to keep posing as a martyr in the pursuit of this disgraceful method of obtaining money.

The statements contained in his interview in the *World* of October 16th are for the most part repetitions of statements that have been proved false over and over again. His first statement is that " railroads would not furnish tank cars to any competitors, while the Standard combination was able by its immense wealth to buy its own cars." As if railroads refused the use of its cars to all shippers but the Standard. The fact is that no railroad except the Pennsylvania ever owned and furnished tank cars. These cars were built only for carrying oil and only a road like the Pennsylvania, having one terminus in the oil region and another at the seaboard, . could be sure of enough oil traffic to warrant the investment in such cars.

Those desiring to ship oil in tank cars over other roads were forced to supply their own cars. This being an improved and cheaper system of transporting oil, all refiners soon availed themselves of it by building their own cars and no up-to-date refiner would now attempt to do business without owning tank cars. George Rice

refused to avail himself of this and other modern improvements and as a natural result failed. For years he
besieged the Inter-State Commerce Commission to make
rulings which would enable him to get to the market by
primitive methods as cheaply as those who availed themselves of improved methods.

One of his most determined efforts was to obtain a
ruling that when oil was shipped in barrels the barrel
should be carred free, urging that the tank of an oil car
was carried free. But the tank is a portion of the car
while a barrel is freight and merchandise. No man
purchases oil in barrels without paying for the barrels.
The commission decided the question against him but
after frequent importunities reversed itself and ruled,
in relation to some eastern roads, that when oil is shipped
in barrels the barrel should be carried free. The railroad companies could not see why oil barrels should be
carried free any more than flour barrels and all other
packages in which merchandise is shipped. They denied
the reasonableness of the ruling and the power of the
Commission to make it. The question is now pending
in the United States Court and it is not believed that
the Commission's ruling will be sustained. Such rulings
would block the wheels of progress. The man who
uses an ox-cart cannot get his goods to market as cheaply
as he who uses modern methods, and no law can enable
him to do so without paralyzing enterprise and improvements.

His next charge is that "The transcontinental
lines charge $105.00 to return an empty cylinder tank-
car from the Pacific coast to the Missouri River, while
they charge the trust nothing at all for the return of
their own exclusive box tank-cars. This gives the
trust an advantage of over $100.00 a car." Unless Mr.
Rice is ignorant of the whole oil shipping business, he
knows this is not true. The Standard Oil Company has

to pay the railroads the same price as other people for the return of empty tank-cars. One of the features, however, which has contributed largely to the immense success of the Standard Oil Company is its constant eagerness for improvements and prevention of waste. It regarded this $100.00 for returning empty cars as waste which should be avoided. To accomplish this it had tank-cars so constructed as to be usable for carrying certain kinds of freight. When the railroads utilize cars for carrying freight on return trips, the Standard is not charged, and as this is generally done the $100.00 is saved. But other shippers can do the same thing if they will only adopt the same improved methods. The Standard does indeed get $105.00 advantage, but this is not by discrimination but by economic improvement. It is in making just such improvements as these that the quality of oil has been improved and the price so greatly reduced to the public, since the Standard Oil Company was organized. Nearly all Mr. Rice's complaints about discrimination in favor of the Standard and against independent producers are of this same character. Many of them have been passed upon by the Inter-State Commerce Commission and pronounced unfounded. For instance, in his interview in the *World* he says:

"Yet another thing helped to ruin me. The railroads allowed the trust to deliver its oils in less than carload quantities at the same rates as for full carloads. They allowed the trust to stop its cars, whether carrying oil in bulk or barrels, at different stations and take it off in small quantities without paying the higher rates which independent competitors were always charged for small quantities thus delivered. Of course, against such discriminations as these the independent competitor of moderate capital could not contend. He was driven to the wall every time, as I was."

These specific complaints were made to the Inter-State Commerce Commisson and the decision thereon is reported in Rice *vs.* Railway Companies, 5 Inter-State

Commerce Commission Reports, p. 660, in these
words :

> "The third ground of complaint appears to be wholly unfounded.
> There is no evidence that 'favored' shippers have secured carload
> rates on less than carload shipments, or through rates on
> local shipments, by being permitted to remove portions of the
> contents of cars at intermediate stations between the points of
> shipment and of destination. The verified answers of the defend-
> ants explicitly deny that any such discriminations have occurred,
> and that denial is fortified by the positive testimony of their witnesses.
> The petitioner did not appear at the hearing, though duly notified
> thereof, and has offered no proof in support of the information and
> belief upon which his allegations were made. As to these charges the
> complaint must be dismissed."

After stringing out much more of this kind of general complaint, Rice re-hashes, as if it were a well-
known fact, that mythical story about the so-called
"South Improvement Company." This was related at
great length in Lloyd's *Wealth against Commonwealth*,
and, as our readers will remember, in reviewing that
book we exposed the utter fallacy of the story. There
was absolutely no truth in it. Mr. Lloyd knew, and
Mr. Rice knows, that this so-called "South Improvement Company" never had any existence. They both
know that it never produced, refined, bought, sold or
transported a gallon of oil of any sort, nor did a dollar's
worth of business of any kind whatever.*

This case would indeed have constituted a scandalous indictment of the Standard Oil Company if it had
been true, but since there is absolutely no truth in it,
and Mr. Rice knows there is no truth in it, it is a base
calumny to circulate it in the public prints, because
each time it is printed thousands of people will read it
and believe it. He then repeats the story of the Marietta Railroad, the story of changing the freight rates to
the advantage of the Standard Oil Company, and says:

> "To show you how the rebate system worked in my own case, let
> me say that in 1885 I was charged 35 cents a barrel for carrying oil

---

*See *Social Economist* for July, 1895, pages 14–17.

from Macksburg to Marietta, a distance of twenty-five miles, while the Standard Oil Company only paid 10 cents a barrel for the same distance.   More than this, out of the 35 cents a barrel that I paid the trust actually received 25 cents.   In other words, the trust received about two-thirds of all the money I paid for freight."

This is another story that was related by Lloyd, the fallacy of which was exposed in the review in the *Social Economist* already referred to.   This affair occurred in 1885.   He relates it in 1898 as one of the means by which he was ruined.   The truth is, this was a temporary arrangement made by a local agent, and lasted but a short time, during which less than $250.00 of overcharge was paid; the arrangement was promptly repudiated by the trust and every penny of overcharge was returned to Mr. Rice, so that instead of being ruined by this, as he pretends, he did not lose a penny.   Yet in his interview this is presented as if it were a permanent arrangement and was chiefly instrumental in driving him out of business.   The truth is that Mr. Rice failed in business because he failed to keep up with modern methods.   Had he devoted half as much energy to the introduction of up-to-date improvements as he has in trying to obtain money by blackmail from the Standard Oil Company he might have been a rich man instead of being a disreputable detractor of progressive industry and the fomenter of false inflammatory public opinion.

The act of this particular man would not be of such great importance were it not that he is aided by an equally disreputable class of journals in circulating falsehoods and unwholesome misrepresentation for the sole purpose, on his part, of exacting blood money, and on the part of all papers like the *World*, of creating a public sensation by debauching public opinion and poisoning the community against capital and the organization of progressive methods of industry,   All this is simply a part of the propaganda of populism and social

ism, maintained not by discussion of industrial facts
and political principles but by wanton misrepresentation
and inciting of class prejudice.   It is high time that a
halt was called on this sort of thing.   If these sensational, conscienceless journals will persist in fattening themselves by this unwholesome and unpatriotic
kind of business, we have a right to expect that the
respectable journals will do something to correct this
work by exposure of the fallacy and presentation of the
facts in such cases, and thus endeavor to neutralize the
evil, as well as contribute to the growth of wholesome
public opinion on industrial and social questions, the
outcome of which may affect the very foundations of
society.

ENGLAND'S FUTURE POLICY

We have several times called attention to the increasing evidences of a growing change in English public opinion on her free trade policy. There are many reasons why to students of public affairs the study of English opinion on this specific subject is specially important. England is the only country that ever adopted a free trade policy based upon a conscious economic theory. She is the most veteran protectionist country in the world, has had more of it in more ways, and received more benefit from it (with perhaps the single exception of the United States) than any other country. When in the course of events, through the development of machine methods, she had changed the relative position of her cost of production as compared with foreign countries, she altered her industrial policy. This she did, just as she had previously maintained protection, by thinking through her immediate interests. Her economists, however, developed the doctrine that free trade between nations is the only true scientific policy. There were many reasons why the immediate effect of this was to increase England's foreign trade and contribute to her industrial prosperity. These reasons are liberally spread upon the pages of most of the economic literature published since the middle of the century.

But this was very much like the advantage that a manufacturer acquires by the exclusive use of a new labor saving device. So long as he has the exclusive use of the instrument, he has an advantage over all competitors; but this disappears just as fast as his competitors adopt the new methods. England's real advantage was obtained by the exclusive use of factory methods, and on the assumption that she would always have that advantage a new policy was made, based on a new economic doctrine. This doctrine was readily adopted by the practical business opinion of England, because its immediate effect was to expand the range of English manufacture. It is not surprising that business men, who usually think only through their immediate interests, became very enthusiastic over this new doctrine; but the same can hardly be said for the economic philosophers or professional economists whose duty it was to consider the doctrine in the light of political philosophy and ultimate effect on national welfare, not merely of England, but of other countries differently situated. Because it seemed to work well in England it has been assumed that it would work equally well everywhere else. The effect of English doctrine and literature upon public opinion in this country has several times been sufficiently strong to induce an experiment with this policy in the United States, and without a single exception it has produced disastrous results.

It has been more than once pointed out that the advantages of this policy to England were necessarily of limited duration ; that her industrial advantage would finally disappear, whenever and just as fast as continental Europe adopted English machinery and methods.* In reality England was and is at a disadvantage with the continent so far as the wage item of cost is concerned. It is only by reason of her use of superior machinery that the balance in the cost account is turned to her advantage. The clumsy methods employed in continental countries were so inferior to the steam driven machinery of England that despite the fact that wages were a third or a half less than in England, the cost of production per unit was actually more. For this reason it has been the boast of English writers, and such writers as Atkinson and Schoenhof in this

---

* Gunton's " Principles of Social Economics," pp. 336–342.

, country, that highly paid labor always produces sufficiently more to make the cost of production less than with
low paid labor. We have frequently explained the
half fallacy of this statement; it is only true when the
superior labor is accompanied by the use of superior
machinery. It is not true as a matter of personal
muscle and dexterity that four dollar a day bricklayers
in America will lay twice as many bricks as two dollar
a day bricklayers in England. The truth is, they will
lay practically no more. The real advantage of high
wage conditions comes when those very conditions necessitate the use of improved machinery. This fact explains why the United States has been compelled as an
economic necessity to adopt a protective policy towards
England. Our higher wages might not have put us to
a competitive disadvantage with England but for the
fact that England had machinery equal to our own. In
respect of tools, therefore, English manufactures were
equal to American, and for a considerable time superior.
In that case it followed that all the difference in the
wages was directly reflected in the difference in the
cost of production in the two countries. Had England
been using hand labor or crude, elementary machinery
the difference in wages in the two countries might not
have caused any difference in the cost of production.
Indeed, if the difference in machinery had been sufficiently great, our cost of production per unit might have
been less than England's, notwithstanding our higher
wages; which is exactly what was the case with England in regard to continental countries for more than
thirty years and to some extent is still true. As already
stated, just in proportion as continental countries adopt
English or American machinery, this advantage disappears, and hence her higher wages become a handicap
to her competitive capacity under free trade.

Whenever the point is reached where the difference in machinery is practically eliminated, and the wage difference operates as the determining element in the comparative cost of production between England and foreign countries, one of four things must necessarily happen. Either wages on the continent must rise to the English level, or English wages fall to the continental level, or England will have to surrender her manufactures, or adopt a protective policy. Continental wages are not likely suddenly to rise to the English level, because, since the permanent rise of wages in any country chiefly depends upon the gradual and permanent growth of the social standard of living, the rise of wage levels must necessarily be slow. The reduction of English wages to the continental level is practically impossible. It would involve strikes and an industrial upheaval which would disrupt industry and probably introduce a large installment of socialism in the process. Under those circumstances, therefore, England will be compelled to choose between surrendering her commercial superiority or adopting a protective policy.

This state of affairs has been gradually developing during the last ten or fifteen years. Germany, France and Belgium are rapidly transforming their methods of production and adopting English and American machinery. The effect of this is that the products of these countries, particularly of Germany, are making steady and dangerous inroads into English trade, and, in many industries, are superseding those of England in foreign markets, and even, in some cases, successfully competing in the home market.

In spite of the indifference of the doctrinaires, this increasing success of continental competition is having its effect upon the practical thinking of English business men. It is difficult for a manufacturer or a class of business men enthusiastically to cling to the theory of free trade when year by year they see their business slipping away from them as the result of foreign competition—a thing which the free trade doctrine denied could ever come.

This doubt of the virtue of free trade and desire for a change of policy, which once was confined to a handful of "fair trade" propagandists, is now finding expression in highly respectable and responsible quarters. On June 27th, 1896, England completed a half century's experience of the free trade *regime*, in celebration of which the Cobden Club held an imposing banquet in London. The President's address on that occasion was doleful indeed. He lamented the fact that English faith in the doctrines of Cobden was waning. The burden of Mr. Courtney's address was "The coming decline of English prestige," but he insisted that "if the catastrophe comes, it will be in spite of the free trade principle—it could not be the result of it." According to the London *Times*, the only thing Mr. Courtney said to cheer Cobdenism was that "when the evil day comes, it will not have been by free trade that it has been caused. The office of free trade will be to mitigate the trouble which it is not within its power to avert." Instead of being a free trade jubilee, it was a convention to apologise for what free trade was failing to do.

This feeling had then been sufficiently translated into public opinion to make its way into practical politics, and Mr. Chamberlain, as Secretary of the Colonies and official representative of the English administration, outlined a scheme for organizing an "imperial federation" which should bring into one industrial union England and all her colonies, giving free trade within, as between, the different states in this country, and imposing a protective tariff against all outsiders; which, in short, was a proposition to return to protection. This scheme was endorsed by the London *Times* and other conspicuous English papers with unmistakable emphasis. "We believe," said the *Times*, "the vast majority of the people of the United Kingdom will heartily endorse Mr. Chamberlain's desire." Since then, the *Saturday Review*, the London *National Review*, the Duke of Devonshire, as well as Lord Salisbury, Mr. Balfour and many other distinguished English statesmen, have given their expressed or tacit endorsement to the new departure. Nothing could be a more accurate indication of the growing distrust in the free trade doctrine and demand for a change of industrial policy.

Of course this sentiment has not yet broken out into a fervent agitation, like that for the repeal of the corn laws and the demand for suffrage, but it is rapidly taking solid form alike with the leaders of opinion and of practical policy. The great dailies are beginning seriously to discuss the question, not as a matter of abstract economic theory, but as a matter for consideration in practical policy. As a contribution to this changing opinion in England, the Sheffield *Daily Telegraph*, one of the leading dailies in Yorkshire, on September 8th, published the following editorial on the subject:

"The Board of Trade returns continue to afford unpleasant reading for those who prefer the welfare and prosperity of the industrial classes to the maintenance of the superstitions of Cobdenism. There is one satisfactory feature in the tables for August, issued yesterday, namely, an increase of £1,412,019 in exports during the month, as compared with August of last year, but with that exception, the effects of hostile tariffs abroad, and of Protection for the foreigner in our home market, are as conspicuous as ever. There is the same phenomenal increase in the import of products which go to displace home labor, the same evidence of decline

in the export of our staple manufactures, the same unfailing disparity in the proportion of imports to exports,
and the same tendency on the part of those rivals who
benefit so hugely by our open ports to dispense with
articles which enter into competition with our own, and
to accept from us only those which enable them to meet
us with success in the markets of the world.   Razors,
in the shape of machinery and coals, which they can
turn against us for the purpose of cutting our industrial
throat, they will take readily enough, but not a morsel
of reciprocity do they bestow upon us in respect of other
descriptions of commodities.   The figures speak for
themselves.   During the month advantage has been
taken of the privilege we accord to the foreigner of
trading here unburdened with the Imperial and local
taxation imposed upon home industries to increase
imports by £3,845,142, the increase for the eight
months of the year being thus raised to £14,511,316—
from £294,565,179 to £309,076,495.   British exports,
on the other hand, in the same period, have been cut
down by £4,901,823—from £157,685,901 to £152,784,-
073.   Imports of manufactures, including such items as
metals, metal goods, yarns, and textiles, have gone up
from £71,224,029 to £72,804,403; corresponding British
exports have gone down, metals and articles manufactured therefrom (except machinery) from £22,593,293
to £21,891,386, and yarns and textiles from £66,283,776
to £63,035,071.   We cannot make any comparison as
regards cutlery, because until the present year it was
included along with hardware, but seeing that the total
exported last month was only £49,910, and in the eight
months of the year only £355,414—a substantial proportion of which, beyond doubt, was of German production—it is safe to assert that the advantage rests
with the foreigner in respect of cutlery also.   As for
exports of bar, angle, bolt, and rod iron, railroad

material, wire other than telegraph wire, hoop iron, sheets, boiler and armour plátes, and tin plates, these are all diminishing quantities. Continental nations which, not many years ago, were largely dependent upon us for supplies of these descriptions, are now in a position to snap their fingers at us. Consequently, they bar the way to competition with them by walls of tariffs so raised that business would be impossible even if the cost of production were brought down by reducing wages to the point of starvation. But, as we have said, machinery which will serve to increase their independence of us, and place them in a position to better compete with us abroad—not to mention our home market—is taken freely enough. Even in the present year of generally declining exports, and notwithstanding the strike in the engineering trade, there has been an increasing demand for machinery and mill work. For the first eight months of 1897, the figures were £11,-676,682; for the eight months of the present year they stand at £11,681,211, with an advance from £1,240,278 to £1,513,371 in August. Were it not, indeed, for this business in machinery, and the coal which moves it, our export trade with foreign countries would exhibit a decline, calculated to startle even one-sided Free Traders out of their smug self-complacency. This will be seen on reference to the statistics of former years. Between 1854–65 the average annual export of these two items was £5,811,738, and it has since grown to an average of £29,886,470. Our so-called Free Traders are, in fact, living upon the credit of a movement comparable to the burning of a candle at both ends. They claim the export of machinery as an evidence of the wisdom of their fiscal system, whereas each loom sent abroad represents an actual or potential deduction from our trade in another direction, and at the best is, in many cases, no more than a temporary compensation for the loss thus occasioned, seeing that it is the practice of our rivals, having secured our models, to supply themselves with imitations thereof. This is the secret of the falling off in the prosperity of our textile industries. At one time, the world was at our feet in the cotton, jute, and linen trades. Now we have made, and are making, great markets virtually independent of us. For this there would be no serious cause of complaint if those markets were left open to British competition, but when they can dispense with our services they are closed to us, although we have fulfilled all the conditions which, according to Cobden and Bright, were to assure us the right of free and equal exchange for ever. Nor is this all. In addition to shutting us out from their particular fields, they add insult to injury by invading our home market, and still further limiting the area of employment. The officials of the Board of Trade apparently do their utmost to screen this view of the subject from the public, but they cannot entirely conceal the damage thus inflicted upon British labor. The figures require a good deal of sifting, but when the operation is completed, it will be found that, whereas between 1854–65, manufactured and semi-manufactured imports—all of the kind we are capable of producing ourselves—averaged no more than about £16,000,000, they now amount to almost £100,000,000. And this total is increasing well-nigh by leaps and bounds, while, as we have shown, the demand for British exports is diminishing. A system such as this may suit Free Traders with capital invested in foreign factories and workshops, or with incomes independent of trade, but whether it is conducive to the prosperity of the working-man, the latter can judge for himself."

The doctrinaires in Oxford and Cambridge may insist upon an abstract theory, and their imitators in this country may repeat the aphorism that taxation is a burden and freedom a virtue, but practical everyday experience is teaching another lesson—a lesson which is likely to have far more influence upon England's policy than any amount of text-books or class-room lectures which advocate a theory directly antagonized by the business experience of the country. It will doubtless be said, as it has often been, that the doctrine is true in theory though not in practice. That is incorrect. No doctrine is true in theory which is false in practice ; because true theory is the logical interpretation of facts and experience. The fault is with the doctrine, not with the experience. Free trade dogma is a part of the habit of thinking in an economic rut, taking a few facts as representing all experience. It is like Mr. Atkinson's explanation of the cost of producing silver, to which we referred in our last issue, generalizing the whole world's production of silver on the experience of two mines, one in Australia and the other in the United States. The free trade doctrine is a generalization on the temporary experience of England under exceptional conditions which will never again exist in any country. It is a doctrine which lacks the element of true economic philosophy and political science. It is a policy which is feasible only under exceptional local conditions, and cannot be raised to the dignity of scientific generalization. As England is the only country which ever assumed to adopt a general free trade policy and live up to it as an economic theory, its ultimate operation in England should be carefully studied, not in the light of English text-books but in the light of the world's experience in general and England's experience in particular.

IV.—M'CULLOCH

The period in the history of English economic thought between Ricardo and Mill (1823–1848) was one of remarkable public interest and vigorous controversy. The most conspicuous economist during this period was John Ramsey M'Culloch, who was born in 1789 and died in 1864. His *Political Economy* was published in 1824, a year after the death of Ricardo. He was a thorough-going disciple of Ricardo, whose theory of rent he re-stated, illustrated and defended in the most effective manner. M'Culloch was not merely an intellectual economist, but was a man intimately acquainted with the history, statistics and policies of public affairs. He enforced his discussion of economics by frequent drafts upon verified data and appeals to industrial experience. He was far more virile and positive than Mill, and in some senses more advanced. He did not systematize the science, in the sense of constructing a body of economic doctrine, in such a comprehensive way as Mill did, yet it may be said that he really gave life to the wage-fund doctrine which Mill put into form. Indeed, in stating the wage-fund proposition Mill almost paraphrases the language of M'Culloch. Thus :

" The well-being and comfort of the laboring classes are, therefore, especially dependent on the relation which their increase bears to the increase of the capital that is to feed and employ them . . . and every scheme for improving the condition of the laborer, which is not bottomed on this principle, or which has not an increase of the ratio of capital to population for its object, must be completely nugatory and ineffectual."—M'CULLÓCH.

" Wages depend, then, on the proportion between the number of the laboring population and the capital or other funds devoted to the purchase of labor. . . . The condition of the class can be bettered in no other way than by altering that proportion to their advantage: and every scheme for their benefit, which does not proceed on this as its foundation, is, for all permanent purposes, a delusion."—MILL.

Although M'Culloch was a victim of this wage-fund fallacy, he had a very clear hold on the idea of differential or marginal cost as a controlling element in value, and he expressed more clearly and emphatically than Mill or any subsequent English economist the idea that the standard of living is really the social basis of wages. In proof of this he compares the standard of living of laborers in India, Ireland and other countries with that in England, and says :—" In consequence of these different habits, there is an extreme difference, not in the rate of necessary wages merely, but in their actual or market rate in this country, so much so, that while the average market price of a day's labor in England may be taken at from 2od. to 2s., it cannot be taken at more than 5d. in Ireland and 3d. in Hindostan." On this phase of economics and also the idea that diversified industries are indispensable to national development, industry and political freedom, M'Culloch was clearer and sounder than most of the economists now occupying chairs in our universities. M'Culloch's *Political Economy* is a work that no student of the subject should ignore. In many respects he is superior to Mill or any other English writer since Ricardo with, perhaps, the single exception of Marshall.

V.—MILL.

We present as a frontispiece to this issue a picture of John Stuart Mill, probably the most universally known of English economists. He was born in 1806 and died in 1873. In some respects Mill was one of the most unique characters in English public life. Though not a college-bred man he had practically all the advantages that a university education would give. He appears to have been almost born to a study of the classics. He could read Greek fluently at six and Latin at eight years of age. In this respect he has had few

equals.   At the age of thirty he became one of the editors of the Westminster Review.   In the field of literature and philosophy he made a lasting mark.   For forty
years he was a continuously active participant in the
discussion of public affairs, including everything from
theology to politics.   No question of philosophy, ethics,
sociology, economics, finance or government came up
for public consideration to which he did not contribute.
It is with his work as a political economist, however,
that we are chiefly concerned.

For twenty years after the publication of his *Principles of Political Economy* (1848), Mill was the recognized leader of economic thought in England, and to a
large extent in this country.   Probably no work on
economics has ever been so generally used as a text-
book as has Mill's *Principles of Political Economy*.   It
cannot be said, however, that he made any striking
addition to the science in the sense of contributing to
fundamental doctrine.   The great contribution that Mill
really made was to systematize and state in orderly
sequence the doctrines that had been evolved during
the discussion that followed the publication of Adam
Smith's *Wealth of Nations* in 1776.   Indeed, he admits
that the object of his work was to bring the subject
down to date, logically incorporating "the more extended knowledge and improved ideas" which had been
evolved during the preceding half century.   This he
did in such an able manner that his work became the
standard classical representative of English economics
throughout the world.   For this work he was eminently
fitted by his scholarship, his masterly logic, and his extraordinary fairness of spirit, singleness of motive and
sympathetic character.   Though not the originator he
was the formulator of the wage-fund theory and its
most tenacious advocate, yet when the defects of that
theory were pointed out by Thornton he was the first

and almost only economist in England who had the courage to renounce it and publicly confess his conversion. He accepted practically without qualification Adam Smith's theory of foreign trade, Malthus's theory of population and Ricardo's theory of rent.

In 1865 he departed from the vocation of expounding economic theory and entered the field of practical politics. In the election of 1865, when Gladstone was making the issue for the Second Reform Bill, John Stuart Mill was elected member of Parliament for Westminster. In this field it may be said that he was a conspicuous failure. The man who had impressed all the world with his philosophy and economic writings, failed to exercise any perceptible influence upon the House of Commons. He was in favor of all the unpopular measures, like woman's suffrage, minority representation, payment of members, etc. His ideas of politics were wholly unlike the modern practice in this country. He was so opposed to the spoils idea that he would not even deliver speeches in his own district nor contribute anything to his own election expenses, and utterly refused to consider the local business of his constituency. He would speak for other people and contribute to the election expenses of other candidates, but he would do nothing to aid his own election.

When standing for re-election in 1868 he lived up to this idea by not only refusing to contribute to his own campaign fund but by contributing £10 towards the election expenses of Charles Bradlaugh, the atheist, at Northampton. As a result Mill was badly defeated and a Tory elected in his place.

EDITORIAL CRUCIBLE.

IF THERE is any truth in the adage that " Whom the gods would destroy they first make mad," Mr. Croker must have had the special attention of the gods. It seemed to be madness enough to dictate the nomination of the brother of Mayor Van Wyck for Governor, but to forbid the renomination of Judge Daly, and boastingly announce that it was because he did not give " proper consideration" to Tammany interests, was political audacity run mad. Nothing but the blind assumption that the Democracy and the people of this state will endorse anything Croker says or does, however vile, could have produced such political insanity. It has aroused the indignation of the whole respectable portion of the legal fraternity throughout the state, and even the *New York Times*, which has been reduced from three cents to one to help elect the ticket, thinks Croker has defeated it,—for which the gods will give universal thanks.

THE STATE election in New York this year, like the municipal election in New York City last year, is a matter of intense interest throughout the nation. The reason for this is that this year as last the contest involves, as in almost no other state, the principle of clean, honest and progressive government, as distinguished from mere hackneyed political rule. It is preeminently, this time, a contest between the best progressive element of the state and the ignorant, debauched and flagrantly defiant methods of Tammany Hall, which has long been a stench in the political nostrils of the entire nation, a discredit to free government and a scandal to the metropolis of the republic. If Mr. Roosevelt is elected, as we hope and believe he will be, the success will be a double triumph, a triumph over Tammany Hall, and also a triumph over the hackneyed and least progressive managers of the Republican party itself.

AT LAST the real missionary work of the United States in China is about to begin. A number of American capitalists, including some of the most conspicuous millionaires in this country, have organized a company to build a railroad in China. In order to obtain permission to do this, the syndicate has agreed to pay eighty per cent. of the net earnings of the railroad to the Chinese Government and, after forty-five years, give it the entire property. This is the entrance of modern industrial civilization into the Walled Empire. It is the true way for the United States to contribute civilizing forces to the Orient. We can help these countries far more by sending them our improved industrial methods than undertaking, either by immigration or annexation, to bring those people under our form of government. China is the best place to civilize the Chinese, and Russia the Russians. Every time we send a machine, or build a factory or railroad, or in any way modernize the methods of industry in these less advanced countries, we are doing a real lasting work in promoting there the natural and most rapid growth of civilization.

In no other way can this be accomplished so successfully and with so little friction. Civilization carried by the tools of industry is always superior, less costly, and far more effective than that carried by war and conquest. Brice, Rockefeller and Morton, as the organizers of the syndicate to take railroads into China, are much better and more effective missionaries for civilization than any number of commodores, generals and military governors could be.

IN A RECENT interview Mr. Andrew Carnegie has expressed himself with his usual emphasis and clearness on the subject of the Philippines. In this interview he is reported as saying: "If the United States is going to undertake the government of the Philippines and go in for expansion throughout the world, putting her hand into the hornets' nest of European rivalry, there can be no prosperous business. We shall be subject to wars and war's alarm. . . . . The development of one state in the union in peace and security will outweigh all the increase of profit we can get from foreign trade in the worthless possessions which we can attempt now to take. The Philippines have a certain trade, which cannot be greatly increased; the wants of the people are few; barbarians are no customers; civilized people are the consumers of our products."

Mr. Carnegie has given expression to his views on many public questions, but never have his words been more fully charged with wisdom, patriotism and political good sense. An increase of twenty-five cents a day in the wages of American labor would do more for industrial prosperity and trade expansion than all the trade of the Philippines. Moreover, that would be a definite contribution to the welfare of our own people and to the prosperity of our own business conditions, while to get the Philippines would probably mean an effort to lower wages here in order to furnish goods for nearly nothing to the Philippinos. Mr. Carnegie is always bright and vigorous, but never before has he seemed quite so much like a philosopher.

———

A FEW MONTHS ago the whole country was stirred by the news that the wages of New England cotton operatives had been cut to the bleeding point. The reason given was the severe competition from southern mills. The operatives consented to the reduction on the assurance that this would keep New England in the race. Now comes the news that the Southern Cotton

Manufacturers' Association has decided to reduce wages
eight to thirteen per cent. President Estes, of the
Association, says; " It is caused by the low prices which
southern mills have had to make to compete with the
North." It is now in order for New England to make
another reduction if wage reductions afford any solution of the problem.

As we pointed out at the time, in this wage cutting business the southerners are sure to win. If New
England is to hold its own in the competition, it must
do so in some other way than by cutting wages. That
never was a remedy for industrial depression, and is to
be hoped never will be. Shorter hours and better conditions in the South, which shall make further reductions of wages socially impossible, and a raise soon
inevitable, is the only true solution of this competition.
between South and East in cotton manufacture. If the
Arkwright Club would contribute a million dollars for
the purpose of industrial education and organization in
the South, it would be a far better investment than paying for the publication of tracts against short hours and
incurring the loss necessarily involved in strikes to enforce lower wages, which tend to bring social disturbances, class hatred, political prejudice and ultimately
an inferior type of citizenship.

CIVICS AND EDUCATION.

A NOVEL EDUCATIONAL EXPERIMENT

LATEST DEVELOPMENTS AT THE GEORGE JUNIOR REPUBLIC

CHARLES BURR TODD

Nine miles awheel from the elms of Cornell, through rolling garden lands rich with tilth and grange, and we see before us a group of detached buildings on the summit of a broad low ridge commanding a view that ought in itself to reform the most incorrigible of evil doers. North, South, East and West lies an expanse of billowy fields green with growing crops, brown with stubble or golden with harvest, with here and there the darker green of noble groves, and the flashing of a river between. This is the Junior Republic. The building nearest the road is the residence of Mr. George. Then follow the school house, court house and jail, capitol, workshop, and the new cottage recently erected through the liberality of Mr. John D. Rockefeller.

We were glad to find Mr. George at home. As the discoverer and successful administrator of a new principle in social reform,—one that is destined, we believe, to work a new departure in sociology,—he possesses for students of that science a real and personal interest. We saw before us a man of thirty-two years, of medium stature, soft voice, winning manners and magnetic personality; large hearted, evidently of infinite tact, patience and perception. In a pleasant informal chat of an hour the philanthropist gave us an interesting account of the inception and gradual rise of his " republic."

He **was** born and grew to manhood here in Freeville, Tompkins County. In 1887, at the age of twenty-one, he went to New York City to engage in business. A natural love for children led him to turn his attention to the neglected boys and girls of New York, and he spent most of his leisure time among them, winning their friendship, teaching them in the Sunday Schools, visiting the boys' clubs, and trying to do them good. Pitying their miserable, narrow lives, he brought with him on his annual vacation to his old home in Freeville, in August, 1890, thirty of the toughest specimens he could collect in the Five Points, Mulberry Street, and Little Italy, their transportation expenses being paid by the *Tribune* Fresh Air Fund. His only object in this was to give them a good time,—fishing, bathing, riding, walking, playing,—pump a little pure country air into their lungs, and fill their stomachs with wholesome country fare—the latter donated by his relatives and neighbors.

The second summer he secured a vacant house near Freeville and brought up a company of 200 boys and girls, who were freely supported by the churches and charitable people of the neighborhood. The next year—'92—he moved to the present site, and has brought to it each year from 150 to 200 children, one-fourth of whom were girls. The fourth year—'93—his eyes were opened to the fact that his work was doing the children more harm than good; that it was degrading, pauperizing them; that one-tenth of the children came there as toughs to fight and quarrel and terrorize the country, robbing orchards, rifling hens' nests, overturning beehives and the like, while the other nine-tenths came for the food and clothing they could get, or carry back to their parents. From the moment of their arrival their constant cry was, "What are dese farmers goin' ter give us ter take back? De woman I was by last year give me two dresses and sent t'ree barrels of potatoes in de winter. What be youse goin' ter give me?"

Here were the two old problems of society for Mr. George to solve—crime and pauperism—the alpha and omega of the political and charitable systems of New York. With 200 budding criminals and paupers on his hands, he fell to thinking, and then were conceived the two great basal principles of his system—necessity and opportunity for the pauper,—punishment, restraint, emulation and reform for the criminal.

One day he expostulated with a crowd of the urchins, who were demanding things as a right.

"Are you not ashamed to beg and ask for these things? Why not go to work and earn them as men do?"

A little Italian girl, self-constituted spokesman, drew herself up and replied : "Mr. George, wot do youse tink we's here fur, anyway?" "That's the talk," chorused the crowd.

During the winter Mr. George continued to do a deal of thinking, and next summer—'94—determined to try the efficacy of work. He bought twelve picks and shovels. The boys came, lounged about, idle, and grumbling about their food, though far better than that they received at home.

"Boys," said he, "you want something to do," and producing the twelve picks and shovels he set them to work on the roads. At first they were most enthusiastic, and said it was just what they wanted. " I was hilarious," remarked Mr. George, "and regretted not having bought more shovels. The second day I had tools enough, the third day there were picks and shovels to spare, the fourth day not a boy appeared,— the experiment was a dead failure. Then about that time I tried another plan. Several boxes of clothing came in. I picked out some of the suits and fitted them on the boys. They were enraptured. 'That's a bute, that's a daisy,' they exclaimed.

" ' How much is it worth?' I asked.

" ' O, dat's wuth five dollars in Baxter Street.' ' Wot youse givin' us; you couldn't git it for six,' said a second.

" ' We'll call it five, the lowest price,' I said. ' Now, what do you boys earn a day in New York?'

" ' O, mebbe a dollar sellin' papers, or when we git a job wid de Superintendent of Public Works.'

" ' Very well,' said I, ' you work five days on the road, and you get this suit.'

" They couldn't have been more astounded had lightning fallen from a clear sky. ' Wy, dat's sent to us,' they cried; ' wese aint to work for dat. '

" I began packing them up. ' Wot youse goin' ter do wid 'em?' ' O, send them back, or put them down cellar. You won't have these clothes till you work for them.'

" They gathered in the tent and held an indignation meeting. Jimmie was for working but the others loudly protested. ' Dey was given ter us. He's goin' ter git five days' work for what cost him nothin',' they said; but next day Jimmie came and said, ' I'll work for 'em, Mr. George.' He labored five days and got his suit. You never saw a boy more proud. It added at least an inch to his stature, and he moved about like a prince. The next day he came to me and begged the loan of a flat iron.

" ' What for?' I asked. ' Ter put a crease in me trowsers,' he replied.

" Jimmie's course provoked an animated discussion in the little commonwealth. The other boys upbraided him. ' Youse a fool. He got five days' work out of you an' it didn't cost him a cent.' ' Wot o' that, fellers,' replied Jimmie, stoutly; ' I feel ten times better over 'em. They're *mine*. I earned 'em. I'm a man an' not a beggar. Try it an' see.'

"Well, Jimmie's example worked wonders. The boys all surrendered and went to work."

The problem of how to deal with crime was equally difficult. Mr. George made rules against stealing, smoking, gambling, fighting and the like, but how to punish the offender when the rules were violated, as they were, caused anxious thought. He tried whipping. but that was of little avail. Then he thought of vicarious punishment, and offered his own back, making the criminal do the whipping. This worked better. "But there was still a gulf between us," said Mr. George. "Our relations placed myself and my helpers in one section, and the boys in another. We were, like the cop, in authority, and therefore to be evaded, outwitted, resisted. One day, pondering over the difficulty, it came to me like a flash that if I could get the boys to try the culprits themselves, pass sentence and execute it, half my point would be gained. One day a neighboring farmer came to me in great wrath. 'Mr. George,' said he, 'my apple orchard has been raided by your boys. I can't keep a King of Tompkins County or a Sweet Harvest on the place. It must be stopped. I expect you to pay the damage.'

" 'Do you know the culprits?' I asked.

" 'I can pick out two of 'em,' he replied.

" I called the boys up. 'That's the one,' he said, singling out Tommie.

" 'Boys,' said I, 'we'll have a court and you shall try Tommie yourselves. Tommie, state your case.'

" The lad hung his head and admitted his guilt. 'All you who think Tommie should be punished hold up your hands,' said I. All hands went up. 'What punishment?' I asked. 'Whipping,' they decreed. 'There is another of 'em.' said the farmer, pointing to Robbie. So I called Robbie before our moot court. 'Anything to say, Robbie?' I asked. 'Tommie coaxed

me off,' sobbed the little lad, beginning to cry. 'All
in favor of punishing Robbie hold up your hands,' I
said, but not a hand went up. 'Those in favor of letting him go free hold up your hands,' and every hand
was raised. I found later that they thought Robbie had
been led astray by Tommie.

"Here was at least one point gained. The boys
had a sense of justice. From that court has grown up
the whole system of punishment followed in the Junior
Republic. The boys themselves try our culprits, convict, and execute justice upon them. At first I was
Judge, but later I found that the boys did better. We
have a complete system of jurisprudence,—police court,
superior court, supreme court, judge, jury and prose-
cuting attorney,—all boys, except the members of the
supreme court, which is composed of the trustees of
the Republic.

"I disliked whipping, and 'one morning when I
had quite a large batch of convicts to sentence, I said:
'Instead of whipping, I'll sentence No. 1 to five hours'
hard labor, No. 2 to six, and No. 3 to seven.' I put
them at the stone pile, and to picking up stone on the
farm. I also had a striped suit made for each, of bed
ticking, which disgrace they felt keenly."

At first the "convict gang" had an adult for over-
seer, but one day he fell ill, and the thought came to
Mr. George, why not put "Banjo" in his place? This
lad, one of the older boys, had been a "tough" in
New York, a member of the Why-o gang, and had
served a term in the Catholic Protectory. Since his
coming Mr. George had made a great effort to gain his
friendship and confidence, but so far in vain. Banjo's
first day as foreman was a veritable eye-opener to Mr.
George. His command of the gang was perfect; he
got double the work out of them, and maintained perfect discipline. "Best of all," said Mr. George, "my

trust in him had gained his confidence; after that he was one of my men. I retained him in office, and the punishment problem was settled. Shortly after, the boys suggested that I select a jury of twelve of the best boys to try culprits, instead of the town meeting, which was followed by excellent results.

"This summer of 1894," continued Mr. George, "gave me a great deal of food for thought, and after the boys went home in the fall I did a deal of thinking. Three things had been demonstrated : first, that the boys had a keen sense of justice and power of discrimination, as shown in all the trials by jury. Second, they were superior in power of discipline and administration over their fellows, to me or my helpers. Third, their suggestions as to government and administration were wiser and more practical than mine. Therefore, I reasoned, they were as capable of making the laws as of executing them, and the idea of a boy legislature came to me. Again, if I compelled them to pay for their clothing by labor, why not also for their food? That was what people in the outside world were doing. Why not copy outside methods, and erect a Republic,— yes, a Junior Republic. The thing came like a flash— an inspiration, it carried me off my feet with a shout. I announced my plan at once, and the next summer, that of 1895, was the first of the Junior Republic. I erred at first in not fully trusting the boys. I made myself president, with a veto on all laws. For chief justice, chief of police, bank president, board of health and civil service examiners I chose adults. A summer's experience convinced me that in all these positions the boys would be superior. They knew much better than we how to deal with their fellows. They would also be more responsible to them, and would have therefore a keener sense of their own responsibility in the execution of their own laws. In the summer of 1896, therefore, all the responsible positions except the presidency were filled by the boy citizens themselves, and in 1897 the man president was abolished, and a boy chosen, by the suffrage of his peers.

" To-day the Junior Republic is a pure democracy, self-governing,—a combination of our federal, state, and city governments. Senators are elected for two weeks, representatives for one week, the president for a year. We follow the Constitution and laws of the State of New York, though subject to amendment by the legislature and president. There is a civil court, police court, superior court, supreme court, police force, jailer,—all (except members of the supreme court) composed of citizens."

One of Mr. George's objects from the beginning has been to give the boys a due sense of the value of money and other property. His financial system has been as much an experiment and an outgrowth as his political. At first he was owner and business manager. He employed the boys and paid them so much per day in the cardboard money of the Republic (later, tin coin). This money was receivable for board and clothing at the hotels and at the Republic's stores. As a matter of form the citizens paid small taxes but Mr. George, as the sole capitalist, paid the great bulk of them. In 1896, in pursuance of his democratic policy, all the mercantile and hotel contracts were let by government to the citizens after being offered at auction, although Mr. George still retained his ownership of the farm of forty acres, and employed a large force in working it. He paid this force daily, and as all the money for board and lodging went to the contractors, and as he had nothing to sell to the citizens—since his crops would not mature until September,—no money came back into his hands. Thus, as he was continually manufacturing money and putting it out, the result was an expansion of the currency which created dire results,— a depreciation to such an extent that a dollar of Republic money was worth only five to ten cents of American money. For a long time neither Mr. George nor the boys could discover the cause of it so as to apply a remedy. The government, finding a large surplus on hand, more money being received than was paid out, projected large internal improvements which were let by contract. The contractors found they could get laborers at fifty cents a day, although the government had been paying one dollar, and as a result grew rich out of their contracts. Then into this pure democracy the "millionaire" obtruded and flaunted his riches, causing discontent and heart burnings. A desire to put down these parvenus was at once manifested, and the People's party was formed for the purpose, with a platform demanding a high tax rate, and the creation from it of a government reserve to contract the currency.

The contractors met this by organizing the "Free Tin" party with a campaign slogan of "High wages, plenty of work, and prosperity." They told the citizens that now they were able to pay fifty cents a day, but that if the currency were contracted they could pay but twenty-five, and as it required fifty cents a day to pay for board, lodging and taxes the condition of the laboring man would then be pitiable in the extreme. These arguments were irresistible and the People's party was overwhelmed.

The next year—1897—Mr. George returned to his former position and became sole owner and capitalist. While this is not in accordance with his theories, he finds it admirable in practice. He is now able to control and regulate the currency, and to prevent the rise of millionaires. He attains the latter end by letting the contracts, not in open competition, but awards them to the more deserving in his own estimation. His present method is to hire and pay all employees himself, or else through his sub-contractors. The sums paid for board and lodging now come into his hands, and with his receipts from other sources enable him to control the currency and keep it at par. In this matter of the currency and finances Mr. George admits that the Republic was a failure. Financially his present system is that of a benevolent despotism. He dislikes this and is now thinking out some plan by which a pure democracy may arrange its financial affairs and yet prevent the fluctuation of its currency and the rise of " millionaires."

The Junior Republic has also solved the pauper problem. In 1895 taxes were levied to support the poor. There were about a dozen boys—"neverworks" —who were content to take the paupers' table rather than engage in honest toil. The boy citizens who supported them rebelled at this. Public opinion and ostracism having no effect, the legislature took the matter up, and passed a law abolishing the paupers' table. The neverworks treated the matter as a huge joke. They allowed that when the time came the boys wouldn't let them starve. But the boys were hard headed, practi cal citizens and taxpayers and when the day came the police told the twelve to move on. They moved, and the same day found work and earned enough to pay for a hearty supper. Since that time there have been no paupers. True, there are no unemployed in the Junior Republic, and the pauper is therefore deprived of his principal excuse for being one. But the sociologist might retort that it is the business of the state to play the part of Mr. George and provide work for all.

Next year the Republic will probably enter upon a new phase of existence. The hotel system will be discarded for the family plan. The cottage just completed, through the generosity of Mr. John D. Rockefeller, puts it in the power of Mr. George to inaugurate a new departure. At present the citizens are lodged in two "hotels," and take their meals at the restaurant,—or rather two restaurants,—one, Delmonico's, where the price of meals is twenty-five cents, and one less elegant where a substantial meal can be had for fifteen cents. By paying in advance a boy may get board and lodging as low as $3 a week, or he may pay as high as $5.50 a week.

Mr. George wishes to exchange this system for the family plan of separate cottages, each holding a "family" of fifteen children, boys and girls, to live as one family and to be managed by the older brothers and sisters and by a capable woman who will serve as aunt or mother. A business corporation will also be organized in each, to own and cultivate separate tracts of land, provide its own table, *etc.* "These children have never known what home life is," says Mr. George, "and it is the duty of the Junior Republic to bestow it upon them." A manual training school is also being instituted, the departments of carpentering, shoe-making and farming being already provided for.

I questioned Mr. George as to results. Had the boys and girls reformed, improved? Did they make good citizens, take an interest in the public policy of their Republic, all vote, and vote conscientiously?

"I wish," he replied, "that every citizen of the greater Republic took as much interest in politics as my boys do, had mastered the science of government half as well, and voted as conscientiously. We have, as you saw, a general library of one thousand volumes, and no books among them are so well thumbed as those on law and government. You will find our boys just out of the slums poring over them at every spare moment. Several of them are already good lawyers. There is of course a great difference in the children that come to us, as to educability and susceptibility, but I have found none wholly insensible to our system of emulation and necessity. As to the reforming influence of the Republic it is wonderful. Boys and girls who were degenerating, almost, coming into the society of our citizens who make and execute the laws which they obey, become new beings. They will have a few lapses, but the fact of being judged and condemned by a jury of themselves goes to the root of their moral consciousness, and, after one or two solitary punishments, the folly of it dawns upon them. To show the power of the principle I may say that our boys have reached and stamped out by their laws secret vices that it has been found impossible to eradicate in seminaries, asylums and reformatories. I do not regard the movement yet as anything more than an experiment. We are hampered by want of funds. We have between fifty and sixty children here, and there are now four hundred applicants on the waiting list.

" I have been offered property worth half a million dollars if I would go over into Pennsylvania and found a Junior Republic there, but I am loth to leave my work here. I wish to reduce it to a system that others of less experience can put into operation, and shall then feel at liberty to accept other calls."

CIVIC AND EDUCATIONAL NOTES

At a recent convention of Factory Inspectors in Boston, Chief O'Leary, of New York, declared in an address that "The only cure for the sweating system is in the restriction of immigration." Certainly this is the indispensable preventive of any further increase in the system, although more direct measures will be needed to stamp out what we already have. Sweatshops are in no sense a product of American conditions, but are purely an imported survival of foreign mediævalism.

Sweatshops
A Mediæval
Survival,

The relative meagerness of the Russian government's expenditures for public education is shown in a discussion of the question in the *Novoe Vremia*, a Russian paper, quoted in a recent Consular Report. Only about 4 per cent. ($20,560,000) of the Imperial budget is devoted annually to education, while it is estimated that the middle-class Russian families, having incomes of from $514 to $2,570 per annum, spend from $154 to $359 per annum for the education of their children. That is, private families of this grade spend from two to four times as much, proportionately, as does the state for educational purposes. These middle-class incomes, however, are extremely few in Russia, and the millions of peasant and artisan population cannot possibly provide for their children's education at all, even if they spend a no greater proportion of their incomes than does the Russian government. The educational facilities furnished by the state to the masses of the population will not equal even those provided by the middle-class families for their own children, until it spends three or four times as much as at present.

Public
Education in
Russia

Mr. Todd's article describing the system and latest developments at the George Junior Republic is

The George Junior Republic

one of exceptional interest. The subject is no stranger to magazine literature, but this article brings out points in the evolution of the system that are new and have far more significance than any mere description of the buildings at Freeville or of the boys who form the working material of Mr. George's Republic.

This experiment must be considered largely tentative as yet, and whether the idea of reforming young city "toughs" by means of self-responsibility and self-government is capable of general application—and hence general adoption as a part of our educational methods—can hardly be determined until more thorough and varied experience has been had. It does not appear as yet, for instance, whether the scheme succeeds because it applies a truly scientific treatment to the problems in hand, or because it is a fascinating novelty and offers the boys an entertaining diversion for the summer months. The real test of the practical value of this experiment is not to be found in the way it works at Freeville but in its effect on the habits, character, and purposes of the boys when they return to their city homes. If the lessons of self-reliance, self-respect, responsibility, duty and regular habits do really take root in the minds of the boys and alter their conduct and influence among the slum children with whom they mingle on their return to the city, then Mr. George has hit upon a really important and valuable discovery, and Junior Republics ought to be established within reach of all large cities and come to fill a permanent niche in our educational and reform systems.

We do not think it at all necessary to the full success of the Freeville experiment that Mr. George should entirely relinquish his personal direction of affairs. In

fact, the present arrangement whereby he retains control of the finances will probably have to be continued
permanently, and there is no particular benefit that could
result to the boys by giving them a pretended management of matters that must in the nature of the case be
really handled by the proprietor himself.   So many of
the essential conditions of real life are necessarily wanting at this Junior Republic that any attempt to illustrate
such vital matters as the money question, the capitalist
and wages problem, and the " rise of millionaires,"
would probably result in more harm than good.

In attempting to illustrate important economic laws
with only half the necessary conditions present, the boys
would be given radically wrong ideas which might even
viciously affect their action on similar problems in real
life later on.   For instance, when the boy "contractors " at the George Republic began to "get rich" by
paying low wages to their hands, the citizens at once
tried to suppress them by high taxation, and finally Mr.
George had to let the contracts himself to what he considered "good boys,"—that is, boys who were content
to work along with the scheme submissively, in the way
it was intended to go, and not manifest any inconvenient
desire to make any money.

Now, this was almost an exact duplication in minia-
ture of the Populist method of dealing with the question of wealth, that is, confiscate it by means of excessive taxation.   If the boys learned any lesson at all from
this incident it was that the way to prevent employers from oppressing their employees is to tax the employer's wealth away from him.   Nothing less could have
been expected, of course, since there was no opportunity
in this Junior Republic for organization of trades unions
which would demand better wages at the penalty of
strikes, *etc.*, nor could there be any such thing as competition between contractors in the use of improved
machine methods of production.

In real life these two forces operate, on the one
hand to maintain a rate of wages equivalent to the
standard of living of the most expensive laborers needed
in any given industrial community, and on the other hand
to prevent any individual accumulation of wealth except
by those who can render superior and cheaper service
to the public. It is right here that the vital points
necessary to an accurate understanding of the capitalist
and wages question are absent in the conditions at the
George Junior Republic; and hence it is far better that
no attempt at all be made to illustrate the workings of
this matter than that the boys should be allowed to carry
away the wrong-headed ideas which an experiment
with such absurdly incomplete conditions would give.
To attempt to illustrate the capitalist and wages problem without reference to the law of competition, on the
one hand, and of wages determined by the standard of
living maintained by labor groups, on the other, is like
endeavoring to explain the solar system with the sun
left out. The matter is too seriously important to be
handled in such a way as to spread misinformation and
false, ill-digested ideas among the boys who will eventually have to decide the public policy of the nation in
regard to just this class of problems.

Nevertheless, in the field of education in political
forms, customs and duties, and inculcation of self-
reliance and orderly, responsible, intelligent conduct of
affairs, there seems to be large possibilities in the
scheme described so interestingly by Mr. Todd. If
Mr. George has the saving faculty of knowing just where
to stop, and how to balance the necessary limitations of
his experiment with his own enthusiasm for it, we may
expect to see some large and permanent benefits develop
from this Junior Republic idea.

SCIENCE AND INDUSTRY

EIGHT HOURS AND THE CONSTITUTION

Legal limitation of the hours of labor is an industrial and social necessity. It is a social necessity because progress in the tastes, customs, general culture and intelligence of the people is a social necessity, and any important advance in these respects is nearly impossible without increase of leisure. A broader social life cannot come unless opportunity is afforded for its cultivation. Reduction of the hours of labor gives that opportunity, in two ways. First, by actually increasing the amount of time available for recreation, education and social life; second, by diminishing the physical exhaustion of prolonged labor, thus leaving mind and body in better condition for the reception of these higher influences.

By following out a little longer chain of cause and effect, it becomes clear that limitation of the hours of labor is also an industrial necessity. Industrial prosperity depends upon an adequate and increasing market for the products of industry. This market, in turn, depends upon the consuming power of the people, and since the bulk of our population is in the wage or salary class, the consuming power of the people depends upon the amount of their wages. In other words, high wages are the basis of industrial prosperity. Now wages are determined by the customary standard of living of the different groups of laborers, and are high in proportion as the social demands and requirements insisted upon by the wage receivers are broad and varied. Without leisure this broad social life cannot exist; and hence it is that one of the most effective—probably the most effective—way of starting the current towards a general and steady increase of wages is to shorten the hours

of labor.   Experience has proved the truth of this, both
in England and some of our eastern states, where legislation has been adopted reducing the hours of labor.   In
each case it was predicted that there would come a corresponding fall in wages, but, on the contrary, the social
life and standards of the laboring class were so improved by these measures that their wages rose in
every instance in response to the pressure of increased
demands.

Anyone trained to think only along the lines of old
school economics finds it almost impossible to understand how such a thing could take place.   On the old
supply and demand theory of prices it could not be explained at all.   It is only when we substitute the cost
for the quantity idea that light begins to break in on
the subject.   If prices were governed solely by supply
and demand, any general reduction of working hours
and increase of wages would mean universal bankruptcy.   But prices are not governed by supply and
demand.   They are determined by the cost of producing the dearest portion of the supply of any commodity
that is continuously required by the market.   The chief
item in this cost of production is wages ; in fact,
when each item entering into production is traced back
to its source, the entire cost is found to consist of
wages or payment for human service of some kind.

Now, the first effect of shortening the hours of
labor is slightly to increase the cost of the product, and
the manufacturer at once tries to recoup himself either
by paying less wages or by raising the price of his product.   Both of these things he may be able for a short
time to do, but all the economic forces of the community are against the permanence of any such state of
affairs.   The producer who can retain or soon go back
to the old price scale is sure of capturing a good portion
of his competitors' trade.   Knowledge of this fact nat-

urally leads the more enterprising capitalists to introduce improved methods, either of machinery or organization, by means of which they can produce as cheaply
as before.   Indeed, it often happens when anything
occurs to increase the cost of production of a given
commodity, like a shortening of the hours of labor or
increase of wages, that those producers who are already
making a liberal profit will continue to sell at the old
rate, accepting a smaller profit for the time being, in
the expectation of gaining the trade of those competitors who are obliged to put up their prices.   The most
expensive manufacturers, who had been selling practically at cost, are thus forced either to adopt improved
methods or withdraw from the field.   Maintain prices
at a higher level, permanently, they cannot.

Neither can they permanently enforce a reduction
of wages.   Very soon a demand for restoration of the
former wage scale, or even for an increase beyond that
scale, is made.   These demands are refused for a time,
until they become so general—threatening costly
strikes—that compliance is cheaper than resistance.
This involves, of course, another increase in the cost of
production, and it is met just as in the case of reduced
hours; first, by an attempt on the part of the more
hard-pressed producers to raise prices, and finally by
the introduction of improved methods of production
and withdrawal of those competitors who fail to procure
these improvements.

The better methods to which we refer may not be
such as actually lessen the cost of production, but generally they make it possible to produce a larger quantity
at the same expense as before, and the market for this
larger output has already been provided in the increased
wages granted to the laborers.   Thus the final net result
is, that the laborers are working shorter hours and getting the same or more pay, and the manufacturers are

doing a larger business with practically the same aggregate profit, though the rate of profit on each item of product is smaller, and nature, as represented by the improved machinery and more economical system of organization, is defraying the increased cost.

Of course, it is not pretended that this process works with clock-like regularity, or that it can be observed in detail in any one establishment. Economic movements are generally group tendencies, and all that can be intelligently discussed and acted upon is the aggregate trend and outcome in each class of phenomena, after allowing for all the exceptional circumstances. The general movement outlined above, however, is being illustrated at some stage of its progress throughout the entire business world every day in the year, and it is by just that process that all our advance in productive methods, wage increases and cheapening of wealth has come about. Not only has it been directly confirmed in experience, but no other theory of the subject whatever offers any logical and consistent explanation of our industrial progress in the past, or throws light on how similar progress is to be achieved in the future.

This is the point—this matter of future progress—that is of real importance. The only object, in fact, of analyzing economic movements so carefully, and ascertaining their laws, is to gain a knowledge of how to apply public policy to these conditions so as to promote and speed along the forces that make for human improvement.

On this question of shortening the hours of labor it cannot be expected that individual employers will, except in rare cases, act from any very long range point of view; nor is it possible for them to do so. It is perfectly clear to the individual employer that to reduce the hours of labor of his employees, or increase their wages, means for the time being at least an increased expense, and the burden of making up for this by improved methods or more economical management falls entirely upon him. Furthermore, he knows that unless all other employers take the · same action he will be placed at a positive competitive disadvantage, and perhaps will have a hard struggle to maintain his position. These things, therefore, are clearly matters for public rather than private action. Voluntary individual philanthropy is altogether too uncertain a force to be relied on for permanent public improvement and permanent maintenance of desirable conditions. The odds against it are too great, and what we need is not isolated cases of philanthropy and fair dealing here and there in the community, but a concentration of the philanthropic sentiment of the community, coupled also with the long range business sense of the community, that shall establish and enforce everywhere, as permanent features of our industrial life, the conditions which the isolated individual can maintain only at great personal inconvenience and hardship.

A reasonable limitation of the hours of labor in factories, mines, mercantile establishments, on railroads, *etc.*, if made general throughout the whole community, imposes no relative disadvantage on any of the competitors, for they then sustain to each other substantially the same relation as before; and the efforts to improve the methods of production and exchange so as to realize the same profit as before, without increasing the price of the product, becomes a general effort, as it should be, instead of a series of specific hardships. Thus, while individual employers in large numbers cannot be expected to inaugurate short-hour systems regardless of their competitors, these employers can and ought to lend their aid to movements looking toward the general establishment of such a system throughout the community. The manufacturer or busi-

ness man in doing this is in reality taking a long-range
view of his own interests, by providing for the ultimate
expansion of his market (as represented in the working
class) while at the same time maintaining for himself the
practical short-range method which he finds absolutely
necessary in the day-to-day conduct of his business. He
need not attempt to solve the problems of the nation
in his own little establishment, but he can help make
the nation solve its own problems, which are the problems of the whole people and of himself as a part thereof.

   If manufacturers and employers generally refuse
to take this action, then it is proper for the community
at large to go ahead and enact this legislation anyway,
in the knowledge that it cannot bring permanent disaster to the manufacturing class but in reality will be
the guaranty of their ultimate success. So important
a social and industrial reform should not be obliged to
wait until that class in the community which' has the
greatest immediate interest in opposing it shall be
thoroughly convinced of its wisdom, especially since
the movement is not against the real interests of the
employing class. It was against the protests of this
class, in fact, that practically all the short-hour legislation of England and this country was adopted. England now has an universal nine and a half hour system
for factory operatives.

   In this country no national legislation on the subject has ever been enacted except with relation to government employees. It has been considered that since
the Constitution did not mention limitation of the hours
of labor as among the specific powers of Congress, that
subject is one of those " reserved to the states respectively, or to the people." A number of states, however,
have established legal limitation of the hours of labor
in certain classes of industry. All the New England
states have done this, Massachusetts leading with a fifty-

eight hour a week system. New York has a ten hour a day system ; New Jersey has limited the hours of labor to fifty-five per week, and so on. Against this system of state instead of national legislation, however, there is something of the same objection that applies in the case of individual employers, *viz.*, that for a time at least it places the manufacturers of one state at something of a competitive disadvantage with those of such other states as take no action at all in the matter. This means that no state can take this progressive, humane, and economically · necessary step ˙ without bringing upon itself the danger, at least, of a temporary penalty; and this ought not to be so. We are getting an illustration of this now in the case of the cotton industry. Massachusetts, with her fifty-eight hour system, finds it increasingly difficult to compete with southern factories working ten and twelve hours, and even more, per day. Thus New England industries are made to suffer and even their very existence is threatened by reason, not of any economic inferiority on their part, but of a definite superiority in the quality of industrial civilization. Everywhere the higher standards of society should be protected from assault and destruction by the lower, and since the South seems in no mood to apply the short-hour system herself, the only practicable way of protecting and preserving the advance that has been made in some sections of the nation is to establish an uniform hours of labor system throughout the whole country, thus equalizing the competitive conditions in that particular at least, and removing the anomalous reproach that any state should be made to suffer because of its broad-minded foresight and humane statesmanship.

Perhaps it is true that a constitutional amendment will be necessary before such a law as this could be enacted by Congress. If so, there ought to be an indefatigable organized agitation all over the country for submission of such an amendment to the vote of the states. The objection has been made that not only does the constitution fail to grant the right of enacting such a measure, but by the fourteenth amendment it is definitely prohibited. The portion of this famous amendment which has been quoted against almost every sort of progressive legislation is as follows :—

" No state shall make or enforce any law which shall abridge the privileges or immunities of citizens of the United States; nor shall any state deprive any person of life, liberty or property without due process of law, nor deny to any person within its jurisdiction the equal protection of the laws."

If literally interpreted, it is easy to see that this provision might be quoted as invalidating a good part of the legislation of all the states. In fact, on the strength of this amendment, the Illinois law restricting the hours of labor of women in factories to eight hours per day was overthrown by the Supreme Court of that state. But the famous decision of the United States Supreme Court, handed down on February 28th, 1898, affirming the constitutionality of the Utah eight-hour law, finally established the labor legislation of the various states on a sound and permanent legal basis. This decision was an epoch-making event. Future experience may show that the rendering of this decision constituted one of the greatest services the Supreme Court has ever rendered to the American people. It has distinctly and formally announced, as a permanent principle of our institutions, that the constitution must be interpreted in the light of the new conditions that arise as our national life expands and as new problems develop that were not foreseen by the framers of our fundamental law; in other words, that the provisions of the constitution must not be considered as carrying along with them perpetually the same interpretation that was given them at the foundation of the nation. It must be treated as an elastic rather than an absolutely inflexible instrument, and thus, while forever safeguarding our liberties, not be allowed to become a stumbling block in our path of national progress.

Briefly, the Utah case was this. A mine owner named Holden had employed a laborer to work in an underground mine ten hours each day, after the eight-hour law previously referred to had gone into effect. The defense was that this eight-hour law, even though in accord with the constitution of Utah, was in violation of the fourteenth amendment to the constitution of the United States. The Supreme Court of Utah sustained the eight-hour law. It was then taken to the United States Supreme Court and, on February 28th last, a decision was rendered affirming that of the Utah Court. Justice Brown, in delivering the opinion of the Supreme Court, said, in part —:

"An examination of both these classes of cases under the fourteenth amendment will demonstrate that, in passing upon the validity of state legislation under that amendment, this court has not failed to recognize the fact that the law is, to a certain extent, a progressive science; that in some of the states methods of procedure, which at the time the constitution was adopted, were deemed essential to the protection and safety of the people, or to the liberty of the citizen, have been found to be no longer necessary; that restrictions which had formerly been laid upon the conduct of individuals, or of classes of individuals, had proved detrimental to their interests; while, upon the other hand, certain other classes of persons, particularly those engaged in dangerous or unhealthful employments, have been found to be in need of additional protection. . . . While the cardinal principles of justice are immutable, the methods by which justice is administered are subject to constant fluctuation, and (that) the constitution of the United States, which is necessarily and to a large extent inflexible and exceedingly difficult of amendment, should not be so construed as to deprive the states of the power to so amend their laws as to make them conform to the wishes of the citizens as they may deem best for the public welfare without bringing them into conflict with the supreme law of the land. . . .

"But if it be within the power of a legislature to adopt (such) means for the protection of the lives of its citizens, it is difficult to see why precautions may not also be adopted for the protection of their health and morals. It is as much for the interest of the state that the public health should be preserved as that life should be made secure. With this end in view quarantine laws have been enacted in most if not all of the states; insane asylums, public hospitals and institutions for the care and education of the blind established, and special measures taken for the exclusion of infected cattle, rags and decayed fruit. In other states laws have been enacted limiting the hours during which women and children shall be employed in factories; and while their constitutionality, at least, as applied to women, has been doubted in some of the states, they have been generally upheld. . . . The former [employers] naturally desire to obtain as much labor as possible from their employees, while the latter are often induced by the fear of discharge to conform to regulations which their judgment, fairly exercised, would pronounce to be detrimental to their health or strength. In other words, the proprietors lay down the rules, and the laborers are practically constrained to obey them. In such cases self-interest is often an unsafe guide, and the legislature may properly interpose its authority.

"It may not be improper to suggest in ,this connection that although the prosection in this case was
against the employer of labor, who apparently under
the statute is the only one liable, his defense is not so
much that his right to contract has been infringed upon,
but that the act works a peculiar hardship to his employees, whose right to labor as long as they please is
alleged to be thereby violated. The argument would
certainly come with better grace and greater cogency
from the latter class. But the fact that both parties are
of full age and competent to contract does not necessarily deprive the state of the power to interfere where
the parties do not stand upon an equality, or where the
public health demands that one party to the contract
shall be protected against himself. The state still retains an interest in his welfare, however reckless he
may be. The whole is no greater than the sum of all
the parts, and when the individual health, safety and welfare are sacrificed or neglected, the state must suffer."

As we have said, this is indeed an epoch-making
decision. Few things were so greatly needed at this
time as this liberal interpretation of the effect of our
national constitution on the legislative rights of the
different states. A view of the constitution which
seems both socially and politically sound and wholesome thus becomes the official pronouncement of the
one institution in this country that is in a sense even
higher than the constitution—because authorized to
interpret it—*viz.*, the Supreme Court. It opens the
way to the progress of rational reform legislation throughout the country, and thus not only establishes the constitution itself on a firmer basis than ever but prevents it from becoming, as it might have become under
the strict interpretation idea, an increasing hindrance
to the industrial and social advance of the republic.

SCIENCE AND INDUSTRY NOTES

It is most interesting to trace the process whereby new elements of material well-being are continually brought, by natural economic forces, down from the point where only a very few can enjoy them, because of their high cost, and become available to larger and larger groups until finally the very profitableness of the business of producing them depends upon their general consumption by the community. This is being illustrated at present in the matter of steel as a material of construction in private buildings. It was not so long ago that the use of steel in the construction of great office buildings was an innovation, and it then seemed probable that this material would always be too expensive for use in any but very large and profitable structures. Now, however, steel is being used in the construction of small buildings, and probably it will be adopted eventually in the erection of private dwellings. As the *Age of Steel* says, on this point:—

"The use of steel in private buildings is an innovation that is not without its significance to steel makers. The iron and steel ribs of the modern sky-scraper were novelties not long since in the anatomy of public structures. They are so no longer. Iron and steel in less pretentious buildings and even in private houses are likely to follow suit. The wedge is entering the block of traditional customs, and it seems to be simply a question of time when for sound and good reasons, such as stability, economy and rapidity of construction, and fire protection, iron and steel will largely displace much of the material now used. We are turning out steel in enormous quantities and at a constant minimizing of cost, and there will be neither lack of material nor any unreasonable burden of cost, when the change is brought about."

Good roads have always been a crying necessity in rural districts, but it seemed to require something more

The Good Roads Movement

than rural agitation to accomplish anything in the matter. The extraordinary development of bicycling, both for reereation and business purposes, put real life and persistence into the good roads movement, and within the last few years considerable progress has been made. At first, of course, the improved roads are built chiefly in the vicinity of cities and large towns, but they are beginning to extend out into the country, as for instance in Massachusetts, which is being gridironed with a magnificent system of paved highways. There are publications and associations in different states devoted exclusively to road improvement. One result of all this has been a rapid decline in the cost of street pavement. " A few years ago," says the *Scientific American*, quoting from an address by General Roy Stone, of the United States Department of Agriculture, " the macadam roads of New Jersey cost $10,000 per mile; now equally good roads are being built for $3,000, even where railway transportation of material is required; and in localities better supplied with road material, and where a narrower road is deemed sufficient, $1,500, or even less, will make a mile of good stone road."

This is the almost universal process in the case of all improvements. At first they are in what might be called the "luxury" stage, but as their use and adoption becomes more and more general, the proportionate cost of production is constantly diminished, and improvements in the methods of production are introduced, until the new thing is finally brought within reach of practically the whole community. The industrial progress of the world is but an illustration, in a myriad of forms, of the workings of this simple but all-powerful law.

CURRENT LITERATURE

LOOM AND SPINDLE.*

This book is the story of the life of the early mill girls in Lowell, Massachusetts. Lowell was one of the earliest seats of cotton manufacture in this country. It also has the distinction of having been the home of probably the first publication in the interest of labor in the United States, called the *Lowell Offering*. This paper was unique in that it was published and edited by the factory girls themselves; indeed, its title page, which was a highly artistic production, was LOWELL OFFERING, *A Repository of Original Articles, written by " Factory Girls."* Its publication began in 1845, and it was not only the first but the only one of its kind, so far as we know, ever published. In no other instance has there been a labor paper published for women, conducted entirely by women, especially women working in factories.

Mrs. Robinson was one of these factory girls herself and writes chiefly from practical experience. In places the book has something the character of an autobiography. It is very readable and is a contribution to the history of factory life. In the narratives and biographies of women connected with the publication of the *Offering*, data are furnished which otherwise it would be difficult to obtain, if indeed they could be obtained at all.

The introduction by Hon. Carroll D. Wright gives a real economic and historical touch to the book. Perhaps no person in this country is more familiar with the

---

* *Loom and Spindle ; or, Life Among the Early Mill Girls.* By Harriet H. Robinson. Introduction by Hon. Carroll D. Wright. Thomas Y. Crowell & Co., New York and Boston. Cloth, gilt top. 216 pp.

history of the factory system than is Colonel Wright,
and it was therefore very fitting that he should write an
introduction to Mrs. Robinson's book.

Colonel Wright also gives a mild suggestive cor-
rection to the last chapter of the book, in which is compared the condition of the present factory operatives
with those of forty years ago, and, as Col. Wright says,
"gives the surface appearance of deterioration, when
the real fact is that through the factory the lower orders,
so far as mental capacity is concerned, are being constantly elevated."

There seems to be an inherent tendency in the
human mind to throw some kind of a halo around the
past as compared with the present, especially with present defects. This is probably due to the fact that we
are very conscious of the defects of the present, under
which we see or feel the chafing ; whereas in viewing
the past we are apt to remember in comparison only the
more pleasant features. Thus it is that we are constantly hearing the Middle Ages praised for simplicity
of life, the kindly paternal care of the rich and employers, and the fatherly attention of the priests to the
needs of the poor, and so work up the feeling that,
judged by the condition of the poor to-day, those were
good old times. In all such pictures we fail to see the
groveling, plodding hardship and suffering for the want
of the common necessaries of life, and lack of sufficient
freedom and independence even to refer to the fact.
In the same way the people of the South will talk of
the attractive side of slavery—how good the masters
were to the "Uncle Toms."

This attitude has been assumed toward no feature
of the labor question in this country so much as toward
the condition of factory operatives in New England.
The laborers themselves, and many people who are
honestly interested in the labor problem, never tire of

affirming that the condition of the factory operatives in Massachusetts and New England is worse to-day than it was forty years ago, and the very existence of the *Lowell Offering*, with factory girls sufficiently intelligent to creditably edit and conduct such a periodical, is pointed to as conclusive evidence of the superior condition of factory operatives in the '40's as compared with the '90's.

Mrs. Robinson, even, is somewhat affected with the same view. There is a certain seeming of truth in this statement, but it is only seeming. When the factory system began in New England, as is clearly pointed out in the little book under consideration, the operatives consisted for the most part of farmers' children. Now, the New England farmers at this time were a rather superior class. New England was settled by a people who were the cream of centuries of social progress in old England. Consequently, the New England farmer was not the traditional agricultural laborer, but in reality a spirited, independent, intelligent personality. Children of New England farmers, therefore, were accustomed to some kind of inspiring home environment and, as a class, were vigorous, active and intelligent. The *Lowell Offering* would have been an impossible product from a collection of the children of English agricultural laborers or the agricultural laborers of any other country.

When the factory system began in England, it could appeal to the poor-law authorities to drive the people out of the poor-houses and force them into the factories, and thus obtain a cowed, crouching, menial class of laborers, whose previous environment had been poverty and pauperism. In New England the case was the reverse. There were no poor-houses to be emptied into the factories. On the contrary, the factory owners had to attract the children of the farmers into their factories, and in order to do so they necessarily could not impose too much discipline or·imitate the early English factory *regime*.   It is true that the hours of labor were from five in the morning till seven at night, with half an hour for breakfast and half an hour for dinner ; but none of the rushing or harsh discipline was enforced, and for the most part factory girls went to the mill only as a sort of temporary occupation, not as a necessary means of supplying the family income.

As the factory developed, the early New England male operatives graduated into overseers and heads of departments, and, as the factory towns grew, entered business and their places were taken by immigrants. "The first immigrants," as Mrs. Robinson tells us (page 12) "to come to Lowell were from England. The Irishman soon followed ; but not for many years did the Frenchman, Italian and German come to take possession of the cotton mills. The English were of the artisan class, but the Irish came as ' hewers of wood and drawers of water.' The first Irishwomen to work in the Lowell mills were usually scrubbers and waste-pickers."   Here is the secret of what seems to be the deterioration of the New England operative class. Those who are there now are neither the same nor descendants of the same people who were there at the time of the *Lowell Offering* in the '40's. As the factories multiplied, the operative population began to consist more and more exclusively of immigrants from Europe, first, as Mrs. Robinson says, the English.   But the English soon moved toward the top, into more responsible positions, and the Irish became the rank and file; and as years passed on the French, Norwegians, and others of a still poorer type were introduced. To-day these latter are the representatives of the factory population.   It is true that the French Canadian and Norwegian now working in the New England factory is not so intelligent a type, and does not represent so high a social standard as did the early factory operatives composed of the children of New England farmers; but this does not mean that there has been no progress. It means that the early class has progressed out at the top, and a fresh supply, furnished up through the bottom from an entirely inferior stock, has taken their place. But the way fairly to estimate the progress of the factory population is not to compare the condition of those who were there forty years ago with the condition of those who are there to-day. Compare the condition of the Irish or French Canadians in Massachusetts to-day with the condition of the same Canadians or Irishmen thirty years ago, in Canada and Ireland where they were, and it will be found that the progress in the condition of the present operatives has been no less conspicuous than in the case of the original New England operatives.

It is true that the social status of the operatives employed in these factories, has not risen during the last thirty years in anything like the same proportion that the general conditions of the country and of civilization have advanced. This is because they are not the same people who have been there during this progressive period. It is a kind of panorama in which, every decade or thereabouts, a new class has appeared, but always from a much inferior position. This is a fact which should never be lost sight of in any discussion of the history and condition of New England factory operatives. It is not a feature in the life of English factory operatives or those of any other country, because they are practically the same people, or their descendants ; they have not been supplanted by immigrants from countries with definitely inferior industrial and social conditions.

ADDITIONAL REVIEWS.

HAWAII: OUR NEW POSSESSIONS. By John R. Musick. Funk & Wagnalls Co., New York and London. 1898. 534 pp.

The author of the Columbian historical novels puts his account of Hawaii into narrative form, relating his experiences and observations during a tour of the islands. This method adds somewhat to the interest of the book in reading, but does not increase its value as permanent literature. Indeed, the work is so voluminous that it becomes something of a task to pick out here and there the important facts recorded by Mr. Musick in the course of his travels. The book is handsomely gotten up and profusely illustrated with half tones and pen sketches.

Of course, just at present, the point of interest in such a book as this lies in the light it can throw on the character of the population of this newly annexed territory. Mr. Musick enlarges on the scenic beauties of these islands, but it can hardly be maintained that annexation of Hawaii was justified by reason of luxuriant foliage or imposing cliffs, for of both of these we have an abundance here at home, as well as vast tracts of undeveloped country promising as rich returns as anything to be found in the islands of the Pacific. The real question of interest, as we have said, relates to the people of these islands.

A few of Mr. Musick's scattered comments throw some light on this. For instance: "One is more than ever convinced that monarchy is a relic of barbarism by a visit to the Hawaiian Islands. The idea of equality of people can not yet be driven into the Hawaiian's head any more than it can be into the heads of some of our Europeans. The divine right of kings is still a prominent idea with the average native. They would not object to President Dole as a king, but they do not understand how a republic of the people, by the people, and for the people can be strong enough to last." So much for Hawaiian comprehension of the fundamental principle of American political institutions.

Furthermore, it appears from Mr. Musick's account that leprosy, while ostensibly confined to the island of Molokai, in reality constitutes an ever present possibility throughout the whole group. "There are some," says Mr. Musick, "who conceal their afflicted relatives and friends to prevent their being sent, thus propagating the disease and endangering their own homes."

Again, in annexing Hawaii, we have acquired, among other valuable possessions, the contract-labor system in its worst form. Of course, it cannot be imagined that this will continue after American laws are applied in the islands, but some idea of what the general quality of labor in Hawaii must be is conveyed by the very fact of the existence of such a system. Mr. Musick calls it "simply diabolical," and says : "It is one of the relics of monarchy, controlled and manipulated by designing men, *and not easy to get rid of.*" (Italics ours.) Elsewhere he says : "The contract laborer has no more privileges than the negro slave had. His government, for a certain stipulated sum, by some sort of contract, hires him to the Hawaiian Government, and that government, for a given period and a given sum, hires him to the planters and business men of the country. It is the most wretched of all slavery. . . . I have heard it said that some of the lower classes live on $1 per month." A country whose free labor approached anywhere near the standard of living and political capacity necessary for participation in American institutions would not tolerate a system so utterly degrading as this. Its very existence is a reflection on the quality not only of the contract but of the free labor.

Yet it now appears that the Commission appointed to recommend a form of government for Hawaii is about to report in favor of admitting the islands as a territory, which is only one step from statehood. It seems difficult, in the present state of expansionist fever, sufficiently to emphasize what this will mean, in view of the fact that territories can be converted into states at almost any time, when the interests of the party in power seem to demand it. Of course, now that these islands belong to the United States it is not the part of political wisdom nor of patriotism to neglect them because of former opposition to the policy that has already been carried out. Nevertheless, it is apparent that we have acquired some extremely troublesome and dangerous problems in these new possessions, which will require most careful treatment if they are to be prevented from reacting on our own institutions and progress.

The problems we would have forced upon us in annexing the Philippines, with a population one hundred times that of Hawaii, become all the more significant and menacing in view of those now developing in the islands just annexed. Mr. Musick, in discussing the question of annexation, though he might be expected to favor that policy, takes no very definite position on the matter and was evidently impressed by the fact that, in his own language, "The Hawaiian Islands are not Paradise."

AMONG THE MAGAZINES.

In the *Journal of Political Economy* for September there is a somewhat extensive review of "The Present Condition of Social Democracy in Germany," by Conrad Schmidt. This review is especially interesting because, as the writer says, "Germany has become the classic land of modern socialism." The German mind is naturally methodical and bureaucratic, and the leading apostles of the socialist movement have come from Germany. Consequently, the strength of the socialist movement there is not surprising, but it is certainly a source of apprehension to the government, in view of the fact that at the election of June, 1898, the socialist party polled over two million one hundred thousand votes throughout the empire. With this increase, however, as Mr. Schmidt points out, there is a growing conservatism in the socialist party and a disposition to adopt the evolutionary rather than revolutionary theory of social progress. This is a good tendency, because, despite the fallacy of the socialist theory *per se*, it is probable that whatever industrial reform is developed in Germany will come as a result of socialist influence.

Social Democracy in Germany.

Clinton Rogers Woodruff, Secretary of the National Municipal League, says in the October *North American Review* that "Municipal reformers now quite generally believe that the municipal problem is in a large part one of men. We must get the right men in the right place, and then keep them there." So far as it may be true that particular men stand for particular ideas or principles of municipal reform this is undoubtedly true. When it happens that in dearth of any proclaimed platform of principles the man himself has to be the platform, of

Methods of Municipal Reform.

course the question of good municipal government is a question of the men nominated. It is important to note, however, that after all it is the principles represented, rather than the individuals *per se*, that are important. The difficulty at present is not that the mayors of our great cities lack personal integrity but that the political parties have not reached the point of presenting definite propositions of municipal reform and making municipal campaigns upon the issues thus raised. Ordinarily, about the only question that is vigorously discussed is that of taxation, and both parties seek to show a record of low taxes as though that were the crowning and only test of good government in city affairs. What is needed more than anything else is a public opinion definitely in favor of numerous lines of municipal reform policy, so strong that the political parties will be literally obliged to embody these demands in their platforms. This would realize the ideal so long sought of having municipal campaigns fought on municipal issues. Associations for the creation of public opinion along these lines are, therefore, in the right direction and will help to bring about just this result. It is encouraging to find Mr. Woodruff saying that, "What we may call, for want of a better designation, policy determining organizations, are growing in number. In this class may be placed municipal ownership leagues, park and playground associations, public education and improvement societies." Whether all of these are aiming at desirable ends or not (and with reference to municipal ownership leagues the wisdom of the end sought is extremely doubtful) they at least embody the correct idea so far as the method of promoting municipal reforms is concerned, It is for these educative organizations to create public opinion, and, by holding the balance of power, compel the political organizations to make issues along these new and progressive lines.

INSTITUTE WORK

POLITICAL EVOLUTION

Political institutions are an evolution from industrial and social conditions. They are really the legal framework of society, and are created, modified and abolished as the growing industrial and social needs of the community require. Ownership of property, personal, social and political freedom, are the real causes which lead to the formation, maintenance and modification of forms of government and political institutions. Where private ownership of property is unknown, and hunting, fishing and reliance upon the voluntary productions of nature are the means of getting a living, political institutions are practically impossible. Chaos reigns supreme. In the absence of economic, not to say social, interests, there is no motive to which an appeal can be made for order and institutional government, and superstitious appeal to the unknown in some form has to be resorted to. Theocracy, or government by God, which was largely an appeal to fear, was the earliest form of government. Even Moses, in order to govern the unruly tribes of Israel with any success, adopted a theocratic form. All his edicts were " Thus saith the Lord."

The first great change in industrial life, as affecting civilization and government, was the transition from pastoral to agricultural life. This change in the character of industry brought with it the necessity of a new type of society. Agriculture necessitated some degree of industrial precision and order, such, for instance, as the planting and harvesting of crops, fencing in the fields from destruction by cattle, and other conditions which were of a similar orderly and precise character, as compared with the loose, irresponsible, hap-hazard methods of nomadic life. The raising of crops and tending domesticated flocks and herds also involved relatively permanent domiciles, which localized the population, in order to be able to secure the results of the labor expended. This evolution of personal property, as the result of persistent labor, made necessary the recognition of a rule of social conduct, or moral code. Since the means of living were no longer gratuitously supplied by nature but could be secured only by individual labor, each one wanted the results of his own industry, and the idea that everything was everybody's ceased. Thus the right to take everything in sight had to be forbidden in order to restrain the predatory habits developed in pastoral life.

As industrial life became the established order and the rights of property were generally recognized, theocracy was superseded by autocracy. The earliest form of temporal authority was naturally crude and despotic. The predatory habit, like all long established customs, died slowly. Not only was protection needed by individuals against other individuals, but protection of the interests and property of the group, whether tribe or nation, against the onslaught of other groups, was a dominant feature of early society, and made militarism essential. Successful military leaders naturally were heroes and grew to acquire absolute authority. Thus the increase of industrial interests and rise of militarism evolved—if not the earliest—a very early form of political institutions, which may be characterized as autocracy, specimens of which still exist in such countries as Persia, Turkey and Russia.

The next great social transition is from agriculture to a commercial and manufacturing type of industrial society. It is peculiar that wherever and whenever agriculture is the industrial type of society, despotism, social, political and religious, is sure to be the form of government. With the evolution of industry towards manufacture and commerce comes a new class of interests. The growth of new industrial interests brings new ideas and demands, and thus industrial groups arise, each demanding something peculiar to itself. We have in the Middle Ages the growth of the walled town and charter cities, and within these towns arose different economic and social organizations, as the religious guilds, the frith guilds, the merchant guilds, the craft guilds. These were the nuclei of new social and political forces. They began to demand certain laws regulating this, that and the other thing, as affecting their particular interests, and thus arose a modification in the political government of the cities. Later, to protect their interests, the cities demanded recognition in the general government, and so we find that with the growth or transition from purely agricultural to manufacturing and commercial industries absolute despotism was first modified by the concession of numerous charters giving special privileges, and ultimately superseded by parliamentary government. This came very slowly, because the change in the industrial composition of society was very slow. It was over four hundred years from the calling of the first Parliament in England to the final establishment of parliamentary government (1265–1688). It was during this time that the industrial transformation took place. The cities arose, which finally overthrew feudalism, and as industrial interests increased people asserted their rights to more and more political power, until the power of landed aristocracy and the monarch was ultimately subordinated to that of Parliament. In the Revolution of 1688, constitutional monarchy with representative government was established.

During the eighteenth century another industrial revolution occurred, and the era of factory methods was ushered in. The development of this new type of industry has been the chief industrial characteristic of the nineteenth century. This separated home from the workshop, cut the last thread of wardship between the state and labor, established a wage system, and differentiated the wage class into industrial groups, with definite social and economic interests. Out of this complex industrial life have come constantly increasing demands for new laws and modification or repeal of old ones, which has resulted in a radical change in the type of political institutions, expanding the principles of representation, which were dimly visible in the thirteenth century in the meagre representation of towns, into full-fledged democracy as represented both in theory and practice in the United States, and in fact in England.

Thus it will be seen that the evolution of political institutions follows the evolution of industry. Of course it is true that political institutions are sometimes cause as well as effect. Each modification of old laws or establishment of new, extends or confirms some new privilege or right, or protects some interest previously neglected. This gives security, encouragement and opportunity for the still further expansion and expression of new industrial wants and social demands, which gradually crystallize into political sentiment and result in still further expansion of political institutions. But through it all there remains the constant relation of demand and result, the demand always arising from industrial and social sources, the result always being the conversion of public opinion thus created into public policy and legislative enactment.

For instance, the evolution of the factory system in the eighteenth and the first quarter of the nineteenth

century radically changed not only the industrial conditions but the social status of the laboring class. In
separating home from workshop and employer from
employed it destroyed the last remnants of wardship in
laborers and responsibility for their personal welfare in
employers. This, together with the new character of
the employment under the factory system, gave rise to
a multitude of new interests which rapidly grew into
new problems. The health of operatives was impaired
by the bad condition of the new workshops and the oppressive driving and long hours of work. This gave
rise to an intense discussion of the labor question,
which, in its various bearings under the factory system,
became a matter not only of social but of political concern. Legislation was demanded for lessening the
hours of the working day, improving the sanitary conditions of the workshops, and finally providing education for factory children. This agitation was a source
of education to the masses, through which the people
began to participate in the discussion of these and other
public questions. The class to which political power
was entrusted was very small, and, as is always the
case, those in power were averse to any invasion which
threatened to lessen their authority, and hence were
reluctant to give ear to the new and what seemed to be
democratic demands. A very natural outcome was that
a new class began to demand the right to vote.

The demand for extension of the franchise began
as early as 1815, with the Henry Hunt movement,
which received its great impetus at the Peterloo Massacre on August 16th, 1819. This movement continued
with little break until 1832, when it culminated in what
is known as the First Reform Bill, which gave the merchants and middle class of England the right to vote.
In the new parliament thus created, Gladstone first entered public life. The middle class who had been

enfranchised by the Reform Bill of 1832 thought the millennium of political freedom had arrived when they were admitted to power, and like the aristocracy who had opposed their enfranchisment, they resisted any demands for giving the franchise to the laborers. Consequently a new agitation began, which gave birth to the Chartist movement, the Ten-Hour movement, and the Trades-Union movement, all acting concurrently, one for political representation, another for industrial legislation and the third for economic organization.

The Chartist movement ended in 1848 by the imprisonment of most of its leaders. The Ten-Hour movement culminated in 1847 in the adoption of the Ten-Hour factory law, and the Trades-Union movement has continued on, to give birth to still new demands. On the ruins of the Chartist movement, in the early '60s, a political reform movement began, demanding the franchise for laborers, and this time enlisted the leadership of Gladstone, who made it a political issue in 1865 and introduced his measure in 1866. This was defeated by the Tories under Disraeli, but the party defeating it was compelled the next year to introduce a measure itself of a still more radical character, which became law in 1867. This, the Second Reform Bill, extended the franchise only to laborers in boroughs. So completely did this whet the appetite of the workingmen for political power that a new agitation set in and, in 1874, again under Gladstone's leadership, the franchise was extended to the agricultural laborers, which gave England practical democracy, though theoretical monarchy.

All this conclusively shows how thoroughly knitted together are the economic interests, political ideas and political institutions of society in all its varying phases. No matter by how rapid or insensible a gradation the

changes come, they are always in obedience to the same
economic and social forces.   If we fully recognize the
significance of this fact, which constitutes the unvary-
ing law in all human society, we shall never make the
mistake of getting the cart before the horse and assuming that the political institutions of a country are the
guaranty of prosperity and freedom.   On the contrary,
we clearly see that the real source of prosperity and
freedom is in the economic and social conditions of the
people, of which political institutions are but the outward expression and flexible instrument.   It is for this
reason that we so often say that laws can only be enforced when there is a public opinion behind them.
Statutes without public sentiment are practically impotent; consequently all efforts permanently to improve
the intelligence, integrity and efficiency of political life
must be sought through the forces which differentiate,
widen and elevate the industrial and social life of the
masses.   Take away the conditions of industrial welfare, and freedom-giving institutions will grow impotent
and crumble.   First corruption and then despotism will
take their place, democracy will be superseded by lower
and more aristocratic and despotic forms, simply in
order to adjust the political institutions to the industrial
needs, capacities and aspirations of the people.

The tree of freedom grows in economic soil, blos-
soms in the sunshine of social welfare, and by collective action finally ripens into political institutions.
Hence the safety of popular government and free
institutions must ever rest on the social and industrial
welfare of the common people.

WORK FOR NOVEMBER

In our October lesson we covered the general theory of national development as the great, conspicuous method of societary evolution, and discussed the nature of the state and the proper functions of government. We saw that there is no one particular form of government that is absolutely superior to all others, under all conditions, but that governmental institutions should be adapted to the needs and peculiarities of each several nation, and hence will vary with varying degrees of civilization. Democracy, for instance, is no more adapted to Chinese conditions than despotism would be to American; probably the results of an arbitrary exchange of institutions between the two countries would be equally disastrous in each case.

It is interesting to note, right in this connection, that even the moderate reforms proposed by the lately deposed Emperor of China were not popular, and some of them, had they been practically applied, would have stirred up open rebellion. Unquestionably the government of China is fairly representative of Chinese conditions, ideas and wishes; and the only way to alter or improve the political institutions of that or of any other country is to introduce forces which will expand and develop the social character of the people.

This month we proceed to study the " Evolution of Political Institutions;" showing how the general principles of government and theory of national development outlined last month are deduced from experience itself; that is, are not mere *a priori* assumptions but are in reality *history systematized and interpreted*. Needless to say, this is the accepted scientific method of investigation, and the only one capable of leading to sound theoretical propositions.

The topic for November is No. III in the curriculum, sub-divided as follows :

III. EVOLUTION OF POLITICAL INSTITUTIONS.
  a Theocracy.
  b Autocracy.
  c Rise of representative government.
  d Constitutional monarchy.
  e Democracy.

REQUIRED READING

In " Principles of Social Economics," Chapters I to VII inclusive, of Part I. In GUNTON'S MAGAZINE for November, the class lecture on " Political Evolution." In GUNTON INSTITUTE BULLETIN No. 2 (Sept. 17th), lecture on " How Shall Our New Possessions be Governed ? "

SUGGESTED READING *

In Maine's " Ancient Law," Chapter V, to page 133. In Maine's " Popular Government," Essay II. In Pollock's " History of the Science of Politics," Chapter IV. In Gneist's " History of the English Parliament," from Section 8 of Chapter II to Section 5 of Chapter III, both inclusive. In Guizot's " History of Civilization," Lecture VII.

NOTES AND SUGGESTIONS

Required Reading. — The chapters assigned in " Principles of Social Economics " this month treat of the progress of civilization in all its aspects, industrial and social as well as political, whereas the class lecture in the magazine deals specifically with *political* ad-

* Books here suggested may be obtained of publishers as follows, if not available in local or traveling libraries: *Ancient Law*, by Sir Henry Maine; Henry Holt & Co., New York; $3.50. *Popular Government*, by Sir Henry Maine; Henry Holt & Co,. New York; 412 pp.; $3.50. *Introduction to the History of the Science of Politics*, by Sir Frederick Pollock, M.A.; The Macmillan Company, New York; 128 pp.; 75c. *History of the English Parliament*, by Dr. Rudolf von Gneist; G. P. Putnam's Sons, New York; 462 pp.; $3.00. *History of Civilization*, by M. Guizot; Appleton & Co., New York; 403 pp.; $1.50

vance, tracing the process of development from despotic
autocracy to democratic self-government. Thus the
lecture gives a more definite idea of the particular topic
in hand, but in reality the method of treatment pursued in "Principles" is the more philosophical, since
political progress never actually comes alone but is
always accompanied by—indeed, is the result of—industrial and social improvement. It is very important
to remember this point; because one cannot have any
accurate idea of political evolution dissociated from the
material and social conditions which produce and shape
any given type of governmental institutions. It is impossible to separate these different lines of progress,
because they are interdependent; political freedom cannot be secured or permanently maintained by any people that has not first come well out of the agricultural
and hand-labor type of industry into the era of capitalistic production, relatively high wages and broad social
life. This, in brief, is the deduction to be drawn from
the historical record traced in the seven chapters assigned in "Principles."

Suggested Reading.—The passages selected in Maine's
"Ancient Law" treat of what may be considered the
primitive foundation of all political organization, namely,
the family groups. The author shows how the patriarchal
system of government expanded "by the absorption of
strangers within its circle," and developed successively
into the House, the Tribe and the State. Of course the
patriarchal system could only exist under the simplest,
crudest conditions of industrial life, and the progress
to tribal and national organizations merely reflects the
growing interdependence of interests and complexity of
relations which settled life, with agriculture, manufacture and trade, necessarily involved.

In the same author's work on "Popular Government," there is a very discerning and judicious essay

on "The Nature of Democracy," which might well be read in connection with this month's topic. He shows that in reality democracy is merely a form of government, not different in *essence* from monarchy, even; having the same conditions to satisfy and discharging practically the same functions, though through different organs. The powers and obligations of government may be substantially the same under either form, the difference being that in the one case these powers are exercised by an individual or group of rulers, and in the other by the subjects themselves. Which system is best is not a question of absolute, inherent superiority, but of *adaptibility* to given conditions. Some of the author's comments on democracy are seemingly influenced by his background of British conservatism, but nevertheless they are in the main just, and philosophically sound. Their import to us is not at all that democracy is a failure here, or that any other form of government would work better, but simply that in our just and proper belief in democratic institutions for ourselves we should not make the mistake of assuming that our system can be extended with good results to all sorts and conditions of men. In other words, our real mission to less advanced races is not necessarily to impose a democratic government upon them, under the mistaken notion that democracy always means liberty, but to help introduce among them the forces of *industrial* civilization—the necessary groundwork of any genuine political capacity for self-government.

Sir Frederick Pollock's small volume deals more with the history of political theories than of political institutions, but it is important inasmuch as the theories discussed reflect the type of political ideas prevalent at various periods. In the particular chapter suggested, however, the discussion treats chiefly of the political doctrines of the nineteenth century. In his concluding remarks the author makes certain suggestions of his own with regard to the proper functions of the state, which are eminently sound and reasonable. Rejecting the Spencerian *laissez faire* idea, he says : " Not only material security, but the perfection of human and social life, is what we aim at in that organized co-operation of many men's lives and works which is called the State."

From Magna Charta down to the complete establishment of the two houses of Parliament is the period covered in the reading suggested in Gneist's " History of the English Parliament." This whole volume might be read with profit, but perhaps the most significant portion, from the standpoint of our particular subject of study, is that which we have selected, describing the beginnings of representative government in England. Our own free democratic institutions were, in reality, made possible only by the centuries of struggle for political representation in the mother country.

Guizot's lectures on the " History of Civilization" all have a bearing on political evolution, but, if any one lecture is to be singled out as specially significant, it is the seventh, on " Rise of Free Cities." Out of the relatively complex industrial relations and social life of the towns and cities of the twelfth and thirteenth centuries sprang the ideas and demands which compelled successive concessions of freedom and gradually transformed, in England at least, autocratic into representative government.

LOCAL CENTER WORK

It happened that the reading mapped out last month included one of the most abstruse discussions, for the beginner at least, in the whole field of political science; namely, that relating to the nature of the state, particularly as to whether the state should be considered an organism or an organization. It is not important or even desirable that students should spend a great amount of time in endeavoring to get a thorough comprehension of this point just at present, because it is one of the things that becomes entirely clear only as we get familiar, later on, with various practical phases of the subject which throw light back on the question of what the state is and what functions it should perform. It seemed necessary, for the sake of logical development of the subject, to place this discussion first, but students should not by any means get the impression at the outset that the succeeding topics in the course are equally intricate and abstract. The only point of immediate importance here is that the state should always be thought of, not as a sort of *larger man* (or organism), of which individual human beings are only inferior fractional parts, but merely as an institution inferior to man and meant only to serve him; a means to an end; an *organization* for the purpose of doing by joint action certain things which will promote the welfare of all.

The reading this month is chiefly historical, and offers a good range of topics for local center programmes. There might be, for instance, papers on: What is theocracy? What is autocracy? How did representative government arise ; How constitutional monarchies differ from republics ; Influence of the free cities on political progress; Industrial progress and political freedom. Debates might be held on the questions: *Resolved*, that political liberty is the result rather than the cause of industrial progress. *Resolved*, that all governments, in a broad sense, represent the character of the people and can be permanently improved only by raising social and industrial conditions. Questions on readings to date would prove interesting; also, informal discussions on unclear points, or readings from works mentioned in the suggested literature and not available to all members.

KARL MARX

ECONOMICS AND PUBLIC AFFAIRS

NEW YORK IN THE SENATE

In order to give to our government the maximum democracy with the minimum danger, the Fathers of the Republic wisely aimed to have the people's voice expressed in our governing machinery through group or state representation, as well as by direct expression of individual citizens. To this end the constitution provides that one branch of the federal government shall represent the direct and frequently expressed opinions of the entire people. Hence the members of Congress are elected by direct vote of the people, and for the short term of two years. In this way the most rapid changes in public opinion on all important questions find immediate expression in the popular branch of the federal government. With our federation of states into a nation, there are really group or state interests somewhat distinct from the national interest. The extent of territory, variety of climate and industrial resources, give rise to certain distinctly local industrial and political interests. It is universally true that the quality, character and direction of social development in any community is largely influenced by the character of the industries and employment of the people. This industrial or group interest necessarily gives rise to a certain degree of group ideas of public policy. This was the stronger in this country from the fact that the different states were previously separated colonies, with political individuality. After the revolution this group or state individuality assumed a form of political sovereignty on the theory of the maximum freedom in group or state interests and the minimum central or federal authority.

Before the civil war state sovereignty was a very conspicuous feature of our national life. After the rebellion it underwent some modification and the republic became a nation rather than a confederacy of little sovereignties. The idea that the federal government stood for a nation, and not a comparatively loose association of states, was more thoroughly established, but the theory of group representation as distinguished from individual and direct representation, remained, and if possible became more important.

This group representation is expressed through the United States Senate. Members of that body are elected by the legislatures of the different states, as representing in each case a political entity. There are certain phases of this system which have given rise to doubt as to its ultimate soundness. In order that the group representation shall be complete the constitution provides that each state shall have equal representation in the United States Senate; while in the House of Representatives each state is represented proportionately to its population; and so in the popular branch of the government every citizen is represented equally with every other, or as nearly as that can be accomplished by a numerical division of the population into political districts. In the Senate population is entirely ignored, and the state as a political organization is recognized. Nevada, with forty-five thousand population, less than a fifth-rate state, has the same representation in the United States Senate as New York State with nearly seven millions of population.

On the face of it this seems like anomaly, and, but for the fact that in the lower branch the population is fully represented, it would be an anomaly. Certain disadvantages have arisen from this through the fact

that the new states are not only small but often crude
and inexperienced in the affairs of national statesmanship. Their interests, and hence their ideas of public
policy, are associated with simple extractive industries
like forestry, mining, ranching and agriculture, with
almost none of the influences of manufacture, commerce,
large financiering and the complex industries of modern
civilization. Naturally enough, in these states the
ideas of public policy will be the result of the economic
interests and business experience of the states themselves. Hence, much of the tendency toward modern
methods in the numerous lines of industrial and commercial evolution is not appreciated, and sometimes is
antagonized. A conspicuous example of this was the
enmity with which this class of states opposed modern
ideas of currency and banking and demanded the
crude, belated greenback policy and free coinage of
silver.

This tendency has been so marked that the question has been raised in many quarters of electing the
members of the United States Senate by direct popular
vote, the same as members of the lower house. That
would be a misfortune, because it would destroy the
group representation in the government, which is really
a conservative force greatly needed in the machinery of
our democratic institutions. It may properly be said
that through the habit of creating new states merely for
partisan purposes we are in great danger of lowering the
quality and character of the United States Senate.
There is undoubtedly room for some amendment to the
constitution in this respect. While the principle of
group representation is eminently sound, and should be
maintained even with some disadvantages, it is becoming
clearer year by year that the arrangement which gives
Nevada, with forty-five thousand population, and Wyom-
ing with eighty-five thousand population each the same

representation in the Senate as New York and Pennsylvania is simply anomalous. Under this condition there are fifteen states whose joint population is two millions less than the population of New York, and they have thirty senators, while New York has but two. That some modification of this must ultimately come is a growing conviction, at least as regards the admission of new states. It has been urged with some force that no new territory should be admitted to statehood with less population than would entitle it to one member of Congress, and that it should only have one senator until the population had reached a million.

Reform in this direction may ultimately come; but in the meantime the influence of large states in the Senate can be increased only by raising the standard of their representatives. In this respect New York has abundant room for improvement. Senator Murphy, whose term expires on the fourth of next March, is a dumb politician whose capacity for the position of United States Senator would not do credit to the smallest and rawest mountain state. He in no sense represents the intelligence, or the financial, industrial and political interests of the Empire State. He is merely a rich brewer, entirely innocent of any elements of statesmanship. Neither before his election to the United States Senate nor since has he even shown the least evidence of intelligent acquaintance with public affairs. The most that ever could be said or expected of him is that he might be a lobbyist of the Croker sort. He was made senator solely because he had been a successful chairman of the Democratic state committee. It may be the proper thing to pay the chairman of a state committee a salary, for the laborer in any field is worthy of his hire; but it is discreditable to the public spirit and intelligence of New York to make that the claim for a seat in the United States Senate. That is the one position in the

republic that should be filled by statesmen,—more so
even than the Presidency.

The Senate should be, as it was intended to be, a
body composed of ripe, experienced leaders of public
thought,—statesmen, not local managers of political
caucuses nor mere party workers of the hackneyed sort.
United States senators are not representatives of districts and caucuses, but of whole states.   To this branch
of the national Congress the nation and the world look.
as they have a right to look, for the ripest, most experienced and ablest statesmen the nation can furnish.
Election to it should ever be regarded as the crowning
result of successful public service and broad statesmanship.   In too many instances, as in the case of Senator
Murphy, it has been made the reward for mere clever
political work.

When the New York Legislature meets in January,
one of its first duties will be to select a successor to
Murphy, who has discredited this state in the Senate
for six years.   Already names are beginning to be discussed, and one that is mentioned in party circles with
some frequency is that of Mr. Odell, present chairman
of the Republican state committee.   The selection of
Mr. Odell for that high position would go far to establish a precedent in this state of making United States
senators out of mere chairmen of campaign committees.
a rule which, in all probability, would, in nine cases
out of ten, give us small calibre politicians instead of
statesmen.   Mr. Odell is a young man of rather good
presence, who could be relied on for party regularity.
Beyond that, little if anything can be said.   Of course
he would not vote for free silver; but he is not the material out of which United States senators should be
made.   There are positions that Mr. Odell could fill
with credit to himself and to the public service, but to
put him in the United States Senate would be unkind

to him, unfair to the state and discreditable to the
nation. Some consideration should be had for the fitness of things. New York should have a senator who,
besides being a man of affairs, of comprehension, and
statesmanlike qualities, can voice her interests in the
Senate; one who can plead her cause and defend her
rights in the forum of the nation.

Among other candidates named is Mr. Joseph H.
Choate. Of course Mr. Choate would not be a dummy.
He is eloquent and sarcastic, and sometimes even funny;
but on all except well-threshed subjects Mr. Choate is
practically unacquainted with public affairs. He has
never shown an interest in, much less an intelligent
comprehension of, any great national question. On the
subject of finance, beyond the mere general phrase of
" sound money " he has no views of which the public is
aware. On the important question of banking, and
public finance generally, he probably is not superior to
Mr. Odell or Mr. Murphy. He is an eminent lawyer,—
would make an admirable judge; but in the domain of
political science, statesmanship and public policy, he is
a man for whose opinions nobody has any special regard.
Indeed, on most great questions it is doubtful if he has
any well digested opinion. On the question of protection, for instance, Mr. Choate is not ordinarily intelligent. In short, Mr. Choate is a lawyer and not a statesman. Besides being a doubtful Republican, more than
half a free trader, he lacks public spirit, patriotism and
that familiarity with great industrial and political questions so eminently necessary in a competent representative of the Empire State in the national Senate.

Moreover, there is no need of selecting persons
who by nature and training lack the qualifications, when
so many competent men are available. The legislature
just elected should give New York the influence in the
Senate that it is entitled to, and look for a candidate for

this position solely with the object of finding the most capable and best qualified man for the place, providing, of course, that he shall be a Republican of unquestioned character.   There need be no difficulty in finding such a man.   Dr. Chauncey M. Depew would fill the position completely.   Mr. Depew is wholly untainted with mugwumpery in any form, and is a thorough protectionist.   Perhaps no man in the state has rendered, year after year, such constant gratuitous service to his party as has Mr. Depew.   He has never had an office, except once as member of the legislature, yet he is always ready to lend his aid in campaign work with an enthusiasm that in many could only be created by the assurance of reward.

Mr. Depew is more conversant with the industrial interests of New York State than almost any other man in public life.   His interest and acquaintance extend to nearly all the important affairs of the state.   He has a national reputation and a wide international acquaintance and influence.   There is perhaps no man in America who is more widely known, and widely known as one intelligently familiar with and intensely interested in American interests and American welfare.   He is a scholar, a peerless orator, and a successful business man.   Indeed, he is almost unique in combining a wide range of business experience with intense, intelligent comprehension of public affairs.

With Mr. Depew in the United States Senate, New York would have a representation fully equal to thirty times—nay, perhaps an hundred times--that given by a Murphy.   Mr. Depew's knowledge, his personality and his eloquence would make him a power in leadership, as New York should be in the Senate.   No great question of national import would be up for consideration without New York being heard from, and heard from by a masterly presentation of the case.   Not merely New York's interests but the United States' interests would be voiced by New York, the richest and largest state in the Union. Mr. Depew is peculiarly the man for the position, because, besides having all the personal qualifications and remarkably wide experience, he is at once an interested representative of all that is best in New York and a specimen of the best type of national spirit and statesmanship. He has the advantage of age ripeness, a superior personal presence and attractiveness, wide range of information, intense patriotism, and almost an unequalled power of oratory, which would make him supreme in the national forum.

It would be difficult indeed to find a man in the whole country who is in all respects more peculiarly fitted to represent the Empire State in the national Senate than Dr. Chauncey M. Depew. If political service is any criterion, he has earned it. If interest in affairs and ability to understand and present the state's and the nation's interests is required, he is supremely qualified.

If, when the legislature meets, an Odell or a Choate is selected for that position when a Depew is available, it will be a disgrace to the state of New York, and justify much that has been said against the leadership of the party organization in the state. There is no excuse for it and we cannot believe it will be done. If Mr. Depew will accept the position no other candidate ought to be spoken of, and it is doubtful if any other would seriously be considered. This is a great opportunity to put New York State to the front where she belongs.

In its issue of October twenty-first, the *Manufacturers' Record* quotes approvingly from our criticism of Mr. Edward Atkinson's pamphlet on "The Cost of Producing Silver." In this pamphlet, as the *Record* says, Mr. Atkinson "used the figures of the two best mining companies of the world to illustrate his article."

In a reply addressed to the Editor of the *Manufacturers' Record*, Mr. Atkinson discusses the point as to whether the mining companies he quoted are really the two " best " mining companies in the business, and says:

" Now if you or Mr. Gunton have any information by which you can prove that the Anaconda and Broken Hill Mines are the two best, i. e., most profitable mining companies of the world, you must have succeeded in procuring statements where I have failed. I therefore ask you to produce your evidence and to let me have the facts. Can you do so? If not, is it not incumbent upon you to withdraw your erroneous version of the pamphlet published by the sound currency committee, of which a copy is enclosed?"

He then cites the opinion of a Denver editor, " that Ananias had been very discreet in getting himself born early in history, since if he had waited until now he would have had no reputation as compared to Atkinson." After which he devotes the remainder of his article to an attack on the free silver doctrine, charging that free coinage at sixteen to one is an effort to swindle the American people.

As our readers will remember, our criticism was of Mr. Atkinson's economic treatment of the subject, not of any mis-statement of facts. Our contention was that Mr. Atkinson's statement that the cost of producing silver is " from twenty-five cents an ounce down to nothing," is a misrepresentation of the case. We insisted that any such unfair and essentially untrue statement of the question injured the cause of sound money, by intensifying the prejudice of the western people against the fairness of eastern discussion of the subject.

We regret to find that in returning to the subject in the *Manufacturers' Record*, Mr. Atkinson makes no reference whatever to this, the real point of the criticism. As to whether the Broken Hill and Anaconda mining companies are literally the most profitable mines in the world is a matter of no importance whatever to the discussion. Yet Mr. Atkinson presented them as two of the largest producers of silver, and added that "What is true of the great Broken Hill Proprietary mine is or may be true of all the mines in New South Wales, in the Broken Hill district, provided they are managed with the same skill and energy, as some of them evidently are."

The burden of Mr. Atkinson's whole contention was that the Broken Hill Company could produce and market silver at twenty-five cents an ounce and less, and that the Anaconda Mine, in Montana, could produce silver without any cost at all—get it for nothing as a by-product of copper. Obviously, it would be difficult to find anywhere in the world a more profitable concern than that which gets its silver for nothing. If Mr. Atkinson desires to save himself by getting upon that fence, then his position will become clear to everybody as pure quibbling. Certainly there are no silver mines where silver can be mined for less than nothing; and in very few, indeed, of those where silver is not a by-product, is the cost of mining and marketing less than twenty-five cents. Hence, for Mr. Atkinson to try to escape the issue on the plea that absolute proof has not been presented that these are literally the most profitable mines in the world is a little worse than begging the question. Silence would have been more dignified, and altogether more creditable to a reputation for economic fairness.

As to the motives and methods of the advocates of free silver in demanding the unlimited coinage of silver at a ratio of sixteen to one, we have no issue with Mr. Atkinson. That is a heresy that should be combated at every turn. Mr. Atkinson is on the right side of that subject, and it is because he is on the right side that we criticised his unfair treatment of the facts, as calculated more to stimulate the heresy than to promote the cause of truth.

As a matter of fact, the people in the mining districts of Colorado and Utah and other of the mining states know from actual experience that it is not true to say that the cost of producing silver is "from twenty-five cents an ounce down to nothing." They know that in their own localities, in many instances, it costs over fifty cents an ounce, and in some over sixty, and that many have had to close down because it costs more than the market price will now yield. We cited Park City, where last August the doors and windows of whole rows of houses were nailed up and the miners had wandered away to find employment elsewhere or in other industries, because it cost more than sixty-five cents an ounce to market silver from the Ontario and other mines.

We repeat, that the fallacy of Mr. Atkinson's position is not in any mis-statement of facts about the Anaconda and Broken Hill mining companies, but in the economic error of deducing from the cost in these two mines the general cost of the market supply of silver The truth is that neither the Anaconda nor the Broken Hill Company's cost of production exercises any appreciable influence upon the market price of silver. It is because the cost of producing silver by these two companies is so much lower than the cost of a considerable portion of the aggregate supply, that they can make enormous profits. If silver produced by the Anaconda Company costs nothing, then the profit on its entire product of silver is the whole selling price, sixty-one cents per ounce. Does Mr. Atkinson want the public to believe that this costless silver of the Anaconda Company in any way represents the general cost of marketing silver? We refuse to believe that he indulges in any such absurdity. If all the silver that comes to the market were costless, like the product of the Anaconda Mining Company, then it could not be sold for any price at all, any more than can air and sunshine. There is no principle in economics more obvious than that costless utilities cannot command a price. This we supposed Mr. Atkinson understood. The price of silver, like that of all other commodities, has relation to its cost of production, but obviously it cannot be to that portion of the supply which has no cost. Since the Anaconda product costs nothing, clearly it cannot be a quotable quantity in discussing the cost of producing silver, as affecting the price.

What is true of the Anaconda product is true of the product of all other mines whose cost is materially below that of the most expensive mines, whose output is a permanent part of the market supply. It is because the cost of producing silver at the Anaconda mine (being *nil*) is so much below that of the most expensive that the profit on that product is the greatest (being the whole price). The product of the Broken Hill Company, in New South Wales, is like that of the Anaconda Mines to the extent that it is less costly than the dearest portion of the market supply. For example, the present price of silver, (Nov. 19,) is sixty-one cents an ounce and hence the profit of the Anaconda Company is sixty-one cents an ounce, and that of the Broken Hill Company, taking Mr. Atkinson's figures as correct, is thirty-six cents an ounce. Why is it that the Anaconda Company can get sixty-one cents an ounce for what costs it nothing, and the Broken Hill Company get sixty-one cents an ounce for what costs it only twenty-five cents? Why cannot they both get a dollar an ounce? The obvious reason is that the poorest competitor in the market, whose supply is demanded, can afford to furnish his silver at sixty-one cents an ounce, which is probably about what it costs him to supply it. If the price were much less he would discontinue the business. If his supply were not needed, it would be rejected at that price. That is exactly what has happened to the product of the Ontario mine and several others where the cost of production is seventy cents an ounce and upwards. In short, it is because the product of more fertile or more easily worked mines will supply the market without the output of these less fertile and more expensive mines; and the price has fallen to the point that the dearest producer whose supply is needed can continuously accept. If the Anaconda and Broken Hill companies could supply the entire world's market, silver would be about twenty-five cents an ounce. The Broken Hill company would be the dearest, and would keep the price at its cost of production. Then the Anaconda Company, instead of getting sixty-one cents an ounce profit would only get twenty-five cents. In other words it would only get for its silver what the Broken Hill Company had to have; but so long as the product of numerous other mines is needed, whose cost of production is about sixty-one cents, then the price will be kept up to sixty-one cents in order to get the supply of these less fertile mines, and, so long as this price is paid for any silver that comes into the market, why it can be secured for all the silver, and hence the Anaconda and Broken Hill companies can continue to get sixty-one cents an ounce for what costs only twenty-five cents in one instance and nothing in the other.

This is what every observer knows to be the fact in the case. It is what every competing mine owner has to confront every time he comes to the market. It is what the people in Utah and Colorado and Idaho, and other mining states, painfully realize. We repeat, that Mr. Atkinson's whole attitude on this question is wrong. His reasoning is unsound, his handling of the facts is misleading, and his influence on the discussion cannot be other than injurious to wholesome public opinion. It is useless for him to say, "My rule in dealing with the silver question was wherever I saw a silver head to hit it, and that I was very glad to have his [Denver editor's] personal assurance that in his case I had cracked a skull which was empty of everything except courtesy," and expect that to pass for argument. People in the West know something about the cost of producing silver, and every time they are introduced to such an absurd and incorrect presentation of the case as Mr. Atkinson's pamphlet contains, they are strengthened in their view that Mr. Atkinson, and the eastern people he represents, know very little about the subject.

If Mr. Atkinson decides again to return to the subject, we trust that he will have the frankness either to defend his pamphlet or to confess that it is indefensible.

DR. SAVAGE ON PESSIMISM

True optimism does not imply shutting one's eyes to the evils and difficulties that arise in the path either of an individual or a nation and allowing affairs to run themselves, in the complacent belief that they will come out all right in the end. It consists, rather, in belief in the possibilities of humanity, belief in the possibility of progress, but it never overlooks the fact that this progress is brought about and these possibilities of humanity realized only by our own efforts. Progress is conditional, and the use of optimism is to furnish us always with the strength and courage that comes from the conviction that we can fulfill those conditions. It is the belief, not that the triumph of right is inevitable anyway, but that it can always be made certain by energetic, determined, persistent effort. The optimism which merely leads to relaxation and happy-go-lucky neglect of the serious side of life, allowing the world to wag on as it may, is in reality the worst form of pessimism in disguise. The optimism which nerves us with the absolute conviction that success is possible and sure, if we are but wise in our labors, is one of the great energizing, propelling forces in and behind the whole upward struggle of man.

On the Sunday before the late elections a very able sermon was preached by Rev. Minot J. Savage, D.D., Minister of the Church of the Messiah, New York City, on "The Evils of Religious and Political Pessimism." Dr. Savage is, least of all things, a pessimist, yet his optimism is of the sort we have attempted to outline above, and not a mere flowery, good-natured, easy-going notion that everything is infallibly destined to move in the right direction whether we aid or oppose. The purpose of his sermon was to dispel the hopelessness in which very very many good people seem to have immersed themselves with regard to our social, political and religions affairs, first, by unqualifiedly refuting the ever-present latter-day prophets of evil, and next by setting forth, as ground for confidence in the future, some of the enormous benefits to humanity that have sprung from toil and conflict in the past.

We have obtained Dr. Savage's permission to re-print a portion of this sermon. After describing the pessimistic attitude of mind among a large class of people, and drawing from religious and secular history a number of illustrations of the opposition and discouragement that the world's great movements and leaders of progress have always had to encounter and overcome, he proceeds:—

I speak of these historical incidents, I say, because they are living issues with us to-day. We have here in New York, and in the United States, these prophets of evil, these over-critical reformers, these people who have identified their peculiar methods and ideas with the absolute truth of God, these people who preach and write and talk in such a way that they become obstructions, they become sources of discouragement, they take the heart out of the people, they make them feel that it is not worth while to try.

Since the sermon which I preached two Sundays ago, I have received letters which probably have suggested to me the work in which I am engaged this morning. One young man writes me that he considers the political situation absolutely hopeless. He thinks that whichever side he looks at is a little worse than the other. And what is the outcome of this attitude? Simply, he says: "I haven't voted for years, and I don't propose to until things get better." I wonder how he expects them to get better. Who is it that is to make things better? The people who hold aloof and become discouraged and disheartened after this fashion?

And I think, friends, that it is the class of people that I
am referring to who are largely responsible for this utterly discouraged and disheartened state of mind.

I received another letter, the writer of it an educated lawyer in this city; and he thinks that it is the
work of these religious and political teachers that has
created such a general apathy, so that there are thousands on thousands who have given it up. Now it is
not my business, and I am not going to assume that it
is, this morning, to tell you which way you ought to
vote or which way you ought to believe in religious
matters. The one thing I have in mind, if I may, is to
hearten the people that I reach a little, and help them
to believe that there is ground for hope, that there is a
field for successful effort. that God has not forgotten
the world, and that all the men in it are not absolutely
foolish or hopelessly bad.

If I believed, for example, that either one of the
political parties at the present time was all ignorant or
all vicious, why, I should give it up, too. I should see
no use in making any effort whatsoever. Friends, it is
not true. The great majority of the people in both
parties are not overwise, perhaps; but they are sound at
heart. They believe in God, they believe in men, they
believe in the city, they believe in the country, they
believe in the possibilities of the future. . . . .

The idea seems to be that the stream of human
history must run down hill. I believe it runs up hill.
Any stream of water may run up hill; and thousands on
thousands of them do, when the force at the head is adequate or is higher than its present level. And, since
God is the force at the head of the stream of human
history and human tendency, I believe it is capable of
demonstration that human nature, left to itself,—if it
ever is left to itself,—does not tend downward, but is
ever sloping upward through the ages towards some

higher, finer issue than we have yet discovered or obtained.

If I believed, for example,—and here let me come to
a little very practical plain talk with you,—that our
office-holders were all vicious men, that they were all
seeking, in underhand and dishonest ways, their own
advantage, why, what would be the use of trying?
Why should we elect men if this is the condition of the
majority of them? And yet some of our superfine
critics, it seems to me, if you accept their almost daily
utterances on the subject, are hammering the idea into
us that this is the condition of our State legislatures,
of our Congress, our Senate, of all the men managing
to-day our public affairs. Friends, I do not believe one
word of it. I believe that the great majority of the
men in Washington are true and earnest and noble men,
seeking according to their light the best welfare of the
country. I believe that on the average, year by year,
there never was in any country nobler and less selfish,
more unselfish men than they are, more devoted to the
highest and finest things. Of course, incidentally, some
may desire to help a friend or cannot refuse to, when
appealed to. But that many of them are corrupt men,
as our wise critics constantly declare, I do not for a
moment believe.

I have a friend, whom I have trusted and honored
for years, who was elected to Congress ; and he said
the one thing that impressed him more than anything
else year by year was the good sense, the uprightness,
the honor, the integrity, of the men with whom he had
daily to deal.

These critics point us now and then, by way of making us more discouraged, to the condition of things in
England. Do you know, friends, that fifty or a hundred
years ago, at least during the latter part of the last century
the condition of things in England was infinitely worse

than it ever was in this country during its entire history ?
No one could be appointed to civil service or in the army
unless he was a member of some of the noble families or
connected with them in some way ; it was by favor or
purchase.   Thousands of pounds were openly, freely,
unblushingly, spent in carrying certain elections.   Boroughs were bought and carried in the pocket, places in
Parliament were given away, and even the religious
guides and teachers in the churches were appointed to
their places, not for learning, not for piety, but because
of social influence, because they were younger members
of noble families.   And yet England is outliving this.
She was not lost or sunk by this condition of things.
She has been grandly outgrowing it, and sloughing off
these conditions year by year ; and so may we.   .   .

I used to hear,—and this illustrates what I had in
mind,—I used to hear temperance reformers preach
and lecture.   These were men who had some peculiar
pet method of curing the evils of society; and, in order
to impress their hearers and rouse them to the necessary
energy and enthusiasm to accept their particular fancy,
they represented every method of failure, and pictured
the world in this direction as getting worse and worse.
And I used to have the feeling, while I listened to them,
If half what you say is true, let us give up the attempt.
If the world at the end of two thousand years of Christian history is getting worse and worse, cannot be trusted out of sight for five minutes, if its tendencies are all
wrong, why, then, where is any ground for faith in
God, faith in man ?

And yet, in spite of these temperance prophets of
evil, the world—very inconsistently, to be sure—went
on getting some better every year, as it has from that
day to this.   And so in every department of human life
the world has been going on getting better and in a more
hopeful condition every year.

I wonder why it is, I wonder what is that tendency
in certain people that makes them see all the good things
in the past and all the bad things right around them at
the present time.   I was talking with a lady on the train
coming home from Washington the other day; and she
was deploring the amount of machinery that was being
invented and used in the world, because she thought it
was supplanting hand-labor, throwing people out of employment, and leaving them in a worse condition than
they were before.   I consulted Carroll D. Wright, who
is probably the best authority on this subject in America; and he told me that the actual fact was that the invention of machinery creates so many new methods of
production that it employs more people than were ever
employed by any hand process, and the result is that
the lowest stratum of society is becoming lifted day by
day and year by year, so that one of the most hopeful
things that ever happened was the wide-spread introduction of machinery.

And then they forget another thing,—the people
who are competent to manage the machines are more
intelligent, better read, of better habits.   A drunken
man cannot manage a delicate machine, so that there is
more temperance in this whole department of human
life than there ever was before.

Another illustration.   There are hosts of ministers
who are deploring the wide-spread use of the bicycle,
so many people wickedly ride on wheels on Sunday and
do not go to church so much as they used to before
wheels were introduced.   And then I was much interested and instructed by a conversation I had with one
of the leading manufacturers of one of the shoe cities of
Massachusetts, who told me that nothing that had happened in fifty years had done so much to elevate the
morals of the workingmen in their great shoe-shops as
the wide-spread, almost universal use of the wheel.

Why? It is simple enough, if you stop and think. Men cannot enjoy smoking when they are rushing at such rapid speed on a wheel. A man who is intoxicated cannot ride a wheel; and, then, those who ride the wheel are taken out into the country, they have fine physical exercise, they are brought into contact with nature, they are taught to discern and notice some of the fair, sweet, healthful things they see about them, they breathe the fresh air, they are lifted to higher realms and better issues. And so, at any rate, he said that the influence of the wheel had been of more avail in lifting the moral level of the city than all the preaching and teaching together for the last fifty years. . . . .

If I had time this morning to glance over human life, I could show you that almost every single one of the human conceptions as to human degeneracy are contradicted flatly by the fact. Men live longer now than they ever did before. There are fewer deaths by disease in comparison with the population than there ever were before. Men are more and more getting control of the sources of human disease, and more and more power to control human conditions. Houses are better, clothing is better, food is better. And then the work people—day laborers as they are called—are infinitely better off than they ever were before during the last fifty years. In every direction is a tendency to increase of wages and the lessening of the cost of living, with the exception of house rent; and this means that the houses are better than they used to be; for you can get the same kind of house cheaper than it was seventy-five years ago.

And so, in spite of all these prophets of evil, the level of the world is lifting; and men are coming ever nearer and nearer to God. There never was so much love, there never was so much tenderness, so much kindness and brotherliness and human help in the world

as there is to-day. And, if you read the newspapers
and note the criminal statistics, you will get an entirely
false impression. This great, seething city of New
York, is a hotbed of crime? No. It is a magnificent
flower garden of all the virtues. The number of
crimes committed in a year is infinitesimal as compared with the number of people that are here. The
great majority of all political faiths and all religious
faiths are living helpful, honest, loving, manly lives.
And all these qualities are increasing year by year.

Why is it, then, that some of these people get such
contrary impressions? It seems to me that in the religious world we may find a little guidance here; A
man assumes that his particular way of looking at God
and the universe is the only way, and that, if people
are not religious after his fashion, they are not religious at all; and so you get the hopeless pessimism of
a man like Mr. Moody. I am not sure whether I have
quoted it to you since I have been here; but it indicates
the way a great many religious people are thinking.
Mr. Moody says there is no use in hoping to better the
general condition of this world. He says it is a wreck,
bound to sink, and the only thing we can do is to get
off as many of the crew and passengers as we can, and
let her go. That is his philosophy of the universe and
human life. Why? Because Mr. Moody is perfectly
sure that his theory of God and the Bible and the condition of man is the only true theory, and, because so
few people agree with him, all the world is hopelessly
lost.

If we could only get rid of a little of this conceit
of infallibility, perhaps we should be able to believe a
little more in the virtue of hope. Take some of the
political critics I have referred to, who are always telling us that the office-holders and the people looking
after our affairs are seeking their own advantage. I

get so weary of this civic omniscience and infallibility that I feel almost as if, for the sake of getting out of that kind of atmosphere, I am ready to be as wicked as they think we are.   I cannot help feeling a good deal of sympathy with the people of Athens before they banished Aristides the Just; for, if he went around airing his political and civic virtues and talking about his infallible wisdom so much as some of our modern religious and political prigs do, I certainly cannot blame the people for wishing to be relieved from the tension and strain by putting the man outside of the walls.

It is this assumption of infallibility in religious and in political matters as well that leads so many of these people to do what they can to fling the control of the city and State and country into the hands of the people whom they think, at any rate, all bad.   It seems to me that we need to learn that the world does not go ahead by leaps and bounds.   There never was a political or religious situation yet, where there were two sides, where there was not one side a little better than the other; and the way this world gets on is by our casting our influence in with the little better, taking the world a step ahead, taking what we can get if we cannot get everything we desire, and holding on to that if we may, and trying another year to take the next step.

And yet there are thousands of the best and most respectable people we have who are hopelessly casting away their influence, shall I say?   No, they are doing worse than that even from their own point of view. They are casting the balance of power which they might hold into the hands of those that they declare to be the worst element of the community.   And, if this is re- form, then let me have nothing more to do with reform the rest of my life.

EQUITABLE BASIS OF INTEREST

THEODORE B. STORK

The payment of interest on money depends on the natural observation that a man with a scythe can cut more blades of grass than he can pluck with his hands.

It is a fact of universal experience that with the aid of tools a man may do more work in a day than without them. It matters not, therefore, by what fine-spun theories we may try to explain away the increased product due to the employment of tools; the fact remains that it is only by the use of tools that the increased product can be obtained.

It is the obtaining of this increased product that prompts the use and the making or the borrowing of the tools. If the laborer can make his own tools then the whole of the increased product becomes his, and he is better off than if he borrows his tools and has to pay part of the increased product to the owner; but even if he borrows his tools he will be better off than if he works without tools, unless he is compelled to pay the whole of the increase gained by the use of tools to the owner.

The universality of the custom of borrowing would seem to show that borrowing, to the practical man of affairs at least, appears to be an advantageous transaction to the borrower as well as to the lender, that is, a transaction by which he makes a gain which he would not make if he did not borrow.

That he should pay something to the owner of the tools is justified by the fact, on the one side, that he has a fund out of which to make such payment which he would not have without the tool, namely, the increased product, and on the other side that the owner of the tools might himself have made that increased product had he chosen to use the tool. That the owner should not receive the whole of the increase, however, is plain from the consideration that he has been at no exertion to make the increase; that he should receive something is equally clear, because otherwise he would have no inducement to lend the tool or to make it for the purpose of lending.

That part of the increased product paid to the owner for the use of the tools is the hire of the tools, and if we translate the term into ordinary commercial language it is] the interest paid on the money represented by the tools; for, in modern industrial affairs the borrower of the tools, as a matter of convenience, borrows money and afterwards converts that into the tools out of which he expects to make the product by the sale of which he will pay the interest on the money borrowed.

Henry George, Karl Marx, and other equally eminent economic authorities, have undertaken to explain away this question of interest on money or of profit derived from the use of tools, as a delusion. Mr. George has explained that the increased efficiency of labor by the use of tools is the common property of the race, but this remark is either utterly beside the question at issue or amounts to merely saying that every man has the right common to all of increasing the product of his labor by the use of tools, which, while undoubtedly true, does not contribute anything to the solution of the problem.

It is true that when by the use of tools the production of a given useful thing is made easier, and is cheapened, the advantage gained by the use of the tools becomes the common property of all men—that is to say, all men share the advantage of getting a given amount of produce utility for a less amount of exertion than was requisite before the use of tools. Thus understood there is value in the remark; for, undoubtedly,

if by his unaided hands a man may harvest say 100
pounds of hay by a day's labor, and by a scythe he can
with the same amount of labor harvest 200 pounds of
hay, then, of course, as soon as the use of scythes for
harvesting becomes common, as it eventually will, the
user of the scythe will get very nearly the same amount
of goods in exchange for the two hundred pounds of
hay as he did previously for the one hundred pounds,
supposing, always, that the other goods offered in
exchange have not altered in respect to the amount of
labor required to produce them.   And in this sense the
advantage of the use of the scythe is shared by the producers of other goods, who thus, by a day's labor of
their products by exchange, get nearly two hundred
pounds of hay where formerly they only received one
hundred pounds.

It will be observed that the whole two hundred
pounds of hay will not be given instead of the one
hundred pounds; part of the two hundred pounds of
hay must be reserved by the maker of the hay to pay
for the wear and tear of the scythe, otherwise at the
end of his work he may wear out his scythe and be thus
left worse off, measured in the goods of other producers,
than when he began his labor with the scythe; and
there must also be reserved for the maker of the hay
something over and above the amount reserved for
making good the wear and tear of the scythe, something to represent the value of the use of the scythe.

The necessity or propriety of allowing anything for
the use of the scythe, as distinct from the amount required to make good wear and tear, is denied by many
authors; but the absurdity of their denial will appear if
we suppose that a scythe costs in labor expressed in hay
one hundred pounds and that the owner of the scythe
loans it to a neighbor who uses it and returns its value,
say in hay, one hundred pounds, having used up the

original scythe.   Now, what inducement would there
be to the owner of the scythe to loan it upon such terms?
He has spent the labor required for one hundred pounds
of hay to make or procure a scythe, and at the end of
the life of the scythe he receives a new scythe from the
owner.   Had he retained the scythe himself and used
it he would have received as much, for we must suppose if the use of scythes is profitable that it must increase the product of hay sufficiently not only to replace
itself, but also leave a margin of hay over and above as
the advantage obtained in product by its use over the
haymaker's unaided efforts.

Thus the borrower of the scythe and the owner are
practically put on the same terms for its use ; the use
of the scythe on sole condition of returning as good a
scythe as was borrowed simply means that the borrower
enjoys the same profitable use as would the owner, and
has the additional advantage of not being compelled to
expend the previous exertion required to make or get
a scythe before beginning his labor.   Under such circumstances everybody would prefer and seek to borrow
scythes rather than make and own them, and there being
thus a demand to borrow but none to lend or to make
scythes a premium greater or less as the case might be
would be offered to the owners or makers of scythes, for
their use, which premium would be the hire of the use
of the scythe and must exceed, as already shown, the
mere amount necessary to replace the scythe when
worn out.

In other words and conversely, the perpetual use of
a thing on condition of replacing wear and tear is practically the ownership of the thing, and no owner of an
article would under ordinary circumstances lend it on
any such terms, while every one would gladly borrow
on such terms, as much more advantageous than any
ownership could possibly be.

Another illustration of the point may be made by supposing the two hay-makers to start each without a a scythe, and that a day's labor will produce a scythe or one hundred pounds of hay. A takes two days and makes two scythes, B works the first day unaided by a scythe and makes one hundred pounds of hay, on the second he borrows A's first scythe and goes to work with it, agreeing to return it as good as new when worn out, let us say at the end of ten days. A takes his second scythe and goes to work on the third day. Compare now the results at the end of ten days. A has eight days' work with the scythe, making two hundred pounds of hay per day, sixteen hundred pounds of hay and two-tenths of his original scythe left, which, expressed in hay, would be twenty pounds of hay, also let us say one hundred pounds of hay (one-tenth represented by what remains of his loaned scythe, and nine-tenths due for its use), altogether seventeen hundred and twenty pounds of hay, while B, the borrower, who has been expending the same amount of labor for his ten days, has nine days' labor, with the scythe, eighteen hundred pounds of hay, also one hundred pounds of hay made the first day without the scythe, altogether nineteen hundred pounds of hay, from which he must pay out the value of the nine-tenths of the scythe destroyed, say ninety pounds of hay, leaving B a net product in hay of eighteen hundred and ten pounds, or a profit of ninety pounds of hay over the results of labor expended by A and expended in a more intelligent and diverse method, in making scythes as well as making hay.

Moreover, A has only sixteen hundred and ninety pounds of actual hay, the remaining thirty pounds are locked up in the unused three-tenths of a scythe, while B has eighteen hundred and ten pounds of actual marketable hay: thus B, the borrower, is better off than if he had made his own scythe, for in that case he would have only eighteen hundred pounds of marketable hay and one unused tenth of a scythe, which has an estimated but contingent value.   No one would make but everybody would borrow scythes on such terms as these, and, thus, there being a strong demand to borrow and none to lend, a premium on lending would naturally arise.   In other words, something over and above the mere replacing of the tool would have to be offered to makers and lenders of tools to induce them to make and lend them, and this would be, commercially speaking, interest.

The amount of this premium would depend on various elements of the question which need not now be considered further than to remark that abundant margin may be found for the means of such payment without disadvantage to the borrower in the difference between the product with the borrowed tool and the product without any tool, or even between the former and the product with the tool made by the owner, which, as has been shown, is less in value than that made with a borrowed tool.

All that is here insisted on is that something more than mere replacement would necessarily be given as hire of the tool.

When the hay-maker came to exchange his hay with the products of other labors he could not expect to get the whole advantage gained by the use of the scythe: the exchange value of hay would fall.   It is on this fact that the whole argument is based by which it is sought to show that for the use of tools or things no payment is properly due.   It will be instructive to trace the manner in which this fall in the exchange value of the hay will be effected.   At first A, the user and maker of the scythe, will exact for one hundred pounds of hay as much of the products of his neighbors as before, the use value of the hay being as great as ever, although now obtained at about half the amount of the former labor.   But B, perceiving that A by his scythe is able to double his day's product of hay, will also make a scythe and obtain the increased product of hay; this will gradually make the product of hay greater than the ·demand and depreciate the exchange value in other goods, and thus other producers will get hay for less goods of theirs than before and in this way some of the advantage of the easier way of making hay with scythes will extend to other producers.   And so, if the use of other tools should cheapen the production of other goods the producers would, by competition and the increased quantities of such goods pressing for exchange with the produced hay, be compelled to share the advantage with the haymakers.

But always there would be something more than merely the cost of replacing the tools used paid over to the owners and users of the tools to induce them to make and use the tools in their labor.   For, to repeat in a somewhat different form the argument already advanced, if we suppose that the whole industrial community enjoys equally the advantage of the use of tools ‚and that the owners and makers of the tools receive no more than the bare replacing of the tools, above the advantage that all enjoy in common from the use of the tools, such owners would at once reason that there was no profit to them in making and employing tools, since they who made the tools got no more advantage than those who simply exchanged their goods with those goods made by the tools.   The mere replacing of the value of the tool, by the other producers giving gradually to the producers of goods with tools a small part ·of the value of the tool, each day it wore out, would be no advantage, of any kind, but rather a disadvantage from the fact that the labor expended to make the tool,

instead of coming back in exchangeable or useful product at once, as ordinary labor would be rewarded by
immediate return, would have its repayment (the reward of the tool-making labor) spread over a long series
of days and possibly years. And there would be added
to the postponement that which always accompanies it,
the possibility or risk that the repayment might never
take place, the possibility that the tool, before it was
paid for, might have its value partially or wholly destroyed by innumerable industrial contingencies such
as the failure of employment for it, the making of a
better tool in its place, etc.

Therefore, perceiving on these terms that the
rest of the community would have the advantage, the
makers and users of tools would cease to make or use
them until better terms were offered, which probably
would speedily come about, there being an absence of
tool makers and users and a demand for the same.

These better terms might be anything, only they
would have to include something by way of reward
beyond the mere replacing of the tools.

What this something might be called or how the
reasons for its payment might be explained is not so
important as the fact of its necessity. The plain common sense view of the matter is that in the nature of
the things themselves there is yielded to the man making and using a scythe a greater product of hay than to
the same amount of labor expended in simply making
hay without a scythe, and it is for that increased product that the man makes and uses a scythe ; to answer
that anybody else may do the same thing is no proof
that there is no advantage due to the use of the scythe ;
nor is it possible to show by any system of reasoning
either that it is fair or equitable that the scythe-using
haymaker should be deprived of this natural advantage
by exchange and placed in an even worse position than

if he had never made and used a scythe, nor is it possible to explain how the natural advantage is lost by exchange without injustice to such maker and user.

To sum up the discussion in a concisely metaphysical form, it may be said that the right to use and enjoy a tool on the simple condition of replacing it is practically the ownership, for all economical use of a tool presupposes this and thus owners and borrowers of tools on these terms are in reality on an exact equality, except that owners are at the disadvantage of having been compelled to expend their labor to make the tools.

So much for the reward or premium paid over to the owner or user of tools as compensation, not for wear and tear or the replacing of them, but for their use, that is, their hire, understanding by that the part paid over and above the mere replacing of wear and tear ; for hire must cover both items.   Out of this hire of things springs the commercial term interest and by this hire it is justified and explained.

DISTINGUISHED ECONOMISTS

VI—Karl Marx

The advent of Karl Marx into the arena of economics constituted something of a new departure. John
Stuart Mill's work ended the period exclusively dominated by the classic English School. For the first fifty
years after the publication of the "Wealth of Nations"
the doctrines of Adam Smith and Ricardo were offered
as conclusive, and assumed the form of economic dogma. The various phases of industrial and economic
agitation during the first half of the century, however,
created the Chartist movement for political democracy,
and the trades union movement for industrial protection through the factory acts, which were all contrary
in spirit to the doctrines of the classic School. The
only movement which had the sanction of economic
scholarship was the Whig movement for free trade.
This was the movement of the factory masters, which
was hostile to all the other concurrent agitations for
social, political and industrial reform. Christian Socialism raised its head in moral protest against the blood-
less doctrine of *laissez'faire*, but it lacked scientific precision and logical statement.

The general whirl of economic discontent throughout Europe culminated in 1845–50, in France with the
revolution of Napoleon III, in Germany by the exile
of the revolutionists, and in England by the repeal
of the corn laws in 1846, enactment of the factory acts
in 1847, and suppression of the Chartist movement by
sending most of its leaders to jail in 1848. Thus England was the only country in which the revolutionary
spirit produced any constructive economic result
through peaceful means. The adoption of the factory
acts, the repeal of the corn laws, and the introduction

of a general free trade policy made England at once the country of industrial evolution and experiment and peaceful political security.

Karl Marx, being one of the punished revolutionists of Germany, went to London, as at once the place offering the greatest personal security and the best opportunity for completing his economic studies. He was essentially a political revolutionist, but unlike most revolutionists he was philosopher enough to know that political institutions rest upon industrial conditions. Marx therefore set out to construct an economic philosophy which could justify social and political revolution. Scientifically to prove that profits and all other forms of capitalistic income are robbery, was the task Marx set for himself. The result was "Das Kapital," the first edition of which, in German, appeared in 1867. A Russian translation appeared in 1872, and an English translation in 1873, the year John Stuart Mill died. The literature and phenomena studied by Marx were mostly English, although the method of thinking and statement is eminently German.

It must be admitted that this was the first comprehensive attempt to establish by scientific process, devoid of sentiment and sympathy, the doctrine that profits are robbery and that capitalistic enterprise is an unconscious process of exploiting the laboring classes. Although much literature has been published on socialism, Marx's "Capital" is the Bible of the movement. The cornerstone of the Marxian theory is the doctrine of surplus value, which is the general name he gives to all forms of profit increment. His reasoning on many of the related subjects is close, sometimes profound, and altogether in advance of the English economists down to his time, both for scientific precision and sociological comprehension.

This is especially true of his reasoning on the doctrine of wages, or "Value of Labor Power," and also on the cost of production and the creation of value by improved machinery; but the real pivot upon which the value of all his writing turns was his theorem of "surplus value." The validity of his whole philosophy turned upon the security with which this proposition was established. It is not our purpose here to discuss the merits of this doctrine. That will be found elsewhere.* The fact remains, however, that Marx's work was a sufficient broadside against standard literature on the subject to create a new current in economic discussion.

About this time, or soon after, Cliffe Leslie's essays, criticising the English doctrine, and Stanley Jevons' attack upon Mill and Ricardo, and the tentative presentation of the idea of marginal utility, started a new current of discussion, taken up principally in Germany, which has since received scholarly elaboration by Prof. Bohm-Bawerk, of Vienna, and found considerable favor among the young economists of this country. This has been dignified by the name of the "Austrian School." But Marx's "Capital" has remained the unrevised and unimpaired standard authority of socialism. The numerous socialistic movements in England, Germany, France, Belgium, Russia, Austria, and in this country, even the crude expression of it in the Populist movement, all have for their foundation, directly or indirectly, the Marxian doctrine that profits are robbery, and that the robbery is not in the moral delinquency of individuals but the consequence of the capitalistic organization of society, the only remedy for which is the overthrow of modern industrial institutions and substitution of some form of socialism or collective ownership of the means of production.

---

* "Principles of Social Economics," p. 252. Pamphlet, "Economic Basis of Socialism."

EDITORIAL CRUCIBLE

IT IS ASTONISHING what kind of arguments are made to do duty in political discussions. The *American Economist* quotes approvingly an article from the *Ogden* (Utah) *Standard* on trusts, in which the Utah journal argues that trusts are not fostered by tariffs, because more trusts were organized under Cleveland's administration than under Republican administrations. It is now in order for some Tammanyite to show that deaths from dyspepsia have increased during McKinley's term, as a good reason for electing Croker President in 1900.

THE AMERICAN ECONOMIST announces that it has lately completed an investigation of the leading industries in forty-seven states and territories, which shows that since the change of administration and the adoption of the new tariff law an aggregate increase in wages paid has taken place amounting to $1,004,615,272.

If half of this be true, it is worth more to this country than all the trade which the annexation of Hawaii, Porto Rico, the Philippines and Cuba together would afford. Another such increase during the next five years would do more for the welfare of the United States and civilization in general than would the conquest of all Asia. Development of trade here, the increase of wages, and improvement in the social conditions of the people of this country is what will do most for the prosperity, power, political purity and world influence of the United States.

THE HUNGER of the administration for foreign possessions seems to be rapidly growing. At the outbreak of the war we declared absolutely against even a remote desire in that direction. Now that we have acquired Porto Rico, and for a time at least control of

Cuba, the administration is demanding the Philippines. According to the latest advices from Paris, we are willing either to buy them or fight for them, if they cannot be obtained by any other means.

It is time that this drift of the administration towards a wholly un-American policy should receive a check. The lukewarmness of the nation towards the administration policy, indicated by the election, seems not to have been understood. The fact that the entire majority in Congress was not wiped out and an unequivocal vote of censure upon the President's attitude definitely expressed, is mistaken for support and approval of his Philippine policy. This illusion might possibly be dispelled by a few mass meetings in the large cities of the country, petitioning the President against taking the Philippines. Mr. McKinley is very impressionable; no President was ever more so. Massachusetts, which has frequently taken the lead in true American movements, has started an anti-annexation movement in which the Reform Club, the Home Market Club, and the free trade and protection organizations of Boston are all co-operating. If the leading cities of New York and other states will promptly join Massachusetts in voicing public opinion on this matter, a saving influence may yet be exercised.

COLONEL ROOSEVELT is at least living up to his ante-election statements. The assertion that "I meant every word I said on labor during the campaign" is being literally verified by his willingness to confer with the level-headed labor leaders regarding labor legislation and policy. No Governor-elect ever showed such a frank willingness to listen favorably to the serious desires of organized labor as does Colonel Roosevelt. It is to be hoped that the representatives of labor will recognize the significance of this fact, and be judicious in their demands.   The old adage that, If you give an ell they will take a yard, ought not to be true in this case. It is really the first opportunity organized labor has ever had to get the ear of a Governor who has a real desire to do something.   If the labor organizations avoid any attempt at extreme "ideal legislation," and show a disposition to ask only for a feasible and conservative policy, they will strengthen the position of organized labor everywhere.

IN A RECENT editorial on "Protection and Cotton Mills," the *Boston Herald* undertook to show that the Wilson Bill increased the dividends of the cotton mills and the Dingley Bill reduced them.   Here is its own summary of the argument which is expected to carry conviction to the minds of New Englanders:

"In the year 1897 the average rate of dividend for these thirty-four mills was 3⅞ per cent.   The dividends for the year 1898 are not known, because the year has not ended, but it is generally believed that they will not show a material change from those of the year 1897. In other words, during the three years covered by the time in which the Wilson tariff law was in force, the dividends of the Fall River mills averaged above 6½ per cent.   During the two years covered by the term of the Dingley tariff law the dividends of the Fall River mills promise to be about 4 per cent."

Really this almost equals the logic of the Tammany "Colored Democracy," which during the recent campaign issued an appeal to the colored voters of New York to support Van Wyck because more colored men were lynched during Harrison's administration than during Cleveland's.

The people of Fall River and Massachusetts know, if the *Herald* does not, that the Dingley tariff made no change in the duty on cotton cloth, hence it could have no effect on the dividends of cotton mills. It is notorious that the depressed condition of the Massachusetts cotton industry is not due to foreign competition, but to southern, the facts concerning which are too familiar to need stating. While the *Boston Herald* is frequently wrong, generally it is not stupid. Alas, "How are the mighty fallen!"

———

AND NOW comes the news that three thousand cotton mill operatives in Augusta, Georgia, are on strike against a reduction of wages. It will be interesting to see what the Massachusetts mill owners will say to this, and quite as interesting on the other hand to see how the southern press, particularly the *Atlanta Constitution*, will treat the matter. We have insisted that the reduction of wages in Massachusetts to save New England manufacturers from southern competition would be ineffective. The South can always beat Massachusetts in a mere low wage race; and it was for this reason that we suggested that the remedy lay in extending the ten-hour factory acts to the South. This brought forth columns of editorial dissertation, not entirely free from abuse, from the *Atlanta Constitution.* That journal loudly proclaimed that the southern mill owners were prosperous, making profits, and that their operatives were happy and contented. The three thousand striking operatives of Augusta, Georgia, are in evidence against the *Constitution's* statement and reasoning. The South will some day learn, perhaps only through bitter experience, that cutting wages is not the road to industrial superiority. Wages must rise and not fall in the South, or the South will not be permitted to make any perceptible advance in industrial development. Slave labor and exceptionally cheap labor are incompatible with a high state of industrial efficiency and progress.

Civics and Education

CIVIC AND SOCIAL REFORMS

The early history of a new movement in society is generally a record of mistakes, extravagances and failures. This is not surprising, and ought not to be discouraging. It is what might normally be expected. It is an incident and signmark not of regression but of progress. The new has idealism in front, but lacks experience behind. It has with it the motive forces of progress—enthusiasm and conviction,—but the knowledge and judgment by which the new must be modified, adjusted and fitted into the social organization come only with time and experiment. Even when an innovation has successfully gone through this process of testing and reduction to a practical working basis in any one social or political group, it is not always possible to transfer the results of that experience to new fields without considerable friction and error. There are differences of condition and circumstance which demand a different method of applying the selfsame thing that may elsewhere have been successfully installed.

This is even more marked in the case of political or civic innovations than of industrial. The test of a new political arrangement or institution is its adaptability to the needs, desires and customs of the people. The test of an industrial innovation, of the sort at least that directly affects wage workers, is its capacity for creating social opportunity or protecting health and morals. Many of the English factory labor regulations, for instance, could be applied with little modification wherever a factory system is established in any quarter of the globe, as at present in Japan. This is particularly true in respect to sanitary construction laws, boxing of machinery, and prohibition or restriction of the labor of women and children. To a large extent it is true also of legal limitation of working hours, though it would doubtless be unwise to begin in Japan with a nine and one-half hour system, such as England adopted only after nearly a half century of agitation and gradual progress toward that point. What England has done in these respects is to demonstrate the necessity and feasibility of these measures, and it thus becomes possible for other countries to apply them just as fast as conditions will warrant, and instead of repressing and punishing the people's demands for these reforms the statesmanship of countries entering the modern industrial era has now a logical and established precedent for encouraging and stimulating any such demands, with a view to developing the people's capacity for properly using the opportunities which it is proposed to confer. Japanese statesmen are, in fact, actually working along these lines and have sent commissioners to Europe to study the factory regulations, with a view to copying them in Japan.

In the case of political or civic institutions it is much more difficult to transfer the results of one nation's experience to another. There is a great difference between the doing of a thing and the instrument by which it is done. The effectiveness of a given reform measure depends upon its necessity and feasibility under the conditions present. The effectiveness of the governmental system under which such innovation is to be introduced depends upon the ability of that system to maintain itself and utilize the forces of the nation in carrying out its policies. In order to possess this ability it must in a general sense typify the population over which it rules; represent its general desires, customs and tendencies, and be able to command its allegiance.

For this reason there is much less in political institutions that can be arbitrarily transferred from one type of population to another than there is in industrial institutions. Factories, for instance, can be set up in Japan, laborers employed and business successfully carried on; and the Imperial government of Japan can say under what conditions, from the standpoint of public welfare, these factories shall be built, and how the machinery shall be guarded, and how long the laborers shall be permitted to toil, and so on;—all this can take place successfully almost as a full-fledged innovation or a direct transfer from foreign communities where factories and factory regulations have previously been developed. But it would be quite another matter suddenly and arbitrarily to establish jury trial, for instance, or town meetings, or universal suffrage, or an American public school system, or a state Christian Church, in Japan. Almost inevitably the consequences would be either total failure or violent revolution. Institutions of this class depend for their very existence and success upon either the implied consent or voluntary participation of the people, and hence the line of change or evolution must be up through the people and thence out into the institution. In industrial affairs, however, success depends upon the wealth-producing efficiency of the industry, and hence the line of evolution is up through the industry itself, resulting in specialization, organization and scientific improvement.

Civic, social or religious innovations, therefore, generally encounter hostility and repeated failures before they are finally established, and this is almost equally true whether the new thing is being proposed for the first time anywhere or has already been introduced, tested and adopted in some other quarter. The advantage to be gained from others' experience in this line is that it shows what errors are to be avoided and furnishes the incentive and encouragement of demonstrated success, that is, shows that the thing sought after is possible of attainment; but practically the same course of gradual testing and familiarization must be gone through in the case of each new people before the innovation is an established success.   Nothing can fully take the place of the direct experience of the people themselves.   Unlike a factory, these institutions must command the general acceptance and support of a considerable majority of the population before they can succeed, and this general acceptance must always be a matter of slow growth and readjustment of popular sentiment.

The social democratic party in Germany and the civil service reform movement in the United States are two decidedly apt illustrations of the erratic early history of social and civic innovations.   One is the case of a movement originating and developing first hand, without previous experience of the same sort to guide it; and the other is, or was at first, an example of an effort to establish somewhat too rapidly a civic institution fully developed elsewhere but radically hostile to the customs that had grown up here and become an accepted part of our political system.   It may be, of course, that in view of the rank evils which this reform aimed to correct, any more moderate or reasonable method of introducing it could not have been expected from the enthusiastic and determined advocates ot the new *regime*.   Nevertheless, it is just this suddenness of application and frequent disregard of circumstances and long established traditions that is responsible for most of the absurdities and mistakes that have characterized the competitive system in the public service of this country.   Both movements, the social democracy in Germany and the civil service reform agitation here, began with radicalism; the one holding that an ideal social system could be successfully organized and operated without further delay, if only opportunity were given; the other believ-

ing that a full grown civic institution could be trans-
planted in American from European soil, and made to
take root at once.   Both movements have encountered
hard knocks and worn off their rough edges; both have
lost much of their impracticableness through contact
with the practical, and are learning the folly of absoluteness and the wisdom of step-by-step progress and reasonable adjustment to conditions.   In proportion as experience is modifying these movements and directing
them into really wholesome and feasible lines of effort,
they are heading towards success; German socialism
has almost within its grasp the accomplishment of many
important social reforms, and the modified competitive
system in the American public service is becoming more
and more susceptible of smooth, successful operation on
a wide scale.

As the social democratic party in Germany gains in
strength and gets within sight of the actual burdens
and responsibilities of power, it is growing more conservative and losing its revolutionary character.   It is
learning that reform cannot be accomplished wholesale,
but must come piecemeal, and, instead of standing together as a mere inert mass and protesting against anything and everything that is done in the legislative
councils of the empire, the members of this party are
beginning to take an active hand in legislation themselves, working for whatever important practical results
they can obtain in the direction of bettering the condition of the lower social classes.   At the late socialist
congress at Stuttgart, says the *Literary Digest*, it was
made very clear that "many of the best men believe that
the time is past for purely revolutionary agitation and
mere obstruction in the Reichstag.   'You can't get
political power by the mere waving of the red rag,' said
Frohme.   Vollmar declared, in so many words, that the
social-democratic party would be very unfortunate if

it came to power, as it is economically and politically
not yet fit to wield power.   Bebel was non-committal,
but he did not oppose Vollmar.   Gradnauer thought
there was a lamentable dearth of talented and educated
men in the party."

Another of the socialist leaders, Bernstein, sent in
his views of the future policy of the party, to the following effect:

"The idea that bourgeois society must soon break
down is a fallacy, and it is useless to deny this.   The
number of affluent people is not decreasing, but increasing.   The middle classes are changing their character, but they are not vanishing, as has been predicted.
In some branches of industry the monopolists prevail,
but in others small establishments hold their own.   In
agriculture the concentration of property progresses
very slowly.   Since, therefore, the chances of a violent
upheaval are very small, the social-democratic party
should actively take part in legislation, and obtain what
advantages they can for their constituents."

To the extent that this change of thought and purpose goes on the socialist party of Germany will become
a practical and genuinely helpful constructive force of
progress towards democratic political institutions and
important social reforms, instead of a merely negative
body of criticism, opposition and disruption.

In this country the civil service reform movement
has probably suffered as much from the indiscretions
of its friends as from the actual hostility of spoils
system beneficiaries.   As a class, the promoters of the
movement demanded that the power of selection of employees be taken away wholesale from public officials
and put in the hands of examining commissions, and
the tests required were at first, in a large proportion of
cases, absurdly crude and inappropriate and brought
ridicule upon the whole system.   The dominating idea

of the whole movement seemed to be that the impersonal, competitive system of appointment was an absolute good in itself, under all circumstances and conditions. It was not recognized that efficient service
requires that a man shall have at least some degree of
personal choice in the selection of his subordinates, nor
was it admitted that the carrying out of public policies
is no less important than mere discharging of perfunctory duties, and that, in order to carry out the policies
demanded by the people at the polls, a considerable
proportion of the leading positions must be of a political
and not merely bookkeeping nature, and likewise that
political opinions are an important consideration even
in the case of certain of the appointive places under
these officials.

In addition to this, it was the disposition of those
most actively interested in the reform to make most
sweeping and violent denunciations of the party system
of government and all connected with it, indiscriminately charging dishonesty, corruption and venality
upon politicians and office-holders right and left. Now,
while there was of course considerable truth in many of
these attacks, there was even more often a great deal of
untruth, and the injustice of such a wholesale crusade
was felt and resented, not only by those directly accused but by their friends and constituents. Most of
these people were simply pursuing what seemed to be
the necessary and customary method of political management, conferring rewards and benefits on the traditional spoils plan as the most effective way of commanding support, and without, in most cases, any consciousness of intentional dishonesty or of the immorality of
these practices.

The movement, therefore, aroused against itself
the opposition of a very large class; first, the real corruptionists and beneficiaries of the spoils system; next,

the great body of average politicians, trained into this system, regarding it as a necessity, and resenting the charges of deliberate villainy heaped upon them by the reformers; next, all those people more or less directly connected with practical politics who recognized the importance of party uniformity in a large class of public offices in order successfully to carry out party pledges made to the people, and to whom, therefore, the sweeping programme of the new movement appeared utterly undemocratic and unfeasible; and finally, those not directly interested in the matter one way or the other, but with whom the red tape and absurdities of the early competitive examinations brought the whole system into contempt.

With experience, however, has come a growth of common sense, less violent denunciation, less unpracticable absoluteness, and a steady improvement in the character and appropriateness of the examinations. The system is by no means perfect or satisfactory yet, certain of the more iron-clad features may require modification, and there will gradually come a more intelligent discrimination as to what kinds of positions should be included in the classified list and what reserved for individual appointment. During the present and two preceding national administrations there have been wholesale additions to the classified list, and yet it has been found that some positions ought not to have been so transferred, and they have been returned to the old status. It is now reported that several thousand other places are shortly to be taken out of the classified list chiefly for same reason that the nature of the services requires a larger measure of personal and confidential choice. This prospective change is already being furiously denounced by extreme civil service reformers as a step backward; but in reality it may be an important and necessary step in rationalizing the system, adjusting it better to the conditions, and increasing the efficiency of our public service. It does not seem probable that this action is proposed merely in order to gain opportunities for distribution of spoils, because the whole disposition of the administration has been in the opposite direction, even to the extent of having put in the classified list a majority of the public places not so included when the last administration went out of power.

The fourteenth annual report of the national Civil Service Commission shows the marked improvement that has been made in the matter of examinations. Experience has shown that the tests should be specialized in accordance with the needs of the different classes of service, and furthermore that the ideas of public officials themselves should be embodied in the tests, with regard to the qualifications that are important in their subordinates. The Commission now regularly confers with heads of departments in regard to the preparation of examinations. The chief examiner, Mr. Serven, in his report, says:—

"During the past year the most cordial co-operation has continued between the departments and the commission in this work, and it is believed that spirit has added largely to the practical value of the examinations as now held. It is manifestly true that the officers of the departments must be assumed to be thoroughly familiar with the needs and requirements of their respective services. Therefore deference has uniformly been given to their opinions in this respect. A case has seldom arisen where it has been necessary to call attention to any seeming inconsistency in their suggestions in reference to the preparation of examinations. In all such cases the matters have been promptly settled by amicable conferences."

Continuing, with respect to the general purposes and character of the examinations, he says:—

" It is the aim of these examinations to apply the same general rules and tests in the selection of employees for the Government service as are now employed with the best results in the management of the most successful private business concerns. It is believed that the nearer this method is approached by the Commission the more satisfactory will be the results. . . .

" From a careful review of the conditions prevailing in the public service, it appears that three general classes of examinations are required to properly meet the demands upon the Commission. The first general class embraces those designed to test merely the general intelligence and adaptability of the competitors. These examinations are used to test the qualifications for positions where a greater or less amount of intelligence is necessary as a measure of ability, but where there are no special duties to be performed which require a special character of qualifications, as for ordinary clerks, messengers, etc. For such positions a series of examinations has been arranged, graduated in character from a mere educational test of the most simple kind to an examination requiring scholastic ability about equal to that obtained in the ordinary common or graded schools. They are known as the first-grade, the second-grade, and the third-grade basis examinations. The third grade requires merely the ability to read, write, add, subtract, multiply, and divide whole numbers, and a knowledge of United States money. The second grade requires, in addition to these, a knowledge of simple operations in common and decimal fractions, while the first grade requires a knowledge of the use of the English language in business correspondence and of such arithmetical operations, including interest and discount, as embrace those principles necessary to solve ordinary business problems.

" The examinations of the second general class

contain appropriate tests of general intelligence combined with those specially designed to bring out the
particular information needed to satisfactorily perform
the duties of technical positions in the service. These
positions require scholastic ability usually of a high
order, in connection with some special or unusual training or experience. In this class are the examinations
for bookkeeper, stenographers and typewriters, examiners of patents, weather observers, the various kinds
of draftsmen, civil engineers, etc.

" The third general class of examinations are those
where no educational qualifications are necessary to
satisfy the requirements of the service, but where some
peculiar experience or skill is demanded, either in a
mechanical or other special line. In these examinations
occasionally applicants have been accepted as competent
although unable to read or write, the Commission having been satisfied that they were fully qualified to perform the duties required. The specific name applied
to this class of examinations is the fourth-grade or
trades examinations. They are employed to test applicants as skilled mechanics, etc. "

The most important and sensible modification in
the examination system is that of including experience
as one of the tests of fitness for public positions. This
is one more step away from the arbitrary, unreasonable
idea that certain scholastic qualifications only are necessary in sifting out an efficient body of public officials.
On this point the Chief Examiner says:—

" During the past year it has seemed wise to include in many of the examinations an investigation into
the business experience as well as capacity of the competitors. This course has been so eminently satisfactory that several important examinations recently held
by the Commission were based largely upon that idea.
Where the requirements are such as can be best deter-

mined by an examination of the previous record of competitors in similar work, it is believed that this method
of testing such competitors cannot fail to be satisfactory.
Many of the extremely technical positions in the Government service will probably be filled in the future as
the result of similar examinations.

"It is proposed that the subject of experience shall
be included in future as a part of each examination
where experience is of practical value in determining
the relative qualifications of applicants. In all examinations prepared for the purpose of testing some
acquired skill it is proposed that the full industrial history of each competitor shall be obtained for the purpose of affording as complete information as possible to
the Commission and to the appointing officers."

These are tendencies in the right direction. To the
extent that they go on, the competitive system will
throw off the extravagances and mistaken methods of
its early career, become capable of rendering increasingly useful service and develop into a successful and
permanent feature of our political system.

CIVIC AND EDUCATIONAL NOTES

The city of Boston has recently investigated the question of municipal lighting, with results decidedly in favor of the private enterprise system.

Against Municipal Lighting Plants

Boston pays a private company an average price of $127.25 per annum for street and park electric lamps, as against $134.57 in Detroit and $154.80 in Chicago, these latter cities having municipal lighting plants. The investigating commission, after reviewing all phases of the question, recommends that Boston do not build a municipal plant but renew its contract with the present company, under certain conditions as to improvements and progressive regulation of the price by an arbitration committee in which all interested parties shall be represented.

The report of W. T. Harris, United States Commissioner of Education, for the year ending June 30th last, shows that the increase in the number of pupils in our elementary schools during the year 1896–97 was 257,896 over the previous year.

Educational Progress

The total number of pupils enrolled in these schools was 15,452,426, and about 800,000 more were in attendance at colleges, universities, high schools and academies. The proportionate increase in attendance in this class of institutions is larger than in the common schools; in 1872 there were 590 persons in the million attending higher institutions; in 1897 there were 1216 in the million, and this notwithstanding the fact that the educational standards in high schools and colleges have been steadily advanced during all of this period. Such facts have an important place among the evidences that indicate the upward trend of our many-sided national progress.

SCIENCE AND INDUSTRY

SUGAR BEET INDUSTRY IN AMERICA

KATHERINE LOUISE SMITH

The manufacture of beet sugar in this country is a matter for serious consideration. There are practically no limits to the possible amount of sugar which can be made. The raising of the beet and manufacture of the sugar represents a remarkable advance in mechanical improvement and is a science in itself.

Everyone who desires to see the prosperity of American ingenuity, machinery and agriculture should favor the development of beet sugar industry. The total consumption of sugar in the civilized world is 7,000,000 tons, of which the United States consumes two-sevenths. Four millions of the 7,000,000 is made of sugar beets, and in the race for the market of the world the beet is ahead of the sugar cane.

Botanically it traces its genealogy back to the family of beets from whence our common beet proceeds, but it resembles it only in outward appearance. The sugar beet is long, spiral and more delicately tinted. It is of a fine pink color and the leaves are of a lighter green than the common beet.

In this country beet sugar manufacture is in its initial state but in Europe it has been developed on an elaborate and scientific scale. A sugar beet means years of careful study—the kind of study that produces the thoroughbred of to-day. A careful selection is made for seeding and it is stated that out of 2,782,000 examinations made in one place in Germany only 3,043 were preserved for seeding purposes. One of the essentials in obtaining roots with sugar is this judicious choice of the seed.

In 1747 Maggraf, a German, read a paper before the Berlin Academy of Science, in which he announced a method of procuring sugar from beets. The Academy received his announcement with surprise. Maggraf was one of the men who devote themselves to the investigation of those sciences whose possibilities they see. He was poor and without influence but he had watched and experimented and finally put it before the people. His discovery, however, slept for half a century when, in 1747 Achard, a pupil of Maggraf, announced to the Berlin Academy the results of his own methods of producing sugar from beets. In 1805 a wealthy baron devoted one of his estates to beet culture and erected a factory for the manufacture of beet sugar. The industry grew and soon France became interested. The war then existing between France and England deprived the French people of their usual supply of sugar from the West Indies. Napoleon I, Emperor of France, offered a reward of 1,000,000 francs for a practical process of extracting sugar from beets. This rich prize stimulated invention and several successful methods of manufacturing beet sugar were brought forward. The growth of the industry has not been without drawbacks. Indeed, for a while it was the butt of wits, newspapers thought it a subject for ridicule and Webster in his speech on the tariff in 1824 referred to it in sarcastic terms as equal to the philosopher "who so longed to extract sunbeams from cucumbers." Still the industry grew and in 1835 both Germany and France had fairly started, the culture of beets was largely increased and the number of factories multiplied. Beet culture and the sugar therefrom was no longer an experiment but had gained a place among the industries of nations which it had won after many reverses. There was still, however, a disagreeable flavor of molasses left in the sugar and for a long time all at-

tempts to get it out failed.   Chemistry finally overcame
this.   Sugar of a fine grade is now daily produced from
tons of beets.   But for the chemists beet sugar would
not have been a success.

In 1889 Europe made 1,800,000 tons of beet sugar
and 20,000,000 tons of beets were brought to the factories.   The United States at that time paid to manufacturers of Germany $16,000,000 for about 200,000 tons
of beet sugar.

One factory in France makes sugar from the juice
obtained from 12,000 acres of beets.   An ordinary beet
factory has a capacity of 250 tons of beets per day and
should make from 200 to 240 pounds of sugar per ton.
More than 500 factories would be required to supply the
sugar we consume annually in the United States.

As early as 1830 began a long list of unsuccessful
attempts to make beet sugar in this country.   Recent
experiments have been so successful however that
capitalists no longer consider it a venture.   The establishment of the industry has been a hard undertaking,
a struggle of capital and brain to convince farmers of
the new era of prosperity in the cultivation of this simple vegetable.

The culture of the beet is intensive and requires
more than ordinary care.   The seed is sown in northern
climates from the middle of April to May, in soil plowed
deeply and of a rich sandy loam, in drills 18 inches
apart.   It is dropped thickly and after the first leaves
appear the plants are thinned out to allow the formation
of perfect roots.   By the middle of July the roots have
begun to develop and sugar is secreted through the
action of the sun's rays on the leaves.   It is important
that harvesting be done just at the proper time.   In
California harvesting may commence in July, but in
the northern belt it may be late in the fall and risks
are run of the beets freezing in the ground.

In the fall the farmer proceeds to pull the beet. In hard ground this is difficult and often the beets must be removed with a fork in order that women and children who follow the workmen may pick them up. The tapering part of the beet and the leaves are then cut off. A sample is taken to test the value of a load.

The essential thing is to shelter the beets from moisture after they are gathered, for if water penetrates they begin to sprout, at the expense of the sugar.

Of course insects have to be combated, and inclemencies of weather and frost in spring which may compel the farmer to sow again. The value of beets is based upon the density of the juice, not upon the weight. The more sugar the denser will be the juice. Sugar is extracted much as it is obtained from the cane. The beet roots are cleaned and macerated by machinery. Presses are used to extract the juice from the pulp. This pulp is an excellent fattening food for cattle. Filtration follows. The juice is then pumped into an iron cistern, heated to boiling point and run through filters packed with bone charcoal. In order to get the liquid dense enough to crystallize, evaporation and a second filtering through charcoal are employed. The juice is like syrup and contains water which is removed by boiling. The labor and cost of conveying enormous quantities of roots long distances to the factories caused the invention of some kind of system which would take the juice alone. A method of underground piping from farms supplying beets to a central factory works well, and an apparatus is used on each farm to extract the juice.

The mass of impure sugar crystals secured from the vats has next to undergo a treatment that will separate sugar from molasses. A centrifugal machine is made to revolve rapidly while a small quantity of pure syrup is poured into the sugar. Dry steam is now in-jected into the machine and the sugar becomes white. This is "first sugar." The liquor flowing from the centrifugal is reheated and the filtering and boiling that follow make a crystallized "second sugar." The whole process takes from 18 to 24 hours.

There is a vast belt in the United States of no mean width, in the latitude of the Lakes and stretching from ocean to ocean, which invites the culture of the sugar beet and seems to unite in happy proportions all the elements that tend to the production of beet sugar. The soil and climate are there, the sunbeams, and most important of all the farmer to cultivate the ground.

It is in northern California however, that the industry was first started with success. This state, New Mexico and Utah leave no want unsupplied so far as warmth and sunshine are concerned. Kansas, Nebraska, the Dakotas and now Minnesota have already been taking up the cultivation of the sugar beet. The natural richness of soil brings the beet to maturity early, and a better knowledge of cultivation which tends to increase the yield of beet fields has solved the problem of profitable cultivation.

The late improvements in the methods of manufacturing the sugar have also helped toward success. Nebraska has one of the most successful manufactories of beet sugar. The oldest manufactory is in Alvaredo, California, and was erected nearly twenty years ago. Next are the Grand Island, Nebraska, and Watsonville, Calif., factories. In 1894 there were only seven manufactories in this country, now there are many more.

The yield varies from 12 to 40 tons per acre on an average. There is land that has yielded from 20 to 35 tons an acre. The estimated cost of production per acre is $50. This varies of course in localities. In respect of quality and sweetness there is no question but that beet sugar is the equal of cane.

SCIENCE AND INDUSTRY NOTES

It is reported that the Japanese government is making overtures to an American syndicate to install all the
Electricity in Japan electric plants for street cars, lighting, etc., which are to be established in Japan, the franchise to be an exclusive one. In a country just entering the era of modern progress it may be necessary to grant an exclusive privilege of this nature, in order to tempt capital to enter the field and take the risks of developing in a proper manner these new and, to them, strange enterprises. We imagine, however, that when Japan has once become accustomed to electric railways, electric lights, etc., it will be very difficult for any one concern to maintain a monopoly of the business of furnishing these facilities. We do not understand that this proposed franchise is perpetual, and after its termination the question of whether the syndicate retains control of all or the bulk of the electric service in the Japanese Empire will depend upon whether it can furnish these facilities more cheaply and effectively than its competitors. A temporary legal monopoly may be necessary under the conditions of the moment, but a permanent economic monopoly can only be the result of exceptional and superior services to the public.

Every little while some sensational alarmist comes out in a magazine article or interview with the discovery that the world has reached the limit
No Famine Ahead of possible wheat production and that we are from henceforth to encounter famines. Despite the apparent show of learning and statistics with which these arguments are accompanied, we have invariably remarked in comment upon them that

the question is not so much one of wheat-raising capacity as of the amount of incentive which the market offers for the production of wheat; in other words, that, granted a sufficient price inducement, we can depend upon having all the wheat raised that the race demands, not only on the basis of the present population but almost indefinitely in the future. The *Scientific American* takes much this same view of the matter, and says, with reference to the doleful prophecy made by Sir William Crookes at the annual meeting of the British Association for the Advancement of Science, September 8th, last:—

"The shortage of last year was due, not to the fact that the wheat-producing land had nearly all of it been brought under the plow, nor to the fact that the land was becoming exhausted and calling for artificial fertilization, but it was directly traceable to the fact that, as the result of the prevailing low prices of the past three years, the wheat production had been allowed to decline. The financial question is a far more powerful factor in determining the amount of wheat that will be brought to the warehouse each year than any of the causes named by Sir William Crookes. Evidence of this is seen in the increase of over 300,000,000 bushels of wheat this year over the supply of 1897, due very largely to the better prices encouraging farmers to devote a larger area to this cereal."

The day will come when wheat bread will be a common article of consumption, not only throughout Christendom but in the Orient and elsewhere, and there is no manner of doubt that the improvement of productive methods, fertilization and utilization of new areas will render possible the supplying of all this immense demand.

CURRENT LITERATURE

LABOR COPARTNERSHIP*

This book is quite unlike Mr. Lloyd's previous book "Wealth against Commonwealth." That work was devoted to an attack on a certain great corporation. The spirit of sourness, disappointment, and even malice pervaded every page. Half-statements, amounting to mis-statements, improper deductions, and the use of mythical matter were so prevalent as to destroy the value of the book as a contribution to respectable economic literature. We are glad to note that the spirit of the present work is altogether different. It is an account of the author's visit to the various co-operative societies in England. It consists chiefly of a description of the working of co-operative efforts among agricultural laborers. The book is quite commonplace, yet interesting, because it is an account of the wholesome effort of English laborers to improve their condition through the means of industrial organization, real self-help. It is written in Mr. Lloyd's best style, buoyant, hopeful and "catchy," as well as "newsy." It contains many facts of real interest not readily obtained elsewhere. It gives an account of the most recent phases of co-operative effort. Like all enthusiastic writers, the author presents this one idea as the great social solvent. The one thing about most co-operative enterprises in England is that they are bound to make a profit. If it cannot be made by superior economy, it is made by fixing a higher price for the wares. This is especially true of what is called "distributive" co-operative stores, the dividends going to the proprietors and in some cases to all purchasers, whether proprietors or not, so that it is

---

*Labor Copartnership. By Henry Demarest Lloyd. Cloth, 351 pp. Harper & Bros., New York. 1898.

generally recognized that the prices of commodities in co-operative stores are higher than in the stores of their individual or capitalistic competitors, but what they pay in higher prices they usually receive in dividends, which is a form of savings, and it is usually defended on that ground. In chapter VI, entitled "From Capitalism to Co-operation," Mr. Lloyd gives an account of something of a controversy on this particular point. "The Wholesale was a success in merchandising," he says, "from the very beginning. It then went into production because, in the flush times following 1870, the manufacturers of Great Britain, overwhelmed with business, supplied their regular customers in preference to the co-operative societies, though glad to sell to them in slack times." The "Wholesale" began to manufacture its own wares, making the co-operative societies its customers. "The profit for the six months [1896] was $33,-225. There have been two strikes in this factory, as has been told by Mr. Jones in his book. The hours at the Wheat Sheaf are fifty-two and one-half a week; the usual hours in Leicester are fifty-four. All the men are trades-unionists.

"The manager of the Wheat Sheaf was outspoken in his condemnation of the labor copartnership idea. It was 'the creation,' he said, 'of an aristocracy of labor.' In his opinion, the duty of co-operative manufacturers is to get the goods to the consumer at the cheapest possible price, and they have no right to make this price dearer by paying more than the market rate of wages."

This discussion, which he gives at length, clearly reveals the fact that co-operation is not the solution of the labor question, but it is a real advantage to owners of small capital, as furnishing a means of investment in which they will have the satisfaction at least of participating in the management.

AMONG THE MAGAZINES

The leading reviews are not slow to recognize the rapidly growing interest and enthusiasm in the Nicaragua Canal project. In the November *Forum*, Ex-Senator Warner Miller, for years identified with the canal scheme, discusses the question and presents arguments and statistics to show that this canal would be entirely feasible from an engineering standpoint, would greatly benefit American interests, would add to our means of defence, and would pay for itself. In the November *Review of Reviews* there is a discussion of the political aspects, past and present, of the Nicaragua Canal, by Lindley M. Keasbey; also an article by Emory R. Johnson, on the commercial advantages that would be gained. And in the *Chautauquan*, also for November, D. A. Willey summarizes nearly all the important points bearing on the question, and urges the importance and necessity of the project. There can be no question that the ball has been set rolling in earnest in this matter, and we shall not be surprised to see legislation during the coming session of Congress of such a character as will make the Nicaragua Canal an accomplished fact within a relatively short space of time.

In discussing territorial expansion in the *International Journal of Ethics* for October, Dr. Adler goes directly to the heart of the matter in making the policy of annexation turn finally upon its effect on the working classes of our own country. He says: " The wage-earning class in particular and all who believe that the progress of society as a whole depends on the improvement of the condition of the wage-earning class have reason to oppose the new policy. And this is not only, as has often been said, because the degraded labor of the tropics may thus be brought into direct competition with American labor, and tend to lower the rate of remuneration and the standard of living, but for another reason." This other reason, Dr. Adler proceeds to explain, is that so long as we rely chiefly on a home market for our products it is to our interest "to enhance the power of consumption on the part of the wage-earners at home," and further, "to accomplish this it will be necessary to think less of the market and more of the 'home,' to regard labor less in the light of a commodity, and more as a condition upon which men, women and children depend for the attainment of their human ends." On the other hand, if, with a policy of expansion, we come to rely more and more upon foreign markets, there is less interest in maintaining a high standard of living and large consumption at home, and thus a colonial policy would probably mean growing indifference to internal problems affecting the labor movement.

Going on to discuss the question of America's duty to civilization Dr. Adler is equally clear. He points out that "the attitude of the advanced towards the backward races should be educational," not by attempting to keep school and "having backward peoples for our pupils," but by developing within the nation a standard of civilization which by its example and by the light it throws on how to solve the problems of civilization, shall be an inspiration and an education to the less advanced nations of the earth.

INSTITUTE WORK

ANNOUNCEMENT

A NEW LOCAL CENTER PLAN

We have a plan to suggest with regard to the formation of local centers for economic and political study, which we think will be found entirely practicable and easy in hundreds of cases where any more formal undertaking would be difficult to carry out.

Let all of our active friends, those of you who would be interested in having a live organization in your community devoted to the study and discussion of public questions and improvements, take steps to have a meeting called in some public place, or else a group of people brought together in your own home. Then propose the formation of a society, composed of both men and women, who shall agree to follow, with as much care as possible, the discussion in standard current literature of important public questions, and to take an interest also in matters of local policy, perhaps, looking towards local improvements, whether in respect of better school facilities, public libraries, water-works, street improvements, new industries, or whatever. Let it be arranged that meetings be regularly held for the discussion of these questions, preferably by persons especially selected to work up the two sides of each concrete case and present the results perhaps in the form of a debate, to which all the others interested should be freely admitted, even though not caring to take part. Besides local matters, all such questions as wages, machinery and labor, trusts, agricultural conditions, city slums, negro problem, education, university settlement work, tariffs, the money question, labor insurance, the eight hour day, socialism, single tax, the liquor problem, unemployment, panics, the social reform work of churches, foreign affairs, city government, housing of the poor, political parties, election and caucus reforms, and so on almost indefinitely, are proper subjects for discussion and study by these clubs or societies.

This would seem to be a particularly useful and popular kind of organization for ministers to form in connection with their churches; for it is a notable fact that the church is more and more coming to take a hand in the active work of social, industrial and political reforms. To furnish serious, helpful education in these subjects, therefore, is practical, applied Christianity, far more so than most forms of charitable work, because its object is to discover permanent remedies for the social and economic evils which charity can at best only palliate and often actually aggravates. Moreover, this is also an opportunity, for such organizations can be made positive sources of strength to the churches themselves. They will attract the interest and sympathy of intelligent young people, because they will show that the church is disposed to become a special instrument of social and industrial, as well as religious and moral, welfare.

When the interest of a group of people, large or small, has been aroused in this way, the home study work of the GUNTON INSTITUTE can be introduced and explained, so that if any in this group of people desire to make a closer study of economic and social principles, in order to be able to understand and discuss public questions more intelligently and satisfactorily to themselves, they may have an opportunity to do so. Even if there are only a few who decide to do this it will form an important nucleus, and the influence of these people in the discussions and debates of the associations will be stimulative and valuable. It is impossible that those who do seriously take up the study course referred to, and stick to it, should not before long exhibit a firmer grasp of public questions and a superior capacity to handle them in discussion with those not so equipped. This fact might gradually induce others to undertake the work ; but at any rate such a nucleus of serious students would constitute a real backbone for the association, which would greatly help in holding it together and giving point and direction to its work.

This, we think, would be a more feasible undertaking than simply organizing centers composed exclusively of Institute students, because it would permit a much larger membership and draw in many people who might not have the time or inclination to pursue a definite course of study. This method, too, would greatly simplify the matter in the case of ministers particularly, and increase the probabilities of success; offering something which could be conducted as a popular feature of their church work. Such societies would afford, on the one hand, a free opportunity for all who would like to become better informed in a general way on public questions, whether of local or national interest, and to hear them discussed, or take part in discussing them; and, on the other hand, furnish both an opportunity and an incentive, right in the same organization, for those who might want to do more serious work and study the economic and political principles which ought to determine the course of our public policies. Several large societies, in fact, projected on just this plan, are already under way in connection with important churches here in New York, and it is equally feasible nearly everywhere.

The course of study given in the MAGAZINE and one or two text-books is made as popular and easy of comprehension as possible, and no topic is discussed without some practical illustration or suggestion giving it meaning and point, the aim being to thoroughly

equip each student for intelligent and convincing discussion and action upon this class of questions.   Therefore, it is important to the permanent success of these
local organizations that this more serious work should
be introduced and its necessity urged; but we think that,
as a general rule, local centers will succeed better in
themselves and be found more interesting and useful
to a wider range of people if they are formed in the
broad way we have suggested.   We earnestly invite the
attention of all our friends, and particularly of ministers, to this line of work.   We shall co-operate with
them in every possible way, in furnishing literature,
suggestions, data, programmes, *etc.*, not only with reference to the topics included in the Institute courses
of study, but, so far as possible, on important questions
that any of these centers may find it of interest to discuss in their local meetings.   We should especially like
those whom this may interest in any way to write **us**
for any further particulars in regard to plans of organ-
ization or practical methods of enlisting support and
co-operation.

INSTITUTE WORK

PRACTICAL STATESMANSHIP

The Institute work this month covers the subject of statesmanship. Clear ideas here, as in every other branch of science or philosophy, depend largely on intelligible definitions. In every community habit and custom have much to do with the method of thinking and terms of discussion. In some countries politics and statesmanship are equivalent terms. In this country they are not. Rightly or wrongly, the word "politician" has come to signify an active worker in local politics, and the phrase "practical politics" is frequently employed to mean subordinating public policy to party exigencies,—in other words, doing that which for the moment will bring the largest number of votes.

Statesmanship, even in this country, is used to signify the making and carrying out of wise public policy. The statesman, therefore, is one who represents certain political principles as doctrines or rules in national policy, and differs from the politician, not merely in integrity as is often supposed, but in character and function. The politician is devoted to the details of political organization, and may be honest, high-minded and patriotic. It is a mistake to assume that the politician is necessarily lacking in the attributes of ethical conduct. The politician and the statesman have different functions, and we should not, therefore, expect the same things from each. Consequently, in studying political science and the duties of citizenship it is important to distinguish between these different functions.

For obvious reasons which cannot be discussed here, we have drifted into the almost national habit of thinking of a politician as one to be avoided and distrusted, and of business men as the real material out of which to make statesmen. This is fundamentally wrong. As a rule the business man is least of all qualified to make a broad-gauge statesman, and the greater the success as a business man usually the less the qualifications for a statesman. The reason for this is, as intimated, that the functions and point of view of these three classes of men are different.

For instance, the point of view of the politician is the efficiency of the party organization. He takes it for granted that the party is right, and that the safety of public welfare depends on the completeness and efficiency of the organized machinery of the party for accomplishing and carrying out the party's programme. This is a useful function, but the point of view through which the state's or nation's welfare is seen is the party organization. Principles beyond platform expressions are seldom considered by the politician. He deals with the concrete.

With the business man the point of view is market activity, ready sale of goods and easy collections. Everything is seen through the immediate conditions of the market-place. He deals not with political machinery, much less with political ideas, but with concrete industrial facts. The business man is eminently interested in public welfare, because he is identified with industry, which is the very life-blood of social welfare. He deals not with the economic and political principles which underlie the industrial movement of society, but with concrete, observable business facts. For instance, he knows that if the market demand for goods is always active prosperous business is assured. He knows that prosperous customers make profitable business, but he knows very little of the social forces which stimulate the growth of purchasing power in the community, upon which prosperity in the long run necessarily depends, and he knows little about this because his habit of life—his very success—has forced his thought and attention and experience in the direction of dealing with concrete existing facts.

The statesman's point of view is different from either of the other two. The successful statesman may be, and often is, almost unacquainted with the details of business life and experience. He knows little of the working machinery of the business mart. His point of view is that of the national welfare, and with him as with the business man and politician, the national welfare is necessarily identified with industrial prosperity. His function, however, is not to deal with bargains, shadings of profits, dickering for wages, the immediate supply and demand, and the daily market price. His concern is with the tendencies and conditions which permanently affect the direction of business development. While the business man deals with the industrial facts that exist, the statesman deals with the policy which shall govern future conditions. In short, the statesman's point of view is the long range point of view,—seeing around the corner. His conduct is governed, or should be, by the industrial and political principles which control the tendency of industrial and social institutions.

For this reason, therefore, statesmanship is to some extent, and ought to be to a much greater extent, a profession. The successful running of a factory or a department store is not a training for statesmanship. It rather unfits a man for the larger and equally important function of leading the nation's public policy. It is no criticism upon the business man to say that usually when he enters politics he is a narrow-gauge, short-sighted, penny-wise public character. It is what ought to be expected, and if he exhibits the characteristics of comprehensive statesmanship it is a matter for surprise. The habitual notion that a successful business man is sure to be a successful statesman, coupled with the democratic idea of rotation in office, has done much to prevent the development of a high class of statesmen in this country, which we otherwise ought to and might have had. The great statesmen of the world have not been business men. The habit in Europe, which has grown into a recognized rule, is, when a man exhibits ability in statecraft, to keep him in the public service—witness Gladstone, Disraeli, Bright, and nearly all the distinguished statesmen of the century, in England. From whatever social rank or party, when once in Parliament such men are kept there for life. If they offend one constituency, another is sought for them. Gladstone, for instance, in 1868 was a candidate for two constituencies, so that if he should be defeated in the one he could accept the other. He has several times been defeated, but, if no vacancy existed, party loyalty demanded that some member of Parliament in a sure liberal district should resign in his favor. In the South before the war the habit was, when once a man in Congress showed capacity, to keep him there, and hence the South had the cream of the ability in Congress.

A few constituencies are adhering to this habit, like the state of Maine, which kept James G. Blaine and now keeps Thomas B. Reed in Congress; but the rule is rotation in office, and when a man has been to Congress once, or filled any public position for a term, he must give way for some successful business man who has contributed to the campaign fund. Many of the most conspicuous English statesmen showed no capacity for business—died poor, but the habit we have spoken of warranted their reliance on the public service. We have a few instances of the same kind in this country, but the habit and theory of rotation in office in this country takes the active men from the public service in order that the promises of political managers may be redeemed. Thus with a few exceptions, like Reed and Hoar, Congress is composed largely of men unacquainted with political science and theory of government—in short, with the principles and practice of statecraft.

If the United States Senate were really the goal of highest promotion for ripe statesmanship, graduated chiefly from experience in the House of Representatives, as it should be, the great problems of national concern, like banking and currency and the problems immediately arising out of the war, would be treated in accordance with some generally recognized national policy. The Monroe Doctrine, for instance, which is the American doctrine of territorial policy, would be relied upon as the guiding principle in the present peace negotiations. The Monroe Doctrine is the doctrine that Old World monarchies shall not increase their influence and authority in this hemisphere, and that the growing movements for freedom and self-government under democratic institutions, in all American territory, shall be aided and encouraged by this republic; but it equally forbids the incursion of the United States into European and Asiatic territory.

If Congress were imbued, through experience and education, with the principles of statesmanship and indoctrinated into the American policy based upon the Monroe Doctrine as the guiding rule of action, the administration would not have thought of demanding, much less of paying or fighting for, the possession of the Philippine Islands. They might have been held as security for indemnity to make Spain pay all the expenses of the war, which she ought to have done; they might even have been sold for that purpose; they might have been given to the Filipinos themselves, if a reasonable guaranty of peaceful free government could have been furnished; but no such departure from the traditional policy of the republic as demanding the Philippine Islands as a permanent part of American territory would have been thought of. General principle is the guiding star of conduct. The person, the city or the nation without a principle or policy drifts and experiments, with the certainty of wasting its resources, losing its influence, and possibly disintegrating.

In no country is an intelligent understanding of the correct theory of statesmanship so important to the average citizen as in the United States, because social caste, political tradition and national habit have done almost nothing for us. In the older countries custom itself is at least a landmark, but here, if we are to have any consistency of conduct and persistency of national purpose, we must have a conscious, teachable, practical doctrine of national policy. To secure this it should be recognized that statesmanship is distinct from and needs an entirely different training and experience from business management. In short, we should recognize that the statesman must necessarily be guided by principles of political science, and that a competent statesman can only be graduated from the school of continuous public experience; that it is a mistaken idea of political usefulness to assume that the successful business man is likely to make an equally successful statesman. The business man's service to the community is not in making laws, but in furnishing good and cheap products. The politician's usefulness to society consists in efficiently and honestly organizing political machinery for converting the consensus of public opinion into public policy. The statesman's function is to direct public policy along the line of the principles of industrial development and political freedom.

WORK FOR DECEMBER

This month we are to study the general theory of statesmanship and its particular application to certain branches of foreign policy, especially colonization and annexation. Under the first head, also, we shall discuss the political machinery by means of which we are enabled to carry on government and get our views realized in public policy. The topics are Nos. IV and V in the curriculum, as follows:

IV. THEORY OF STATESMANSHIP.
   a The business man's *vs.* statesman's point of view.
   b Political parties.
   c Civil Service; spoils *vs.* merit system.
   d The laborer's position in national welfare.
   e The viewpoint of public policy.
V. FOREIGN POLICY.
   a Territorial policy.
     1 The doctrine of colonization.
     2 The doctrine of annexation.
     3 The Monroe Doctrine.
     4 The position of the Republic.

REQUIRED READING

In " Wealth and Progress," the Introduction, and Chapter II of Part III. In GUNTON'S MAGAZINE for December, the class lecture on " Practical Statesmanship," the Notes on Required and Suggested Readings ; and article on "Civic and Social Reforms." In GUNTON INSTITUTE BULLETIN No. 4, of Vol. II, lecture on " Political Parties and Popular Government." In Bulletin No. 9, lecture on " Taking the Philippines."

SUGGESTED READING *

In Bryce's " American Commonwealth," Part IV, and Chapter 111 in Part VI (both in Vol. II.) In

---

* See Notes on Suggested Reading, for statement of what these references cover. Books here suggested may be obtained of publishers as follows, if not available in local or traveling libraries:

The American Commonwealth, by James Bryce; The Macmillan

"Orations and Addresses of George William Curtis,"
Vol. II, Addresses Nos. VI and XIII.

In McMaster's "With the Fathers," Chapter I. In
Dr. Lujo Brentano's "Relation of Labor to the Law of
To-day," Chapter XII. In "The United States and
Foreign Powers," by W. E. Curtis, Chapter VII; Chap-
ter XIII from p. 194; Chapter XIV from p. 208. In
Roosevelt's "American Ideals," Chapters III, VI, VII,
and XI. In *Harper's Magazine* for September, 1898,
article on "Thoughts on the Policy of the United
States," by Rt. Hon. James Bryce. In GUNTON'S MAG-
AZINE for July, 1898, the article "Can We Stand Vic-
tory?" by Prof. George Gunton. Also, lecture on
"How Shall Our New Possessions Be Governed?" in
Institute Bulletin No. 2, might profitably be re-read in
this connection.

NOTES AND SUGGESTIONS

Required Reading.—The subject of the chapter assigned in "Wealth and Progress" is "How to Enlarge
the Social Opportunities of the Masses." This chapter,
and the Introduction to the book, come under the curriculum topic "The laborer's position in national welfare." In the Introduction it is shown that the welfare
and prosperity of the community, under modern conditions, rests upon the material and social conditions of
the wage-earning population, and in the subsequent
chapter mentioned it is suggested, briefly, in what ways

Company, New York; 2 vols., 1488 pp., $6. *Orations and Addresses
of George William Curtis*, Harper & Bros., New York; 2 vols., 1462 pp.,
$3.50 each. *With the Fathers*, by John Bach McMaster; Appleton
& Co., New York; 334 pp., $1.50. *The Relation of Labor to the
Law of To-Day*, by Dr. Lujo Brentano; G. P. Putnam's Sons, New
York; 305 pp., $1.75. *The United States and Foreign Powers*, by
Wm. Eleroy Curtis; Flood & Vincent, Meadville, Pa.; 313 pp., $1.00.
American Ideals, by Theodore Roosevelt; G. P. Putnam's Sons, New
York; 354 pp., $1.50.

we can enlarge the workingman's opportunities for higher wages and broader social life.

The topic "Political Parties" is covered in Bulletin lecture No. 4; "Civil Service: spoils vs. merit system," in the magazine article "Civic and Social Reforms;" "Territorial Policy" is treated in Bulletin lecture No. 9. The other curriculum topics included in the study outline for December are covered in the class lecture on "Practical Statesmanship," briefly, but with the object of giving a clear and definite point of view from which the details of each subject may be interpreted and understood. The suggested reading is of more than usual importance this month, as several of the points deserve wider reading than the necessary limits of the required work make it possible to give.

Suggested Reading.—It would be an excellent thing if every student of this course would read the whole of James Bryce's "American Commonwealth." It is the ablest, fairest and most masterly commentary on American institutions that has appeared since De Tocqueville's "Democracy in America." Part IV, which we have particularly recommended, deals with "Public Opinion," and is appropriate both to the present and last month's reading. Mr. Bryce's purpose in this section is to show in what way public opinion does rule in this country, and likewise to point out in what directions it succeeds and where it fails. Chapter 111 in Part VI is on "The Pleasantness of American Life," and is suggested not because of its direct relation to our December studies but because it is one of the most delightfully interesting passages in the whole work, and students who get the volume from libraries especially to read the section on "Public Opinion" ought not to miss this little fragment.

The second volume of the "Orations and Addresses of George William Curtis" contains seventeen of Mr.

Curtis's more important public deliverances on Civil Service Reform. The two addresses which we have recommended for reading are " The Spoils System and the Progress of Civil Service Reform," delivered at Saratoga in 1881, and " The Reason and the Result of Civil Service Reform," delivered in New York City in 1888. These two orations summarize rather completely the rise and progress of the movement, and therefore will, in a sense, stand for all the rest.

The chapter suggested in McMaster's " With the Fathers," is important chiefly because of its historical, rather than philosophical, treatment of the Monroe Doctrine, and the same applies to chapter VII in Curtis's " The United States and Foreign Powers.". The other chapters suggested in this latter book deal with the manner in which we acquired Florida and Louisiana from Spain and France respectively. This directly bears on our December study topic, " Territorial Policy," and is particularly significant because the fact of our acquisition of Florida and Louisiana, and later Alaska, is now cited as sufficient precedent for further expansion in annexing the Philippines. A very brief consideration of this point, however, shows that the conditions were utterly dissimilar. The dominions acquired from France and Spain were very thinly settled, and were desired mainly because they offered additional territory to which our own citizens could emigrate. It was never even hinted that the Indians in these regions should be embodied in our political system, then or ever; in fact, the policy pursued towards them was no better than extermination, and later it has been to fence them off in groups and treat them simply as the nation's wards. Furthermore, it goes without saying that the sparse French and Spanish population which came to us with these new sections was many times nearer our own standard of civilization at that time than are the half-savage natives we now propose to take in. We were at that time chiefly an agricultural people. The wage system had hardly made its appearance, industry was individualistic, and hence the addition of new groups of population under these simple, primitive conditions was by no means so serious a matter as it is to-day, when any considerable new influence introduced into our complex, interdependent industrial conditions may affect the whole wage status of the country, as well as its political complexion.

Furthermore, Florida and Louisiana were naturally in the line of our necessary national growth, in a geographical sense, and fulfilled all the conditions for becoming part of a homogeneous, unified nation. This by no means applies to a group of savage islands on the other side of the world. Alaska, it may be granted, is a more appropriate precedent for annexing far-away regions, but it would puzzle the most enthusiastic expansionist to show in what degree our national greatness has been increased by bringing in that bleak, isolated and relatively barren country. The larger part of the Klondike gold field is in Canada, and would unquestionably have been developed sometime regardless of annexation. The only conspicuous feature of our presence there has been a long and irritating sealing controversy with Great Britain, more annoying and costly, probably, than the whole matter was ever worth. In the case of the Philippines, we are not annexing the islands because of any need of territory, for we have extensive regions as yet practically undeveloped in our own great West, and no American workingman has the least idea of ever emigrating from this country to compete with Oriental barbarism at 10 cents a day. It might prove some advantage to a few exporters and franchise holders and a small army of carpet-bag officeholders but that is about all. The proposition is so utterly and radically different from that involved in the early annexation of Florida and Louisiana that comparisons between the two are hardly entitled even to respectable standing in the arena of scientific political controversy.

Mr. Bryce's article in the September "Harper's" is seriously recommended to all those who imagine that the necessary destiny of the American nation is to enter upon a policy of land acquisition in the Orient. Mr. Bryce's great work, to which we have referred, entitles his view on so momentous a question as this to serious consideration, and in the article mentioned he emphasizes his solid reputation as a broad-minded, comprehensive political philosopher. He points out the fact that America's great contribution to the world is to be expansion upward rather than outward; expansion of civilization rather than of territory. We have here problems which will tax the resources of our statesmanship for generations to come, and, as Mr. Bryce says: "The United States will render a far greater service to humanity by developing a high type of industrial civilization on her own continent—a civilization conspicuously free, enlightened, and pacific—than by any foreign conquests."

The chapters suggested in Roosevelt's "American Ideals" discuss in a wholesome, patriotic and vigorously practical way the duties of American citizenship, practical politics, civil service reform, and the Monroe Doctrine. In the chapter on "Six Years of Civil Service Reform" he writes from personal knowledge as a member of the National Civil Service Commission.

LOCAL CENTER WORK

At the head of the Institute Work department we have made a suggestion in regard to the formation and conduct of local centers, which we hope will be widely read and produce important practical results. We propose, however, to continue our suggestions as to work for centers organized distinctly to follow the Gunton Institute study course, as well as for those in which these studies form only a portion of the work carried on. The topics covered this month afford opportunity for very interesting programmes, which might include such items as these:—

Papers on: The statesman's point of view; History of ¡American political parties; Civil Service Reform; How high wages affect the national welfare; Sketch of the Monroe Doctrine; What does the Monroe Doctrine mean? The United States' duty to the world. Review of work to date, questions and answers, debates or discussions on local questions. Debates on: *Resolved:*—That political parties are necessary instruments of democratic government; *Resolved:*—That merit rather than political opinion should be the test of fitness in our public service; *Resolved:*—That the United States should retain control of the Philippines only until they reach the point of safe self-government; *Resolved:*—That our position regarding the Monroe Doctrine ought morally to restrain us from interfering in the affairs of Europe or the Orient.

We are particularly anxious that any questions that may be raised or unclear points developed in the discussions at meetings of local centers should be forwarded to this office, in order that we may have the opportunity to clear up any such matters, either by direct correspondence or through the Magazine. Let every individual student, as well as officer of a local center, feel the utmost freedom in this regard. We are not only willing but extremely desirous to render just this assistance wherever the need of it may exist.

H
1
G9
v.15

Gunton's magazine

**PLEASE DO NOT REMOVE
CARDS OR SLIPS FROM THIS POCKET**

UNIVERSITY OF TORONTO LIBRARY

Lightning Source UK Ltd.
Milton Keynes UK
UKHW021927180219
337529UK00011B/943/P